THE GREEK CHRONICLES

PART I

SUPPLEMENTS

TO

VETUS TESTAMENTUM

EDITED BY

THE BOARD OF THE QUARTERLY

VOLUME XXV

LEIDEN
E. J. BRILL
1974

THE GREEK CHRONICLES

THE RELATION OF THE SEPTUAGINT OF I AND II CHRONICLES

TO THE MASSORETIC TEXT

BY

LESLIE C. ALLEN

PART I

THE TRANSLATOR'S CRAFT

LEIDEN

E. J. BRILL

1974

ISBN 90 04 03913 9

To my wife

CONTENTS

PREFACE

This work is a revised and, one trusts, improved form of a thesis submitted to the University of London for the degree of Doctor of Philosophy in 1968. It is being published in two parts: the sequel to this one is due to appear shorty in the present series. Intended as a contribution to the study of the text of the Bible, the work was inspired by an appreciation of the worth of God's Word.

"No man is an island" in the world of research. Many have considerately given time and thought to my concerns, too many to mention here. But acknowledgement must be given of the help of Dr. D. W. Gooding, The Queen's University, Belfast, who originally suggested this subject to me and criticised an earlier form of chapters i-viii. Thanks are due to Professor S. Stein, my patient supervisor, and to his helpful colleague Mr. R. Loewe, both of University College London. I am indebted to Professor P. A. H. de Boer, editor of the Supplements, and to Dr. W. Baars for their criticism and encouragement; and also to Mr. F. C. Wieder, Jr., Director of E. J. Brill, for his kindly efforts in overcoming obstacles to publication. The laborious task of typing the original dissertation was willingly undertaken by my friend Miss Cleone Prins. Not least I am grateful to my wife for practical support as well as moral : she acted as a sounding board for my ideas and their literary expression, and compiled the biblical index.

Financial aid to enable publication was generously given and gratefully received from the British Academy, the Managers of the Hort Memorial Fund, the Trustees of the Bethune-Baker Fund and the Board of Governors of the London Bible College.

London Bible College   Leslie C. Allen

ABBREVIATIONS

AJSL	*American Journal of Semitic Languages and Literatures*
Arm	Armenian Version
Boh	Bohairic Version
CBQ	*Catholic Biblical Quarterly*
ET	*Expository Times*
Eth	Ethiopic Version
Gk	Greek
Heb	Hebrew
HTR	*Harvard Theological Review*
HUCA	*Hebrew Union College Annual*
ICC	*International Critical Commentary*
IEJ	*Israel Exploration Journal*
JAOS	*Journal of the American Oriental Society*
JBL	*Journal of Biblical Literature*
JNES	*Journal of Near Eastern Studies*
Jos	Josephus
JQR	*Jewish Quarterly Review*
JSS	*Journal of Semitic Studies*
JTS	*Journal of Theological Studies*
La	Old Latin Version
LXX	Septuagint, Septuaginta
ms., mss.	manuscript(s)
MT	Massoretic Text, according to *Biblia Hebraica*³
NTS	*New Testament Studies*
OT	Old Testament
OTS	*Oudtestamentische Studiën*
PSBA	*Proceedings of the Society of Biblical Archaeology*
Pesh	Peshitta, cited according to Lee's edition and Barnes' *Apparatus Criticus*
RB	*Revue biblique*
SBOT	*Sacred Books of the Old Testament*
Syh	Syro-Hexaplar Version
Targ	Targum, cited according to Sperber's edition
TLZ	*Theologische Literaturzeitung*
TQ	*Theologische Quartalschrift*
TR	*Theologische Rundschau*
TZ	*Theologische Zeitschrift*
VT	*Vetus Testamentum*
Vulg	Vulgate
ZAW	*Zeitschrift für die alttestamentliche Wissenschaft*

The following abbreviations are used for OT and Apocryphal books. Where different the LXX is bracketed. Gen Exod Lev Num Deut Jos Jud Sam (Rg) Ki (Rg) Isa Jer Ezek Hos Jon Hab Zeph Zech Mal Psa Prov Lam Eccles Esth Dan Neh (Esdr) Chron (Par and Esdr) Ecclus Macc.

INTRODUCTION

All too often the LXX is used atomistically as an aid to solve difficulties in this or that verse of the Massoretic Text. The only antidote to this "lucky dip" type of approach is an exhaustive analysis undertaken with respect for the individual Greek books as works in their own right. The non-Septuagintalist is apt to assume that the LXX is a monolithic entity somehow immune from the change and decay that time has wrought in the Hebrew text. C. C. Torrey has deplored somewhere "the folly of 'criticising' our MT by the use of a Greek text which has not itself been criticised at all". A major task of this necessary criticism is to hack out a path from the fifty extant manuscripts of Paralipomena and a number of daughter versions back to the probable text of the translator via a jungle of recensional « improvements" and transcriptional blunders.

As to recensions the manuscripts and versions fall roughly into four groups. Which of the four is to be taken as our principal guide ? The one led by Codex Vaticanus, most have said; the one headed by Codex Alexandrinus, aver Torrey and his supporters. All the groups seem to be revisions of an earlier text; so they are all witnesses to that text in places where they left it unchanged. Enough common ground remains to establish hallmarks of the old version. These and other criteria enable an assessment of the groups in terms of the degree of revision that they contain. One group has generally been recognized as Lucianic, an ascription that raises further questions these days. Another has rightly been related to the recension "R" which Rahlfs found in Reigns. A third is now proved by comparison with fragments of the Syro-Hexapla to be linked with Origen's work. The fourth is claimed substantially to underlie the rest, but in its present form to contain a considerable amount of secondary material.

Jerome was shocked at the discrepancies between the Greek and Latin manuscripts of his day and his Hebrew text of Chronicles. In the extant preface to his lost revised Old Latin text of Paralipomena he complains that "ita et in grecis et in latinis codicibus hic nominum liber vitiosus est ut non tam hebrea quam barbara et sarmatica nomina congesta arbitrandum sit". Undoubtedly many of these discrepancies were perpetrated in the course of Greek transmission, as Jerome went on to claim. The aid of Greek textual criticism has to be invoked in order to restore the pristine bloom of the translator's product.

The methodology of the translator is a crucial area of study. How high or low were his standards of accuracy ? Was he inclined to paraphrase, to abbreviate, to expatiate ? It is only when armed with answers to these and similar questions that one can assess the relation between the basic Greek text and our Hebrew one by resurrecting the missing link, that ancient manuscript of Chronicles which lay on the translator's table. The relation it bore to the Massoretic Text can then be analysed in detail, down to its likely script and date. At what points did it diverge from our present text, and why ? Which, if any, of its deviations are superior to today's readings ? Miswritings, misreadings, omissions, explanatory glosses, the influence of synoptic passages — the *Vorlage* was the victim of all these and still more types of textual adaptation. At times the tables are turned, and the Massoretic Text has to be judged inferior.

Much of this work is an evaluation of previous labours in this field of study. Commentators on Chronicles have frequently dipped into Paralipomena and drawn — their own conclusions. Torrey has already been mentioned. Is his claim true that Theodotion was the translator ? Or even a proto-Theodotion ? Rehm did much detailed textual work, especially in the synoptic passages. Gerleman has done important work in certain areas of this field. Rahlfs and Ziegler have established patterns of study in the LXX which need to be applied to Paralipomena. These and many another scholar are no less contributors to this study than the author.

Full particulars of books and articles are supplied in the Bibliography. Elsewhere they are cited with sufficient detail to enable reference to the Bibliography.

Chapter and verse numeration in Reigns, Paralipomena and I and II Esdras are given from Brooke-McLean ; in other books either Swete's edition or Rahlfs' has been used.

CHAPTER ONE

GREEK TEXTUAL MATERIAL

Some forty six mss. of Par have been consulted to a greater or lesser degree. Indirect evidence is available from versions dependent upon the Gk translation: the Ethiopic, Bohairic, Old Latin, Armenian and Syro-Hexapla. The Old Latin and the fragments of the Syro-Hexapla have been investigated fully. Ignorance of the languages of the others has necessitated dependence upon the apparatus of BM for the most part. Ancient writers such as Josephus and the Church Fathers quote or allude to Par. The citations of Josephus in BM have been checked and amplified. Of the patristic evidence, quotations of Justin, Origen, Eusebius and Chrysostom have been taken into account and wherever possible checked with editions.

The critical apparatus of BM has generally been followed, apart from a few instances. Its evidence has been supplemented by study of Gk mss. on microfilm.

1. Uncials

The capital letters used in BM tally with those employed in Rahlfs' *Verzeichnis der griechischen Handschriften des AT*, except that the latter calls N V.

Egerton Papyrus 4 (971 in the *Verzeichnis* numeration), IIIrd century, two fragments of a leaf of a codex.[1]

Papyrus Barcinonensis 3, IIIrd century, three fragments of a leaf of a codex.[2]

S   Codex Sinaiticus, IVth century, extant from I 9.27 τὸ πρωί to 19.17.

B   Codex Vaticanus, IVth century.

A   Codex Alexandrinus, Vth century.

N   Codex Venetus, VIIIth century.

---

[1] See p. 104.

[2] See p. 105.

2. Minuscules

Twenty one minuscule mss. are designated in BM with small letters. They are set out below according to their age, as dated by Rahlfs. The latter's numeration is given in brackets.

IXth century:

o (412), a fragment[1].

Xth century:

a (60), missing I 12.32-21.16 $\Delta av\iota\delta$[2].

c (64), missing after II 24.20 $\dot{\epsilon}\nu\kappa\alpha\tau\epsilon\lambda\dot{\iota}\pi\epsilon\tau\epsilon$ till 25.18.

f (489).

h (55).

j (243).

n (119).

y (121).

c (127), missing from II 36.5.

XIth century:

i (56), dated 1093, extant only as far as II 13.15.

q (120).

t (134).

XIIth century:

b' (19).

XIIIth century:

b (108). This ms. and b' are cited together in BM as b when they agree.

g (158).

m (71), missing I 25.9-26.11; 26.20 $\kappa\alpha\dot{\iota}$ $\dot{\epsilon}\pi\dot{\iota}$ — v. 26 $\Sigma\alpha\lambda\omega\mu\omega\theta$.

e₂ (93), missing after $\alpha\dot{v}\tau\sigma\hat{v}$ I 1.45 till $\ddot{\epsilon}\tau\epsilon\kappa\epsilon\nu$ 2.29 and from II 32.26 onwards.

XIVth century:

d (107), dated 1334.

e (52).

p (106).

z (554).

---

[1] See p. 85.

The following are cited occasionally in BM from Holmes-Parsons' apparatus:

44, XVth century.

74, XIIIth century.

144 (130 according to Rahlfs), XVth century.

236, XIth century.

Two chapters of 125, XIVth century, are collated in Holmes-Parsons, Addenda to vol. ii.

Of these numbered mss., microfilm copies of 74, 144 and 236 were obtained, but 44 (Staatsbibliothek A.1, Zittau, XVth century) and 125 (Lenin Library, Graeci 30, Moscow, XIVth century) [1] proved unobtainable.

Microfilm reproductions in whole or part were also obtained of the following :

46, XIIIth-XIVth centuries.

68, XVth century.

98, XIIIth century.

122, XVth century.

246, dated 1195 A.D., extant from II 1.1 to 13.15.

314, XIIIth century.

321, XIVth century.[2]

346, dated 1326 A.D.

350, dated 1540 A.D.

379, XVIth century.

381, XIth century.

610, XIVth century.

728, XIth-XIIIth centuries.

731, XIVth century.

The following mss., apart from 44 and 125, proved unavailable:

442 = Biblioteca de la Universidad Central, E.1.10, Madrid, XVth-XVIth centuries.

571 = Bibliothèque de l'Arsenal 8415, Paris, XIVth century.

762 = Mt. Athos Βατοπαιδίου 599 (formerly 512), Xth century.

---

[1] The Director of the Department of Manuscripts reports that in fact their Gr. 30 is a XVIth century liturgical text; she suggests confusion with Gr. 30, a XVth century LXX ms., including Par, in the Synodic collection kept in the State Museum of History, Moscow.

[2] The Hexaplaric notes this ms. has been said to contain prove to be merely quotations from Theodoret.

CHAPTER TWO

THE LIE OF THE LAND

1. Theodotion — the case for and against

The subtitle of this book has prejudged an important issue. Can the Gk version of Chron rightly be called "the Septuagint" in the loose sense that it may take its place among other early Gk translations of the OT? Or is it rather, as some have claimed, a product of Theodotion, traditionally assigned to the second century A.D., or of an *Ur*-Theodotion? Apparently the issue turns on the relation between Par and II Esdr on the one hand and I Esdr on the other: II Par 35-36 is paralleled in I Esdr 1-2.3 and much of II Esdr in I 2-9.[1]

The suggestion that Par is the work of Theodotion was first made in 1644. Hugo Grotius remarked on II Chron 35.5 : "פסח semper Theodotion vertit φασεκ non ut alii interpretes πασχα. Theodotionis autem interpretationem in Paralipomenis et aliis quibusdam libris recepit Graeca Ecclesia. In Graecis quibus utimur libris, initio Esdrae positum est caput xxxv Paralipomenon et magna pars xxxvi ex LXX, ubi semper πασχα non φασεκ."[2] The basis of Grotius' argument appears to be erroneous.[3]

In 1722 William Whiston made a related suggestion.[4] He claimed that I Esdr was used by Josephus and by the Church Fathers, Clement of Alexandria, Tertullian, Origen, Cyprian and Eusebius and concluded: «I cannot but fear that the present Gk version of that book [Neh], as well as of the Heb Ezra, is only Theodotion's and no part of the old Septuagint version, any further, I mean, than Theodotion, as is well known, used very much to imitate those translators in his own

---

[1] Full details are given in Rudolph, *Esra und Nehemia*, p. iv.

[2] *Annotata ad Vetus Testamentum*, i, p. 367.

[3] Cf. Walde, *Die Esdrasbücher*, pp. 38ff., for evidence that πασχα is used in material ascribed to Theodotion. Torrey, *Ezra Studies*, p. 67, calls Grotius' argument too sweeping, but goes on to suggest that πασχα has been *replaced* by φασεχ/κ in most mss. of Par and II Esdr and that the ascription of φασεχ to Symmachus in mss. of the LXX is erroneous.

[4] *An Essay Towards Restoring the True Text of the OT.*

version".[1] He added, "I have already proved that the first book of Esdras among the Apocrypha is that true Septuagint version and no other. Probably the other Esdras, now in our Gk Bibles, is the version of Theodotion".[2]

Henry Howorth was the first to develop the case for Theodotion to any length. In correspondence from the Athenaeum Club, published in *The Academy*,[3] he gave evidence that Josephus used I Esdr and argued that it was therefore the true LXX and II Esdr was another translation, probably by Theodotion. He compared the case of the LXX translation of Daniel being replaced by Theodotion's.[4] I Esdr was in his view a section of a continuous book comprising all the Chronicler's work. So Par also represents a later translation.[5] In vol. xliv of *The Academy* he passed on information from J. Gwynn that a ms. of Paul of Tella's Syriac version of the Hexapla contained I Esdr with the notice that it was taken from the LXX.[6] This to Howorth was very strong proof that I Esdr represents the LXX of Ezra-Neh, and by implication that II Esdr does not.[7]

In *PSBA* he presented the same views more fully. He stated concerning II Esdr that since it is "a very literal and servile translation" of MT it must be attributed to either Aquila, Symmachus or Theodotion.[8] Since, further, the Church seems to have favoured Theodotion's translation, as witnessed by its displacing the LXX text in Daniel, then probably it too belongs to him. "The problem is at least worth testing minutely by someone with more leisure and skill than I." Whereas the Theodotionic text of Dan displaced the LXX, his II Esdr — "for so I shall take it to be until the reverse is proved" — existed side by side

---

[1] *Op.cit.*, p. 55.

[2] *Op.cit.*, p. 114.

[3] xliii, 1893.

[4] *Loc. cit.*, p. 13f.

[5] *Loc. cit.*, p. 60.

[6] It should be noted that according to Gwynn, *Remnants of the Later Syriac Versions*, part ii, p. xvi, it also contains parts of Par and II Esdr with the same notice. On p. xxii he suggested that "Origen only inserted in his Hexapla so much of I Esdras as extends from ii. 1 to x. 45, thus omitting the parts which coincide with 2 Chronicles and with Nehemiah".

[7] *Loc. cit.*, p 74.

[8] xxiii, 1901, p. 151.

with another translation. He cited[1] Thackeray[2] and Pohlmann[3] for evidence that Josephus followed I Esdr, and argues that if Josephus used it then it must precede the period of the Three and be older than II Esdr.[4] The closeness of the latter's text to MT points to its lateness.[5]

Howorth devoted further study to his thesis the following year.[6] Thackeray's demonstration of I Esdr's links with Alexandria suggested to Howorth that it is the LXX text.[7] He expressed his firm conviction that the so-called LXX versions of Chron-Ezra-Neh were all taken not from the LXX but from one of the versions of the Massoretic text, probably Theodotion's. Field's work on the Hexapla had shown that there existed virtually no Hexaplaric readings from the Three in Par and II Esdr. It therefore seemed conclusive that, as with Daniel, Origen had substituted Theodotion for the LXX of Chron-Ezra-Neh.[8] But later Howorth modified his views to the extent of supposing Symmachus to be the translator.[9]

At this point C. C. Torrey took over from Howorth.[10] He assessed Howorth's arguments and defined them as full and vigorous but not compelling. He had merely shown that Par and II Esdr might well be later than I Esdr, without proving his case. His assumption that because the former closely followed MT they must be derived from the Three was hardly acceptable. Beyond citing the analogous case of the Gk Daniel he had taken the case little further than Grotius and Whiston before him.[11]

The following year Torrey endeavoured to undergird the viewpoint

---

[1] *Loc. cit.*, p. 154.

[2] *HDB* i, p. 759.

[3] *TQ* xli, pp. 258ff.

[4] *Loc. cit.*, p. 154.

[5] *Loc. cit.*, p. 157.

[6] *PSBA* xxiv.

[7] *Loc. cit.*, p. 166.

[8] *Loc. cit.*, p. 167.

[9] *PSBA* xxix, p. 32f.

[10] *AJSL* xxiii, 1907, pp. 116ff., reprinted as ch. ii of *Ezra Studies*, 1910. Four years before, in *PSBA* xxv, p. 139f., he had cited Grotius and briefly stated his conviction that Theodotion was the author of Par and II Esdr: in fact he had so lectured since 1894. Another follower of Howorth was J. Theis: in *Geschichtliche und literarkritische Fragen in Esra 1-6*, 1910, he claimed that II Esdr was Theodotion's work, largely echoing Howorth, and finally suggested (p. 34) that the same conclusion applied to Par.

[11] *Ezra Studies*, p. 16.

of Howorth, etc., with more weighty arguments,[1] although he significantly confessed: "The following discussion of the critical apparatus
is only fragmentary, leaving a good many important matters either
half treated or not touched upon at all".[2] He took up Grotius' point
about Theodotion's transliteration and developed it comprehensively.
The absence of any readings from Theodotion was very noticeable. His
tendency to transcribe, demonstrated by Field[3] and Swete[4], is matched
in Par and II Esdr. A few are shared by those works and concur with
citations of Theodotion's version elsewhere.[5] Indeed there are six or
so translation links with Theodotion's version of Dan: "Undoubtedly
other examples of the kind can be found. I have made no thorough
search". He also appeals to Theodotion's custom of transliterating
names exactly instead of using Gk endings. Par has examples of both,
but Torrey claims that the latter have been substituted later.

He suggests that probably the number of transliterations were greater
than now appears and that those found in the so-called Lucianic witnesses b e₂ are original. If Par is Theodotion's version, it follows easily
that they are survivals from it. He explains away the embarrassing
fact that transliterations appear in many parts of the Gk OT by assuming that Theodotion's readings have there supplanted those of the
LXX.[6] Torrey appears to be remarkably adept at evading the brunt of
conflicting evidence.

As to the relation between the Gk Chron-Ezra-Neh and I Esdr he
considers it improbable that in the former Theodotion was revising
the latter, for unlike the LXX of Dan and Theodotion's version these
two works are not very close.[7] I Esdr originally formed part of a larger
work translated not long before the middle of the second century B. C.
Eupolemus, a Jewish historian generally assigned to about 150 B.C.,[8]
cited II Chron 2.12ff. in a Gk form, including ὃς τὸν οὐρανον καὶ τὴν
γῆν ἔκτισεν (= עשׂה): compare the use of the same verb in I Esdr. 6.12

---

[1] *OT and Semitic Studies*, ii, pp. 55ff., reprinted as ch. iv of *Ezra Studies*.

[2] *Ezra Studies*, p. 63 note 3.

[3] *Hexapla*, pp. xxxix-xlii.

[4] *Introduction*, p. 46.

[5] *Op.cit.*, pp. 70-78.

[6] *Op.cit.*, pp. 79-81.

[7] *Op.cit.*, p. 81.

[8] He is generally identified with the Eupolemus sent by Judas Maccabaeus to make
a treaty with Rome in 161 (I Macc 8.17 ; II 4.11). Cf. F. Jacoby, *Paulys Real-Encyclopädie*,
vi, col. 1228. Eusebius incorporated extracts from his history in *Praeparatio Evangelica*,
ix, 30-34.

τοῦ κτίσαντος (= עבד) τ. ο. καὶ τ. γ. and contrast II Par ἐποίησεν and II Esdr 19.6 ἐποίησας (= עשׂה). Here is a somewhat free citation of a Gk version of Chron: there is every reason to believe and none to doubt that this translation was the same one of which a part has survived in the I Esdr fragment.[1] On p. 84f. Torrey goes on to refer to the resemblance between the Gk of I Esdr and that of Dan LXX shown by several scholars.[2] He suggests a few more and concludes that probably both translations are by one and the same man.[3]

In 1945 Torrey reaffirmed his position: Chron-Ezra-Neh, revised into its present form at about the beginning of the second century A.D. or a little later, was eventually translated into Gk by Theodotion, whose version was adopted as the standard and in modern times has generally been called "the Septuagint".[4]

E. L. Curtis wrote his *ICC* on Chron (1910) in full flush of reading Torrey. He embraced his views with enthusiasm. Curtis enumerated Torrey's three points of (1) transliterations, (2) parallels with the late version of Dan, and (3) frequent non-Hellenised transliterations of names, and gives examples of Josephus' use of I Esdr as well as of Eupolemus' supposed use.[5] He concludes that "the accepted Greek text (Theodotion's), therefore, is only of value for recovering the authoritative Hebrew of the second century A.D.". On the other hand, "the true Septuagint" is preserved in I Esdr. 1, dating from before 150 B.C.

Support for Torrey's views has been forthcoming elsewhere. G. F. Moore considered that he "proves what had been previously surmised".[6] W. A. L. Elmslie calls Par "a later Greek translation, which most scholars (esp. Torrey, *Ezra Studies*) consider to be the rendering of Theodotion".[7] Much later he repeats this view: Par is "the LXX [sic] translated in the second century A.D.".[8] R. H. Pfeiffer, discussing I Esdr, follows Torrey in viewing it as the extant portion of a lost

---

[1] *Op.cit.*, p. 82. If Torrey's thesis is rendered doubtful on other grounds, the reference is to be viewed as a loose citation, probably influenced by the similar phrases in Gen. 14. 19, 22.

[2] E.g., Swete, *op.cit.*, pp. 48f., 310f.

[3] *Op. cit.*, p. 84f.

[4] *Louis Ginzberg Jubilee Volume*, p. 396.

[5] *Op. cit.*, pp. 38ff.

[6] *AJSL* xxix, 1913, p. 54.

[7] *Chronicles, Cambridge Bible*[2], 1916, p. lviii.

[8] *The Interpreter's Bible*, iii, 1954, p. 394.

translation of the whole of Chron-Ezra-Neh.[1] Correspondingly he
regards Par-II Esdr as a later rendering, made in the first or second
century A.D.; but he rejects its attribution to Theodotion because of
inadequate evidence. B. J. Roberts states categorically that "B gives
us the revised text of Theodotion as do the other uncials".[2] S. Jellicoe
has made a fascinating suggestion as to how Par-II Esdr came to
Egypt, "if Torrey be correct".[3] It hails from Ephesus and is the work
of an *Ur*-Theodotion. Along with the proto-Theodotionic texts of
Daniel and portions of Reigns, it was brought to Alexandria as part
of Mark Antony's gift of the Library of Pergamum to Cleopatra some
time after 41 B.C. In *The LXX and Modern Study* he repeats this
suggestion.[4] He also gives a glowing account of Torrey's view of
Par-II Esdr: "it is likely to gain in attractiveness, at least in essentials"
in view of its parallel with the current theory of *Ur*-Theodotion in
Reigns.[5] As for Gerleman's presentation of evidence that Par existed
by 150 B.C., he grants the fact but parries its force by implying that
proto-Theodotion can be that early. He criticises Torrey's assertion that
the use of I Esdr by Josephus proves the priority of that version : II
Esdr "might well have been in existence but rejected by Josephus"
in favour of I Esdr's superior Gk style.

Such is the case and such are the witnesses for Theodotion. A view
with such drastic implications has naturally not gone unchallenged. In
1875, before the development of the controversy, J. Freudenthal maintained that Eupolemus used Par as one of his sources, in addition to
Chron.[6] He found five echoes of Par in the phraseology of Eupolemus,
as cited in Eusebius, *Praeparatio Evangelica* ix. 34:

II 3.5 ἐξύλωσεν ξύλοις κεδρίνοις ; cf. ξυλῶσαι κεδρ. ξύλοις.

v. 17 καὶ ἔστησεν τοὺς στύλους ... ἕνα ἐκ δεξιῶν καὶ τὸν ἕνα ἐξ
εὐωνύμων ; cf. στῆσαι δὲ αὐτοὺς (i.e. τοὺς στύλους) ... ὃν μὲν ἐκ
δεξιῶν ὃν δὲ ἐξ εὐων.

4.3 ἐχώνευσαν ... χωνεύσει ; cf. χωνευτάς [7].

---

[1] *History of NT Times*, 1949, p. 249f.

[2] *OT Text and Versions*, 1951, p. 154.

[3] *NTS* iii, 1966, p. 148.

[4] 1968, pp. 88-93. Cf. *VT* xxiii, 1973, p. 23f.

[5] *Op. cit.*, pp. 290-294.

[6] *Hellenistische Studien*, i, pp. 108, 114, 119, 185, 211. His citations of Eupolemus
have been checked with E.H. Gifford's edition of Eusebius, *Praeparatio Evangelica*, 1903.

[7] Freudenthal, p. 211, proposed reading ταύρους χωνευτούς for τορευτὰς χωνευτάς
thus achieving a closer link with the OT material.

v. 13 κώδωνας ... τετρακοσίους εἰς τὰ δύο δίκτυα ; cf. ἑκάστῃ δικτύι κώδωνας ... τετρακ.

6.13 ἐποίησεν ... βάσιν χαλκῆν ; ποιῆσαι ... βάσιν χαλκῆν.

So in the middle of the second century B.C. Par was already known and in use.[1]

In 1907 H. St. J. Thackeray criticised Howorth's position on the score that Par itself has unmistakable early Egyptian colouring.[2] The Sukiim and the Meunim are identified with the Troglodytes (II 12.3) and the Mineans (I 4.41; II 26.7; cf. 20.1; 26.8) respectively, two tribes living by the Red Sea. The translator used the titles of the Alexandrian court: διάδοχος (II 26.11; 28.7) or διαδεχόμενος (I 26.18; II 31.12), οἱ πρῶτοι διάδοχοι τοῦ βασιλέως (I 18.7), ὁ πρῶτος φίλος (I 27.33). The word he uses for a chamber attached to the Temple is the name for a cell in the Serapeum (παστοφόριον: I 9.26, etc.). The phrase τῆς ἐπιγονῆς (II 31.16, cf. 18) is very frequent in the papyri, apparently referring to a second generation of Macedonian Greeks who had later settled in Egypt. The Egyptian colouring of Par makes it impossible to hold that Theodotion is the translator.

But Thackeray made a concession in the light of Torrey's work. Two years later he agreed with Howorth that II Esdr was the work of Theodotion, but Egyptian traits and a rather greater freedom of style made him hesitate to attribute Par to him.[3] However, Torrey had made out a strong case and if he and Howorth were right, it was necessary to suppose what Torrey denied, that Theodotion made use of an earlier version of Par such as was not available for II Esdr.

A. Rahlfs wrote that he did not consider compelling Torrey's proof that Par and II Esdr were Theodotion's.[4] Torrey's chief and really only proof was the many transliterated words. But transliteration is not merely a feature of Theodotion, but occurs elsewhere. Moreover in Par

---

[1] Five other links with Par can be claimed:

II 2.13 ἀπέσταλκά σοι (Chron v. 12 only שלחת): cf. P.E. ix. 34 σοὶ ἀπέστ. (Swete, Introduction, p. 370).

v. 16 κατὰ πᾶσαν τὴν χρείαν σου : cf. P.E. ix. 31 κατὰ τὴν χρείαν.

4.6 εἰς τὸ νίπτεσθαι τοὺς ἱερεῖς : cf. P.E. ix. 34 τοὺς ἱερεῖς ... νίπτεσθαι.

5.4f καὶ ἔλαβον ... τὴν σκήνην (III Rg 8.3f. κ. ἦραν ... σκήνωμα) : cf. P.E. ix. 34 λαβόντα ... τὴν σκήνην.

v. 6 μόσχους (III Rg 8.5 βόας) = P.E. ix. 34.

[2] JTS viii, p. 276f.

[3] Addendum to p. 13 of Grammar, vol. i.

[4] LXX-Studien, iii, 1911, p. 85 note 2.

and II Esdr, as Torrey remarked, many transliterations render a corrupted Heb consonantal text, but such cases are very seldom in known Theodotionic examples. One cannot explain this phenomenon by saying as Torrey does that such readings were not preserved because "the fact that they originated in such blunders was apparent": this assumes too accurate a knowledge of Heb to ring true.

A. T. Olmstead was emphatic: "The Greek Chronicles is not from Theodotion".[1] He had maintained the view that IV Rg had emanated from Theodotion,[2] and went on to show that II Par 36 and the parallel chapter in IV Rg exhibit striking differences, and so independence, in translation. But he had six other reasons: (1) the likeness of Par's phraseology to that of the papyri;[3] (2) the references to the Troglodytes and Mineans, betokening a rather early translation; (3) the use of certain words in a particularly Ptolemaic sense;[4] (4) Par's use of $\theta\epsilon\acute{o}s$ for Yahweh, a usage found otherwise only in early books;[5] (5) the actual attribution of a reading to Theodotion in Par in a Gk fragment then recently found[6] and another in II Esdr in codex S.[7] The first reference is worth pausing over. Thomsen's ms. (= 412 in Rahlfs' reckoning and o in BM) has two marginal notes at 33.14, the first giving Symmachus' rendering and the second Theodotion's, the latter as follows: $\kappa\alpha\grave{\imath}\ \pi\epsilon\rho\iota\epsilon\kappa\acute{u}\kappa\lambda\omega\sigma\epsilon\nu\ \tau\grave{o}\ \check{\alpha}\delta\upsilon\tau o\nu\ \kappa\acute{u}\kappa\lambda\omega\ \epsilon\grave{\imath}s\ \tau\grave{o}\nu\ O\phi\lambda\alpha.$[8] The first half of this reading is taken up in B[ab], A and nine minuscules cited in BM. To return to Olmstead, his sixth reason was one of style: although I Esdr is an earlier translation, yet Par is written in better and less literal Gk than one finds in Theodotion; the article is better handled and more used. Gk endings are given where Theodotion exactly transcribes: Olmstead is here stressing the other half of the evidence on this matter which Torrey had dismissed with a wave of the hand.

---

[1] *AJSL* xxx, 1913, p. 14.

[2] Thackeray, *The LXX and Jewish Worship*, pp. 24ff., considered it rather the work of an *Ur*-Theodotion, a pioneer of the literal school and a predecessor of Aquila, partly because Josephus appears to use it. Barthélemy, *Les devanciers d'Aquila*, has identified it with a first century A.D. recension undertaken, he suggests, by Theodotion, who lived a century earlier than tradition claims. Cross, *HTR* lvii, p. 283 note 11, has called this last point "highly speculative".

[3] No examples were given : he had Thackeray's article in mind.

[4] Note 6 refers to Thackeray.

[5] P. 15 note 1 refers to Redpath, *JTS* vii, p. 608.

[6] P. 15 note 2 refers to P. Thomsen, *ZAW* xxxi, p. 308f.

[7] See the note on 13.15 in Rahlfs, *LXX*.

[8] See further p. 82.

1913 also saw the publication of B. Walde's work on Esdras.[1] He held firmly that Par is a pre-Christian translation already existing in the first half of the second century B.C., referring to Swete, *Introduction*, p. 24f.:[2] this is a reference to Eupolemus' citation of II Par 2, which Torrey had already claimed to be linked with I Esdr. Walde does not delve into this point. He points out that the text form of II Par 35-36 is partly divergent from MT and so it must be older than the Three since these translators used a Heb text which later was vocalised as MT.[3] He endeavours to show from comparative translations of the same vocabulary that Par and II Esdr come from two different hands.[4] Howorth and Torrey had lumped the books together as Theodotion's, but Walde drives a wedge between the two documents. He goes on to deal with Torrey's argument concerning transliteration.[5] Some of the instances are found in the LXX OT or in other translations, and most are not attested as Theodotionic. There are parallels in a number of other books for the use of transliteration. As one cannot conclude that all the parts of the LXX containing transliterations emanate from Theodotion, so it is unnecessary in this case. Walde does not mention, and clearly does not accept, Torrey's view that the transliterations elsewhere represent replacements of the LXX text. As to Torrey's point that many transcriptions were later removed from Par and II Esdr, as partially witnesses the fact that some survive only in Lucianic mss., Walde argues that, if so, it cannot be established whether they are peculiarly Theodotionic, and so the phenomenon is excluded from discussion. He is stressing that the mere fact of transliteration is not necessarily an indelible mark of Theodotion.

M. Rehm has made a few germane points.[6] Eupolemus quoted II Par 4.13 in referring to κώδωνας, which is there the unusual rendering for רמונים.[7] He goes into the matter of Theodotion's suggested authorship of Par.[8] He finds that quotations from Theodotion in Rg have some unexpected agreements with the parallels in Par: in I Rg 31.3, 13; II

---

[1] *Die Esdrasbücher der LXX.*

[2] *Op. cit.*, p. 50 note 2.

[3] *Op. cit.*, p. 50 note 3.

[4] *Op. cit.*, p. 37.

[5] *Op. cit.*, pp. 40ff.

[6] *Textkritische Untersuchungen zu den Parallelstellen der Samuel-Königsbücher und der Chronik*, 1937.

[7] *Op. cit.*, p. 13 and note 1.

[8] *Op. cit.*, p. 33.

5.18, 22; 10.8; 23.8; 24.16; IV 11.12.[1] But there are also differences: two in III Rg 15.14, and also in IV 11.9,12; 14.14. At IV 15.5 Syh has a note attesting as Theodotion's a free rendering of II Chron 26.16, 18 (it has no clear links with Par). Par itself has only two possible Theodotionic quotations: one at II 4.16 with no ms. authority but suggested by Field,[2] and one at 26.1 in BM,[3] but Rehm does not consider this scanty evidence conclusive either way. On the whole he deems it more probable that Par is Septuagintal, especially in view of the striking rendering attested by Eupolemos.

The most comprehensive attack on Torrey, etc., was launched by G. Gerleman.[4] He makes three points: (1) stylistic and linguistic considerations, (2) Eupolemus' and Josephus' use of Par, and (3) reflections of second century B.C. Egypt in Par. In ch. i "The Age of the Paralipomena" he gives first a brief resumé of the discussion. Howorth's "main contention, namely that a Gk translation which closely follows the text of the Masoretes cannot have been taken from the LXX, is totally devoid of foundation". He regards as "very rash" Howorth and Torrey's view that Par and II Esdr come from the same hand. He admits that the small differences between II Par 36.22f. and the parallel II Esdr 1 are perhaps not very conclusive, but he gives a string of general stylistic and linguistic differences between the two books. As to transcription he reiterates that it is not a characteristic only or mainly of Par and Theodotion. In fact he presents a number of examples where Rg transliterates and the parallel in Par translates: II 8.13; 21.18; III 7.7; IV 11.8, 12.[5]

Moreover, Thackeray had pointed out Par's strong Egyptian colouring: Gerleman himself developed this argument.[6] His treatment may be left till later.[7]

---

[1] Of these and the following examples II 23.8; 24.16; IV 11.9, 12; 14.14 must now be ruled out of consideration. θ' and the Lucianic mss. attest in fact a B.C. recension of Rg: see Barthélemy, *op. cit.*, pp. 128ff., and the discussion at the beginning of chapter ix.

[2] *Hexapla*, ad loc. But it is doubtful: see p. 170.

[3] Actually there is another one in BM at II 23.13: b e₂'s reading σύνδεσμὸς σύνδεσμός is ascribed to θ' in b. But is this merely referring to so-called Theodotion in IV Rg? In the parallel IV Rg 11.14 this reading is shared by all ms. groups.

[4] *Studies in the LXX II. Chronicles*, 1946.

[5] The cases in II 21.18; IV 11.8, 12 are less clear than Gerleman thought. The Lucianic mss. containing the earliest extant form of text have ασηδωθ γιγάντων (= Par) and τὸ ἁγίασμα respectively.

[6] *Op. cit.*, chapter ii.

[7] See pp. 21ff.

Another pointer away from a second century A.D. dating for Par is that Josephus apparently used it, especially in the case of material which has no equivalent in Sam-Ki/Rg. He admits that the question whether Josephus used Chron or Par is a difficult one, but he finds evidence of the latter where Par has unexpected renderings of the Heb. The "daily offerings" of *Ant.* viii. 104; ix. 155 seem to be a misunderstanding of ἐφημερία, Par's term for the priestly divisions, especially in II 5.11; 23.18. Ahaziah's medical treatment (θεραπευόμενος) in *Ant.* ix. 121 more probably goes back to ἰατρευόμενον in II Par 22.9 than to a use of a Heb text with the same reading as Par's *Vorlage.* The interpretation of קֶשֶׁר as "attack" in II Par 23.13 seems to underlie Josephus' description of Athaliah's ordering the death of her enemy in *Ant.* ix. 151. With regard to numbers he sometimes follows Par, not Chron: Rehoboam's concubines number 30 in II Par 11.21 (B h c₂) and *Ant.* viii. 250, instead of 60 as in II Chron. Asa's Benjaminite soldiers are 250,000 in II Par 14.8 and *Ant.* viii, 291, but 280,000 in II Chron 14.7.

Gerleman also refers to Eupolemus' mention of κώδωνας in the Temple, independently of Rehm. II Par 4.13 can be the only source. "Eupolemos' curious idea about the bells clearly indicates that the Gk translation of the Chronicles which he used and which must thus have already existed in the middle of the second century B.C., was no other than our Paralipomena".

H.M. Orlinsky in the course of a review of Gerleman's book agreed that Par is not the work of Theodotion.[1]

P. Kahle criticised Thackeray for suspecting the influence of a late Theodotion merely on the grounds of transliteration.[2] Rather, this feature must rationally be regarded as an early phenomenon in Gk texts used in Jewish circles where the transcriptions would be understood. Kahle maintained that in Gk mss. used by Christians original transliterations had been replaced, but this was not done with equal thoroughness in different books.

An important service rendered by the critics of Howorth and Torrey has been a redress of balance. An evaluation of I Esdr has no bearing *per se* on the age of Par. Moreover, Par must be evaluated independently of II Esdr. Freudenthal and Gerleman's argument from early external testimony to Par is a strong one. Internal study of Par, beyond the

---

[1] *JBL* lxvii, pp. 381ff.

[2] *Cairo Geniza*[1], 1947, p. 169f.; [2], 1959, p. 254f.

controverted factor of transliteration, has yielded an important discovery in Thackeray and Gerleman's detection of Ptolemaic colouring. In the course of the thesis other factors will emerge which weigh down the scales further in favour of an early date. Jellicoe's ascription of Par to proto-Theodotion will be discussed further at the end of ch. vii.

2. GROUPING AND VALUE OF MSS.

This section might reasonably be expected to precede the former one and follow hard upon ch. i, but because certain views of ms. value depend upon the issue of the former section, this order has been deemed preferable.

In 1937 M. Rehm made a brief survey of the main mss. of Par.[1] b (y) e₂ offer the form of text generally recognized as Lucianic. S c₂ are associated with B, concerning which he considered that in Rg and Par "hat B die ursprüngliche Übersetzung in ihrem Bestand und in einzelnen Formen am reinsten bewahrt". d p q t z form another group, and A N, etc., yet another. The two latter groups and the Lucianic mss. agree more with the MT. Their text is the result of a later revision according to the Heb text then current. So they may not be used as witnesses to the original condition of Par. But since they are revisions and not new translations, they attest old readings at times.

In a number of these observations Rehm was saying little new but was heir to half a century of intermittent study of Par. P. de Lagarde in his Lucianic edition of 1883 had used b e₂ for the Lucianic text in Par. Some twenty years later A. Rahlfs in a study of Theodoret's quotations from Rg and II Par had noted his value for verifying that b e₂ represents the Lucianic recension;[2] and he later stated that "L = 19 93 108 et saepe 121" (b e₂ and y).[3] P. Vannutelli in 1931 had termed b e₂ Lucianic and g i m sub-Lucianic.[4] He could find no Origenic mss. in Par. d e p q t 44 74 144 236 belong to a "junior recensio", discovered in Rg by Rahlfs.[5]

As to the respective merits of the two major mss., the uncials A and

---

[1] *Untersuchungen*, 1937, p. 13.

[2] *LXX-Studien*, i, 1904, pp. 16ff.

[3] *LXX* i, p. 752.

[4] *Libri synoptici Veteris Testamenti*, i, p. vi.

[5] *LXX-Studien*, iii, pp. 20, 162.

B, Rehm was travelling in the mainstream of scholarly tradition. As long ago as 1897 H. J. Gilbert, in the course of a study of names in I Chron, said of codices A and B in Par: "Of these two codices B is by far the more independent of our present Hebrew text in the matter of proper names; its variants are striking, and it probably represents an independent Hebrew text. At the same time its errors and self-contradictions are more numerous than those of A, which bear undoubted traces not only of having been, in Chronicles, carefully compared with, and revised by, the parallel passages in Genesis, but also of having followed a text which, if not the same as our present Hebrew text, is one very similar to it."[1]

I. Benzinger in his commentary published in 1901 made this general survey: "A kennzeichnet sich auch hier durch engen Anschluss an den hebraischen Text. Luc. dagegen ist häufig mit dem Wortlaut vom Gen, Sam, Reg gleich gemacht ... Noch häufiger ist auch Luc. in auffallender Weise nach heb. korrigiert... Vat. zeichnet sich durch ein im Vergleich zu Vat. zu Sam und Reg (oft auch im Vergleich zu Luc.) wesentlich besseres griechisch aus. Unter diesen Umständen wird man principiell dem Vat. den Vorzug geben müssen, als die echte LXX am meisten repräsentierend."[2]

A year later R. Kittel came to a similar conclusion: "B hat nun trotz vieler Schriebfehler doch im ganzen den besseren Text, auch bei den Namen, wahrend A sich fast durchweg Angleichung an den MT zu Schulden kommen lässt."[3]

Rehm's successors in the study of Par have seen no reason to dispute this view of B. J. Goettsberger in the commentary brought out in 1939 judged B to be the most valuable of the mss. when not defective through corruption or omission.[4] More recently D. Barthélemy has spoken of "la Septante ancienne (attestée par B S c₂)" in I Par 10.5; of B c₂ "qui témoignent vraisemblement pour la Septante ancienne" in II 18.21; and of "la traduction originale, attestée par B c₂" in II 15.14.[5]

None of the writers from Vannutelli on give any hint of a rift of opinion. This is surprising since in 1910 C. C. Torrey shattered the peaceful scene of scholarly unanimity by propounding a contrary view. After

---

[1] *AJSL* xiii, p. 281.

[2] *Die Bücher der Chronik*, p. xvii.

[3] *Bücher der Chronik*, 1902, p. 24.

[4] *Die Bücher der Chronik*, p. 19.

[5] *Les devanciers d'Aquila*, 1963, pp. 42, 62.

citing the conventional view from Kittel as "the current (and so far as I know, unchallenged) opinion as to the best Greek text", Torrey went on to describe it as "altogether mistaken" and rated A as standing nearest the original translation and B furthest away.[1] This new evaluation goes hand in hand with the theory that Par is a product of Theodotion. "We are not dealing here with the Pentateuch or the books of Samuel or with a translation made in the third century B.C. Theodotion had before him a Hebrew text which very closely resembled our MT; he rendered it exactly and transliterated it very carefully; and we happen to have in codex A a pretty old and unusually trustworthy copy of the original version. That is all."[2] If Par is only a second century A.D. creation, it follows that copies with little corruption among the Gk mss. are very likely authentic as representing the original text. Indeed on Torrey's view of Par's authorship it would hardly be feasible that no ms. in good condition has survived. So interlocked are his higher and lower critical views.

He is uncertain about codex N in Par : it either represents an intermediate stage between the older and more correct text of A and the type selected by Origen, or else it is eclectic.[3]

Torrey believed the mss. of the B group to be Hexaplaric.[4] This belief is based first upon his conviction that Syh of I, II Esdr comes closest to the B group, apart from asterisked passages, and secondly upon a note in S at the end of II Esdr stating that the ms. had been carefully collated with one of the oldest and most correct of all Hexaplaric mss. Torrey holds that the Gk Chron-Ezra-Neh all stem from Theodotion, and he assumes that B has the same character throughout. Therefore, although finding it "necessary to speak with more caution" where the B group in Par is concerned, he enunciates that "it is hardly to be doubted that here also these same mss. [S, B, 55=h] contain the Hexaplar text". He means by this that B, etc., in Par represent a copy of Origen's fifth column with the asterisked passages removed.[5] But why should Origen have chosen for his LXX column a ms. which had suffered such monstrous corruption over the century or so that its text had existed ? Perhaps "he made the same mistake which modern scholars have made. Not knowing that Theodotion was the author of

---

[1] *Ezra Studies*, p. 92.

[2] *Op. cit.*, p. 93.

[3] *Op. cit.*, p. 97 note 41.

[4] *Op. cit.*, p. 96.

[5] *Op. cit.*, p. 97.

this version ... he may have looked with suspicion on the Gk text that agreed closely with MT and have preferred the one that showed somewhat more divergence".[1] It is highly regrettable that although Torrey was aware of the existence of extant fragments of Syh of Par[2] he made no textual study of it. Consciousness of this particular deficiency no doubt underlies his confession cited in section 1.

Torrey's dissentient voice has since 1910 been amplified to students through the megaphone of the *ICC* on Chron. E. L. Curtis took over uncritically Torrey's views of B and A in Par.[3] His Heb textual criticism is often affected by his assumptions that A represents the oldest text of Par and that the testimony of B is of comparatively little value. G. F. Moore also accepted that Torrey had established in Par "the superiority of the A class over the B class".[4]

But J. H. Ropes disagreed with Torrey's conclusions.[5] For Ropes the divergence of Syh of I, II Esdr from B in the matter of asterisked additions pointed in the opposite direction: to the inference that B is pre-Hexaplaric and closely similar to the text which Origen took as the basis of his LXX column. As to Torrey's view that B has had additions removed, he counters it with the consideration that no such treatment of Hexaplaric mss. is otherwise known. As to the note in S, Ropes retorts that Tischendorf and Lake, acknowledged experts, both hold it to be the product not of the original copyist but of a later corrector referring to his own corrections.[6] By a strange inconsistency, when discussing A (p. ci), Ropes agrees with Torrey that A is pre-Hexaplaric : he appears to have left uncoordinated the two sections on B and A.

3. CHARACTERISTICS OF THE TRANSLATION

Hitherto there has been a certain amount of discussion both in general and in detail concerning the characteristics of Par. Most of it may

---

[1] *Op. cit.*, p. 99.

[2] Cf. *AJSL* xxiii, p. 68.

[3] *Chronicles, ICC*, p. 40f.

[4] *AJSL* xxix, 1913, p. 54.

[5] *Beginnings of Christianity*, iii, 1926, p. xcv.

[6] Ropes cites C. Tischendorf, *Bibliorum Codex Sinaiticus Petropolitanus*, i, 1862, p. 13*; H. and K. Lake, *Codex Sinaiticus, OT*, 1922, p. xff. According to Lake the corrector belongs to the C group variously dated between the fifth and the seventh centuries. There may be added the testimony of H.J. Milne and T.C. Skeat, *Scribes and Correctors of the Codex Sinaiticus*, 1938, p. 65 : "As regards the correctors the conclusions formed by Lake still hold the field".

be left until chapters iv and vii, at which points previous suggestions can be considered in their individual contexts more profitably than in the vacuum of a hurried survey. But two significant traits which Gerleman has extensively discussed may conveniently be summarised at this point.

(a) *Egyptian colouring*

It has been observed already in section 1 that H. St. J. Thackeray attacked Howorth's position on the ground that Par contains certain signs of an Egyptian provenance.[1] Gerleman took up Thackeray's points, although unfortunately he did not acknowledge his debt to him in detailed instances so that it is impossible to see from his own writings when he is echoing Thackeray and when he is covering new ground. Chapter ii of Gerleman's *Studies in the LXX II. Chronicles* is devoted to a study of the links between Par and the culture of the Egypt of the Ptolemy period. The great merit of his work compared with Thackeray's is that he does what the latter could not do in the heat of controversy: he provides detailed documentation from Egyptian sources, wherever possible.

He first mentions a little detail that points to Egypt as the source of the translation. מערב in II Par 32.30; 33.14 is rendered λίψ, which Aristotle includes among the south winds, and in the LXX elsewhere means "south". But in the Egyptian papyri λίψ is used for "west".

He next traces the links between the technical terminology of the religious cult in Hellenistic Egypt and the wording of Par. Although in many cases the translator leaned heavily upon the Gk Pentateuch, in other cases he resorts to what were evidently features of his environment. When the Temple is designated τὸ ἱερόν, "an extremely rare designation in the LXX except for the Apocrypha, this is in complete conformity with the current Hellenistic Alexandrian usage".[2] παστοφόριον, used to render לשכה three times in Par (also used in Isa, Jer and Ezek a total of four times and in the Apocrypha four times)

---

[1] *JTS* viii, p. 276f.

[2] G. Schrenk, *s.v.* τὸ ἱερόν, *Theological Dictionary of the NT*, III, p. 233, enumerates its use in I 9.27; 29.4; II 6.13, and comments that "only Chronicles offers rare exceptions to the basic attitude". He goes on to say that the case is very different in I Esdr, I-IV Macc; and Josephus and Philo use it freely. But the word does occur in Ezek 45.19, as Schrenk notes earlier, and on p. 226 he observes that in Dan. 1.2 LXX the Temple vessels are called ἱερὰ σκεύη.

was a feature of the Serapeum. καταλύματα, used only in I Par 28.12
expressly of special chambers in the Temple, was also used with
reference to the Serapeum. In addition, κώδωνες, used incorrectly
for רמונים in II 4.13, refer to temple fittings just as κωδώνια do in
the papyri.

Civil administration and military organisation under the Ptolemies
seem to be reflected in the vocabulary of Par. διάδοχος appears in
I 18.17; II 16.11; 28.7. "So far as has been found, it was not used in
any other Hellenistic states than that of the Ptolemies, not has it any
comparable parallel at the courts of the Pharoahs or the Persian kings."
It was apparently a title of honour bestowed by the king. The title
"towards the end of the second century B.C. gradually fell into disuse.
For the first century B.C. not a single holder of that rank has been
discovered. That the Paralipomena still use this ephemeral, genuine
second century title corresponds well with our dating of the translation
to about 150 B.C."

At this point may be interjected the criticism of E. J. Bickerman.[1]
He calls the evidence in this chapter of Gerleman's "unconvincing".
It is unfortunate that he does not refute him point by point. But he
does single out the use of διάδοχος, and claims that Par uses it merely
in the general sense of "lieutenant" with no reference to Alexandrian
court officials. One wonders how Gerleman's critic reached this conclusion. In all three cases the word is followed by "of the king". In the
first instance it is used of David's sons in a list of officials, including
ὑπομνηματογράφος and γραμματεύς, for both of which Gerleman
claims Hellenistic links, as well be noted presently. In the second it
accompanies γραμ. and κριτής: for the latter Gerleman makes the
same claim. In the third case it is linked with the royal chamberlain.
Both the court and its officials feature in the semantic environment
of the word; it is difficult, for the present writer at least, to avoid
seeing a remarkable link with the Ptolemaic διάδοχος.

In I 27.33 הארכי רע המלך is rendered ὁ πρῶτος φίλος τοῦ βασ
The Heb רע המ׳ is itself a title, for part of which the parallel in Rg.
uses ἑταῖρος, an older title than Par's term. The translator "has
doubtless deliberately sought a parallel among the titles at the court
of the Ptolemies". "At the court of the Ptolemies ἑταῖρος, as a title,

---

[1] "Some Notes on the Transmission of the LXX", *Alexander Marx Jubilee Volume*,
p. 161 note 39.

was soon superseded by φίλος." ὑπομνηματογράφος, used in I 18.15;
II 34.8 (and also in Isa 36.3, 22) is employed in the papyri as a title for
a secretary of high rank at the court of the Ptolemies. γραμματεύς
and κρίτης are used in a military context in II 26.11:[1] in Ptolemaic
Egypt the former was "not an exclusively civil official, but also an
officer holding a rather high military rank", and the latter was a
general title for a high official rather than a technical term.

Gerleman also mentions the rendering of אבני–שיש in I 29.2 as
(λίθον) Πάριον, Parian marble, much famed and used in antiquity. He
observes that in an Egyptian papyrus from the middle of the second
century B.C. temple fittings are stated to be of Parian stone, a significant parallel to its use in Par for material to be used for the Temple
at Jerusalem.

The rendering Τρωγ(λ)οδύται for סכיים in II 12.3 "emanates from
associations which were familiar to the Alexandrians of the Ptolemy
period. The papyri contain numerous indications of the busy traffic
between Egypt and the Trodogyte country on the east coast of Africa".[2]
Gerleman might usefully have added the observation of D.S. Margoliouth: "The LXX was probably suggested by the fact of a place called
'Suche' (Pliny, *Historia Naturalis* vi 172) being mentioned among Tro-
godyte possessions".[3]

All this evidence of links with Egypt, and often with Ptolemaic
Egypt, has a strong cumulative effect. It is difficult to avoid the
conclusion that Par is a pre-Christian Egyptian creation, probably of
second century origin.

(b) *Echoes of the Pentateuch*

Gerleman devotes the third chapter of his work on Par to the
familiarity of the translator with, and dependence upon, the Gk
Pentateuch. Both general vocabulary and cultic details are borrowed.
To point the contrast, he cites the frequency with which certain words
occur in the Gk Pentateuch, in Rg and in Par. For instance, σωτήριον
or (ἡ) θυσία (τοῦ) σωτηρίου renders שלם about fifty times in the
Pentateuch, eight in Par, but not at all in Rg; whereas εἰρηνική is

---

[1] Note the interchange of the two terms observed on p. 128.

[2] Gerleman goes on to explain a supposed reference to Amazons: see p. 167 on II
14.14/15. (The number before the oblique line refers to the numeration of MT, that after
it the LXX numbering = BM in Par.)

[3] *HDB* iv, p. 627.

used twelve times in Rg, but is not found in the Pentateuch or Par. The latter echoes the Pentateuch in preferring ἐναντίον to ἐνώπιον (Rg has the latter more often); in using φυλή for שֵׁבֶט (Rg has more often σκῆπτρον); in preferring παῖς for עבד (Rg prefers δοῦλος), and in using σοφία for חכמה (Rg favours φρόνησις), ζυγός for על (Rg always uses κλοιός) and εὐφραίνειν for שׂמח (Rg also employs χαίρειν).

Gerleman observes that the phrase τὴν σκήνην τοῦ μαρτυρίου in II 5.5 occurs about 120 times in the Pentateuch, while τὸ σκήνωμα τοῦ μ. in the parallel III Rg 8.4 is never found there.[1] The rendering ἀναφορεύς for בד is found apart from Par only in Exod and Num. Comparing IV Rg 12.9f. with II Par 24.8,10f., the Scandinavian again detects "the sensibility of the Paralipomena for words characteristic of the Pentateuch": the collecting box (ארון) is κιβωτός in Rg, but Par calls it γλωσσόκομον and reserves K. for the ark.

The description of the Temple furniture in II 4.11ff. bears detailed resemblance in vocabulary to the account of the sanctuary and its furnishings in Exod 35ff. Gerleman claims that the translator apparently "borrowed several details from the Pentateuch". In each case the parallel III Rg 7.26ff. translates differently. Here are the echoes:

v.11 סירות: κρεάγρας. Compare the use of the Gk word for מזלגת in Exod. 38.3/23. Gerleman's equation, though not his conclusion, is in fact erroneous.[2] The Gk stands for יעים here, and in v. 16 for both יעים and מזלגות: the latter rendering accords perfectly with Exod. In v. 16 Gerleman wrongly considered ποδιστῆρας to be the translator's correspondent to סירות, and unnecessarily sought a parallel in Exod.

v. 14 כירות: λουτῆρας, an equivalent found also in Exod 38.8/28.

v. 11 again, יעים: πυρεῖα, which Gerleman claims is "a rendering which can be traced back to the description" in Exod 38.1, 3f./22ff. He need not have been so vague. The Gk in fact stands for סירות.[3] In the B text of Exod 38.3/23 ואת־הסירת ואת־היעים is rendered καὶ τὸ πυρεῖον αὐτοῦ καὶ τὴν βάσιν in the text of B, while in A's text the order is transposed according to the Heb. It is obvious that the translator knew the Gk Exod in the form of B at this point; he took πυρεῖον to stand for סירת and echoed the supposed rendering.

ibid. את־המזרקות: τὴν ἐσχάραν τοῦ θυσιαστηρίου. Gerleman calls

---

[1] στολὴ βυσσίνη for אפוד בד in I 15.27 Gerleman attempts to take back to Gen and Exod. But see p. 59.

[2] See p. 170 on v. 16.

[3] See p. 170 on v. 16.

this "a characteristically inadequate interpretation" and "a concise rendering of the apparatus described" in Exod 38.4/24: "a grating, a network of bronze, for the altar". Again, the conclusion is right, but the explanation inadequate.[1]

ibid. καὶ πάντα τὰ σκεύη αὐτοῦ has nothing to correspond in MT or in the parallel. Gerleman considers that it is taken from Exod 38.3/23.[2]

v. 13 רמונים: κώδωνας χρυσοῦς (III Rg 7.28 ῥοάς). The Gk word usually stands for פעמן. The nearest parallels are found in Exod 39.25f./36.32f. where reference is also made to κ.χ. (פעמני זהב), while the same passage mentions ῥοΐσκων (רמנים). Apparently the translator took bells and pomegranates as loose equivalents.[3] (Presumably he chose the former here as a stylistic variant to ῥοΐσκων = רמונים later in the verse, according to the principle of ch. iv, section 13.[4]

v. 20f. זהב סגור: χρυσίου καθαροῦ, a rendering found only here. Gerleman compares the same expression for זהב טהור in the Gk Exodus. "It is found, among other places, in the description of the tabernacle, e.g. 36, 22, 38 [actually 37]; 38, 2, 5, 9, 11."

Turning to discuss the reason for "this marked correspondence between the two descriptions" in Exod and this chapter, Gerleman dismisses the possibility of divergence of *Vorlage* as "scarcely probable". Instead, he sees here "a characteristic tendency in the translator" in view of Par's other links with the Gk Pentateuch. He considers that similarity of subject-matter is not the only reason for the translator's inclination to make II Par 4 conform more closely to the description in Exod. Developing Thackeray's idea of the effect of liturgical use of the Old Testament propounded in *The LXX and Jewish Worship*, he asks whether the LXX translators did not at times "accentuate the liturgical allusions in their renderings". He notes that the Babylonian Talmud (*Meg.* 31A) indicates I Ki 7.40-50 (paralleled in II Par 4.11ff.) as an alternative *Haphtarah* on *Chanukkah*. The liturgical connection of that passage with Exod 35-40 "in the modern service, which as a rule is very conservative" leads Gerleman to suggest that the use of I Ki 7 in the ordinary Sabbath readings was ancient

---

[1] See part II, p. 82.

[2] But see p. 199.

[3] Rehm, p. 59, suggested either a reading פעמונים or Wutz-like confusion between ρεμωνειμ and φεμωνειμ. Neither expedient is likely.

[4] See pp. 55ff.

and has been omitted accidentally from our sources. The translator, then, aware of such a liturgical connection between the passages, would have made his translation correspond closely. "The question why the similarities of the texts in regard to minute details are, broadly speaking, confined to a few verses, would be given a perfectly satisfactory explanation: the second lesson comprised only this small passage."

Gerleman has not exhausted the Pentateuchal references in Par. More will be cited in ch. iv, section 14, and ch. v, section 1, ii.[1]

4. PARALLEL ASSIMILATION

The first specialised attempt to face the problem of parallel assimilation in Par was on a minor scale. E. Podechard noted the constant tendency on the part of the Gk author and copyists to conform the text of Chron to that of the Genesis LXX.[2] He went on to trace the parallels between the two texts especially with regard to proper nouns. His examples will be noted in detail, in ch. ix.

Early in the nineteen thirties P. Vannutelli brought out a textual collation of parallel passages in MT and LXX of Sam-Ki and Chron.[3] No doubt these useful reference volumes were the inspiration behind an important work by Martin Rehm which appeared in 1937.[4] It is a painstaking study, especially in the third chapter in which he seeks to establish that the translator of Chron made use of the existing LXX rendering of Sam and Ki. First he notes places where both texts have in common an unusual rendering for the Heb.[5] Then he presents cases of identical or similar renderings where the parallel texts employ a synonym.[6] Common deviations from MT come next under review.[7] Then are examined examples of common or similar renderings based upon a single Heb or Gk error.[8] As to the Heb errors, Rehm considers it improbable that in each case similar errors happened to occur in two parallel places. Moreover it is not to be assumed that assimilation had already occurred in Par's *Vorlage* since (i) the agreement, apart from small details, occurs in the Gk wording, (ii) almost throughout a

---

[1] See pp. 57ff, 71f.

[2] "Le premier chapitre des Paralipomenès", *RB* xiii, 1916, p. 376.

[3] *Libri Synoptici*, i, 1931; ii, 1934.

[4] *Textkritische Untersuchungen*.

[5] *Op. cit.*, pp. 34-36.

[6] *Op. cit.*, p. 36.

[7] *Op. cit.*, pp. 37-39.

[8] *Op. cit.*, pp. 40-43.

worse text has been adopted (which, it is assumed, would be unlikely within the Heb tradition) and (iii) there are supporting indications that the translator used an existing translation of the parallel text. As to similar Gk errors, chiefly concerning names, Rehm holds out two possibilities: either the translator used the names in their present form, which he knew from other Bible books, even when his Heb *Vorlage* did not correspond, or it could be the work of copyists.[1] He notes cases where a common Gk error is repeated in the LXX apart from the parallel places, which seems to indicate that the translator used certain forms automatically as the standard Gk equivalent. Rehm goes on to list instances where Par combines Chron and Rg, judging that here also two explanations are possible: that they are due to the translator or to a later reviser of his work.[2]

The sixth section deals with cases where the text of Rg has been completely taken over into Par.[3] A number of his instances are not verbally identical, but Rehm justifies their inclusion with the supposition that the translator consulted Rg and then made stylistic changes at times before using it in his own rendering. This is why assimilation to Rg is often so dovetailed into Par: clearly this is not the work of a Gk copyist but goes back to the translator. There is no need to suppose that readings similar to the parallel were to be found in the *Vorlage*: in fact it is generally impossible to relate the different readings as palaeographical developments. When they can be related, Chron is generally preferable to the reading of Sam-Ki and a common retrograde step is hardly likely. It is the translator who has used the work of his predecessors even when his own *Vorlage* offered him better readings.

Summing up his position, Rehm maintains that the majority of the striking similarities observed between Par and Rg are due to the translator.[4] It is necessary to assume that he used Rg. But the dependence is by no means complete. In many cases the *Urtext* of Chron has been preserved. His dependence on Rg is limited to those places where Chron has reproduced "im grösseren Ausmass" the wording of Sam-Ki.

Rehm turns to consider the additions in the closing chapters of II Par.[5] Here he takes a completely different view — a view, it may be

---

[1] *Op. cit.*, p. 43.

[2] *Op. cit.*, p. 44.

[3] *Op. cit.*, pp. 44-47.

[4] *Op. cit.*, p. 47f.

[5] *Op. cit.*, pp. 49-51.

observed, generally taken by commentators. There are a few cases
where Par depends on Rg, word for word or with stylistic changes,
but basically the additions represent material which the translator
found in his Heb *Vorlage*.

Apart from the important third chapter there are some other relevant
points. Rehm lists a number of places where Par agrees with the
parallel Rg in small stylistic matters such as suffixes, subjects, number
of verb or noun or word-order.[1] The author considers that the translator was occasionally responsible but that often the changes are due to
subsequent Gk assimilation. In his fifth chapter on the use of the LXX
for Heb textual criticism Rehm maintains that in very many cases
where Par sides with Sam-Ki it represents the original text of Chron.
When Par came into being, its Heb text agreed with the parallel text;
Par has preserved the *Urtext*, while Chron MT represents a degeneration
of the true text preserved in both Par and Sam-Ki.[2] Comments on
Rehm's general position and detailed examples will appear in ch. ix.

Mention should be made of A. Sperber's article "New Testament and
Septuagint".[3] He discusses and illustrates the fact that the various
LXX mss. of Sam-Ki and Chron often reflect the parallel text.[4] At the
outset he states his conclusion that when Origen's sources were com-
posed, perhaps much earlier than his own time, the two recensions had
not yet been finally assigned to their respective Biblical books.

Gillis Gerleman's work must now come under review.[5] He does not
take Rehm's work into account. He notes first that the Gk texts show
much correspondence in their wording, which has no parallel in MT.
Often words and phrases found only in one of the parallel Heb texts
are reproduced in both the Gk versions.[6] Sometimes the Gk parallels
agree with the briefer of two Heb alternatives. After examples of
these phenomena he draws his conclusions. It is not merely a question
of a unilateral dependence, of a younger translation showing influences
from an earlier parallel text, since the Gk parallel texts correspond now
with Sam-Ki, now with Chron.[7] The synoptic correspondence must in
many cases be traced back to the Heb originals. "This is the simplest

---

[1] *Op. cit.*, pp. 28-31.

[2] *Op. cit.*, p. 85.

[3] *JBL* lix, 1940, pp. 193ff.

[4] *Loc. cit.*, pp. 283ff.

[5] "The Paralipomena and the Reigns", *Studies in the LXX*, 1946, ch. iv, pp. 30ff.

[6] *Op. cit.*, p. 31.

[7] *Op. cit.*, p. 34.

explanation of many passages in which the similarity between the texts does not extend to the actual choice of words."[1]

But precise word for word correspondence suggests that another factor has often been at work. "There can scarcely be any doubt that the correspondence in the wording of the Gk synoptic texts is largely due to a process of harmonisation between them, similar to that of the synoptic gospels ... The longer parallel texts have in fact been more exposed to assimilating influences, presenting natural friction surfaces, where 'unevennesses' have been filed away so as to produce greater similarity with the parallel version."[2] Gerleman mentions as cases of this lengthy assimilation I Par 17, II 6, 9, 18 and their parallels. But he notes that despite "the levelling-down, not to say fusion" between the parallel texts, they often show distinct differences, which serve to highlight the individual facets in the style of Par's translator.

Gerleman returned briefly to this field two years later, in 1948.[3] He is mainly concerned now with the LXX witness to the text of Sam-Ki but some points impinge upon the area of the present work. He mentions the "diagonal affinity" in Rg and Par, namely their tendency to deviate from their respective Heb text and conform instead to the parallel one. He notes that often the greater conformity in the Gk synopsis lies not in a literal wording, but extends merely to factual correspondence : he attributes this correspondence to their Heb texts. He does the same when single words or short word-groups are identical in Par and Rg, but the context does not show strict correspondence. He agrees in passing with Rehm that sometimes the translator of Chron has made direct use of Rg, [4] but observes that quite as often the reverse is the case: Rg shows an affinity with Chron MT. Gerleman criticised Rehm for being so concerned with copyists' errors as to overlook the factor of Jewish textual revision.[5]

One of Gerleman's main conclusions has been opposed by J. D. Shenkel.[6] He carefully analyses parallel passages in I Par and I-II Rg. His conclusions are (1) confirmation of his contention, well argued else-

---

[1] *Op. cit.*, p. 35.

[2] *Op. cit.*, p. 37.

[3] *Synoptic Studies in the OT*, esp. pp. 28ff.

[4] H.M. Orlinsky brought Rehm's work to Gerleman's notice in his review of his earlier work on the LXX of Chronicles in *JBL* lxvii, 1948, pp. 381ff.

[5] Gerleman is echoing Orlinsky's criticism of Rehm for appealing overmuch to lower criticism in his review of Rehm's book in *JBL* lviii, 1939, pp. 337ff.

[6] *HTR* lxx, pp. 63ff.

where, that the *kaige* recension in the text of B in II Rg begins at
10.1 and not 11.1, and (2) that the translator of Par made use of a
text of Par older than the *kaige* recension and adapted it to reflect
I Chron, producing a recension of Rg with definite redactional characteristics. Shenkel's thesis is essentially a refinement of Rehm's, to
whom he does not refer. Like Rehm, he considers that the translator
used Rg; but, inspired by Barthélemy and by his own work in Rg, he
goes on to think in terms of a recension of early Rg material. He
maintains that the translator-redactor remained largely faithful to
his Heb text. He does not discuss Gerleman's view of Heb accommo-
dation to the text of Sam, apparently assuming that the text of Chron
which lay before the translator matched our own. But Gerleman's
thesis of subsequent Gk harmonization he dismisses as now outmoded.
His own explanation is "both simpler and more in accord with what is
now known of the recensional history" of Rg.[1] Moreover, since the
early text of Rg in II Rg 10-24 has been preserved in only a small
number of mss., he considers it unlikely that gradual assimilation
occurred: if that had been the case, the form of text found in the
majority of mss. available to us would have been echoed.[2]

This chapter has surveyed only four major areas of this field of study.
Obviously there is much detailed work accomplished hitherto which
will be best left until its subject-matter arises in the course of study.
But a few comments may conveniently be recorded at this point.

It is a truism to speak of the LXX as a medium of interpretation.
This line of approach has been explored by V. M. Rogers, who in an
unpublished thesis has vigorously gleaned possible examples of theolo-
gically motivated renderings in Par.[3] He envisages five levers at work
bending the translation away from its Heb *Vorlage*: an exalted concept of Yahweh, high regard for David, respect for royalty, esteem for
the chosen people and veneration of the Temple and Jerusalem. In
justification of this approach he claims that there is an overwhelming
mass of material in Par which defies such explanations as variant Heb
readings, mistakes in translation and errors in transmission. Unfortunately the narrowness of Rogers' approach has vitiated his work and led
frequently to fanciful speculation. He has a two-tier view of Par: for

---

[1] *Loc. cit.*, p. 65 note 4.

[2] *Loc. cit.*, p. 81.

[3] *The Old Greek Version of Chronicles: a Comparative Study of the LXX with the
Hebrew Text from a Theological Approach*, Ph.D. 1954, Princeton.

him the Gk text of BM is virtually a carbon copy of the translator's handiwork, and the *Vorlage* practically a twin of the MT of Chron. Ideological translation is used as a key to unlock too many doors. He has occasional flashes of insight, but most of his evidence must be attributed either to fumbling or meddling Gk hands later than the translator's or to Heb hands before his time.

The second comment concerns *Biblia Hebraica* [3]. H. M. Orlinsky has amassed a number of references from other scholars and from his own previously published writings concerning the inadequacies of the edition.[1] It is a sad fact that the author must add a similar testimony of his own. BH[3], edited in Chron by J. Begrich, commits errors of fact and judgment on practically every page of Chron. Very many of its errors will be noted in succeeding chapters, and in the Index of Biblical Passages are marked with an asterisk.

A partially important contribution to the study of Par is the two-volume work of F. X. Wutz.[2] It contains many excellent solutions to textual problems of Par and its relation to MT, but they have to be sifted carefully from the chaff of his theory that a Gk transcription of the Heb text lies at the base of the translation. Orlinsky has rendered an invaluable service in surveying the rise and fall of this theory.[3] He notes that apparently Wutz himself finally abandoned it. Generally the work has been ignored in this thesis apart from elements which the present writer esteems of value.

---

[1] "The Textual Criticism of the OT", pp. 114ff.

[2] *Die Transkriptionen von der LXX bis zu Hieronymus*, 1925, 1933.

[3] "Current Progress and Problems in LXX Research," pp. 155-157.

CHAPTER THREE

GROUPING OF MSS.

It has been observed already, in ch. ii, that many of the Gk mss. of Par have been divided into groups and in some cases labelled. The aim of this chapter is to sift the ms. evidence afresh. A suitable sieve lies ready to hand in books like these, which contain so many proper nouns. The different forms of names found in the mss. afford an opportunity to discover the relative grouping of those mss. and the divergence of different types of text. This is the systematic approach which proved so useful to M. L. Margolis in his study of the LXX of Joshua. He wrote on this matter : "The proper names in the book of Joshua are the milestones which guide the investigator in finding his way to texts held together by group affinity".[1] Also H. L. Allrik, discussing names in I Esdr, has spoken thus of their value for analysing and testing the relationship of mss. : "Here so to speak the vicissitudes of the text remain uncovered; the scribe has no clues or hunches by which to smooth out or cover over. Here the half-read word or group of letters cannot be too quickly guessed or grasped at, nor can the unconscious but natural inclination to make sense so easily do its levelling work. Difficulties will be left lying in the open".[2]

In quite a large number of cases the forms of names or other transcriptions in Par may be divided into as many as four consistent groups. A selection of twenty cases of quadruple readings, taken representatively from all over Par, is set out below. Apart from the numbered mss., readings are taken mainly from the critical apparatus of BM. Also cited are five other instances where four forms of text may be distinguished, names apart.

I 1.33 $E\lambda\delta a\delta$ b g y e$_2$ $A\beta\iota\delta a\delta$ f j p q t z 74 144
אלדעה 236 321 346

$E\lambda\delta aa$ A N a c e n $E\lambda\lambda a\delta a$ B h c$_2$
$E\lambda\delta a\nu$ i Arm
$E\lambda\delta a$ m

---

[1] *JAOS* xxxi, p. 367.
[2] *ZAW* lxvi, p. 273.

2.14 רדי	$P\epsilon\eta\lambda\alpha\iota$ b	$P\eta\delta\iota$ d j p q t z 74 144 236 321 346
	$P\epsilon\eta\lambda\alpha$ y $P\epsilon\lambda\alpha\eta$ b′	$P\iota\delta\iota$ f
	$P\alpha\delta\delta\alpha\iota$ A N a c e g h n $Radai$ Arm	$Z\alpha\delta\delta\alpha\iota$ B * h c₂ $Z\alpha\beta\delta\alpha\iota$ B ᵃ ᵇ i $Z\alpha\mu\delta\alpha\iota$ m ܘܟܝܐ Syh
4.2 ראיה	$P\alpha\iota\alpha\lambda$ e₂	$\Sigma\alpha\delta\alpha\iota\acute{\alpha}s$ d f j p t 74 144 236 321 346
	$P\epsilon\eta\lambda$ b	$\Sigma\alpha\delta\delta\alpha\acute{\iota}\alpha s$ q $\Sigma\alpha\beta\alpha\acute{\iota}\alpha s$ z
	$P\epsilon\iota\alpha$ A N g h i m y $Ov\rho\epsilon\iota\alpha$ c n $Ov\rho\sigma\iota\alpha$ e '$I\epsilon\rho\epsilon\acute{\iota}\alpha s$ a $Keria$ Arm	$P\alpha\delta\alpha$ B c₂
7.32 חותם	$Ov\theta\alpha\mu$ b y e₂	$X\omega\theta\alpha\mu\iota$ d j p q t z 144 236 321 346
	$X\omega\theta\alpha\mu$ A N a c f h $Xo\theta\alpha\mu$ e i m $X\omega\mu\alpha\theta$ n $Chothas$ Arm	$X\omega\theta\alpha\nu$ B g c₂
9.8 יבניה	'$I\epsilon\chi ov\acute{\iota}ov$ b y e₂	$I\epsilon\mu\nu\alpha\iota$ d j p q t z 74 236 321 346 $I\epsilon\mu\nu\alpha\alpha$ 144
	$I\epsilon\beta\alpha\nu\alpha\iota$ N a c e h i m n Arm $I\epsilon\beta\alpha\nu\epsilon$ f g $I\epsilon\beta\alpha\nu\alpha\alpha\iota$ A	$B\alpha\nu\alpha\iota\alpha$ B c₂
11.29 חשתי	$\Sigma\omega\sigma\alpha\theta\epsilon\iota$ b e₂	$Ov\sigma\alpha\theta\iota$ d j p q t z 74 144 236 321 346 $\tau o\hat{v}$ $\Sigma\alpha\theta\iota$ m
	$A\sigma\omega\theta\iota$ A N a c e g h i n Arm	$A\theta\epsilon\iota$ B c₂ $I\alpha\theta\epsilon\iota$ S
12.7/6 ישיהו	$I\epsilon\sigma\sigma ov\epsilon$ b e₂	$I\epsilon\sigma ov\iota$[1] d j m p q t 74 144 236 321 346

---

[1] Holmes-Parsons, followed by BM, erroneously cite the readings of 74 and 236 as $I\eta\sigma ov\iota$ and $I\epsilon\sigma\sigma ov\iota$ respectively.

$I\epsilon\sigma\iota\alpha$ A N a c e f g h i n Arm $I\eta\sigma\sigma\upsilon\nu\epsilon\iota$ B S c₂

14.8 $\epsilon\grave{\iota}s \ \beta\alpha\sigma\iota\lambda\acute{\epsilon}\alpha$ b f e₂ $\beta\alpha\sigma\iota\lambda\epsilon\hat{\upsilon}\sigma\alpha\iota$ d j p q t z 144 321
למלך 346

om. c e g i m n y $\beta\alpha\sigma\iota\lambda\epsilon\acute{\upsilon}s$ B A N S h c₂ 74 236
Arm

16.5 $I\alpha\eta\lambda$ b e₂ $I\alpha\iota\eta\lambda$ j p q t z 74 144 236
יחיאל 321 346
$I\omega\eta\lambda$ m

$I\alpha\epsilon\iota\eta\lambda$ N c d $E\iota\epsilon\iota\eta\lambda$ B S Boh
e f h i n Arm ... $\iota\epsilon\iota\eta\lambda$ c₂
$I\alpha\theta\iota\eta\lambda$ A
$I\delta\epsilon\iota\eta\lambda$ g

18.8 $T\alpha\beta\alpha\theta$ b e₂ $M\alpha\tau\alpha\beta\eta\theta$ j q t 74 144 321 346
טבחת $T\alpha\beta\eta\theta$ m $M\alpha\tau\alpha\beta\eta\delta$ 236
$M\epsilon\tau\alpha\beta\eta\theta$ p z

$M\alpha\tau\epsilon\beta\epsilon\theta$ A N c e h Arm $M\epsilon\tau\alpha\beta\eta\chi\alpha s$ B S c₂
$M\alpha\tau\epsilon\beta\epsilon\tau$ g
$M\alpha\tau\epsilon\beta\alpha\theta$ f
$M\epsilon\tau\epsilon\beta\epsilon\theta$ i n y

20.4 $\Sigma\alpha\pi\phi\iota$ b e₂ $\Sigma\alpha\phi\sigma\upsilon$ d j m p q t z 74 144
ספי 236 321 346

$\Sigma\epsilon\phi\phi\iota$ A N c f g h i n y $\Sigma\alpha\phi\sigma\upsilon\tau$ B c₂
$\Sigma\epsilon\phi\iota$ e
Sepfias Arm

23.7 $\Gamma\epsilon\delta\sigma\omega\nu$ b i y e₂ $\Gamma\eta\rho\sigma\omega\nu\iota$ d e^a? j p q t z 74
גרשני Gethson Arm 144 236 321 346
$\Gamma\epsilon\rho\sigma\omega\nu$ 44
$\Gamma\eta\rho\sigma\omega\nu$ A N a c e* f g h i n $\Pi\alpha\rho\sigma\sigma\omega\mu$ B
$\Gamma\eta\rho\sigma\alpha\nu$ m $\Pi\alpha\rho\sigma\sigma\sigma\mu$ c₂

24.15 $X\eta\zeta\epsilon\iota\rho$ b e₂ $E\theta\theta\iota$ d j p q t z 74 144 236
חזיר 321 346
$X\eta\zeta\eta\rho$ m $I\epsilon\theta\theta\iota$ 44

$I\epsilon\zeta\epsilon\iota\rho$ A N a c f $A\phi\epsilon\sigma\eta$ B c₂
$I\epsilon\zeta\eta\rho$ i n y $A\phi\epsilon\sigma\iota$ g
$E\zeta\eta\rho$ e h
Ezirai Arm

26.15 $A\sigma\alpha\phi$ b e₂ Arm $\sigma\epsilon\phi\iota\mu$ d j p q z 74 144 236
אספים 321 346
  $\sigma\epsilon\rho\iota\mu$ t

  $\alpha\sigma\alpha\phi\epsilon\iota\nu$ A i n y $\epsilon\sigma\epsilon\phi\epsilon\iota\nu$ B
  $\alpha\sigma\alpha\phi\epsilon\iota\mu$ N c e f g $\epsilon\sigma\epsilon\phi\eta$ c₂
  $\alpha\sigma\alpha\phi\epsilon\iota$ h
  $\sigma\alpha\phi\iota\nu$ m
  $\alpha\alpha\tau\iota\phi$ a

27.21 $I\alpha\sigma\sigma\iota\eta\lambda$ b e₂ $I\alpha\sigma\iota\eta\lambda$ d j p q t z 74 144 236
יעשיאל 321 346
  $A\sigma\iota\eta\lambda$ A N a c e h i m n ArmLa $A\sigma\epsilon\iota\eta\rho$ B h
  $A\epsilon\iota\eta\lambda$ f $A\sigma\eta\rho$ c₂
  $A\sigma\alpha\eta\lambda$ g

II 11.9 $A\delta\omega\rho\alpha\mu$ b e₂ $A\delta o\upsilon\rho\alpha\iota\mu$ d i p (ρ ex λ pᵃ) q
אדורים t y z 74 144 236 321 346
  $A\delta o\upsilon\rho\alpha\mu$ m

  $A\delta\omega\rho\alpha\iota\mu$ A N a c e g h j n Arm $A\delta\omega\rho\alpha\iota$ B c₂
  $A\delta\omega\rho\epsilon\mu$ f

13.3 $\dot{\alpha}\nu\delta\rho\hat{\omega}\nu$ $\dot{\epsilon}\kappa\lambda\epsilon\kappa\tau\hat{\omega}\nu$ $\dot{\alpha}\nu\delta\rho\hat{\omega}\nu$
איש $\delta\upsilon\nu\alpha\tau\hat{\omega}\nu$ $\dot{\iota}\sigma\chi\upsilon\dot{\iota}$ ($+$ $\delta\upsilon\nu\alpha\tau\hat{\omega}\nu$ p)
בחור $\dot{\alpha}\nu\delta\rho\hat{\omega}\nu$ $\pi o\lambda\epsilon\mu\iota\sigma\tau\hat{\omega}\nu$
גבור $\pi o\lambda\epsilon\mu\iota\sigma\tau\hat{\omega}\nu$ b e₂ $\delta\upsilon\nu\dot{\alpha}\mu\epsilon\omega\nu$
חיל *virorum electis potentibus virtute* $\dot{\iota}\sigma\chi\dot{\upsilon}\iota$ i p q t y z 74 144 236
  La 321 346

  $\delta\upsilon\nu\alpha\tau\hat{\omega}\nu$ (om. e h)
  $\pi o\lambda\epsilon\mu\iota\sigma\tau\hat{\omega}\nu$
  $\delta\upsilon\nu\dot{\alpha}\mu\epsilon\omega\varsigma$ A N a c e f g h j n $\delta\upsilon\nu\alpha\tau o\dot{\iota}$
  Arm $\pi o\lambda\epsilon\mu\iota\sigma\tau\dot{\alpha}\iota$ B c₂
  $\delta\upsilon\nu\dot{\alpha}\mu\epsilon\omega\varsigma$

15.8 $\Omega\delta\eta\delta$ b e₂ $A\delta\delta\omega$ d p q t z 144 236 321
עדד 346
  $A\delta\omega$ 74
  $'A\zeta\alpha\rho\acute{\iota}o\upsilon$ A N a c e f g h m n $A\delta\alpha\delta$ B cᵃ₂
  y Arm $\Delta\alpha\delta$ c₂*
  ܥܙܪܝܐ Syh
  cf. *Azarie filii Odet* La

22.7   τοῦ ἐξολεθρεῦσαι   εἰς τὸν οἶκον
להכרית   τὸν οἶκον   Αχααβ d f j m n p q t z 74
את־בית   236 321
אחאב   Αχααβ b y e₂
         ad percutiendam domum Acab La
         om. A N a c e g h 144 346 Arm τὸν οἶκον
                                      Αχααβ B c₂

23.1   Μαασίαν b e₂   ’Αμασίαν a d n p q t y z 74
מעשיהו   144 236 321 346
         Maasiam La   ’Αμασσίαν N
                                      Αμεσια g

         Μασίαν A c e f j m Arm   Μαασαίαν B
                                      Μασαίαν h c₂

25.18   ακχαν e₂   ακχουχ d f n p q t y 74 144
                                      236 321 346
חוח¹   ακαν m   ακχαχ z
         ακχαμ b
         αχαμ b′
         cf. Spina La = ἄκανθα

         αχουχ c e g*   χοζει B
         αχχουχ N a gª? j   χοζ c₂
                                      οχοζ A h Arm

26.11   Μαασσιόυ b e₂   Μαασίου d p q t y z 14 144
                                      236 321 346
מעשיהו Μαασαίου A N a c n   ’Αμασαίου B
         Μασαίου f g h j c₂   ’Αμασίου m
         Μασέου e
         Maseai Arm

28.12   Αλδι b   Ελδαι m p q t y z 74 144 236
                                      321 346
חדלי   Αλλααι e₂

         Αδδι A N a c e f g j n   Χοαδ B c₂
         Αδαι h
         Adli Arm
         Adali La

32.10 καὶ κάθησθε b e₂ 74   καὶ καθήσεσθε d p q t y z c₂
      et sedetis La   144 321 346

וישבים sedetis Arm   καὶ καθίσ. 236

      καθῆσθαι A N c e f g h j n   καθήσεσθε B a m
            o^vid

34.8 ἐκέλευσε τοῦ   ἐκέλευσε καθ.

לטהר   καθαρίσαι b   d p q t y z c₂ 74 144 236 321
                                      346

      ὅτε συνετέλεσεν τοῦ   τοῦ καθ. B
      καθ. A N c e f g h j m n Arm
      cf. cum emundasset La

These four groups will be numbered as follows in the next few chapters:

i   ii
iii iv

La will be considered separately.

CHAPTER FOUR

TRANSLATION TECHNIQUES

It is obvious that a thorough knowledge of a translator's style and method of dealing with his text is necessary if one is to judge aright the nature of the text that lay before him. A casual reference to the LXX of a particular passage without this wider knowledge can lead to unwarranted conclusions. D. R. Ap-Thomas lays down the wise ruling that "every case of discrepancy between the MT and a Version must be decided on its merits, after the main idiosyncrasies of that particular translator have been discovered".[1] But in speaking of a translator's style with regard to Par two as yet unproven assumptions are being made. It is assumed that underlying the mass of ms. variants is a single, consistent attempt to render Chron into Gk. First, as to ms. variants it has already been observed that the Gk mss. fall into four major groups. Their relative value has not yet been analysed and in fact it will eventually be observed that none of these groups can be simply identified *en bloc* with the original translation. But in order to establish methods of translation, only those features are employed which are common to all four groups. Throughout this chapter cited renderings are shared by groups i-iv unless it is otherwise stated. Moreover, the reading of MT is in little doubt in the cases of translation which are quoted, unless otherwise stated.

While the first assumption concerns ms. variants, the second concerns stylistic variety of renderings to be found in Par. The work bears marks of homogeneity in many respects. But alongside this uniformity lies a host of apparently contradictory features. The translation as a whole presents a picture of strong contrasts. Are these in fact marks of different minds at work ? It is a conviction forced upon the writer that this conclusion would be unwarranted and that there is an overall consistency which embraces within it a rich variety of expression. "One man in his time plays many parts", and the reader is invited to note how literal and loose renderings overlap and reappear at every stage of the work.[2]

---

[1] *A Primer of OT Text Criticism*, p. 20.

[2] The preponderance of names in I Par must of course be taken into account as the

Helbing characterised Par as inclining to "mechanischer, wortge-treuer Wiedergabe oft auf Kosten der griechischen Sprache in gram-matischer und stilistischer Hinsicht".[1] In similar vein Rehm speaks of the style of Par as "möglichster Wortlichkeit".[2] Gerleman criticised Helbing's verdict as misleading: "even if the Paralipomena are by no means free from Hebraisms, it must be stated, after a comparison with the Reigns, that the Paralipomena translation, relatively to the original, is linguistically and stylistically the freer version".[3] Barthélemy des-cribed Par's use of ἕκαστος for אִישׁ as "litteralisme intelligent".[4] In fact, considerable stylistic mixture will be noted in the translator's approach, to which no brief summary can do complete justice.

1. ORDER OF WORDS

The translator generally ties himself rigorously to the Heb order. This feature is especially noticeable in the retention of the Semitic order: verb + subject. Clear cases of transposition in translation are attested by all four groups at I 21.22 (δός μοι αὐτόν for תְּנוּהוּ לִי), II 1.7 (σοι δῶ for אֶתֶּן־לָךְ) and 25.8 where ἐν τούτοις appears a few words later in the sentence.[5] These cases at least show that the Heb order is not absolutely followed.

2. THE ARTICLE

Gerleman, p. 40, noted that Par uses the definite article less than Rg, especially in genitival constructions. This trait he saw to be a Hebraism, corresponding to the lack of article with a Heb noun either in the con-struct state or having a suffix. He traced the contrast in this respect between Rg and Par through a number of parallel passages. Unfortuna-

---

reason why examples from II Par are often more numerous. With this paragraph is to be compared the following statement of H.S. Gehman, *Textus* v, p. 125, not about Par but about the LXX generally: "We often meet in the same verse or in adjacent verses both literalism and extreme freedom of translation side by side. At times the reader of the LXX is reminded of the swing of a pendulum from one end of the arc to the other as if the interpreter was working under a tension between literalism and freedom of rendering".

[1] *Kasussyntax*, p. xiii.

[2] *Untersuchungen*, p. 40.

[3] *Studies in the LXX II*, pp. 40ff. Gerleman did not undergird his work with a study of ms. groupings. Some of his examples are not available in all the groups and so cannot be cited in this survey.

[4] *Devanciers*, p. 48.

[5] See further on this verse part II, p. 85.

tely many of his examples are not attested in all the major groups of Gk mss. and so are unsuitable for this survey.[1] But below is set out a bird's eye view of examples representatively selected. It must be understood that the translator does not consistently adopt an anarthrous style. The casual reader will find many examples of the article used in similar constructions throughout Par. The translator is equally at home with or without the article. In fact, to point the contrast as characteristic, contrary cases are below illustrated from the close vicinity of the first set of examples.

I 2.21	πατρὸς Γαλααδ [2]		τὴν θυγατέρα Μαχειρ
4.41	ἐν ἡμέραις Ἐζεκίου [3]		τοὺς οἴκους αὐτῶν
11.3	διὰ χειρὸς Σαμουηλ		κατὰ τὸν λόγον κυρίον
16.40	ἐν νόμῳ κυρίου		τοῦ θυσιαστηρίου τῶν ὁλοκ.
21.19	ἐν ὀνόματι κυριου		κατὰ τὸν λόγον Γαδ
25.6	ἐν οἴκῳ θεοῦ/κυρίου		τοῦ πατρὸς αὐτῶν
II 4.10	ἀπὸ γωνίας τοῦ οἴκου	4.9	τὴν αὐλὴν τῶν ἱερέων
6.15	ἐν χερσίν σου		τῷ πατρί μου
9.4	καθέδραν παίδων αὐτοῦ		τὰ βρώματα τῶν τραπεζῶν
12.16	ἐν πόλει Δαυειδ		τῶν πατέρων αὐτοῦ
18.9	ἐπὶ θρόνου αὐτοῦ		ἐν τῷ εὐρυχώρῳ (τῆς) (θυσίας) (τῆς) πύλης
21.20	ἐν τάφοις τῶν βασίλεων	21.19	ὁ λαὸς αὐτοῦ
25.19	ἐν οἴκῳ σου	25.18	τὰ θηρία τοῦ ἀγροῦ
29.15	διὰ προστάγματος κυρίου		κατὰ τὴν ἐντολὴν τοῦ βασίλεως
32.26	ὀργὴ θεοῦ / κυρίου		ἐν ταῖς ἡμέραις Ἐζεκίου
34.17	ἐν οἴκῳ κυρίου	34.16	τῶν παίδων / δούλων σου

In this section there must also be noted a tendency to use τόν before a proper noun which is the object of a verb. This trait could be merely a Gk device to aid understanding, but it is not insignificant that the article often corresponds to את. Remarkable are the three instances of

---

[1] The author has been aware of the possibility of secondary influence permeating all the groups, and has isolated all recoverable cases in ch. viii. He has accepted as original instances where not only do the four groups agree but also there seems to be no specific reason to suspect revision.

[2] Throughout this chapter names are given in B's form or abbreviated to the initial letter.

[3] It will be noted that many of the examples in the first column involve prepositions. The need to cull contrary examples from the same context has rather over-emphasised this trait.

ὁ before a noun, representing את, in I 2.9, but group ii omits the articles. But the translator is no Aquila:[1] sometimes τὸν appears where את does not occur, e.g. I 2.48 שבר : τὸν Σ.[2]

3. THE CONJUNCTION

καί appears with monotonous frequency throughout most of Par. It is occasionally varied : with πλήν II 15.17, ἀλλά 28.22[3] and δέ 32.8. These all stand for ו. δέ is idiomatically added at 6.34.

The Hebraism καὶ ἐγένετο … καί represents ו … ויהי at I 17.1, 3; 18.1; 20.1, 4; II 8.1-2; 10.2-3; 13.15; 25.14, 16. καί also appears for ו after subordinate clauses, mainly temporal, at I 17.10; 21.28; II 2.3/4, where ו was read by dittography; 7.1, 20; 22.8; 24.11.

The rendering of וגם is in many cases disputed among the groups.[4] But unanimity is frequent enough to perceive two opposing trends. Simply καί is deemed sufficient at I 12.39/38, 41/40; 20.6; 29.9; II 1.11; 9.10; 15.16; 16.12; 21.13, 17; 24.12; 28.8; 29.35; 30.1; 34.27.[5] Highly significant is καὶ γαρ at II 26.20; 28.2 as an attempt to render the two elements distinctly. But this apparent tendency towards literalism is outweighed by the other examples.

4. NEGATIVES

The translator has contrasting methods of dealing with לא before a noun: twice ἐν οὐ is used in II 15.3 for ללא, but on the other hand בלא becomes παρά in 30.18. He can render a positive statement or question negatively: I 17.21 ומי : καὶ οὐκ ἔστιν, 26.27 לחזק : τοῦ μὴ καθυστερῆσαι τὴν οἰκοδομήν.

5. VERBS

(i) Uniformity of translation is illustrated by the consistent use of πονεῖν in the sense "suffer pain, be sick" for חלה scattered at I 10.3; II 18.33; 35.23.[6] The translator has idiomatic renderings of עלה in

---

[1] See Barthélemy, *Devanciers*, p. 17.

[2] There seems to be no necessity to posit a different *Vorlage*. The use of the article is further discussed on p. 142f.

[3] See further p. 160.

[4] See the partial lists in Barthélemy, *op. cit.*, p. 41f.

[5] For the rendering καίγε in II 14.14/15 see p. 167.

[6] The rendering occurs sporadically in other books: see Hatch and Redpath, *Concordance*. For the meaning of the Gk verb see Liddell and Scott, *Lexicon*, For the case in I 10.3 see further p. 129.

artistic or literary usage: κατεχωρίσθη ("entered in a register")
I 27.24, ἔγλυψεν II 3.5, ὕφανεν[1] 3.14, κατέγραψεν 20.34. In translating
נתן in the sense "make, set, appoint" he can be wooden at times,
using διδόναι e.g. I 17.22; II 8.9; 17.19; 23.11; 35.25. But at other
times he is more sensitive to ordinary Gk usage, using κατέστησεν
I 12.18, ἔταξεν 16.4 or τιθέναι, e.g. II 1.15; 6.13; 24.8; 32.6; 36.7.
As Thackeray notes, a Hebraism appears in the rendering ἀναπαύειν
or καταπαύειν τινί at I 22.9, 18; 23.25; II 14.5/6, 6/7; 15.15; 20.30
for הניח לפ'.[2]

(ii) As to tenses, a mixed picture is presented. Heb imperfects mecha-
nically become Gk futures at I 9.28; II 5.6; 23.19. But perfect and
preterite are well turned into Gk imperfects at II 12.11; 17.9; 24.11.

(iii) The Gk participles in Par are often literalistic translations of
Heb ones, so that clauses lack a finite verb: examples are at I 6.33/48;
9.29; 12.16/15; 15.27; 21.3; II 5.6; 7.4; 9.18; 18.9; 29.28. Yet the
translator does know better: he does not fall into this mechanical
error at I 21.20; II 7.3; 13.10; 17.11, for instance.

At times an adjectival participle is turned into a finite verb: II 23.4
בָּאֵי: εἰσπορευέσθωσαν (but Rehm, p. 41, posits בָּאוּ), v.14 הבא :
εἰσέλθατε (groups ii, iii ἐξέλθατε), 31.6 המקדשים: καὶ ἡγίασαν. Thus
the rendering καὶ ὕψωσάς με for המעלה in I 17.17 does not necessarily presuppose ותעלני contra Curtis and BH.

Gk participles in Par are sometimes idiomatic. The use of ἀναφέρων,
to render a Heb infinitive, after συντελεῖν is to be noted at I 16.2;
II 29.29. Parataxis is avoided by using participles at I 12.24/23 באו :
οἱ ἐλθόντες, 29.10 ויאמר: λέγων and v.20 ויקח וישתחוו: καὶ κάμψαντες τὰ
γόνατα προσεκύνησαν.

(iv) The measure of freedom which the translator takes with his
material is illustrated by his transformation of Heb infinitives con-
struct. Subordinate Heb infinitives can be manipulated into coordinate
verbs in translation: II 29.24 לכפר: καὶ ἐξιλάσαντο, 36.6 להליכו :
καὶ (ἀπ/ἀν)ήγαγεν (αὐτόν).[3]

(v) Change of voice is encountered at times, if deemed more con-

---

[1] At II 3.14, in view of Chron's use of עלה and its treatment in Par, there is no need
to assume with Rehm, *Untersuchungen*, pp. 70, 83, a *Vorlage* ויקלע for ויעל in line
with קלע in the parallel I Ki 6.29.

[2] *Grammar*, p. 281.

[3] The reason may be confusion with the use of ל + infinitive as a finite verb, of
which the translator was aware.

venient. Active becomes passive at I 28.4 לְהַמְלִיךְ: τοῦ γενέσθαι με βασιλέα, II 26.22 כָּתַב: γεγραμμένοι ὑπό, 32.6 וַיִּקָּבְצֻם: καὶ συνήχθησαν. Indefinite third plurals are turned into passive verbs: II 24.8 וַיַּעֲשׂוּ: γενηθήτω, וַיִּתְּנֻהוּ: καὶ τεθήτω, 34.24 אֲשֶׁר קָרְאוּ: τῷ ἀνεγνωσμένῳ. Passive verbs are also made active: I 19.16 נִגְּפוּ לִפְנֵי יִשְׂרָאֵל: ἐτρο-πώσατο αὐτὸν Ἰσραηλ,[1] II 2.13/14 יִנָּתֶן־: δῶς.[2] In 23.14 תְּמִיתוּה is rendered: ἀποθανέτω (i θανατωθήτω). Rehm, p. 71, reads תֻּמְתָה (sic) according to II Ki 11.15 תּוּמַת.

(vi) Number is not always strictly adhered to, especially where collective singulars are involved. When אִישׁ is the subject a singular replaces the Heb plural at II 20.27. Likewise frequently with עַם, e.g. at I 19.6; II 7.14; 10.16; 21.19; 27.2; and with קָהָל in I 13.4; II 29.28; 30.25; and with בַּיִת I 10.6; II 21.6. With a double subject a plural Heb verb is made to agree with the first, singular, subject at II 7.5; 13.17; 29.29; 31.8. The indefinite singular מָלֵא at II 16.14 naturally becomes ἔπλησαν.

6. PREPOSITIONS

The translator's attitude to prepositions falls into two distinct categories. On the one hand he can be literalistic. ἐν covers a multitude of uses of בּ. It stands for בּ *pretii* at I 11.19; 21.22; II 24.25; for בּ meaning " by reason of" in I 10.13; 27.24; for בּ meaning "with" I 15.16, 28; II 18.10; 24.24; 25.8. This last use of ἐν is so much part of the translator's thinking that he can use it at II 23.10 in the loose rendering ἕκαστον ἐν τοῖς ὅπλοις αὐτοῦ for וְאִישׁ שִׁלְחוֹ בְיָדוֹ. The temporal use of בּ with infinitive becomes ἐν τῷ *passim*, e.g. I 12.21/20; 16.19; 21.28; II 5.10; 13.15; 22.6; 28.6; 36.2; and בְּעוֹד is so rendered in II 20.22; 29.27. The idiomatic use of בּ after certain Heb verbs is often reproduced word for word with ἐν: after שָׁאַל I 10.13; 14.14; after מָעַל I 5.25; II 10.19; 26.16; after רָצָה I 28.4; after בָּחַר I 28.4ff. (but σέ v.10); 29.1; II 6.5, 34; 7.12. בְיָד frequently becomes ἐν χειρί.

ל frequently has εἰς as its mechanical equivalent: predicatively after the verb to be or γίνεσθαι or a verb of appointing, e.g. I 11.6; 28.6; II 6.5; 12.8; 28.23; 36.20; in the sense of "for, with a view to", e.g. I 12.26/25; 22.1; II 4.13; 23.19; 35.2. εἰς can render ל in its

---

[1] See p. 56.

[2] Rehm, p. 59, here posits נָתֹן (י lost after ר).

adverbial usage to indicate reference to a norm: εἰς πλῆθος often appears for לרב, e.g. I 22.3; 29.21; II 9.1; 30.24. Compare εἰς δόξαν II 3.6. and εἰς ὕψος, e.g. I 14.2; 29.3; II 17.12; 20.19.

מן is at times used in Chron virtually to introduce the subject in the partitive sense "some of". ἀπό takes on this Semitic flavour as its equivalent in I 9.3 (i ἐκ), 30; 12.17/16, 33/32-38/37. ἐκ is so used in I 4.40; 9.29. Even a bare genitive appears in II 32.21 according to groups i-iii, but group iv prefaces it with ἐκ.

Helbing's dictum springs readily to mind in reaction to this display of Semitisms where prepositions are concerned. But it is only half the story. The translator also makes deliberate and persistent efforts to avoid clumsy Heb prepositions in favour of a more elegant, or at least a more natural, Gk rendering. Here is a telling list:

I 4.42	בראשם :	ἄρχοντες αὐτῶν
12.19/18	בראשׁי :	ἄρχοντας
II 5.13	כאחד :	μία φωνὴ
5.13	בהלל :	ἔλεγον Ἐξομολογεῖσθε
9.7	העמדים לפניך :	οἱ παρεστηκότες σοι
14.6/7	לפנינו :	κυριεύ(σ)ομεν [1]
18.16 ... ל	לא־אדנים ל :	οὐκ ἔχουσιν ἡγούμενον
20.27	בראשם :	ἡγούμενος αὐτῶν
21.16	אשׁר על־יד :	τοὺς ὁμόρους
28.9	בחמת :	ὀργή
30.27	וישבקולםעמ :	καὶ (ἐπ)ἠκούσθη ἡ φωνὴ αὐτῶν
31.16	במשמרותם כחלקותיהם :	ἐφημερία(ι)ς, διατάξεως αὐτῶν
32.1	לבקעם אליו :	προκαταλαβέσθαι αὐτάς [2]
32.25	עליו :	ὃ ἔδωκεν αὐτῷ
35.8	לנדבה :	ἀπήρξαντο [3]
v. 25	בקינותיהם :	θρῆνον
II Ki 24.3/36.5c	על־פי :	θυμός [4]

It was noted earlier that לרב appears as εἰς πλῆθος, but nearly as many times πολύς is used instead, e.g. I 22.3; 29.2; II 14.13/14; 30.13.

In view of this practice of avoiding prepositions it is surely hazardous to conclude with BH and Rudoph that in II 26.11 τοῦ διαδόχου

---

[1] Schleusner, *Lexicon*, i, p. 792; ii, p. 341, following L. Bos, unnecessarily considered the Gk corrupt.

[2] The preposition is represented in the middle voice of the verb.

[3] Benzinger wrongly claims that Par omits לנ׳.

[4] על־אף was read: see part II, p. 94.

stands for מִשְׁנֶה as at 28.7 instead of MT מִשְׂרֵי. Compare διάδοχοι for ליד in groups ii-iv at I 18.17.

Here may be mentioned the stylistically good phrase ἐξελθεῖν εἰς ἀπάντησιν so regularly used for יצא לפני on the analogy of יצא לקראת: in I 12.18/17; 14.8; II 15.2; 20.17; 28.9. אל־פני(ו) underlies the Gk at II 19.2. In II 14.9/10 εἰς συνάντησιν instead is used for לפני(ו).

The translator at times likes to insert ἐκ or ἀπό within a genitival phrase. Examples are:

II 2.7/8   עצי לבנון : ξύλα ἐκ τοῦ Λ.

3.6   זהב פרוים : χρυσ(ι)ου τοῦ ἐκ Φ.

9.21   אניות תרשיש : πλοῖα/ον ἐκ Θ.

32.31   שרי בבל : τῶν ἀρχόντων (τῶν) ἀπὸ B.

This practice suggests that at II 3.10 Benzinger, followed by Curtis, was incorrect in suggesting that the LXX presupposes מעשה מעצים for מ' צעצעים on the basis of ἔργον ἐκ ξύλων.

7. NOUNS

(i) בן is widely used in Chron both literally and figuratively. The translator has two ways of dealing with the literal usage: he uses both υἱός and ὁ τοῦ or τοῦ. The latter method of rendering is found quite frequently, e.g. I 26.24; 27.2; II 11.3; 19.2; 28.12. As to the figurative uses both mechanical and periphrastic renderings occur. Here are the literalistic examples:

בני חיל	:	I 5.18 υἱῶν δυνάμεως/ν
		II 26.17 υἱοὶ δυνατοί (i ... δυνάμεως)
בני בליעל	:	13.7 υἱοὶ παράνομοι
בני הגדוד	:	25.13 υἱοὶ τῆς δυνάμεως
בני התערבות	:	25.24 τοὺς υἱοὺς τῶν συμμίξεων[1]
בן of age	:	26.3 υἱός

Yet at times the translator does bestir himself to do better than this and to avoid the odd-sounding "son":

בני חצי	:	I 5.23 οἱ ἡμίσεις (ii οἱ ἥμισυ)
בני־חיל	:	26.9 δυνατοί
		II 28.6 ἀνδρῶν δυνατῶν

[1] The same rendering is found in the parallel IV Rg 14. 14 in a doublet. This root ערב does not recur in Chron; in IV Rg 18.23 התערב is rendered μίχθητε. Therefore the phrase probably originated in Rg.

Compare also II 10.17 בני ישראל: ἄνδρες Ἰσραηλ.

(ii) The Heb language puts nouns to a wider use than Gk does. The translator reflects now Gk usage, now that of his *Vorlage*. In I 12.39/38 ψυχὴ μιά renders לב אחד as a predicate to a personal subject. On the other hand, genitival nouns are often replaced by adjectives, e.g. ὀνομαστός for שׁם(ות) in I 5.24; 11.20; 12.31/30, πολεμι(κ)ός for מלחמה/ות in I 12.34/33; 18.10, I 28.3, ὀχυρός for מצור(ות) in II 8.5; 11.23; μεμηχανευμένας for מחשׁבת in 26.15, and ὡραῖον for מחמדיה in 36.19.

(iii) Gk lacks the fullness of Heb style in respect of repeating nouns within the same sentence or brief context, and prefers to use pronouns. Par very often literally repeats name after name, noun after noun. But the translator can adopt a better style: I 28.16 לשׁלחנות[2]: ὡσαύτως, 29.24 שׁלמה המלך: αὐτῷ, II 36.16 האלהים: αὐτοῦ. Accordingly one is led to query the following case of automatic retroversion in the apparatus of BH:

II 28.24 את־כלי בית האלהים: αὐτά: 'GV אותם'.

(iv) אישׁ in the sense of "each" is well rendered ἕκαστος in II 9.24; 11.4; 18.9, 16; 23.10; 25.22; 31.2.[1] BH wrongly posits כל־אישׁ for ἕκαστος in a note on II 36.4a.

(v) The Heb idiom of repeating a noun to give distributive force is rendered both literally and loosely. On the one hand ἑκάστης τραπέζης translates לשׁלחן ושׁלחן at I 28.16. On the other hand πρωὶ πρωί renders בבקר בבקר in I 9.27, and εἰς πύλην καὶ πύλην for לשׁער ושׁער in II 8.14 (cf. 28.25; 31.19; 35.15 for similar phrases). Two cases could be due to haplography, but certainly need not: I 23.30 בבקר בבקר: πρωί, II 32.28 לכל־בהמה ובהמה: παντὸς κτήνους.

(vi) The translator deals variously with the Heb habit of using a singular noun indicating a part of the body where more than one person is in question. Consider, for example, κεφαλὴν αὐτῶν I 23.3; 25.1, καρδίαν υἱῶν II 6.30, καρδίαν αὐτῶν 11.16, χεῖρα ποιούντων 34.10. The stereotyped ἀπὸ προσώπου for מפני or מלפני with a plural occurs, e.g. at I 5.25; 10.1: II 28.3; 33.2. However, the translator is not always so wooden: e.g.

I 19.5	זקנכם	:	τοὺς πώγωνας ὑμῶν
29.18	לבבם	:	τὰς καρδίας αὐτῶν
II 1.17	בידם	:	ἐν χερσὶν αὐτῶν

---

[1] In I 16.3 τῷ ἀνδρί for לאישׁ is a case of re-interpretation.

13.16   בידם : εἰς τὰς χεῖρας αὐτῶν
29.31   ידכם : τὰς χεῖρας ὑμῶν

(vii) As to number generally, the translator at times feels free to put singular for plural and *vice versa*.

גבול in the sense of "frontier" is generally ὅρια according to Gk idiom, e.g. I 6.39/54; II 11.13.

מנחה in the sense of "tribute" is always δῶρα, e.g. I 18.2; II 9.24; 26.8.

עולה is often ὁλοκαυτώματα, e.g. at I 6.34/49; 21.29; II 4.6; 35.14, as well as ὁλοκαύτωσις. BH has not grasped this fact in the note on II 7.1 העולה (τὰ ὁλοκαυτώμοτα) 'G העולות'. At 9.4, where for עֹלֵיתוֹ Par has τὰ ὁλοκαυτώματα, many commentators, listed by Curtis and including him, read עֲלֹותָיו with 'GVS'. Compare BH: '1 c I R 10, 5 וְעֹלָתוֹ, cf. GVS (וְעֹלֹותָיו)'. In fact, as Rehm, p. 70, perceived, the translator clearly read עָלָתוֹ, the same as the Ki text (BH misquotes). The process works the other way too: עֹולות becomes ὁλοκαύτωσις in I 21.23; II 1.6; 29.34. Rehm, p. 71, is hardly on safe ground in positing לעלה for לעלות at I 21.23 in line with the parallel II Sam. 24.22.

בשמות idiomatically becomes ἐπ᾽ ὀνόματος in I 16.41.

ארצות often becomes γῆ, e.g. at II 12.8; 17.10; 32.17. Therefore at I 13.2 one queries the note in BH '1 prb c G ארץ': Rudolph explains well Chron's plural.

מלחמות becomes πόλεμος in II 27.7; 32.6,8. One therefore doubts the necessity of concluding with BH '3 MSS G S מלחמה' at II 16.9 as far as Par is concerned.

Collective singulars after numerals naturally become plural, e.g. in II 9.15; 18.5; 25.5. So BH, although it claims so categorically '1 c Seb pl MSS G V T גבורי' at II 17.16 and '1 c Seb GVST גבורי' at 25.6, is not necessarily supported by Par.

Collective nouns in general are at times rendered in the plural, e.g. II 25.8 אויב: τῶν ἐχθρῶν. The translator often prefers to make יד plural even without a plural of person, e.g. I 14.10; 29.5; II 6.15; 28.5. Curtis is hardly on safe ground in claiming at II 25.20 that εἰς χεῖρας for ביד implies בידי. Nor is BH in claiming at 18.5 that εἰς χεῖρας for ביד means 'G בידי': oddly the same rendering is found at v.11 without annotation in BH!

8. Comparative adjectives

The same dual treatment repeatedly noted hitherto recurs with regard to comparatives. On the one hand, normal Gk comparatives appear, e.g. at I 27.6 $\delta\upsilon\nu\alpha\tau\acute{\omega}\tau\epsilon\rho\sigma$; II 10.10 $\pi\alpha\chi\acute{\upsilon}\tau\epsilon\rho\sigma$; 17.12 $\mu\epsilon\acute{\iota}\zeta\omega\nu$; 32.7 $\pi\lambda\epsilon\acute{\iota}\sigma\nu\epsilon\varsigma/\pi\lambda\epsilon\acute{\iota}\sigma\upsilon\varsigma$. However, Semitisms like $\acute{\upsilon}\pi\grave{\epsilon}\rho$ $\tau\sigma\grave{\upsilon}\varsigma$ $\delta\acute{\upsilon}\sigma$ $\check{\epsilon}\nu$-$\delta\sigma\xi\sigma\varsigma$ in I 11.21 and $\dot{\alpha}\gamma\alpha\theta\sigma\grave{\upsilon}\varsigma$ $\acute{\upsilon}\pi\acute{\epsilon}\rho$ $\sigma\epsilon$ in II 21.13 also find a place in Par although $\acute{\upsilon}\pi\acute{\epsilon}\rho$ is at least better than $\dot{\alpha}\pi\acute{\sigma}$ or $\dot{\epsilon}\kappa$ would have been for מן. The contrast is highlighted by the rendering of two similar phrases:

II 15.13 למן־קטן ועד גדול : $\dot{\alpha}\pi\grave{\sigma}$ $\nu\epsilon\omega\tau\acute{\epsilon}\rho\sigma\upsilon$ $\check{\epsilon}\omega\varsigma$ $\pi\rho\epsilon\sigma\beta\upsilon\tau\acute{\epsilon}\rho\sigma\upsilon$

34.30 מגדול ועד־קטן : $\dot{\alpha}\pi\grave{\sigma}$ $\mu\epsilon\gamma\acute{\alpha}\lambda\sigma\upsilon$ $\check{\epsilon}\omega\varsigma$ $\mu\iota\kappa\rho\sigma\hat{\upsilon}$.

In 15.13 the comparative form has a superlative sense.

9. Suffixes

(i) *Nominal*. The translator apparently felt free at times to omit suffixes on nouns or to add possessive pronouns. He tends to omit suffixes where there follows a relative clause whose verb has as subject the same person as the suffix. Cases of this omission are עליתו II 9.4, קברתיו 16.14. He omits a suffix where the Heb has a series of nouns, each with a suffix: עליתו I 28.11, מלחמתיו II 27.7, עבודתם 31.16, גבריו 32.3. He omits where there is no obvious antecedent: לבבם II 16.9, לבבו 30.19. Or he omits where the antecedent occurs just before and so is quite clear: קירותיו, דלתותיו II 3.7, שריו 30.2, 6; 36.18. This fact casts doubt on BH's note (so Rothstein) at I 15.3 מקומו: "G המקום". He omits where the antecedent is the subject of the sentence: גבולם II 11.13, קינותיהם 35.25. In the light of this trend the note in BH following Rothstein at I 27.1 שטריהם: '1 c G השטרים' is rendered rather uncertain.

On the other hand, possessive pronouns are freely added idiomatically, even where the link is clear. Here are some typical cases, which seem to be merely liberties taken by the translator in amplifying the Heb.

I 16.15 דבר : $\lambda\acute{\sigma}\gamma\sigma\nu$ $\alpha\dot{\upsilon}\tau\sigma\hat{\upsilon}$ [1]

16.29 הדרת־קדש : $\alpha\dot{\upsilon}\lambda\alpha\hat{\iota}\varsigma$ $\dot{\alpha}\gamma\acute{\iota}\alpha\iota\varsigma$ $\alpha\dot{\upsilon}\tau\sigma\hat{\upsilon}$

17.23 הדבר : $\acute{\sigma}$ $\lambda\acute{\sigma}\gamma\sigma\varsigma$ $\sigma\sigma\hat{\upsilon}$

---

[1] Here and in 17.23 Rogers, pp. 10, 13, sees the translator's reflection of the Jewish stress upon God's Word.

29.19	הבירה	: τοῦ οἴκου σου
II 4.21	הנרות	: οἱ λύχνοι αὐτῶν
5.8	כנפים	: τὰς πτέρυγας αὐτῶν
14.13/14	הערים	: τὰς κώμας αὐτῶν
ibid.	הערים	: τὰς πόλεις αὐτοῦ (i-iii αὐτῶν)
23.17	המזבחות	: τῶν θυσιαστηρίων αὐτοῦ
26.21	בית המלך	: τῆς βασιλείας αὐτοῦ
30.9	פנים	: τὸ πρόσωπον αὐτοῦ
34.8	המזכיר	: τὸν ὑπομνηματογράφον αὐτοῦ
		(ii omits the phrase)
36.17	בתולה	: τὰς παρθένους αὐτῶν
ibid.	זקן	: τοὺς πρεσβυτέρους αὐτῶν

An awareness of this type of Gk addition raises a warning against mechanical re-translation, of which BH is often guilty. In I 20.2 καὶ εὑρέθη ὁ σταθμὸς αὐτοῦ for וימצא משקל calls forth the note inspired by Rothstein '1 ? c G משקלה וימצא'. In fact, as Rehm, p. 21, has seen, Par merely re-divides the same consonantal text, reading as וימצא המשקל. In 21.25 במקום becomes ἐν τῷ τόπῳ (i-iii περὶ τοῦ τόπου) αὐτοῦ: this hardly warrants the note 'G במקומו'.

(ii) *Verbal suffixes.* Again the same trend is noticeable. A suffix is omitted in a series of verbs with the same object, as in these cases: ויחפהו II 3.5, והשיבהו 18.25, ויאכלום ויסכום 28.15.

A resumptive suffix is omitted: עזבנהו II 13.10, הסירה 15.16.

On the other hand, an object is sometimes made more explicit. לסלח in II Ki 24.4 becomes ἐξολεθρεῦσαι αὐτούς in II Par. 36.5d. In I 17.17 for המעלה Par has καὶ ὕψωσάς με, which prompts a note in BH 'G ותעלני'. Already this note has been queried on another ground,[1] and it is surely unnecessary to posit a suffix. Other cases where Gk amplification is likely are:

II 2.3/4 להקדיש : ἁγιάσαι αὐτόν: 'G להקדישי'
21.14 נגף: πατάξει σε: 'G V S + אתך'

(iii) Suffixes which are collectively singular or are so regarded by the translator are rendered *ad sensum* with plural pronouns.[2] Examples are:

---

[1] See p. 42.

[2] Cf. pp. 43 and 46f.

I 29.8	אתו	: παρ' αὐτοῖς
II 15.4	לו	: αὐτούς
28.5	ממנו	: ἐξ αὐτων.

Accordingly in II 3.15 τὰς κεφαλὰς αὐτῶν does not warrant an underlying ראשם, as BH claims.

10. Relative clauses

The ambivalent attitude already evident in many ways recurs in the translator's treatment of relative clauses. On the side of literalism are found the following examples of a pleonastic pronoun or adverb after a relative.[1]

I 6.50/65	ἃς ... αὐτάς
29.1	ὃν ... ἐν αὐτῷ
II 1.3	οὗ ἐκεῖ (כי־שם)
1.11	ἐφ' ὃν ... ἐπ' αὐτόν
6.11	ἐν ᾗ ... ἐκεῖ
6.27	ἐν ᾗ ... ἐν αὐτῇ
6.34	ἣν (i ἐν ᾗ) ... ἐν αὐτῇ
6.37	οὗ ... ἐκεῖ
7.14	ἐφ' οὓς ... ἐπ' αὐτούς
20.10	εἰς οὓς ... δι' αὐτῶν.

Yet side by side with this mechanical translation there goes an avoidance of relative clauses in favour of a less clumsy expression in Gk.

Sometimes the translator uses a genitive:

I 11.11	אשר לדויד	: (τοῦ) Δ.
II 4.19	אשר בית	: (τοῦ) οἴκου.
14.12/13	אשר־עמו	: αὐτοῦ.

At other times an adjective or participle is employed:

I 21.17	אשר־חטאתי	: ὁ ἁμάρτων
II 15.16	אשר־עשׂתה...	: λειτουργοῦσαν
21.16	אשר על־יד	: τοὺς ὁμόρους
34.21	אשר נמצא	: τοῦ εὑρεθέντος
34.24	אשר קראו	: τῷ ἀνεγνωσμένῳ.

---

[1] Cf. Swete, *Introduction*, p. 308.

Before prepositional clauses אֲשֶׁר may become the article:

II 25.18 אשר בלבנון : τὴν ἐν τῷ Λ., τὰ ἐν τῷ Λ.
34.4 אשר למעלה מעליחם : τὰ ἐπ᾽ αὐτῶν

Or it may be omitted:

I 9.2 אשר באחזתם : ἐν ταῖς κατασχέσεσιν αὐτῶν
II 3.4 אשר על־פני : κατὰ πρόσωπον.

Compare I 16.41 הברורים אשר נקבו בשמות: οἱ ... ἐκλεγέντες (ii ἐκλεκτοί) ἐπ᾽ ὀνόματος.

Sometimes אֲשֶׁר is omitted and the relative clause dissolves into a main one, as at II 9.10 ...אשר הביאו הביאו: ἔφερον. There is another instance in 30.17.

11. TYPES OF PARAPHRASE

Examples of loose and periphrastic renderings have already been encountered. In this section some instances of similar paraphrase are to be grouped together, both to illustrate Par's overall consistency and as a warning against overstressing Par's literalism and drawing wrong conclusions as to the *Vorlage*.

(i) Loose reference is made to the sanctuary as follows:

I 6.17/32 אהל : οἴκου (iii, iv only; i, ii omit)
29.4 בתים : ἱεροῦ
II 31.2 מחבדת : οἴκου [1]
35.5 קדש : οἴκῳ.

(ii) Certain cases of paraphrase centre around Jerusalem and may indicate that the translator had some personal knowledge of it. At least they indicate his interest in the city. At II 32.6 the "city gate" is more clearly defined as τῆς πύλης τῆς φάραγγος (but i τ.π.τ. πόλεως), the valley-gate mentioned in 26.9. In II 23.20 שער העליון appears as the "inner gate" (ἐσώτερος), presumably the gate of the inner court of the Temple leading to the outer one.[2] Similarly, in 23.5 the difficult שער היסוד is identified with "the middle gate", i.e. a gate between the Temple precincts and the palace. Rehm, p. 60, posits a different, unknown *Vorlage*. Curtis traces the definition back to a Heb reading שער (ה)תיכון, "a corruption" of MT, similarly BH 'G (ה) תיכון vel התוך

---

[1] Rudolph thinks differently: see p, 161.
[2] Cf. I Ki 6.36; II Ki 23.12 with Ezek 8.3.

(cf. Jer 39,3)', but it is in keeping with the translator's propensity to paraphrase. The topography of the Temple was apparently known to him, for מזבח למזרח becomes κατέναντι τοῦ θυσιαστηρίου in II 5.12. BH's note 'G^BL מנגד ?' is hardly necessary.

(iii) Another category concerns answer to prayer. Par has a fixed formula which is used irrespective of the precise wording of the Heb. ἐπακούειν is employed for ויענהו and ענהו in I 21.26,28, for ויאמר in II 32.24 (ii εἰσήκουσεν) and for ויעתר in 33.13 (i omits by haplography, ii εἰσήκουσεν). At 32.24 BH suggests '1 frt c G ויעתר' (so Rehm, p. 87f): not only does Rudolph rightly regard the change as "graphisch unmöglich", but also the Gk evidence hardly substantiates it. The translator understood the present Heb as "and he (Yahweh) answered him (Hezekiah)".

(iv) Royal accession gives the translator scope for paraphrase of a similar kind. One case is at II 36. 1 וימליכהו: καὶ κατέστησεν αὐτὸν εἰς βασιλέα (cf. too v.4). Another is at 29.3 בשנה הראשנה למלכו: ὡς/ἡνίκα ἔστη ἐπὶ τῆς βασιλείας αὐτοῦ. The third is at 21.5 במלכו: κατέστη ... ἐπὶ τὴν βασιλείαν αὐτοῦ (i ἐν τῷ βασιλεύειν αὐτόν). This example is put last to show the baselessness of BH's note "G^BA קם על ממלכתו, var ad init 4".

(v) The remaining items to be mentioned are miscellaneous. יד is at times paraphrased away in a sophisticated manner: I 29.14 מידך; (ἐκ) τῶν σῶν,[1] v. 24 נתנו יד תחת: ὑπετάγησαν (i ὑπηρέτησαν), II 23.10 ואיש שלחו בידו: ἔκαστον ἐν τοῖς ὅπλοις αὐτοῦ, 30.8 תנו־יד: δότε δόξαν. In the last example there is no need to assume a reading הוד with Goettsberger, who adapts a suggestion made by Wutz.[2] The paraphrase is a straightforward one: compare the same rendering for תנו עז in Psa 68/67.35.

When David stands up in public at I 28.2 על־רגליו is paraphrased ἐν μέσῳ τῆς ἐκκλησίας: Rothstein unnecessarily assumes a different *Vorlage*. In II 20.17 בזאת התיצבו עמדו is interpreted ταῦτα σύνετε (i prefaces ἐν ταύτῃ στῆτε καί), in other words "keep this firmly in your mind, take your stand upon this truth". ויצא שמו in 26.15 becomes καὶ ἠκούσθη ἡ κατασκευὴ αὐτῶν: in the context שמו refers to Uzziah's stockpiling of armaments, and the translator says so. Goettsberger's suggestion that שמע was read for שם (עד follows) and a form of עשה for יצא ignores the word order.

In 36.4a τότε ἤρξατο ἡ γῆ φορολογεῖσθαι renders II Ki 23.35

---

[1] See further p. 121f.

[2] *Transkriptionen*, p. 85. Rogers, p. 38, finds anti-anthropomorphism here.

אַךְ הֶעֱרִיךְ אֶת־הָאָרֶץ. This translation hardly necessitates Curtis and BH's laboured reconstruction of the *Vorlage* as אָז תֶחֱלָה הָאָרֶץ לְהֵעָנֵשׁ. The passive construction has parallels noted in section 5(v). אַךְ is taken temporally "just then", as in Deut 28.29 LXX. הֶעֱרִיךְ means to assess for taxation, i.e. to arrange the preliminaries of taxation, precisely as Par interprets. Other elements in the same verse are rendered loosely: כְּעֶרְכּוֹ becomes κατὰ δύναμιν and the gloss[1] אֶת־עָם παρὰ τοῦ λαοῦ.

12. THE SAME GK FOR DIFFERENT HEB WORDS

A feature of translation technique which appears constantly throughout the two books is the use of the same Gk word for two different Heb ones within a single verse or a space of a few verses.[2] Sometimes the practice is forced upon the translator because a Gk synonym would be difficult to find, e.g. in II 4.9 αὐλή stands for חָצֵר and עֲזָרָה; καθαροῦ represents מָרוּק in 4.16 and סָגוּר in vv. 20, 22/21; while in 14.12/13 and 13/14 σκῦλα appears for שָׁלָל and בִּזָּה. At other times the translator is obviously borrowing a word from the context to render a Heb word he does not know, e.g. when in II 28.15 ἀντελάβοντο is used for וַיְנַהֲלוּם after rendering וַיַּחֲזִקוּ. Further examples of this expedient will be considered when the translator's methods of dealing with unknown words are analysed.

In most cases either a synonym or a more exact equivalent of one of the two terms lies readily to hand. Indeed, it will be noticed later how very often the translator strives for variety. When in I 21.12 ἐχθρῶν appears for צָרֶיךָ and אוֹיְבֶיךָ one wonders why ὑπεναντίων does not appear, as elsewhere in Par. When ἄρχων renders רֹאשׁ and שָׂרֵי in I 27.3 and נָשִׂיא and רָאשֵׁי in II 1.2, and ἡγουμένους stands for both נְצִיבִים[3] and שָׂרָיו in II 17.2, 7, it seems inconsistent for the translator not to ring the changes within the same contexts. Note too κατισχύειν in II 11.17 for וַיְחַזְּקוּ and וַיְאַמְּצוּ, although he can use κραταιοῦν at times. But both this trait and his desire for variety, to be considered in the next section, have a common cause behind them. The translator is not a precisionist. He is literal up to a point, but his literalness is not for its own sake. If the meaning can be adequately brought out simply by repeating a word, why should he make the effort

---

[1] See Montgomery, *Kings, ad loc.*

[2] Ziegler, *Beiträge*, p. 29, notes this practice occurring in the LXX of Jer.

[3] Wutz, *op. cit.*, p. 84, thought that the translator must have read another word. But for נְצִיבִים in a personal sense cf. Montgomery's note on I Ki. 4.7.

to ransack his vocabulary for another word ? If on the other hand he is
in a more active frame of mind and desires to enliven his narrative by
varying his style, he has no scruples whatsoever.

Sometimes an equivalent is chosen which suits better the first word
of the pair. Examples are:

παρατάσσειν	I 19.9, 10, 11 (ו)ויערך, 14 ויגש
καταλείπειν	28.9 תעזבנה, יזניחך
δέησις	II 6.19 תחנתו, רנה
ἐξαίρειν	7.18 יכרת, 20 ונתשתים
λόγων	9.29 רברי, נבואת
ἐν τῇ Ἰουδαίᾳ	17.12 ביהורה, 13 בערי י׳
ἐθανάτωσαν	23.15 וימיתוה, 17 הרגו
αὐτός	26.2 הוא, (וישיבה)
ὀργή	28.9 חמת, זעף
(ἐν) ἐτράπησαν	30.11 נכנעו, 15 נכלמו
πληρωθῆναι	36.21 מלאות, 22 כלות.

At other times, a little less frequently, the translator is obviously
looking ahead, for his equivalent fits the second one of the pair more
closely. Here are examples:

ἀναφωνεῖν	I 16.4 להזכיר, 5 משמיע
φόβος	II 19.7 פחד, 9 יראת
ἐξολεθρεύειν	20.7 הורשת, 10 השמידום
σώζειν	32.8 לעזרנו, 11 יצילנו
πατάξαι	33.24 וימיתהו, 25 ויכו
ἀγιάσματος	36.15 מעון, 17 מקדש.

A knowledge of this trick of translation is essential for sound textual
criticism of both the Gk and Heb texts of Chron, and without it one
could obviously go astray and leap to false conclusions. At I 12.33/32
the note on על־פיהם in BH 'G עמהם' is rendered very questionable
when one considers μετ'αὐτῶν again, for עמהם, in v. 35/34.

Goettsberger at II 3.3 claims that Par's ἤρξατο for הוסד depends
upon the Aramaic שׁרי "begin". Rehm, p. 87, posits יֻסַּד, comparing
the renderings ἠθέλησεν, ἐπέταξεν in Esth. 1.8. A glance at vv. 1,2,
where ἤρξατο occurs for ויחל, reassures that no difference of reading is
necessarily involved.

In 14.4/5 τὰ θυσιαστήρια for הבמות is doubtless a careless rendering
because מזבחות and במות are both the objects of the same verb in

v. 2/3. Probably similar carelessness underlies ἐν πάσαις ταῖς πόλεσιν for בארץ יהודה in 17.2: בכל־ערי י׳ precedes.

At 18.33 BH's note on המחנה '1 prb c G V המלחמה' voices the verdict of most commentators, but πόλεμος is used again in v. 34 to render המלחמה and this must raise a warning signal against assuming a different Heb reading.[1] At 22.9 Curtis states 'G ἰατρευόμενον = מתרפא' for מתחבא. Apparently he is relying on the equation להתרפא: τοῦ ἰατρευθῆναι in v. 6.[2] Certainly the translator did not read מתחבא, for he recognised it in v. 12 and rendered correctly. Here he seems to have read מתחבש[3], miswritten under the influence of the following בש(מרן), and of the thought of v. 6, and renders according to the principle illustrated in this section. This trait is a vital factor to be considered by all who use Par for Heb textual criticism. It underlines the truth that simple retroversion is not always a key to the *Vorlage*.

13. DIFFERENT GK FOR THE SAME HEB WORDS

Another important feature of the translator's approach to his task is his fondness for stylistic variation. A Heb word is repeated, but he is often not content to repeat his own Gk equivalent, but searches instead for an alternative way of expressing the original.[4] One method adopted is the use of synonyms, e.g. as follows:

נולד	I 2.3 ἐγεννήθησαν, 9 ἐτέχθησαν (i transposes)
אבה	11.18 ἤθελεν/ησεν, 19 ἐβούλετο
נפל	12.20/19 ἐπιστρέψει, 20/19, 21/20 προσεχώρησαν
על־ידי	25.2,6 ἐχόμενα/οι, 6 μετά
שמחה	29.17 εὐφροσύνη, 22 χαρᾶς
עבדים	II 2.7/8 δοῦλοι, παῖδες
רחב	3.8 πλάτος/ους, 4.1 εὖρος
משפט	6.35 δικαίωμα, 39 κρίμα(τα)
הודות	7.3 ᾔνουν / ᾔνεσαν, 6 ἐξομολογεῖσθαι
קבץ	15.9 ἐξεκκλησίασεν, 10 συνήχθησαν
אויב	20.27 ἐχθρῶν, 29 ὑπεναντίους/ων
בנים	25.4 τέκνων, υἱοί

---

[1] See further part II, p. 83.

[2] Margolis, *JQR* xvi, p. 119f., also suggested a misreading as מתרפא, caused by aberration of the eye to v.6.

[3] This is an adaptation of a suggestion made by Wutz, *op. cit.*, pp. 5, 93, 104, who thought in terms of a C/Є error in a transcribed text.

[4] This feature is common in the LXX generally: see Swete, *Introduction*, p. 328f.

הסיר 30.14 καθεῖλαν/ον, κατέσπασαν
נגיד 31.12 ἐπιστάτης, 13 ἡγούμενος
כון 35.4 ἑτοιμάσθητε, 10 κατο/ωρθώθη
פרס 36.20 Μήδων, 23 Περσῶν.

Another example is the different rendering of משה משאת in II 24.6,9. In v. 6 the phrase becomes τὸ κεκριμένον ὑπὸ M. (i inserts λῆμμα before ὑπό: this is obviously secondary). משאת is interpreted as "utterance". V. 9 interprets in the same way but has καθὼς εἶπεν M. Curtis unnecessarily suggests כאשר אמר as the basis of the Gk in v.9.

Occasionally variation in a prepositional prefix satisfied the translator:

הניח I 22.9 ἀναπαύσω, 18 ἀνέπαυσεν, 23.25 κατέπαυσεν
לפני (God) II 2.3/4 ἀπέναντι, 5/6 κατέναντι
ויכל/יכ(י)ל 4.5 ἐξετέλεσεν, 11 συνετέλεσεν
לפני 14.9/10 εἰς συνάντησιν,
15.2 εἰς ἀπάντησιν.

Sometimes the translator first gives a literal rendering and then a looser one, e.g.:

לפני (ark) I 16.4 κατὰ πρόσωπον, 6 ἐναντίον (i ἐνώπιον)
ויתן II 17.2 καὶ ἔδωκεν, καὶ κατέστησεν
חבר 20.35 ἐκοινώνησεν, 37 ἐφιλίασας
איש (each) 23.7 ἀνδρός (i ἀνήρ, ii ἄνδρες), 10 ἕκαστον
ארצות 32.13 χωρῶν, πάσης τῆς γῆς
מלפני (God) 33.12 ἀπὸ προσώπου, 23 ἐναντίον (i ἐνώπιον)
הרים 35.7 ἀπήρξατο, 8 ἔδωκεν.

Another time the first instance is rendered rather loosely, then at a second occurrence of the same word the translator falls back on a literal equivalent, e.g.:

(שאל) באלהים I 14.10 διὰ τοῦ θεοῦ, 14 ἐν (τῷ) θεῷ
לפניך (God) 17.24,27 ἐναντίον σου (i ἐνώπιόν σου),
25 κατὰ πρόσωπόν σου
נגפו לפני ישראל 19.16 ἐτροπώσατο αὐτὸν I.,[1] 19 ἐπταίκασιν (i
ἐθραύσθησαν) ἀπὸ προσώπου I.
מגפה 21.17 ἀπώλειαν, 22 πληγή

---

[1] Rehm's suggestion (op. cit., p. 21) that נגפו was read as נגפו ignores לפני. In the second case the verb may have come from the parallel II Rg. 10.15, but the preposition is different.

לרב   22.3 πολύν, εἰς πλῆθος

ערים   II 14.13/14 κώμας, πόλεις

נכנע   33.19 ἐπιστρέψαι, 23 ἐταπεινώθη.

These last two ways of ringing the changes are interesting as an epitome of the translator's general style. They show how differently his mind worked at different times, now lighting upon the literal, now preferring paraphrase. These opposing traits are here worked out within narrow bounds over and over again. This phenomenon confirms that, strange as it appears at first sight, one and the same person is responsible for stilted literal renderings and for more sophisticated paraphrase, both of which styles have been profusely illustrated earlier in this chapter.

The two principles of rendering different Heb words by one Gk one and *vice versa* apply on a wider scale than the range of a few verses or a chapter or two. תורה suggests to the translator mainly νόμος, but also πρόσταγμα, II 19.10 and ἐντολή, 30.16. Par normally makes no distinction between orthodox and pagan altars, using θυσιαστήριον for both, but in II 31.1 המזבחת in a bad sense is rendered τοὺς βωμούς (i τὰ θυσιαστήρια), as in the Gk Pentateuch.[1] אוצר generally becomes θησαυρός, but it is rendered ἀποθήκη in I 28.12 and παράθεσις in II 11.11. Conversely, εἰς ἀπάντησιν appears for לקראת, e.g. I 19.5, for אל־פני in II 19.2, for לפני e.g. in I 12.18/17, and for אל־תא in II 12.11. σῴζειν can render not only עזר and הציל, as was seen above, but also הושיע, e.g. I 16.35, and נמלט in II 16.7. Perhaps the record for number of equivalents is held by δύναμις, which is used for חיל, e.g. II 13.3, צבא, e.g. I 19.16, גדוד, e.g. I 12.19/18, מחנה in II 14.12/13, עז in I 13.8, כח, e.g. II 26.13, גבורה in I 29.11, חלץ in II 20.21 and ערך in II Ki 23.35/II 36.4a. The translator can be either flexible or stereotyped in his approach to individual words and to words of similar meaning.

14. USE OF THE GREEK PENTATEUCH

It has already been noted that Gerleman devotes the third chapter of his *Studies* in Par to the close lexical links between Par and the LXX of the Pentateuch, and finds the resemblance between the two in regard to phraseology a pervading characteristic. In fact, it may be

---

[1] Cf. S. Daniel, *Recherches*, pp. 16-23, 367-369. She rejects on convincing grounds the theory of P. Churgin, *JNES* i, pp. 41ff. that βωμός here and elsewhere in the LXX is the result of a later revision.

said, by way of summarising Gerleman's thesis and the extra, confirmatory material below, that the translator at times uses the Gk Pentateuch both as a commentary and a dictionary, rather like translators of other books of the LXX.[1] Here are some more links with Pentateuchal vocabulary, presented alphabetically.

אסף is rendered προστιθέναι twice in II 34.28. It is also related to יסף in this way eleven times in the Pentateuch according to Hatch and Redpath.

נרתיהם לבערם becomes τοὺς λυχνοὺς τοῦ φωτός in II 4.20. This is another allusion to Exod. 35ff., overlooked by Gerleman. At Exod 35.14, in the course of a similar catalogue of sanctuary furniture, מנרת המאור is rendered τὴν λυχνίαν τοῦ φωτός, which has inspired this paraphrase. However, in 13.11 almost the same phrase is rendered οἱ λυχνοὶ τῆς καύσεως. The Exodus account there appears to be forgotten. The difference of translation supports Gerleman's view that a special link with the Gk of Exod. 35ff. underlies ch. 4. It is unlikely that המאור was read for לבערם, as Rehm, p. 59, lamely suggests.

חלציך in II 6.9 is translated τῆς ὀσφύος σου as in Gen. 35.11. The parallel III Rg. 8.19 renders with πλευρῶν.

ערי (ה)מסכנות in II 8.4, 6; 17.12 becomes (τὰς) πόλεις (τὰς) ὀχυράς.[2] The rendering is found elsewhere only at Exod. 1.11.

יצוך in I 22.12 is translated καὶ κατισχύσαι σε. Compare Exod. 18.23 וצוך: καὶ κατισχύσει σε.[3] Doubtless the thought of authority underlies the translation.[4]

רחבת ידים in I 4.40 becomes πλατεῖα ἐναντίον (ἱ ἐνώπιον) αὐτῶν, which renders ר'־י' לפניהם in Gen. 34.21. The translator has used his Pentateuchal dictionary carelessly.

לשום את־שמו שם or the like is a cultic phrase which the LXX of Deut renders with Hellenistic sophistication. לשום becomes ἐπονομάσαι in Deut 12.5 and ἐπικληθῆναι in 12.21; 14.24. III Rg 9.3; 11.36; 14.21 prefer the blunt θέσθαι. But Par sensitively follows Deut, using ἐπονομάσαι in I 28.3; II 12.13 and ἐπικληθῆναι in II 6.20.

---

[1] Cf. Mozley, *Psalter*, p. xiii: The Pentateuch "was probably ... our translator's textbook in learning Heb and served him to a great extent in place of a dictionary". Seeligmann, *Isaiah*, pp. 45ff., found confirmation of this in the LXX of Isa.

[2] Group ii adds τῶν φόρων in 8.4,6.

[3] Wutz, *op. cit.*, p. 510, related καὶ ἐνισχύσω σε in Isa 42.6 to a reading ואצרך for ואצוך, but on p. 76 he inconsistently linked it with אזר.

[4] See further p. 127.

שׁנִינָה in II 7.20 becomes διήγημα, as in Deut 28.37. Contrast λάλημα in the parallel III Rg 9.7.

תְּרוּעָה is rendered σημασία in Num 10.5, 6; 29.1; 31.6. Apart from II Esdr 3.12f., the translation recurs only in I Par 15.28; II 13.12.

The use of the Gk Pentateuch, so consistently illustrated, is an important external influence upon the translator which exercised a certain amount of control over his vocabulary and his interpretation. An awareness of it provides both insight into the mind of the translator at work and a caution that new factors appear in his translation which were not present in his *Vorlage*.

15. TREATMENT OF UNKNOWN WORDS

It is not difficult to perceive that now and then the translator came across words whose meaning he did not know and could not discover. He seems to have had three distinct methods of dealing with the situation, upon which he draws throughout Par, and on occasion he applies more than one method to the same word in different places.

(i) The first and most common expedient is guesswork. The cases will be dealt with alphabetically.

אוּלָם is translated ναός in I 28.11; II 8.12 (ii λαοῦ); 15.8; 29.7, 17. This rendering is in fact the standard one for הֵיכָל: the translator haphazardly equates the two quite different parts of the Temple. But this he cannot do in II 3.4, since ναός obviously would not fit. He resorts instead to transliteration: αιλαμ.

אֵפוֹד בַּד. It was noted in section 12 that sometimes the translator borrows a word from the context to render a Heb word he does not know. At I 15.27 is a case in point. אֵפוֹד בַּד becomes στολὴ βυσσίνη, but earlier in the same verse this phrase has been used for מְעִיל בּוּץ.[1]

הַחֻמָּנִים is guessed as εἴδωλα in II 14.4/5 and as ὑψηλά[2] in 34.4, 7. The different renderings probably signify the translator's uncertainty.

הִתְחַפֵּשׂ in II 35.22 becomes ἐκραταιώθη. The rendering has been hailed as the answer to a difficulty. The Gk verb represents חזק elsewhere in Par, e.g. at 34.8. Many commentators, listed by and including Curtis, accordingly read הִתְחַזֵּק: cf. BH '1 c G הִתְחַזֵּק vel c G^Esr V

---

[1] אֵפוֹד and בַּד (= linen) are ἅπ. λεγ. in Chron. It is less likely that στολή was used deliberately to avoid the impression that David was wearing a priestly garment.

[2] The first rendering recurs in Isa 27.9 LXX, while βδελύγματα is used in 17.8. In Lev 26.30 ξύλινα χειροποίητα is the equivalent and in Ezek 6.4,6 τεμένη.

חֹשֵׁב'.[1] But Rudolph is on surer ground in maintaining that Par, along with the other versions, merely translates according to context.

בחר בתיהם in 34.6 is difficult, and so the translator found it. He renders vaguely (ἐν) τοῖς τόποις αὐτῶν. Surprisingly BH annotates "1 c G S ברחובותיהם". Rudolph rightly criticises BH for citing Par as a witness since the Gk is only a guess. Schleusner unnecessarily conjectured that ἐρήμοις had fallen out after τοῖς.[2]

יִשִּׁי at 36.17 obviously presented a problem to the translator. He attempted to solve it by rendering ἀπήγαγον, as if it were a verb. He "borrows" the verb from v. 6. Did he link the Heb with נשא ?[3]

מסכנות was evidently viewed with perplexity. In some places he translated with the aid of his Pentateuchal dictionary, as noted in section 14. Naturally enough, that rendering did not always fit. At 32.28 the translator obviously reasoned that the mysterious מסכנות must be closely linked in meaning with ערים, which elsewhere always accompanies it: it becomes πόλεις. Curtis' suggestion, partly on the basis of Par, to import ערים from v. 29 is unnecessary. In 16.4 the translator's uncertainty is reflected by yet another rendering: περιχώρους "surrounding". It is hardly necessary to presuppose סביבות or the like with Benzinger, Curtis and Rudolph. Rehm, pp. 71, 84, supposed that ככרות was an error for כנרות I Ki 15.20 and that in Chron a copyist was reminded by the following ערי (for עד) of the standard phrase.

מפלצת occurs twice in II 15.16. In the first case the translator can indirectly render אשר עשתה לאשרה מפלצת as τῇ Ἀστάρτῃ λειτουργοῦσαν. Rehm's suggestion (p.60), followed by Rudolph, that אשר עשתה was overlooked before לאשרה and that מִפְלֶחַת was read for מפלצת is hardly necessary. The paraphrase is a cloak for uncertainty. But in the second case the unknown word demands a direct translation and the translator settles for the vague εἴδωλον.[4]

In I 11.25 משמעתו "bodyguard" (BDB) becomes τὴν πατρίαν αὐτοῦ. Rothstein, BH and Rehm, p. 58, claim a *Vorlage* משפחתו, but more probably Gerleman, p. 42, is right in seeing here a conjectural paraphrase.

---

[1] Surely ἐπεχείρει in I Esdr 1. 26 is merely a paraphrase of חפש "search".

[2] *Lexicon*, iii, p. 283.

[3] Cf. Isa 42.11 where יְשׁוּשׁוּן is generally read for יִשְׂאוּ.

[4] Cf. Targ טעותא in *both* cases in Ki 15.13 and here.

פוך in I 29.2 is guessed as πολυτελεῖς with the help of אבן יקרה a little later in the verse.[1]

פרבר in I 26.18 means "temple precinct".[2] The rendering διαδεχομέ-νους "relief gatekeepers" is a conjecture.

בצלחות in II 35.13 puzzled the translator. The only root he knew meant "be successful". So, ignoring the initial ב and the final ות, he rendered εὐο/ωδώθη.

צעצעים in II 3.10 is a hapax legomenon. It is rendered ξύλων in terms of the similar looking עץ in v. 5. As in the last example, part of the word is ignored. There is no need to assume with Curtis and Rehm, p. 59, that עצים was read. Cf. ξύλῳ for נעצוצים at Isa. 7.19.

שדרות in II 23.14 is vaguely guessed as οἴκου. But the very guess causes difficulty: אל־מבית הש׳ can hardly be rendered "inside the Temple" since the end of the verse states that Athaliah's death is not to take place on holy ground. Accordingly the phrase is rationalised into ἐκτὸς τοῦ οἴκου despite the incongruity of the following εἰσέλθατε.[3]

אל־תא in II 12.11 is translated according to context εἰς ἀπάντησιν, a rendering elsewhere used in Par for אל־פני, לפני and לקראת.[4] Rehm, p. 60, assumes a different, unknown *Vorlage*.

התרים becomes τῶν ὑποτεταγμένων in II 9.14 and III Rg 10.15, where Montgomery calls it a guess. In Rg it is most probably a later gloss assimilating to Par.[5]

(ii) The second method of dealing with unknown words was simply to omit them.[6] There are a few instances attested by all four groups. In II 15.16 ... מגבירה אשר becomes simply τοῦ μὴ εἶναι + participle. צפת in 3.15 is omitted: והצפת אשר־על־ראשו is rendered καὶ τὰς κεφαλὰς (ii κεφαλίδας) αὐτῶν. BH's note 'G V sol וראשם' is hardly warranted. The phrase הוא מכלות זהב in 4.21 is left out, doubtless

---

[1] With this generic rendering contrast the specific ἄνθρακα in Isa 54.11 LXX.

[2] See Montgomery, *Kings*, p. 539f.

[3] Rahlfs, *LXX-Studien*, i, p. 40f., notes that Theodoret, in citing IV Rg 11.15, emends ἔσωθεν to ἔξωθεν according to Par, apparently following the same reasoning given above.

[4] In the parallel III Rg. 14. 28 the rendering ܡܓܐܠܐ is ascribed to Symmachus in Syh. Field, p. 627, comments: "in qua voce omnino nos haerere fatemur". It is perhaps to be related to the rare ܡܓܐܒܠ "coram, ante" (cf. R. Payne Smith, *Thesaurus Syriacus*, ii, 3495f.) and is then either inspired by Par or is an independent conjecture.

[5] In Rg ומסחר הרכלים was probably omitted by homoeoteleuton, so that τῶν ἐμπόρων is Rg's (correct, cf. Montgomery) equivalent for התרים. ὑποτάσσειν does not occur elsewhere in Rg but comes twice in Par: I 22.18; 29.24 (ii-iv).

[6] Ziegler, *Untersuchungen*, p. 7, found this expedient used in the LXX of Isa.

because the translator is fighting shy of מכלות. It is scarcely justified to conclude with Curtis and Rudolph that the phrase is a gloss because it is wanting in Ki and Par.

(iii) The translator's third method of coping with unknown words was to transliterate. The case of αιλαμ has already been noted. Here is a list of other examples. Exact forms vary often among the groups, and the forms of B in group i are given for convenience.

עבדת הבץ: εφραθ αβακ I 4.21. Presumably עבדת was corrupted in the *Vorlage* or else the word would have been translated. בוץ is known in 15.27: doubtless the lack of vowel letter and the less informative context foiled the translator.

אריאל : αριηλ 11.22

גדוד: γεδδουρ 12.22/21 (i adds ἐν τῇ ἐξοδίᾳ). גדוד is elsewhere in Par translated: e.g. in v. 19/18 it becomes δυναμέων/s. Here again apparently the *Vorlage* is to blame: גדור was read.[1]

שׁופר	:	σωφερ 15.28
האספים	:	εσεφειν 26.15
כתרות	:	χωθαρεθ II 4.12, 13
מכנות	:	μεχωνωθ 4.14
החפשׁות	:	αφφουσιων 26.21
(קדשׁים)	:	καρασειμ II Ki 23.24/35.19a [2].

Here again it appears that a corrupted word baffled the translator.

16. TRANSLITERATION

In the previous section it was noted that one use the translator makes of transliteration is as a method of representing Heb words not known to him. But in some cases it is clear that the translator did know the meaning but yet found cause to keep certain words in their Heb form. These and the remaining instances attested by all four groups appear to fall into two further categories.

(i) Some instances can reasonably be listed as names, whether actual or so taken by the translator.[3] Again the forms of B are given for convenience.

---

[1] See part II, p. 91.

[2] Cf. Seeligmann, *Isaieh*, p. 66: "the word שִׁקּוּצִים of the Massoretic text turns out to be a theological correction of an earlier word קְדָשִׁים". Cf. further S. p. 123.

[3] Wevers, *CBQ* xiv, p. 42; xv, p. 32, found the same factor underlying the transliterations of II Rg 11-III 2 and III Rg-IV 25.

אסר : Ασειρ I 3.17

מלכת : Μαλεχεθ 7.18

נחלי : Ναχαλει 11.32.

BM does not capitalise. Rahlfs, *Septuaginta*, does, and so better represents the intent of the translator. נחל is translated in II 7.8; 20.16; 32.4.

במה : Βαμα I 16.39, Βαμωθ 21.29, Μαβα II 1.13. [1]

שפלה : Σεφηλα II 26.10.

The word is translated in 28.18 but the translator here needs that rendering for the next word, מישׁור. Strangely neither BM nor Rahlfs capitalises.

משׁנה : Μαασαναι 34.22.

The translator appears to recognise as a place-name this suburb of Jerusalem.

(גן־עזא) : Γανοζαη 36.8.

BM does not capitalise, but Rahlfs does. This and the preceding cases are interesting examples of transliterated places in Jerusalem. Taken along with the instances of paraphrase centring round Jerusalem mentioned in section 11, they seem to indicate that the translator had some personal knowledge of Jerusalem.

(ii) The third and last class of transliteration is made up of religious words, which may reasonably be supposed to have been carried over into the Gk language of a Jewish community.[2]

אמן : αμην I 16.36

כרוב (ים) : χερουβ(ειν) 28.18, also II 3.7, (8), 10, 11, 13, 14; 5.7,8.

דביר : δαβειρ II 3.16, also 4.20; 5.7,9.

It is difficult to decide whether this is transliterated as a known cultic word or as an unknown word like αιλαμ.[3]

---

[1] For τὴν ὑψηλήν in II 1.3 see p. 166.

[2] Cf. Kahle, *Cairo Geniza*[2], p. 254: "How many Hebrew words are to be found in the Yiddish language which is used by Jews who do not understand Hebrew!"

[3] See p. 59.

פסח   : φασεκ/χ 30.1ff.; 35.1ff.
תרפים   : θαραφειν II Ki 23.24/35.19a.

Here again this could be classed in the category of unknown words.

CHAPTER FIVE

GROUPS I AND II

It was observed in ch. iii that the mss. cited in BM give consistent evidence of falling into four groups. In this chapter and the next it is proposed to look more closely at those groups, one at a time, and to investigate their membership and some of their characteristics. For this latter purpose use will be made of the material presented in ch. iv, which points to readings shared by all four groups and containing consistent characteristics as evidence of a single translator. It will be shown that groups i-iii have in turn a special relationship with group iv.

1. GROUP i

(i) *Mss. in the group*

b (= b'+b) e₂ are regular members of the group. e₂ is missing between αὐτοῦ I 1.45 and αὐτῷ 2.29, and is extant only as far as II 32.25.[1] y is a member until I 11.4: at 11.5 it joins group iii. The group's readings are sometimes shared by the mixed mss. f j (in II Par) m, by the group iii mss. g and some or all of its sub-group i n y, and sporadically by other mss. Arm, mainly a member of group iii, has at times readings of this group.

350, a Catena ms., belongs to this group. In LXX Sam Johnson observed: "350 geht mit b + und besonders mit Thdt [= Theodoret] zusammen".[2] The same is true in Par, as the following examples illustrate. The first reading is that of B in BM.

I 5.1	οὗτος : αὐτός b y e₂ Arm Thdt
10.13	ζητῆσαι : ἐκζητῆσαι b y e₂ Thdt
II 2.6	οὐ φέρουσιν αὐτοῦ τὴν δόξαν : οὐχ ὑποίσουσιν αὐτόν b e₂ Thdt
15.4	ἐπιστρέψαι : ἐπιστρέψουσιν Thdt
21.13	ὡς : ὃν τρόπον b e₂ Thdt
24.25	αὐτῷ : τῷ Ιωας b e₂ Thdt

---

[1] For the cause of these omissions see Rahlfs, *LXX-Studien*. iii, p. 10f.

[2] *Die hexaplarische Rezension des I Samuelbuches*, p. 20.

28.23   αὐτοῖς τοίνυν θύσω : θ. τ. αὐτ. Thdt
32.31   ἀπό : pr. τῶν b e g Thdt
33.17   κύριος ὁ θεός : εἰς κενὸν κῷ τῷ θ͞ῷ b z Thdt.

The fragments of the Bohairic version collated in BM cover I 15.2-16.37; 28.2-29.22; II 3.1-7.16. Boh has a very mixed text in these fragments, with a pronounced leaning towards L. Out of 65 variants exclusively agreeing with one of the four textforms, it follows L 39 times, group ii 10, group iii 5, group iv 11.

The portion of the Ethiopic version collated in BM, I 12.18-29, reveals closest affinity with L. Its evidence accords with information supplied by J. W. Wevers in a private communication concerning the Ethiopic of II Chron : "Nine mss. are presumably extant, though the one in Frankfurt/Main cannot be found. The others are in Paris (3), London, B.M. (3), Oxford (1) and Rome, P.B.I (1). Two of these, A and B (both Paris), represent the Old Eth. text and are based on the Antiochian text... The remainder constitute a Revised Text but also based on the same Greek textform. Within the Revised Text there is evidence of a further revision, but no revision lies outside the textform of b and e₂, though there is a slight influence of the d group on the *Vorlage* of Eth."[1]

(ii) *A revised textform*

The group has customarily been identified with the Lucianic recension.[2] Its close links with Theodoret, investigated by Rahlfs, mark it as a text current in Syria in the fifth century A.D. Chrysostom's citation of II Par 26.16, 18 confirms this association.[3] The group exhibits the

---

[1] One of Prof. Wevers' students, J. Clear, has researched in this field. Cf. his own report in the *Bulletin of the International Organization for Septuagint and Cognate Studies*, v, Summer 1972, p. 13f., where he notes links with La. S. Grébaut's edition, *Les Paralipomènes livres I et II:version éthiopienne editée et traduite*, Patrologia Orientalis, xxiii, 4, 1934, is judged to be very inaccurate.

[2] See p. 17.

[3] Of five relevant readings, checked with Montfaucon's edition, vi, 1835, in three cases Chrysostom agrees with L:

    v. 16 + (ὁ) 'Οζίας L Syh Chr Thdt

    ibid. διαφθεῖραι L Chr Thdt

    v. 18 τοῖς υἱοῖς O L Chr Cyr Thdt.

In one case, involving a less striking reading, the text of Chr sides with other textforms against L;

    v. 18 θυμιάσαι O R Chr Cyr: pr. τοῦ L Thdt.

In the last case BM cited Chrysostom's reading, again in v. 18, as ἀλλά = R over against ἀλλ' ἤ G O L. In fact, he quotes twice, first reading ἀλλά, then a little later ἀλλ' ἤ.

characteristics normally associated with the Lucianic recension. For instance, it frequently adds names and replaces pronouns by names; it substitutes synonyms, such as δοῦλος very often for παῖς, and indulges in neo-Atticisms, like εἶπον and ἐγένετο which are constantly read in place of εἶπαν and ἐγενήθη.[1] In the light of such characteristics "L" will be used as a convenient designation of this textform.

Some of the traits of translation which emerged in ch. iv may be used as criteria by which to prove the revised character of L. L gives the impression of being most carefully corrected according to MT. Sometimes recognised features of the translation are thereby disfigured, but enough evidence was left unchanged to enable the compilation of ch. iv. It was there demonstrated that the translator characteristically avoids a clumsy literal rendering of phrases involving prepositions.[2] In seven cases L adapts such renderings, attested by the three other groups, in order to render the Heb more exactly. In the following examples and all through this section the first Gk rendering represents the reading of groups ii-iv, unless otherwise stated, and the second the reading of L.

I 5.20	שעמהם	: τὰ σκηνώματα αὐτῶν	: οἱ μετ' αὐτῶν
18.17	ליד	: διάδοχοι	: ἐπὶ χεῖρα e₂
28.12	ברוח עמו	: ἐν πνεύματι αὐτοῦ[3]	: ἐν πν. μετ' αὐτοῦ
29.11	לך ... הממלכה	: σὺ ... δεσπόζεις	: + σὰ ἡ βασίλεια
II 4.2	משפתו אל־ש'	: τὴν διαμέτρησιν	: + ἀπὸ τοῦ χείλους αὐτῆς εἰς τὸ χεῖλος αὐτῆς
20.32	סר ממנה	: ἐξέκλινεν	: + ἀπ' αὐτῶν
26.6	ערים באשדוד	: πόλεις Ἀζώτου	: π. ἐν Ἀζώτῳ[4].

Section 12 of ch. iv showed the translator's rather lazy habit of repeating a Gk word to render two roughly synonymous Heb words in

---

[1] Moreover, doublets are very numerous: see the references to conflate readings in this group on p. 126. Other examples of substituted synonyms are as follows. The first Gk reading is that of the other three groups.

I 2.3	נולד	: ἐγεννήθησαν	: ἐτέχθησαν
v. 9	נולד	: ἐτέχθησαν	: ἐγεννήθησαν
6.39/54	טירותם	: κώμαις	: ἐπαύλεσιν
v.41/56	חצריה	: κωμας	: ἐπαύλεις
II16.14	משכב	: κλίνης	: κοίτης
32.8	בשר	: σάρκινοι	: σαρκικοί

[2] See p. 44.

[3] Rothstein unnecessarily posited ברוחו.

[4] BH's note "GᴮᴬΑ' ערי" is unwarranted.

the same context. L frequently blots out this feature for the sake of greater accuracy.

I 2.10-44	ἐγέννησεν	=	הוליד	
vv. 46, 48		=	ילד(ה)	: ἔτεκε
6.4/19	πατριαί	=	משפחות	: συγγένειαι
	πατριὰς αὐτῶν	=	אבותיהם	
7.2	ἰσχυροὶ	=	גבורי	: δυνατοί
v. 4		=	גדודי	: δυνάμει

There is hardly need to posit גבורי in v. 4 with BH, Rothstein and Rudolph.

7.40	(ὁ) ἀριθμὸς αὐτῶν	=	התיחשם	: τῶν γενεαλογηθέντων
		=	מספרם	
10.10	καὶ ἔθηκαν	=	וישימו	
	ἔθηκαν [1]	=	תקעו	: ἔπηξαν
15.1	καὶ ἐπόιησεν	=	ויעש	
		=	ויט	: καὶ ἔπηξεν

P. Katz suggested that in the second case ἐπόιησεν was a corruption of the L reading, comparing 16.1 נטה: ἔπηξεν.[2] But the well-attested feature of translation, here destroyed by L, adequately explains the rendering.

21.12	τοῦ ἐξολεθρεῦσαι	=	למשגת	: καταδιώκειν σε
iii, iv				
	ἐξολεθρεύων	=	משחית	

In the first case Rothstein posited להשחית and Rehm unnecessarily queried the *Vorlage* of LXX.[3]

28.11	ἀποθηκῶν	=	חדריו	: ταμιείων αὐτοῦ
v. 12	ἀποθήκας	=	אצרות	
v. 16	σταθμόν	=	משקל	
v. 17		=	כפור	: + κεφφουρε
II 6.23	ἀποδοῦναι	=	להשיב	
		=	לתת	: ἐπιστρέψαι, correcting the wrong word !

---

[1] Rogers, p. 67f., finds here the translator's respect for royalty in toning down the Heb as abhorrent.

[2] *VT* i, p. 266.

[3] *Untersuchungen*, p. 58.

7.19	ἀποστρέψητε	=	תשובון	: ἀποστράφητε
v. 20	ἀποστρέψω	=	אשליך	: ἀπορρίψω
10.11	ἐπάιδευσεν	=	העמיס	: ἐν/ἐπ/ἔθηκεν
		=	יסר	
14.12/13	καὶ ἔσκύλευσαν	=	וישאו	
v. 13/14		=	יבזו	: καὶ διήρπασαν
24.12	ἐπισκευάσαι	=	לחדש	
		=	לחוק	: τοῦ κραταιῶσαι
26.11	εἰς ἀριθμόν	=	במספר	: om.
	ὁ ἀριθμὸς αὐτῶν	=	פקדתס	: ὁ ἀρ. τῆς ἐπισκέψεως αὐτῶν
29.24	καὶ ἐξιλάσαντο	=	ויחטאו	: περιεράντησαν
		=	לכפר	
34.12	ἐπίσκοποι	=	מפקדים	: + καθεσταμένοι
	ἐπισκοπεῖν	=	לנצח	: ἐπισπουδάζειν
35.4	διὰ χειρός	=	במכתב	: κατὰ τὴν ἀπογραφήν
v. 6		=	ביד	

The translator's desire for stylistic variety appears to account for his trick of using two different Gk words for two occurrences of the same Heb one.[1] But often L painstakingly destroys this characteristic, as follows.

I 15.2	(ark) לשאת	: ἆραι : αἴρειν
v. 15	(ark) וישאו	: καὶ ἔλαβον : καὶ ἦραν
19.14	מפניו	: ἀπ' αὐτοῦ : ἀπὸ προσώπου αὐτοῦ
19.15	מפני	: ἀπὸ προσώπου
21.20	חטים	: πυρούς
v. 23		σῖτον : πυρόν
25.2	על־ידי	: ἐχόμενοι/a
v. 3		μετά : ἐχόμενοι
28.4	ויבחר	: καὶ ἐξελέξατο
	בחר	: ἠρέτικεν : ἐξελέξατο (but L keeps ἠρέτ. in 29.1)
29.29	על־דברי	: ἐν λόγοις : ἐπὶ λόγων
		ἐπὶ λόγων
II 1.17	ויוציאו	: καὶ ἐξῆγον
	יוציאו	: ἔφερον : ἐξέφερον
4.2	ם	: θάλασσαν
v. 3		λουτῆρα : θάλασσαν. Rehm, p. 59,

---

[1] See p. 55.

unnecessarily suggested that כיור was read for ים by errors of כ/מ, י/ר.

v. 7	משמאול	: ἐξ ἀριστερῶν
v. 8		ἐξ εὐωνύμων : ἐξ ἀριστερῶν
v. 11	סירות	: κρεάγρας , pr. λέβητας
v. 16		λέβητας
6.24	והודו	: καὶ ἐξομολογήσονται
v. 26		καὶ αἰνέσουσιν : καὶ ἐξομ.
10.5	שובו	: ἔρχεσθε : ἐπιστρέψατε
v. 12		ἐπιστρ.
v. 6	ויועץ	: καὶ συνήγαγεν : + καὶ συνεβουλεύσατο
v. 8		καὶ συνεβ.

Rehm, pp. 42, 111, claimed a *Vorlage* וַיְצַו here and in the parallel I Ki 12.6 (Rg καὶ παρήγγειλεν). But here the translator's practice is certainly sufficient explanation of the Gk as a rendering of MT. As for Rg Montgomery has judged that "there is no reason for emendation on basis of Gr".

12.6	ויכנעו	: καὶ ἠσχύνθησαν : καὶ ἐνετράπησαν
v. 7	נכנעו	: ἐνετράπησαν
20.26	עמק	: αυλῶνα : κοιλάδα
		κοιλάς
35.4	בכתב	: κατὰ τὴν γραφήν
	במכתב	: διὰ χειρός : κατὰ τὴν ἀπογραφήν.

Gerleman demonstrated that the translator often harked back to the Pentateuch, and more examples were supplied in ch. iv, section 14. At times L does not accept this influence and rejects it in favour of greater fidelity to the Heb.

| I 5.1 | ובחללו יצועי | : καὶ ἐν τῷ ἀναβῆναι ἐπὶ τὴν κοίτην ii-iv. |

The euphemistic paraphrase is based upon Gen. 49.4 LXX, where ἀνέβης γὰρ ἐπὶ τὴν κοίτην ... ἐμίανας renders חללת ... כי עלית משכבי. The Heb phrase in Chron is interpreted with the aid of the parallel verb in Gen. It is interesting to note that here Targ also paraphrases in terms of Gen: באפסותיה קדושתיה כד סליק לדרגשא דאביו. But L prefers to render literally ἐν τῷ βεβηλῶσαι τὴν στρώμνην.

החבתים in 9.31 is explained at length in the text of ii-iv as τῆς θυσίας τοῦ τηγάνου τοῦ μεγάλου ἱερέως. Rothstein and Goettsberger rightly note that the source of this interpretation is the LXX of Lev 6.13ff. It is there laid down that a cereal offering ($\theta v\sigma ia$) made $\dot{\epsilon}\pi\dot{\iota}$ $\tau\eta\gamma\acute{a}\nu ov$ (עֹל מחבת) is to be made by Aaron's successor. L makes the clearly secondary addition of $\tau\hat{\omega}\nu$ $\tau\eta\gamma a\nu\iota\sigma\tau\hat{\omega}\nu$ after $\tau\eta\gamma\acute{a}\nu ov$.

It was observed in ch. iv that ערי מסכנות is given the Pentateuchal rendering $\pi\acute{o}\lambda\epsilon\iota s$ $\dot{o}\chi\upsilon\rho\acute{a}s$ in several places. A footnote stated that L adds $(\tau\grave{a}s)$ $\tau\hat{\omega}\nu$ $\phi\acute{o}\rho\omega\nu$ in II 8.4, 6, breaking the link with Exod. Is the basis of this rendering מכס "tax", or ܡܟܣܢܘܬܐ "tax-collection"?

In II 23.11 העדות is translated $\tau\grave{a}$ $\mu a\rho\tau\acute{\upsilon}\rho\iota a$ in ii-iv, but $\tau\grave{o}$ $\mu a\rho\tau\acute{\upsilon}\rho\iota o\nu$ in L. The plural Gk word is used in a material sense in the LXX only in Exod 25.16/15, 21/20; 30.6; 40.20; Lev 16.13; Num 17.25 and is some mss. of Deut 9.15. The translator apparently identified העדות with the tables of the Decalogue or a copy. This interpretation features elsewhere in Jewish tradition: Rashi explained "he placed beside him the Torah, which is עדות".[1] But L snaps the link with the Gk Pentateuch.

(iii) L's basic text

One could go on citing evidence of a similar kind, but the evidence cited above is enough to stamp L as a revision of an earlier form of text. Can that text be identified from among the other three groups? There are signs that group iv represents a type of text most similar to that which underlies the revision. The following links with iv. not shared by ii or iii,[2] appear to be places where L has left its basic text unrevised or insufficiently revised.[3] Some of these instances might conceivably be coincidental, but most of them probably are not. Innergroup variations are noted.

In 17 cases L shares group iv's reading:

I 1.9	חוילה	: $E\upsilon\epsilon\iota\lambda a\tau$
4.14	יואב	: $I\omega\beta a\beta$
v. 24	יריב	: $I a\rho\epsilon\iota\mu$ ($I a\rho\epsilon\iota\nu$ B)
5.11	סלכה	: $E\lambda\chi a$

---

[1] Montgomery, *Kings, ad* II 11.12.

[2] Occasionally individual mss. of these groups may share the reading, but in such cases it is clear that it is not the group reading.

[3] Identical readings due to parallel assimilation have not been taken into consideration. It will be demonstrated later that the text of group iv has been contaminated from synoptic passages. L too assimilates, as Rehm has shown, and so shared readings could be coincidental.

7.10	אהוד	:	$A\omega\theta$ ($I\omega a\theta$ c₂, $\varDelta\omega\theta$ e₂)
ibid.	כנענה	:	$Xavaav$
8.26	שחריה	:	$\Sigma a\rho a\iota a$
9.7	סלוא	:	$\Sigma a\lambda\omega\mu$
v. 16	גלל	:	$\Gamma a\lambda a a\delta$
11.35	אור	:	$\Sigma o\upsilon\rho$ ($\Sigma\theta\upsilon\rho$ B)
18.9, 10	תעו	:	$\Theta\omega a$($\Theta o\lambda a$ b' b* v. 9, b v. 10)
26.23	יצהרי	:	$I\sigma\sigma a a\rho$ ($I\sigma a\rho\epsilon\iota$ c₂)
II 21.17	יהואחז	:	$'O\chi o\zeta\epsilon i a s$
35.6	והתקדשו והכינו	:	$\kappa a\iota\ \dot{\epsilon}\tau o\iota\mu\dot{a}\sigma a\tau\epsilon$
v. 18	וכל־מלכי	:	$\kappa a\iota\ \pi a v\tau\dot{o}s\ \beta a\sigma\iota\lambda\dot{\epsilon}\omega s$
II Ki 24.3/36.5c	להסיר	:	$\tau o\hat{\upsilon}\ \dot{a}\pi o\sigma\tau\hat{\eta}v a\iota\ a\dot{\upsilon}\tau\dot{o}v$
36.23	כל־ממלכות	:	$\pi\dot{a}\sigma a\iota s\ \tau a\hat{\iota}s\ \beta a\sigma\iota\lambda\epsilon i a\iota s$ [1]

In 3 cases L's reading is a further development of that of group iv:

I 1.32	מדן	:	$Ma\delta\iota a\mu : Ma\delta a\iota\mu$
v. 40	אונם	:	$\Omega vav : I\omega vav$ ($I\omega a vav$ e₂)
II 30.18 הפסח בלא ככתוב		:	$\tau\dot{o}\ \phi a\sigma\epsilon\chi\ \pi a\rho\dot{a}\ \tau\dot{\eta}v\ \gamma\rho a\phi\dot{\eta}v\ \tau o\hat{\upsilon}\tau o$: $\tau\dot{o}\ \phi a\sigma\epsilon\chi\ \tau o\hat{\upsilon}\tau o\ \pi.\tau.\gamma.$

In 3 cases L preserves the older reading of group iv, which has
degenerated in the text of that group

I 8.35	מלך	:	$M\epsilon\lambda\chi\eta\lambda : M\epsilon\lambda\chi\iota\eta\lambda$
23.9	שלמות	:	$A\lambda\omega\theta\epsilon\iota\mu : A\lambda\omega\mu\iota\theta$ ($A\delta\omega\mu\epsilon\iota\theta$ e₂)
II 11.6	עיטם	:	$A\pi av$ (TI/Π): $A\iota\tau av$ e₂ = L ($A\iota\tau a\mu$ b, following group ii).[2]

In I 8.35 L's reading undoubtedly represents the original LXX. In
the other two cases both L and group iv exhibit corrupt forms, but
L preserves forms at an earlier stage of inner-Gk corruption.

The results of this study of group i may be summed up as follows.
The group is marked by many departures from the basic text, whose
features were illustrated in ch. iv. The form of text underlying the
revision bears most resemblance to that of group iv, and in some cases
attests it at an earlier stage. Similar conclusions will later be drawn
concerning the pre-revised text-form of groups ii and iii.

---

[1] "Ad praec tracta" (Rahlfs, *LXX*).
[2] Other cases of an old text in L are in II 9.20; 22.7; 35.16.

(iv) *Proto-Lucian*

L evidently has a history stretching back long before Lucian.[1] An earlier form of the recension is apparently attested by Josephus. It is notoriously difficult to establish beyond shadow of doubt Josephus' source at any particular point on account of his propensity to paraphrase and of the variety of possible sources — Sam-Ki or Chron, Rg or Par. But there are at least seventeen cases where it seems most likely that Josephus depended upon a proto-Lucianic text.[2]

I 13.1 $+ \pi\rho\epsilon\sigma\beta\upsilon\tau\acute{\epsilon}\rho\omega\nu$ L cf. $\gamma\epsilon\rho\acute{o}\nu\tau\omega\nu$ *Ant.* vii. 78.

II 13.8   עגלי זהב : $\mu\acute{o}\sigma\chi o\iota \chi\rho\upsilon\sigma o\hat{\iota}$ G O R, $\delta\alpha\mu\acute{\alpha}\lambda\epsilon\iota\varsigma \chi\rho\upsilon\sigma a\hat{\iota}$ L cf. $\tau a\hat{\iota}\varsigma \chi\rho\upsilon\sigma a\hat{\iota}\varsigma \delta\alpha\mu\acute{\alpha}\lambda\epsilon\sigma\iota$ *Ant.* viii. 279.

v. 13   הסב : $\mathring{\alpha}\pi\acute{\epsilon}\sigma\tau\rho\epsilon\psi\epsilon\nu$ G O R, $\pi\epsilon\rho\iota\epsilon\kappa\acute{\upsilon}\kappa\lambda\omega\sigma\epsilon$ L cf. $\pi\epsilon\rho\iota\kappa\upsilon\kappa\lambda\omega\sigma\alpha\mu\acute{\epsilon}\nu o\upsilon\varsigma$ 282.

v. 15   ויריעו : $\mathring{\epsilon}\beta\acute{o}\eta\sigma\alpha\nu$ G O R, $\mathring{\eta}\lambda\acute{\alpha}\lambda\alpha\xi\epsilon\nu$ L cf. $\mathring{\alpha}\lambda\alpha\lambda\alpha\xi\acute{\alpha}\nu\tau\epsilon\varsigma$ 283.

ibid.   נגף : $\mathring{\epsilon}\pi\acute{\alpha}\tau\alpha\xi\epsilon\nu$ G O R, $\mathring{\epsilon}\theta\rho\alpha\upsilon\sigma\epsilon$ L 283.

14.13/14   ויבזו : $\mathring{\epsilon}\sigma\kappa\acute{\upsilon}\lambda\epsilon\upsilon\sigma\alpha\nu$ G O R, $\delta\iota\acute{\eta}\rho\pi\alpha\sigma\alpha\nu$ L cf. $\delta\iota\alpha\rho\pi\alpha\gamma\eta\nu$ 294.

17.12   בירניות : $o\mathring{\iota}\kappa\acute{\eta}\sigma\epsilon\iota\varsigma$ G O R, $\beta\acute{\alpha}\rho\epsilon\iota\varsigma$ L 396.

20.16   הציץ : $A\sigma\alpha\epsilon$,, etc. G O R, $\tau\hat{\eta}\varsigma \mathring{\epsilon}\xi o\chi\hat{\eta}\varsigma A\sigma.$ L cf. $\tau\hat{\eta}\varsigma \ldots \mathring{\alpha}\nu\alpha\beta\acute{\alpha}\sigma\epsilon\omega\varsigma \lambda\epsilon\gamma o\mu\acute{\epsilon}\nu\eta\varsigma$ δ' $'E\xi o\chi\hat{\eta}\varsigma$ ix.11.

v. 17   התיצבו עמדו : $\sigma\acute{\upsilon}\nu\epsilon\tau\epsilon$ G O R, $\sigma\tau\hat{\eta}\tau\epsilon$ L cf. $\sigma\tau\acute{\alpha}\nu\tau\alpha\varsigma$.

v. 18   נפלו : $\mathring{\epsilon}\pi\epsilon\sigma\alpha\nu/o\nu$ G O R, $+ \mathring{\epsilon}\pi\grave{\iota} \pi\rho\acute{o}\sigma\omega\pi o\nu$ L cf. $\pi\epsilon\sigma\acute{o}\nu\tau\epsilon\varsigma \mathring{\epsilon}\pi\grave{\iota} \pi\rho\acute{o}\sigma\omega\pi o\nu$

v. 24   פליטה : $\sigma\omega\zeta\acute{o}\mu\epsilon\nu o\varsigma$ G O R, $\mathring{\alpha}\nu\alpha\sigma\omega\zeta.$ L cf. $\mathring{\alpha}\nu\alpha\sigma\omega\theta\hat{\eta}\nu\alpha\iota$ 13.

21.15   מעיך : $\mathring{\eta} \kappa o\iota\lambda\acute{\iota}\alpha \sigma o\upsilon$ G O R, $\tau\grave{\alpha} \mathring{\epsilon}\nu\tau\epsilon\rho\acute{\alpha} \sigma o\upsilon$ L cf. $\tau\hat{\omega}\nu \mathring{\epsilon}\nu\tau\acute{\epsilon}\rho\omega\nu$ 101.

26.16   להשחית : $\kappa\alpha\tau\alpha\phi\theta\epsilon\hat{\iota}\rho\alpha\iota,$ G O R, $\delta\iota\alpha\phi\theta\epsilon\hat{\iota}\rho\alpha\iota$ L cf. $\delta\iota\epsilon\phi\theta\acute{\alpha}\rho\eta$ 222.

28.24   ויסגר : $\mathring{\epsilon}\kappa\lambda\epsilon\iota\sigma\epsilon\nu$ G O, $\mathring{\epsilon}\kappa o\psi\epsilon$ R, $\mathring{\alpha}\pi\acute{\epsilon}\kappa\lambda\epsilon\iota\sigma\epsilon\nu$ L cf. $\mathring{\alpha}\pi o\kappa\lambda\epsilon\hat{\iota}\sigma\alpha\iota$ 257.

33.12   חלה : $\mathring{\epsilon}\zeta\acute{\eta}\tau\eta\sigma\epsilon\nu$ G O R, $\mathring{\epsilon}\delta\epsilon\acute{\eta}\theta\eta$ L cf. $\mathring{\epsilon}\delta\epsilon\hat{\iota}\tau o$ x.41.

34.4   וינתצו : $\kappa\alpha\tau\acute{\epsilon}\sigma\pi\alpha\sigma\epsilon\nu$ G, $\kappa\alpha\tau\acute{\epsilon}\sigma\kappa\alpha\psi\alpha\nu$ O, $\kappa\alpha\tau\acute{\epsilon}\sigma\kappa\alpha\psi\epsilon$ L R cf. $\kappa\alpha\tau\acute{\epsilon}\sigma\kappa\alpha\psi\epsilon\nu$ 52.

v. 8   גדע : $\mathring{\epsilon}\kappa o\psi\epsilon\nu$ G O R, $\mathring{\epsilon}\xi\acute{\epsilon}\kappa o\psi\epsilon$ L Jos.

Justin cited part of the psalm of I Par 16 in *Apol.* i.41.[3] His text, like

---

[1] For the relation between L and the Rg *kaige* recension see p. 140.

[2] BM's citations have been checked with Vannutelli, who gives the text of B. Niese's edition.

[3] BM's citations have been checked with both Migne and J.M. Pfättisch, *Justinus' des Philosophen und Martyrers Apologien,* 1912.

so many patristic quotations, is marked by much assimilation to the
parallel Psa 95, some of which overlaps with L. But it would be
hazardous to claim more than coincidence in such shared readings,
since it is probable that quotation from a memory that played tricks is
responsible for the confusion in Justin's text.[1] There are two striking
alignments.

v. 27   ἔπαινος : αἶνος Just cf. αἶνος L for δόξα earlier.

v. 29   ἐνέγκατε : εἰσέλθετε L Just cf. Psa 95.8 εἰσπορεύεσθε.

(v) *L and the Three*

The translations of Chron made by Aquila, Theodotion and Symmachus have unfortunately been poorly preserved. There are very few
variants extant with specific labels attached. BM records twenty six
quotations from σ′, two from α′ and two from θ′, little of which is
reflected in O, L or R. Much of the secondary material preserved in
the later textforms is too nondescript to label, but there are a number
of snatches of translation which contain elements distinctive enough
to attach them with some confidence to one of the Three.[2] Over
against BM's purely objective reckoning Field can attribute by conjecture three readings to σ′ and one to θ′. The text of L contains four
named variants, of which one, in II 23.13 ascribed to θ′, is of uncertain
interpretation.[3] There is no reason to doubt ὁράσει for ראת *sub* θ′
in *b* at II 26.5 nor ἐξώσθη for נגזר ascribed to θ′ in *b* at v. 21. In
33.14 o^mg ascribes to θ′ κύκλῳ εἰς τὸν οφλα for וסבב לעפל, which
reappears in L (but τὸ οφλαα).[4]

The following readings in L may be deductively attributed to α′.

I 6.33/48 עבודת : δουλείαν, similarly 9.13; 25.1; 28.14. S. Daniel,
         Recherches, p. 115, has suggested this provenance.

18.15   מזכיר : ἀναμνημνίσκων e₂. So α′ renders in II Rg 8.16.

29.18   שמרה־זאת ליצר מחשבות לבב עמך : φύλαξον αὐτὴν εἰς πλάσ-
         μα διανοιῶν καρδίας λαοῦ σου. Katz, *Philo's Bible*, p. 23
         note 1, saw Aquila's handiwork here.

II 4.2   קו : σπαρτίον, ascribed to α′ in Ezek. 27.19 = קוה, by
         error for קדה (Reider-Turner, *Index to Aquila*, p. 219).

---

[1] Cf. Wevers, "Proto-LXX Studies", *The Seed of Wisdom*, p. 73.

[2] Apart from literature cited below, Hatch and Redpath's Hexaplaric index has been
used.

[3] See p. 15 note 3.

[4] Thomsen, *ZAW* xxxi, p. 309.

12.11   והשבום : an equivalent found only in α' at Jer 12.15
         (*Index*, p. 26).
13.3   איש בחור גבור חיל : ἀνδρῶν ἐκλεκτῶν δυνατῶν ἰσχυί.

The second word points to α'.

15.8   לכד : κατελάβετο, an equivalent found only in α' (*Index*,
         p. 129).

Probable echoes of θ' are as follows.

I 4.8   משפחת : πατριαί, ascribed to θ' in Jer 33 (40).24; Ezek 20.32
         and by Ziegler (*Index*, p. 186) in Jer 15.3.
v. 38   פרצו : ἐχύθησαν. So θ' renders at Isa 54.3.
15.27   אפוד בד : εφουδ μόνον (also in z^mg): cf. θ' at Exod 39.2
         (36.9).[1]
16.29;   II 7.7 מנחה : θυσίας, attributed to θ' by Daniel, p. 232.
II 2.3/4 סמים : ἀρωμάτων, ascribed to θ' at Exod 30.7 (Katz,
         Philo's Bible, pp. 63 note 3, 64).
20.13   טפם : ὄχλος L, probably θ': cf. *Index*, p. 180.

σ' was probably the author of the following.

II 20.7 אהב : φίλω/ου : cf. τοῦ φίλου μου σ' in Isa 41.8 (Katz,
         p. 85).
29.24   ויחטאו : περιεράντησαν. Cf. περιρραντισμός σ' used for נדה
         in Zech 13.1.

Undoubtedly much more of L's material is derived from the Three
than can be attributed to them individually either through ms. ascription or by deduction. Obviously their renderings were an important
source of L's text, whether via the Hexapla or independently of Origen.

2. Group ii

(i) *Mss. in the group*

Rehm pointed out, and chapter iii illustrated, that d p q t z are the
regular members of a second group. 74 144 236 321 346 show close
affinity with the group, and so does 44 when cited in BM.j is a full-time

---

[1] In I Rg 21.9 (10) θ' ἐπώμιδος, σ' εφουδ have probably been confused: cf. σ' ἐπώμιδα
here according to b^mg and z^mg.

member throughout I Par, but in II Par is a mixed ms., at times siding with this group. The other mixed mss. f m frequently exhibit its readings. i belongs to the group from II 1.2 until the ms. stops at 13.15. While i belongs to the group, it sides often with L, together with y, e.g. at 2.7; 3.17; 6.34; 7.21; 9.7; 12.15. y joins the group from II 1.2 and stays with it until the end of the book. n joins its ranks from II 21.8 to 25.23. c₂ forsakes group iv in favour of this one at II 31.6b and stays with it until it finishes at 36.5 Ἰερουσαλημ.[1]

Microfilm samples of 314 show that it is related to this group. It belongs not to the sub-group d p, to be mentioned below, but to the main stream of the group. In the following examples the first reading is that of B, the second shared by 314 and the cited ms. evidence.

I 13.1	τῶν [1] : pr τῶν ἀρχόντων καί ii
v. 8	δυνάμει : pr τῇ ii
v. 10	ἐπάταξεν : ἀπέκτεινεν ii
14.5	Βααρ : Ιεβαρ ii
v. 7	Ελεισαμαε : Ελισαφα ii
II 11.8	Μάρεισαν : Μαρισαθ ii
v. 12	αὐτῷ : τῷ d p q t z 74 144 236 321 346
v. 20	ἑαυτῷ : αὐτῷ p q t z 74 144 236 321 346
34.4	ἐπί : κατά ii
v. 9	πύλην : φυλακήν ii

246 is extant from II 1.1 to 13.15. The very extent of the ms. suggests that it is related to i, which stops at the same point. Detailed study confirms this relationship, as the following examples illustrate. The second reading is shared by 246.

1.10	κρινεῖ : κρίνῃ i
v. 13	Ισραηλ : Ιλημ g* i
v. 17	ἀργυρίου : ἀργυρίων e i y
2.7	ἅ : ὅν a i
v. 16	ἄξομεν : ἄξωμεν a d i
3.16	σερσερωθ : σερωθ i
8.5	Βαιθωρωμ [2] : Βεθωρων i y
v. 18	Σωφειρα : Σοφειρα i
11.6	Βαιθσεεμ : Βιθλεεμ i

---

[1] There is no reason to include e as a regular member of the group, as Vannutelli does. The text of e shares its readings on only a few occasions. Sometimes a corrector of e adds them to the text.

68 is among the list of collated mss. in Holmes-Parsons' edition of
Par. But Rahlfs pointed out that it was not in fact collated.[1] Study of
microfilmed extracts has revealed that in the main it is closest to y.
Now y has chequered affinities: it belongs to group i in the first ten
chapters of I Par, to iii in the rest of I Par and to ii in II Par. But the
extract of 68 from I 12 breaks this pattern: it sides with ii, instead of
iii as expected. But in succeeding chapters it follows the pattern of y.

I 12.24	δορατοφόροι : δορυφόροι ii
v. 31	οἵ : οὗτοι ii
v. 40	σταφίδας : σταφυλάς ii
13.5	Ιαρειμ : Καριαθιαρειμ i y
v. 10	κύριος : + ὀργῇ A i n y Arm
14.5	Εκταε : Ελισου c e f g i n y
v. 8	αὐτοῖς : αὐτῶν b i n y
II 10.3	Ροβοαμ : pr τὸν βασιλέα ii
v. 15	ἤκουσεν ... λαοῦ : ᾔδει ὁ βασιλεὺς Ροβοαμ i p-z 74 144 236 321 346
v. 18	Ροβοαμ :+ ὁ βασιλεύς L i p q y 74 144 236 321 346
33.6	ἐπλήθυνεν τοῦ ποιῆσαι : καὶ ἐπλήθυνε y.

122 is also very similar to y. It has the readings mentioned above in
I 14.5, 8; II 33.6,17. Note also:

II 11.8	Μάρεισαν : Μαρισαθ ii
v. 18	Μολλαθ : Μοολαθ d i m q y 74 236 321 346
v. 21	Αβεσσαλωμ : Αβεσαλωμ g q t y 321 346.

dp form a clearly defined sub-group throughout. In the following
list of selected variants the main group reading is given first.

I 1.32	Ασουριειμ : Ασουριμ
3.1; 11.1; etc.	Χεβρων : Χευρων
6.74; 8.23	Αβδων : Αυδων
12.28	δύο : ἕξ
16.35	αἰνέσεσιν : αἰνέσεις
19.14	παρετάξατο : — αντο
21.10	ἐρῶ : ὁρῶ
25.3	τὸν πατέρα : τῶν πρ͞ων
II 5.6	λογισθήσονται : — εται = L
7.5	βοσκημάτων : — ατα

[1] Verzeichnis, p. 306.

9.11	βασιλεύς : + Σολόμων
11.1	ἑαυτῷ : αὐτῶν
17.7	'Αβδίαν : Αὐδίαν
26.1	ἔλαβον : ἔλαβεν
30.8	ἡγίασεν : — σαν
31.10	ἐξ οὗ : ἐκ σου
33.5	δυσίν : δυνάμεσιν

Holmes and Parsons supplied in the Addenda to vol. ii variants of
125 from I Par 1 ; II 1. A comparison of these readings with the apparatus of BM has revealed two facts. First, 125 is clearly a member of this
group.

The second result is that 125 is very closely aligned with d, as the
following examples show. The first reading is that of B, the second
that shared by 125 and the ms(s). cited.

I 1.19	(ἀδελφὸν) αὐτοῦ : om. d p
II 1.1	(θεὸς) αὐτοῦ : om. d f g j e₂
v. 6	αὐτό : αὐτῷ Σολόμων d
v. 8	πρὸς τὸν θεόν : om. d
v. 14	(χίλια) καί : om. d
	καὶ ὁ ... Ιερουσαλημ : om. d
v. 17	ἑκατὸν καὶ πεντήκοντα : ρν' ἀργυρίου d

610, examined on microfilm, is also closely related to d, as the following examples show. The second reading is shared by 610.

I 1.8	Φουδ : Φογγ d
3.12	Ιωαθαν : Ιωθαμ b d p z
6.62	υἱοῖς : χῆς d
v. 74	Αβαραν : Αυδων d p Arm
14.4	Ισοβοαμ : Ουσωβαθ d p
29.8	Βεσιηλ : Ιαηλ d
II 11.19	Σαμαρίαν : Σομορίαν d
21.2	Ιηλ : Ιεηλ d g
35.8	Ιειηλ : Ιεηλ d g m
v. 15	ἁγίων : αὐτῶν b d.

(ii) *The archetype of the group*

The group appears to stem from a single ms. according to the evidence
of errors shared by all or most members. Omission by homoeoteleuton

occurs, e.g. I 6.35f.; 11.2; 24.24f.; 29.22f.; II 2.18; 4.13; 9.10; 18.2; 23.11; 27.3f; 30.25; 34.10; 35.22. Common variants due to corruption occur as follows.

The reading of group ii comes after that of the other three groups.

I 13.7	καινήν : κενήν
25.8	ἔβαλον : ἔλαβον
29.3	εὐδοκῆσαι : οἰκοδομῆσαι
II 8.12	ναοῦ : λαοῦ
15.6	ἐξέστησεν αὐτούς : ἐξετάστης ἐν αὐτοῖς
24.23	λαῷ : ναῷ
27.5	αὐτόν : αὐτῶν
32.12	αὐτῷ : αὐτό
34.32	εὑρεθέντας : πορευθέντας
35.21	καταφθείρῃ σε : καταφθαρήσῃ

(iii) *A revised textform*

Vannutelli and Rehm claimed from general observation that the group represents a revision of an earlier Gk text. Close examination reveals that this is indeed so and that the revision is twofold. On the one hand, the changes made solely by the group are stylistic and explanatory, and even at times amount to an independent re-writing of the text. In II 10.15 "did not listen to the people because" becomes "did not know that". At 27.3; 33.14 Οπλα is misunderstood as ὅπλα, and (ἀπ)έθετο is added to suit this new view.[1] γεγραμμένας ἐν τῷ νόμῳ in 31.3 is adapted to γινόμενας ἐν τῷ οἴκῳ.

It was noted in ch. iv[2] that the translator frequently renders anarthrously a Heb construct noun or a noun with a suffix. The group, independently of the others, improves the style by inserting the article in such cases at I 2.23; 3.21; 5.1; 21.18; 23.14; II 1.9; 4.20, 21; 7.9; 9.20; 12.13; 18.11, 18; 21.11; 24.13; 28.10; 36.17.

Alongside the stylistic and paraphrastic changes there also appears a certain amount of revision more closely approximating to the Heb, which occurs only within this group. Instances may be cited where L too corrects, but with different vocabulary, and clearly L and this group are correcting independently.

---

[1] Torrey, *Ezra Studies*, p. 104, is mistaken in thinking that B as well as this group interprets as "weapons" in 33.14.

[2] P. 39f.

Group ii adds with MT as follows. The first Gk reading is that of other groups.

I 11.2	גם בהיות	: ὄντος : pr ἔτι
12.38/37	כלי צבא מלחמה	: ἐν πασιν σκεύεσιν πολεμικοῖς iii, iv + εἰς πόλεμον (+ ἐν δυνάμει L)
19.5	²האנשים	: om. iii, iv : οἱ ἀνοι (οἱ ἄνδρες L)
28.4	למלך	: βασιλέα : pr εἰς
II 10.12	ביום	: τῇ ἡμέρᾳ : pr εἰς
11.1	בית	: om. : οἶκον
20.22	החלו	: (ἐν)ἄρξασθαι : + αὐτούς
v. 31	בן	: om. iii, iv : ὦν (υἱός L)
v. 33	לא סרו	: ἔτι ὑπῆρχεν iii, iv : οὔκετι ὑπ. (οὐκ ἐξήρθη L)
22.2	במלכו	: ἐβασίλευσεν iii, iv : pr ὅτε (ἐν τῷ βασιλευέιν αὐτόν L)
23.13	עומד	: om. iii, iv : ἑστώς (εἱστήκει L)
24.6	ומירושלם	: καὶ Ιερουσαλημ : καὶ ἀπὸ I.
25.23	בן יהואחז	: om. iii, iv : υἱοῦ Ιωαχαζ (υἱοῦ Ὀχοζίου L = Rg)

The group has unique omissions according to MT:

I 4.28	καὶ Σαμα
II 9.30	ὁ βασιλεύς
13.10	αὐτοῦ
18.1	ἔτι
20.22	αὐτοῦ
25.14	αὐτός
v. 26	ἰδόυ
31.2	(ἐν ταῖς) αὐλαῖς
36.8	οὐκ

The group has unique variants according to MT:

I 12.19/18	הגדוד	: τῶν δυνάμεων : τῆς δυνάμεως
II 6.30	וסלחת	: καὶ ἰάσῃ : καὶ ἰλάσῃ
13.15	איש	: ἄνδρες/ας : ἄνδρα
25.15	נביא	: προφήτας : προφήτην
v. 21	פנים	: ἀλλήλοις : προσώποις
29.9	נו–²,³,⁴	: ὑμῶν : ἡμῶν

The group changes the word-order according to MT:

I 12.19/18   דויד ועמך בך ישי : καὶ ὁ λαός σου Δαυειδ υἱὸς Ιεσσαι iv
(Δ. υἱ. Ι. σὺ [om. iii] καὶ ὁ λ. σου L, iii): Δ. καὶ ὁ λ. σου
υἱ. Ι.

II 4.3   הבקר יצוקים : ἐχώνευσαν τοὺς μόσχους iii, iv: τοὺς μ. ἐχ.
(βόες χωνευτοί L)

14.5/6   יהוה לו : αὐτῷ κύριος : κ. αὐτῷ

15.15   יהוה להם : αὐτοῖς / αὐτούς κύριος : κ. αὐτοῖς

17.12   ביהודה בירניות : οἰκήσεις ἐν τῇ Ἰουδαίᾳ iii, iv: ἐν τῇ Ι.
οἰκ. (ἐν τῷ Ιουδα βάρεις L)

34.6   מנשה ואפרים : Εφραιμ καὶ Μανασση : Μ. καὶ Ε.

v. 7   את־המזבחות ואת־האשרים : τὰ ἄλση καὶ τὰ θυσιαστήρια :
θυσιασίηρια αὐτῶν καὶ τὰ ἄλση

v. 8   ובשנת שמונה : καὶ ἐν τῷ ὀκτωκαιδεκάτῳ / ὀγδόῳ καὶ
δεκάτῳ / ἔτει : καὶ ἐν τῷ ἔτει τῷ ὀκτωκ.

36.13   ויאמץ את־לבבו : καὶ τὴν καρδίαν αὐτοῦ κατίσχυσεν iii,
iv (only κατίσχυσεν L) : καὶ κατίσχυσε τὴν κ. αὐτοῦ

v. 21   שבעים שנה : ἐτῶν ἑβδομήκοντα : ἑβδ. ἐτῶν

The textform seems to be identical with the recension "R" which
Rahlfs found represented by the same mss. in Rg,[1] and with the related
recensions R C which he discovered in the LXX of Ruth.[2] It is significant that he observed a double tendency in R C of Ruth: approximation to MT and also departure from it to produce smoother, more
comprehensible Gk. Katz rightly commented that these liberties
"certainly represent a different stratum and, I should say, a more
recent one. For otherwise it is difficult to imagine that its results were
not swept away by the recensor who brought the text so close to the
Hebrew".[3]

His comment is equally applicable to group ii in Par. This group is

---

[1] Cf. p. 17. Bo Johnson, op. cit., p. 88, regards d l p q t z or d+as a secondary group
of witnesses to the Hexaplaric text of I Rg. He notes that "d+ zeigt gelegentlich, besonders bei Eigennamen, eine Textform die besser mit MT überstimmt als es bei A c x
der Fall ist. Dagegen hat d+ kaum eigene Varianten von hexaplarischen Charakter
aufzuweisen". (p. 107).

[2] Studie über den griechischen Text des Buches Ruth, pp. 103ff. P. Katz in Philo's Bible,
pp. 99ff., maintained that in the writings of Philo an interpolator substituted for the LXX
readings from the same recension as Rahlfs found in Ruth, in an attempt to re-introduce
lost lemmata. He believed on the evidence of interpolations in Philo that R once existed
throughout the Pentateuch.

[3] Op. cit., p. 101f.

marked by two completely different traits: now it does not scruple to
take liberties with its text, now it carefully corrects according to the
Heb. The utter diversity of these characteristics suggests that the
present text of group ii has undergone more than one revision. It was
doubtless the former quality that made it eventually the most popular
Gk textform: more extant mss. belong to R than to any other group.

It is not unlikely that Josephus Gk text of Par had occasional affinity
with R. There are three cases of R-type readings:

II 13.20   עצר כח : ἴσχυσεν R, *Ant.* viii. 285 (ἔσχεν ἴσχυν G O L)
28.7   מעשׂיהו : 'Αμασίαν R='Αμασίας *Ant.* ix. 247 (Ma‑G O L).
34.8   מעשׂיהו : 'Αμασίαν R, *Ant.* x. 55 (Ma‑G O L).

(iv) *R and the Three*

A fairly sizeable collection of material from the Three could be
reconstructed from among the variants in L. L is in fact the major
repository of such readings among the textforms of Par. Only a few
can be detected in R. There is a single explicit citation. At II 33.14
καὶ κατὰ τὴν εἴσοδον τὴν διὰ τῆς πύλης τῆς ἰχθυικῆς is ascribed to
σ′ in oᵐᵍ, while the following καὶ περιεκύκλωσε τὸ ἄδυτον is attribu‑
ted to θ′ along with κύκλῳ εἰς τὸν οφλα which reappears in L.
Obviously a copyist has erred slightly: καὶ περιεκ. and κύκλῳ both
render וסבב. Most probably the text as far as ἄδυτον is to be ascribed
to σ′. Anyway, R's text, found also in A and Bᵃᵇ, is a mixture of σ′
and θ′, while L cites only θ′. Yet in I 28.14f. R appears to be building
upon L or upon L's source. L R supply material missing in G O. L has
a more literal rendering than R, and the use of δουλεία for עבודה
points to α′ as his source. R's text seems to be a stylistic rewriting of
L's wording. The frequent identity of text in L R could indicate R's
dependence upon L. But the many differences between the two suggest
rather that L and R at times derived their readings from a common
source.

At II 7.1 ἐτέλεσεν R for συνετέλεσεν (וככלות) has been ascribed to
α′ by Katz, *Philo's Bible*, p. 6 note 1. In 35.19 ἤδρασεν R c e g n for
הכין is probably from σ′: cf. Katz, p. 35.

(v) *The* Grundlage *of the group*

R—for so it may now be called—is evidently a revision of an earlier
text. There is much evidence to suggest that of the extant text-types,

group iv represents the type nearest to that underlying R. Unusual readings are often shared by the two groups. In the light of the foregoing evidence of revision this fact implies that R has kept unchanged readings otherwise found only in the fourth group.

In 25 cases R alone shares group iv's reading:

I 1.37	נחת	: $N\alpha\chi\epsilon\varsigma$
4.2	צרעתי	: $A\rho\alpha\theta\epsilon\iota$
6.39/54	למשפחת	: $\tau\hat{\eta}\ \pi\alpha\tau\rho\acute{\iota}\alpha\ \alpha\mathring{\upsilon}\tau\hat{\omega}\nu$
7.32	שומר	: $\Sigma\alpha\mu\eta\rho$
8.33	אשבעל	: $A\sigma\alpha\beta\alpha\lambda$
v. 39	אולם	: $A\iota\lambda\alpha\mu$
20.3	לכל	: $\tau o\hat{\iota}\varsigma\ \pi\alpha\iota\sigma\acute{\iota}\nu$
21.30	נבעת	: $o\mathring{\upsilon}\ \kappa\alpha\tau\acute{\epsilon}\sigma\pi\epsilon\upsilon\sigma\epsilon\nu$
23.11	ויהיו	: $\kappa\alpha\grave{\iota}\ \acute{\epsilon}\gamma\acute{\epsilon}\nu\epsilon\tau o$
v. 19	אמריה	: $A\mu\alpha\delta\iota\alpha$
24.8	חרם	: $X\alpha\rho\eta\beta$
v. 23	אמריהו	: $A\mu\alpha\delta\iota\alpha$ ($A\iota\mu\alpha\delta\iota\alpha$ t)
v. 24	בני	: om.
25.4	מחזיאות	: $M\epsilon\alpha\zeta\omega\theta$ ($M\epsilon\lambda\zeta\omega\theta$ B)
v. 12	נתניהו	: $N\alpha\theta\alpha\nu$
v. 25	חנוי	: $^{\backprime}A\nu\alpha\nu\acute{\iota}\alpha\varsigma$
26.7	סמכיהו	: $\Sigma\alpha\beta\chi\epsilon\iota\alpha$ ($\Sigma\alpha\beta\alpha\kappa\chi\epsilon\iota\alpha$ c$_2$)
v. 11	טבליהו	: $T\alpha\beta\lambda\alpha\iota$ ($I\alpha\beta\lambda\alpha\iota$ c$_2$)
27.8	שמהות	: $\Sigma\alpha\lambda\alpha\omega\theta$
v. 15	חלדי	: $X o\lambda\delta\epsilon\iota\alpha$ ($B\alpha\nu\alpha\acute{\iota}\alpha\varsigma$ d)
II 1.13	מלפני	: $\pi\rho\grave{o}\ \pi\rho o\sigma\acute{\omega}\pi o\upsilon$
v. 16	הסוסים	: $\tau\hat{\omega}\nu\ \mathring{\iota}\pi\pi\acute{\epsilon}\omega\nu$
3.8	רחבו	: $\tau\grave{o}\ \mu\hat{\eta}\kappa o\varsigma$
11.7	שוכו	: $\Sigma o\kappa\chi\omega\theta$ ($\Sigma o\kappa o\chi\omega\theta$ p)

In 11 cases R's reading is a further development of an unusual rendering in group iv, which is placed first.

I 4.35	ויהוא	: $\kappa\alpha\grave{\iota}\ o\mathring{\upsilon}\tau o\varsigma$: $\kappa\alpha\grave{\iota}\ \alpha\mathring{\upsilon}\tau\acute{o}\varsigma$
9.44	אצל[1]	: $E\sigma\alpha\eta\lambda$ S : $E\sigma\epsilon\lambda$ (from $E\sigma\alpha\iota\lambda$)
16.15	זכר	: $\mu\nu\eta\mu o\nu\epsilon\acute{\upsilon} o\mu\epsilon\nu$: $\mu\nu\eta\mu o\nu\epsilon\acute{\upsilon}\omega\mu\epsilon\nu$
23.9	הרן	: $A\iota\delta\alpha\nu$ B* from $E\delta\alpha\nu$ c$_2$: $A\iota\lambda\alpha\mu$
II 22.7 להכרית את־בית אתאב		: $\tau\grave{o}\nu\ o\mathring{\iota}\kappa o\nu\ A\chi\alpha\alpha\beta$: pr $\epsilon\mathring{\iota}\varsigma$
26.9	שער[2]	: $\tau\grave{\eta}\nu\ \pi\acute{\upsilon}\lambda\eta\nu\ \gamma\omega\nu\acute{\iota}\alpha\varsigma$ B* : $\tau\grave{\eta}\nu\ \gamma\omega\nu\acute{\iota}\alpha\nu$.

B^{ab} corrects according to R.

27.3   העפל   : αὐτοῦ Οπλα : αὐτῆς ὅπλα

28.18 R adds 16 words from v. 21 with B, prefixing καὶ τά.

29.19   המלך אחז   : Αχας ὁ βασιλεύς : Αχαζ ὁ βασιλεύς

v. 33   שלשת אלפים   : τρισχείλια πεντακόσια B* : τριακόσια

33.14   לעפל   : εἰς αὐτὸν Οπλα : εἰς αὐτὴν ὅπλα

In five cases R clearly preserves an older reading found adapted in group iv:

I 4.17   ילון   : Αμων : Ιαμων

8.12   אונו   : Ωναν (Εναν c₂) : Ωνα

v. 30   נדב   : Αδαδ : Ναδαδ

v. 40   אולם   : Αιλειμ : Αιλαμ

20.4   ספי   : Σαφουτ : Σαφου

In conclusion, group ii gives a strong impression of being descended from an archetype which was revised from a text-form most similar to that of group iv.

CHAPTER SIX

GROUPS III AND IV AND THE OLD LATIN

1. Group iii

(i) *Mss. in the group*

A N a c e g h n are regular members, as ch. iii illustrated. In relation to Gk mss. Arm[1] mainly follows this group, although it sometimes attests L-type readings. The mixed mss. f j (in II Par)[2] and, less often, m are at times allied. g sometimes strays into other groups. Often A N h, generally individually, have readings of group iv: this fact will be elaborated later. b temporarily belongs to R from II 21.8 to 25.23, as noted previously. i is attached to group iii in I Par; it is at times aligned with group iv in chs. 1-3. o is a member in its brief extant life of II 32.1 τειχήρεις-15 παντός; 33.11-34.1. y is affiliated from I 11.5 till II 1.1.

---

[1] There is another Armenian version of Chron. S. Lyonnet, *Les origines de la version arménienne et le Diatessaron*, 1950, p. 10, cites authorities who derive it from an underlying Syriac text.

[2] In II Par f j at times exhibit independent readings, often closer to MT. In the following examples the first Gk reading is that of the other mss., the second that of f j.

II 2.3/4 בונה : οἰκοδομῶ : -ῶν

9.15 על־הצנה האחת : τῷ ἑνὶ θυρεῷ : θ. τῷ ἑνί

10.7 — : ἐν τῇ σήμερον : om

20.36 ויעשׂו : καὶ ἐπόιησεν : ... - σαν

22.6 הוא : — : αὐτός

30.9 תשׁבו : ἐπιστρέψωμεν : ἐπιστρέψητε

In 26.11 γραμματέως, instead of βασιλέως, is a misplaced correction of κριτοῦ earlier for שׁוטר.

This pair of mss. also have unique variants unrelated to MT ,e.g.,

9.23 האלהים : ὁ θεός : κ̄ς̄ by parallel assimilation to III Rg 10.27

13.15 לפני : ἐναντίον : ἀπὸ προσώπου

23.5 היסוד : μέσῃ : μεγάλῃ

98 and 379, examined from microfilmed extracts, are related to j. The second ms. is in fact a slavish copy of the first, as M. Faulhaber, *Biblische Zeitschrift*, i, p. 249, reported in a study of Gk mss. in Spain. Another ms. which also has close affinity with j is 731, studied from microfilm. Like j, these three mss. are related to R in I Par and have mixed readings in II Par.

As to sub-groups c e g often diverge from the main group throughout Par. Examples are as follows. The main reading is given first.

I 6.67	αὐτῷ : αὐτοῖς c e g L Arm
11.17	ποτιεῖ : ποτίσει c e
14.10	θεοῦ : κυρίου c e g R
16.39	τῇ ἐν : τῆς c e g
26.24	θησαυρῶν : + οἴκου κυρίου c e
II 6.27	παίδων : δούλων e g L
7.1	ἔπλησεν : ἐπλήρωσε c e
8.16	ἐτελείωσεν : ἐτέλεσε c e
14.8	τριακόσιαι : τετρακόσιαι c e g
16.1	δοῦναι : εἶναι c e g
20.20	ἐμπιστεύσατε : -εύετε c e g
24.23	λαῷ : ναῷ c e R
26.5	Ζαχαρίου : Ἀζαρίου c e g
28.15	ἐπεκλήθησαν : ἐπικληθέντες c e g
32.24	ἔδωκεν : ἔδειξεν c e g
34.4	θυσιαζόντων : θυσιαστηρίων c e g

381, examined on microfilm, is related to this sub-group, as the following examples show. The main group reading is given first, and that shared with 381 second.

I 2.16	ἀδελφή : pr ἡ a c e
v. 23	Γεσσουρ : Γεσουρ N* b e g n Arm
11.1	πρὸς Δαυιδ ἐν Χεβρων : ἐν Χ.π.Δ. c e c₂
v. 8	Ιωαβ : om c e f i
II 1.2	ἐναντίον … ἄρχουσι : om a c e Arm
9.1	εἰς ¹ : om c e
22.1	ἐν : om c e g c₂ Arm
v. 9	κύριον : θ̄ν̄ c e g
32.1	τούτους : om c e g
v. 24	ἔδωκεν : ἔδειξεν c e g.

728 was studied on microfilm samples. It too is related to this sub-group having special affinity with c.

I 14.9	ἐν : om S c e
15.1	τῇ κιβωτῷ : τῆς κιβωτοῦ A c e g j z
II 11.6	Βαιθσεεμ : Βαιθσαιεμ c
v. 18	Ερμουθ : Ιερμουθ c e g j n

34.10   καθιστάμενοι : καθεσταμένοι N * c e Arm
ibid.   αὐτό ² : αὐτῷ a b' c g h.

Another microfilmed ms., 46, also belongs to this sub-group. It is
closely related to e.

I 5.5   Ρηχα : Ριχα e g m
v. 13   Ιαχαν : Ιαχααν e
11.5   εἶπαν : εἶπον d e i p L
21.3   ζητεῖ : ζητῇ e c₂
II 3.4   αιλαμ : ελαμ e g h i z e₂
15.15   θελήσει : θλίψει e
32.2   Σενναχηρειμ : Σεναχ e f z.

i n y represent a second sub-group as long as y is associated with
group iii. Here is a selection of examples:

I 11.12   Ελεαζαρ : Ελεαναν i n y
12.20   αὐτόν : τὸν Δᾱδ i y L
14.9   τῶν γιγάντων : Ραφαιμ/ν i y
16.27   καύχημα : ἔπαινος i n y
21.5   μαχαίραν : ῥομφαίαν i n y L
23.25   κατεσκήνωσεν : κατέστησεν i n y
26.30   ῾Ασαβίας : ῾Ασαίας i n y
29.9   προεθυμήθησαν : — μησαν i n y

In 20.1 i y (cf. g) have a long plus loosely assimilating to II Rg. 12.27ff.[1]

(ii) *A revised textform*

Rehm's observation led him to classify the group containing A N as a
recension, just as others before him had described A's text as the
product of revision. On the other hand, Torrey has claimed the originality of A and its related mss. Detailed examination of the evidence
endorses Rehm's view. The unique readings of group iii are character-
ized both by attempts to improve the rugged style of the Gk, attested
by the other three groups, and by approximations to MT. Both these
features were also noted in R, in different cases, but R takes much
more liberty with the text than this group does. The test of the definite
article stamps the group as a product of revision. Like R this group

---

[1] BH has a note "ins ? c G ...", but "G" is misleading. Rudolph, who substantially
adopts the plus, rightly criticises BH's placing of the note.

often uniquely prefixes the article to a genitival phrase: I 12.18; 15.29; II 6.8; 9.16, 26; 21.13; 28.2, 10; 29.10.

At times the group has readings closer to MT than those common to the other groups. In some cases it is conceivable that it represents a text which was subsequently adapted among the other groups, but the clear impression given by the evidence as a whole is that this group represents a revised text. The evidence set out below may be considered scanty. Certainly this group was less diligent in repairing its basic text than was L or R. There are many more cases where the group appears to be adapting, but since in those cases L and/or R agree with this group, they are not admissible evidence. The instances cited are fortunate chinks in the redactional efficiency of L and R.

It adds with MT as follow:

I 24.21   Ἰεσ(σ)ίας = ישיה

v. 23   καὶ (υἱοί) = ו (בני)

26.10   ἀπό = מן

II 2.16/17   καὶ (ἑξακόσιοι) = (... שׁשׁ) ו

It omits with MT:

I 12.21   ἐν τῇ δυνάμει

21.2   ὁ βασιλεύς

II 10.18   ἐπ' αὐτούς

It changes according to MT, apart from proper nouns:
I 26.28 ἡγίασεν R, iv (ἁγιάζων L): -σαν, a misplaced change according to הקדישׁ v.27, where all groups read ἡγίασεν.

v. 31   τοῦ : τῷ = ל

II 25.22   καὶ ἔφυγεν : καὶ ἔφυγον = וינסו

30.23   ἐν εὐφροσύνῃ : εὐφροσύνην = שמחה

32.6   ἐπὶ (τήν) : εἰς = אל

34.4   κατέσκαψε LR, κατέσπασεν iv : κατέσκαψαν = וינתצו

v. 30   τοὺς εὑρεθέντας : τοῦ εὑρεθέντος = הנמצא

36.5c   ἀποστῆναι L, iv (ἀπολέσαι R) : ἀποστῆσαι = להסיר
       II Ki. 24.3.

(iii) *The basic text of the group*

It was discovered earlier that both L and R depend upon a form of text which bears most similarity to that of group iv. The same may be said of this group. Cited below is a selection of cases where only groups iii and iv share unexpected readings. Clearly the former depends upon the latter. The reviser occasionally let slip through his net readings in his basic text which did not accord with MT, compared either directly or via MT-based translations. Instances are as follows:

I 1.35	יעוש	: $I\epsilon ov\lambda$
2.42	מישע	: $Ma\rho\epsilon\iota\sigma a(s)$ $(M\epsilon\rho\iota\sigma a$ c2, $Ma\beta\rho\iota\sigma a$ n)
3.19	פדיה	: $\Sigma a\lambda a\theta\iota\eta\lambda$
4.27	שש	: $\tau\rho\epsilon\hat{\iota}s$
5.5	ראיה	: $P\eta\chi a$ $(P\eta\chi a\beta$ n)
8.8	אותם	: $a\dot{v}\tau\acute{o}v$
8.15	זבדיה	: $A\zeta a\beta a\beta\iota a : A\zeta a\beta a\delta\iota a$ ($-\beta a\rho\iota a$ g, $Za\beta a$-$\delta\iota a$ i)
11.27	הרורי	: $A\delta\iota$
24.22	יחת	: $Iva\theta$ $(Ia\theta$ i n y R)
26.25	ישעיהו	: $\Omega\sigma a\iota a(s)$ $('I\omega\sigma.$ g R)
II 8.17	אילות	: $A\iota\lambda a\mu$
14.7/8	ושמונים	: $(\kappa a\grave{\iota})$ $\pi\epsilon v\tau\acute{\eta}\kappa ov\tau a$
17.16	עמסיה	: $Ma\sigma a\iota as$ $(Ma\sigma av\iota as$ g)
20.37	דדוהו	: $\Omega\delta\epsilon\iota a$ $(\Sigma\omega\delta\iota a$ a)
24.1	צביה	: $A\beta\iota a$
31.15	עדן	: $O\delta o\mu$ $(\Sigma o\delta o\mu$ N)
34.8	אצליהו	: $\Sigma\epsilon\lambda\iota a$ $(\Sigma\epsilon\delta\iota a$ N, $A\sigma\epsilon\lambda\iota a$ g)

One case may be cited where this group, cited second. appear to preserve an earlier form of group iv:

I 7.29 (יבלעם): $Ba\lambda a\delta : \beta a\lambda aa\delta$

(iv) *The identity of the group*

In the following sections evidence is to be adduced that group iii is the closest witness to the Hexaplaric recension in the Gk ms. tradition.[1] The evidence is twofold: the affinity of the group with the extant fragments of Syh, and the presence of undoubtedly Origenic asterisks in mss. belonging to the group. The double corollary of this evidence is that the text upon which group iii is based is pre-Hexaplaric, and that group iv, as the closest extant representative of that basic text, is also the best witness to the text used as the basis of the Hexaplaric

---

[1] Field's *Origenis Hexaplorum quae supersunt* ... does not live up to its title where Par is concerned. It is a catalogue of extant variants and cites one asterisk in c at I 1.11-23.

revision. Consequently group iii will hereafter be designated "O" and group iv "G" as the oldest extant form of the Gk text of Chron.

Origen's few quotations of Par tend to confirm these conclusions. Of ten significant variants there are five cases of agreement with O or O^{mss}.[1]

I 16.9   *omnes* Or-lat = πάντα c e c₂
v. 22   καὶ ἐν O L R Or
21.1   *diabolus Satan* Or-lat: cf. Σαταν i y, διάβολος Σατανα c₂
29.1   οἰκοδομή c₂ Or: cf. ἡ οἰκ. O L R
II 2.1/2   νωτοφόρων O L R Or

Twice Origen prefers to quote the old, non-Hexaplaric text, a not infrequent phenomenon in his biblical citations.

I 16.8   ἐξομολογεῖσθε G Or: + τῷ κυρίῳ O L R
29.2   πολύ G Or: πολύν O L R .

Eusebius' quotations of Par are slightly nearer to R than to O.[2] Of twenty three significant variants, sixteen are shared by O, eighteen by R, eleven by L and one by G. Of eight exclusive group readings Eusebius' single agreement with G is significantly also shared by Syh: Αβιασαρ for אביסף at I 6.22/37. There are four unique alignments with R: I 2.6 Δαρδα, a corruption of the G O reading Δαρα; a lacuna caused by homoeoteleuton at 6.35f.; 6.37 Ασηρ, an itacism for Ασειρ G O; 17.13 τυμπάνοις for κυμβάλοις G O L. There is one reading shared uniquely with L: I 25.3 κινύραις for κινύρᾳ G O R, conformed to the plural of v.l. Eusebius twice agrees with O alone: 2.6 χαλχαλ, and (ι)Αἰείας at 25.3, related to Ιεεια A H a f h (from Ιεσια c e g).

(v) *The Syro-Hexapla*

J. Gwynn published in 1909 *Remnants of the Later Syriac Versions of the Bible*. From a ninth century Nitrian ms. in the British Museum, Add. 12168, a catena of mainly Biblical extracts, he edited in the second part of his book fragments of Chron in Syriac. These are in fact deli-

---

[1] BM's citations have been checked in *Grieschische christliche Schriftsteller* or with Migne if the text is not available in *GCS*. In I 16.8 Or sides with L by adding καί against MT, both influenced by the Psa parallel; in 29.3 with L R, reading ἠτοίμασα for ἠτοίμακα; in II 16.12 with e₂, reading ἀρρωστίᾳ for μαλακίᾳ.

[2] Of Eusebius' citations of I Par 2, 6, 16, 17, 25 given in BM, the author has been able to track down and check in *GCS* or Migne only those from chapters 2 and 17.

berately selected extracts, taken from parts of Chron which have no or
scanty counterpart in Ki (Gwynn, p. xvii). The extracts comprise
firstly genealogical material (I 1.1-4, 17, 24-28, 34 [whole verses or
parts of verses] 2.1-17; 3.1-20; 6.1-15, 31-49; 23.14-17), and then the
accounts of Uzziah's sacrilege and punishment (II 26.16-21), of the
renewal of worship under Hezekiah (29.30-36; 30.1-5, 13-20), of his
siege preparations (32.2-4), of Manasseh's apostasy, repentance and
reformation (32.33; 33.1-16), and of Josiah's fatal encounter with
Necho (35.20-5).

The evidence that the extracts were taken from Paul of Tella's
Syriac version of the Hexaplaric text, made between A.D. 613 and 617,
mounts up as follows. First, it is known that a Syro-Hexaplar version
of these books was made. Andreas Masius in the 16th century owned
a ms. of Syh which is no longer extant: he recorded that it contained
Par among other books.[1] Secondly the extracts from Par, I and II
Esdr and Dan are headed ⲕⲟⲁⲟⲣⲁⲗⲉⲑ ⲣⲁⲗⲉⲑ, ⲕ "according
to the version of the Seventy", obviously to distinguish them from
other Biblical passages, which are taken from Pesh. The Dan extracts
have been identified by comparison with Codex Ambrosianus as
belonging to the version of Paul of Tella.[2] It is therefore reasonable to
assume that the Par material goes back to the same source.

Since Syh "forms our chief authority for the text of Origen's revision",[3] here is rich evidence indeed for the identification of Hexaplaric
mss. Gwynn himself translated the literal Syriac back into Gk and
compared readings of Gk mss. in an apparatus. The apparatus is
disappointing: "most mss." and "etc." reduce its worth.[4] He did not
seriously attempt to deduce from the apparatus which mss. might be
Hexaplaric or under Hexaplaric influence. The omission is rather
surprising in view of Torrey's claims for A, made in the previous year,
but perhaps Gwynn had already completed his work before Torrey's
appeared in print. But Gwynn does note on p. 68 "a close affinity"
of Syh with 19 93 108, i.e. the L group.

In 1968 W. Baars published further relevant material in *New Syro-
Hexaplaric Texts Edited, Commented Upon and Compared with the LXX.*
His Chron excerpts, drawn from the British Museum ms. Add. 17195,

---

[1] Gwynn, *op. cit.*, p. xi.

[2] *Id., ib.*, p. xvii.

[3] Swete, *Introduction*, cited by Gwynn, *op. cit.*, p. x.

[4] It is not always trustworthy: e.g. the καί in I 6.3 said to be read by Syh alone (p. 41)
is in fact read in six mss. cited by BM.

are as follows: II 15.8-15; 17.3, 7-9; 18.31+19.1-3+25.5-12; 24.6-11; 36.11-13.[1] According to Wright's description the ms. is in a script of the latter half of the tenth century and contains religious and moral exhortations supported by Biblical quotations.[2] The sections 17.3, 7-9 and 18.31 + + are expressly identified as Syro-Hexaplaric (ܣܒܥܝܬܐ),[3] and so is 36.11-13 (ܣܒܥܝܬܐ ܕܣܒܪܐ). The quotations from 15.8-15 and 17. 3, 7-9 have rubrics mentioning the distinctive title of Chron in Syh, ܕܡܠܘܬܐ (= Παραλειπομένων). The section 24.6-11 lacks a rubric because the previous leaf of the ms. is missing, but there is no doubt that its text is Syro-Hexaplaric.

Baars' edition is a model of execution. He has taken great pains to aid the Septuagintalist by comparing the Syriac both with the usage of Paul of Tella known elsewhere, in order to deduce the underlying Gk, and with the text and apparatus of BM.[4] It would obviously have been outside his set task to draw any conclusions as to the significance of the alignment of particular Gk mss. with or against Syh.

Gwynn and Baars seldom compare identical Pesh readings in the apparatus or notes, but in fact Pesh has influenced Syh, in its present form, to no small extent.[5] Examples of common forms of names are:

I 1.25	ܐܪܥܘ (רעוּ, Ραγαυ)
2.16	ܨܪܝܐ (צרויה, Σαρουια(ς))
3.5, etc.	ܫܠܝܡܘܢ (שְׁלמה, Σαλωμών, etc.)
v. 12; 6.30/45	ܐܡܨܝܐ (אמַציה(וּ), Ἀμασίας, Ἀμεσσαι, etc.)

---

[1] M.H. Goshen had earlier drawn attention to this material in *Textus* iv, p. 230f., although he overlooked the section 18.31ff. He also stated that 30.18-20, already included in Gwynn's edition, also occurs in this ms., at fol. 35a, but in a form slightly different from that cited by Gwynn. On investigation the author has found that the differences are of such a minor order as to be irrelevant for comparison with the Gk.

[2] *Catalogue of Syriac Mss. in the British Museum*, p. 914.

[3] Goshen, *Biblica* xxxvii, p. 162 note 6, quoted 19.1-2 from a Cambridge University ms. Add. 2023 fol. 56a, claiming it to be apparently from Syh, but leaving open as an alternative the possibility that its source is Jacob of Edessa's recension. Now that one can compare it with the counterpart from the British Museum ms. edited by Baars, it is obvious that its text is a corrupted form of the latter. It is marked by many omissions and small variants such as a careless copyist would make.

[4] There are occasional slips: e.g. on p. 117 the second Syriac reading in 15.14 agrees with most Gk mss., not merely with e; on p. 118 ܐܠܠܝܐܠ at 17.7 is neither an addition nor a recognisable variant; on p. 123 κυρίου in 19.2 is read by all Gk mss., not merely by La[pars].

[5] Cf. Ziegler, *Beiträge*, p. 9, with regard to Jer: "Syh manchmal die E(igen)N(amen) in der Form der Peschitta oder des masoretischen Textes überliefert".

v. 16	[Syriac] (יְכָנְיָה, Ἰεχονίας)
v. 18	[Syriac] (חושמע, Ωσαμω, etc.)
6.19/34	[Syriac] (אלקנה, Ελκανα)
II 17.7	[Syriac] (עבדיה, Ἀβδίαν, etc.)
v. 8	Syh [Syriac][1] cf. Pesh [Syriac] (עשהאל, Ασιηλ, etc.)
ibid.	[Syriac] (שמעיהו, Σαμουας, etc.)
24.6	[Syriac] (משה, Μωυσῆ,, etc.)
36.12	[Syriac] (ירמיהו, Ιερεμίου).

Apart from names the exclusive influence of Pesh is further seen in the addition at II 26.19 of [Syriac] [Syriac] and of [Syriac] in 33.7, and in the plural form [Syriac] (Pesh [Syriac]) in 33.15.[2]

In view of Syh's tendency to be independent of the Gk, agreement between Syh and Pesh on the one hand and Gk mss. on the other must be taken *cum grano salis*. It is impossible to decide in such cases whether agreement is significant or coincidental. Accordingly, in the following selection of variants, readings shared by Pesh (or by a number of its mss.) are ignored. In order to obtain a manageable yet representative number of variants, a selection has been made of all instances where Syh agrees with mss. belonging to one or two textual groups. Of these instances, out of a total of 89 variants, agreements with group mss. reach these totals: G 10, G O 17, G L 1, G R 1, O 21, O L 9, O R 12, L 12, L R 2, R 4. Variants associated with G number 28, with O 59, with L 24, and with R 19. This latter fact suggests that, in the case of variants attested by O and another group, O is the significant partner.

Correspondences with O mss., alone or together with those of another group, are as follows. Gk orthographical changes which would not affect transcription into Syriac are ignored; later corrections in mss. are excluded. The code "O-ᴬ" indicates the O mss. with the

---

[1] The ms., followed by Baars, p. 118f., actually reads [Syriac], but this is an obvious miswriting of [Syriac]. Another probable type of error is the omission of *seyame*, e.g. [Syriac] 15.8, [Syriac] 24.11.

[2] Other influences have been at work upon Syh. In I 6.32/47 [Syriac] ([Syriac]) is found only in Syh. Par has (υἱοῦ) Μοσει or Ομουσι or the like; Pesh reads [Syriac] ([Syriac]). Presumably the reading goes back to MT בן מושי, read as בן נמושי. In 3.5 [Syriac] [Syriac] looks like an independent translation of בת־שבע (MT בת־שוע).

exception of A. BM's apparatus has been used. For this purpose Arm has been included in O.

I 1.17-24 ܘܐܪܦܟܫܪ ܫܠܚ[1] = καὶ Αρφαξαδ Σαλα B g h
2.3 ܫܠܐ = Σηλω $O^{-ANh\ Arm}$
v. 6 ܟܠܩܢ = Χαλκαν a d* f* j*
ibid. ܕܪܥ = Δαρα G O
v. 9 ܐܘܪܡ cf. ὁ Ραμ G $O^{-a\ g\ n}$, *Oram* Arm
v. 14 ܙܒܕܐ cf. Ζαβδαι i
v. 16 ܐܚ̈ܘܬܐ = (οἱ) ἀδελφοί n L Arm
3.2 ܬܘܠܒܝ[2] = Θολβει n
v. 4 ܘܐܡܠܟ ... ܝܪ̈ܚܐ = καὶ ἐβασίλευσεν ... ἑξάμηνον O(i※)R
v. 5 ܫܘܒܒ = Σωβαβ O^{-a}, without καί
v. 8 ܐܠܝܦܠܛ = Ελειφαλα B h[3]
v. 12 ܥܙܪܝܐ = Αζαρια(ς) G O
v. 19 ܫܠܬܐܝܠ = Σαλαθιηλ B O
ibid. ܫܠܡܘܬܝ has no parallel. It is surely an error for ܫܠܘܡܬܝ = Σαλωμεθει G $O^{-g\ Arm}$
v. 20 ܐܘܥ is to be corrected with Gwynn, p. 7, to ܐܘܠ = Οολ O^{-ce}R.
ibid. ܐܘܣܒܐ is a clear error for ܐܣܘܒܐ cf. Ασοβαεσδ, etc., O, Ασοβασοκ c2
6.4 ܕܝܢ = δέ h
ibid. ܦܝܢܚܣ[2] = Φεινεες G A N a h, without καί
v. 5 ܐܒܘܩܝ, ܒܘܩܝ = Βωκαι $O^{-h\ Arm}$, Βοκκι R. The first form is to be corrected to the second with Gwynn, p. 8. No doubt it was assimilated to ܐܒܝܫܘܥ earlier.
ibid. ܒܘܩܝ: καί om. with a g n Arm
v. 6 ܒܘܙܝ: καί om. with G $O^{-i\ Arm}$
v. 39 ܐܚ̈ܐ = ἀδελφοί a g
v. 41 ܐܕܥܝܐ = Αδαια $O^{-n\ Arm}$. BM wrongly prints ܐܕܥܐ
v. 42 ܐܘܪܝ = Ουρι O R
v. 44 ܐܚ̈ܐ = (οἱ) ἀδελφοί a L Arm

---

[1] ܪ is an error for ܕ (Gwynn, p. 36). In his Gk text "24" is an error for 18; in his Syriac text 24 is misplaced.

[2] Gwynn hazardously corrected to ܬܘܠܡܝ in his Syriac text, but left Θολβι in his Gk one.

[3] It has already been noted that at times A, N and h reflect group iv. This may be the case in such an instance as this.

ibid.	ܩܝܫܝ = *Κεισαν* O R
ibid.	ܥܒܕܝ = *Αβδει* G O-a g
v. 45	ܚܫܒܝ = *Ασεβει* G O
ibid.	ܕܒܪܗ ܕܚܠܩܝܐ = *υἱοῦ Χελκια/ου* O L
v. 46	ܡܥܫܝ is surely an error for ܥܡܫܝ = *Αμασῃ/αι* O-c e n Arm L
23.17	ܪܚܒܝܐ[1] = *Ρααβια* G O-N e h Arm
ibid.	ܪܚܒܝܐ[2] = *Ρααβια* G O
II 15.8	ܥܙܪܝܐ = *'Αζαρίου* O
ibid.	*ὃ ... κυριου* om. with N d
v. 11	ܘܕܒܚܘ = *καὶ ἔθυσαν* A or *κ. ἐθυσίασαν* e2
v. 15	ܕܠܗܘܢ = *αὐτῶν* O b f j m
17.7	ܢܬܐܝܠ = *Ναθαηλ* b h
v. 8	ܘܗܢܘܢ = *καὶ οἱ* O-h Arm
19.1	ܒܫܝܢܐ = *ἐν εἰρήνῃ* O L
v. 2	ܐܢ[2] = *εἰ* g n
24.6	ܟܕ = *ὅτε* A N a b c n y
v. 7	ܐܦ : *γάρ* om. with A Theodoret?
25.8	*σε* om. with A n
ibid.	*καί*[2] om. with O-c n
v. 9	*καί*[2] om. with a
ibid.	ܠܗ = *αὐτῷ* f j Arm
ibid.	ܛܒ ܣܓܝ = *πλεῖστα* (Baars, p. 122) G A N a f h j
26.20	ܣܚܦܘܗܝ = *κατέσπασαν* c e g, as BM notes. Gwynn erroneously renders *κατέσπευσαν*.
29.30	ܡܠܟܐ ܚܙܩܝܐ = *ὁ βασιλεὺς 'Εζεκίας* c2 O-h
v. 34	ܐܬܕܟܝܘ ܗܘܘ ܒܢܝܚܐܝܬ = *ἡγνίσθησαν προθύμως* O-a h Arm
30.18	*τοῦτο* om. with O R-y
ibid.	ܗܘ = *ὁ* O-N g R-q
32.33	ܝܗܒ = *ἔδωκεν* g
33.5	ܡܕܒܚܐ = *θυσιαστήριον* 44 Arm
v. 6	ܒܐܢܘܡ = *Βεεννομ* A c e n
ibid.	ܐܣܓܝ ܠܡܥܒܕ = *ἐπλήθυνεν τοῦ ποιῆσαι* G O-A g
v. 14	ܬܝܡܢܐ[2] = *νότον* O-e g R-y
ibid.	ܕܐܙܠ cf. *πορευομένων* A N a f h
35.25	*καὶ (ἰδού)* om. with O-Arm R

There is the following agreement with mss. of G, alone or together with mss. of a group other than O:

I 1.34 ܝܥܩܘܒ ܘܥܣܘ = *Ιακωβ καὶ Ησαυ* G
2.8 ܙܪܗܝܐ = *Ζαρεια* G
3.3 ܫܒܛܝܐ = *Σαβατεια* G
v. 6 ܐܠܝܫܥ = *Ελεισα* G
v. 7 ܢܦܬ = *Ναφαθ* B
ibid. ܝܘܢܘܥ cf. *Ιανουε* G
v. 18 ܦܠܕܝܐ = *Φαλδαίας* G
6.6, 7 ܐܡܪܝܐܠ cf. *Μαρειηλ* G. 'ܐܡܪ is probably an error for 'ܡܪ under the influence of ܐܡܪܝܐ following.
v. 37 ܐܒܣܝܪ is an error for ܐܒܝܣܪ = *Αβιασαρ* G
v. 44 ܐܝܬܡ = *Αιθαμ* G L
II 33.14 ܒܢܐ ܒܬܪ ܗܠܝܢ = *ᾠκοδόμησεν μετὰ ταῦτα* G
ibid. ܙܝܢܐ = *Οπλα* G, *ὅπλα* R

Syh agrees with L mss.[1] or with L R mss. as follows:

I 6.3, 4 ܐܠܝܥܙܪ = *Ελιεζερ* e2 Arm[2]
v. 34 ܝܪܡܝܐܠ = *Ιερεμαηλ* L
II 15.8 +ܐܣܐ = *τὸν Ασα* L = MT
v. 12 ܘܥܒܪܘ = *καὶ διῆλθον* L R = MT
17.8 +ܘܛܘܒܝܐ ܘܛܘܒܕܘܢܝܐ[3] = *καὶ Τωβίας καὶ Τωβαδωνι(α)* Lm = MT
24.11 +ܘܐܩܝܡܘܗܝ = *καὶ κατέστησαν αὐτό(ν)* L = MT
26.16 +ܥܘܙܝܐ = *'Οζίας* L = MT
29.34 ܡܬܕܒܪܝܢ = *ἀντελαμβάνοντο* b t Arm = MT
30.3 ܒܝܪܚܐ ܩܕܡܝܐ cf. *ἐν τῷ μηνὶ τῷ πρώτῳ* L in a different position = MT
v. 5 ܕܢܐܬܘܢ = *τοῦ ἐλθεῖν* L Arm (cf. ܕܬܥܒܪ earlier = *διελθεῖν*) = MT
33.7 ܒܗܘ ܕ = *ἐν ᾧ* L = MT
ibid. ܕܒܐܘܪܫܠܡ = *ἐν* ... b', without *καί*, as BM rightly notes (MT 'ובי). Gwynn wrongly translates *τῷ ἐν*: cf. v. 14 'ܕܒ = *ἐν*
v. 11 +ܐܝܬܝܘܗܝ = *ἦγον αὐτόν* L = MT
35.20 +ܠܡܩܪܒܘ ܠܘܩܒܠܗ ܒܟܪܟܡܝܫ = *τοῦ*

---

[1] At II 24.11 Baars tentatively compares *ἐπί* L with ܒ(ܕܘܟܬܐ) (*εἰς* G O R), but *εἰς* stands for ܒ in v. 10, and perhaps in 15.10.

[2] Since Arm sometimes exhibits L-type readings, it has been deemed preferable to allocate to this section readings shared by Arm and L mss.

[3] The ms. actually reads ܘܛܘܒܕܢܝܐ, but this is surely a Syriac error.

πολεμῆσαι αὐτὸν ἐν Χαρχαμεις L = MT, but differently placed.

Finally, here are agreements with R mss. alone:

I 1.28   ܐܒܪܡ = Αβραμ d
II 24.7   ܕܡܪܝܐ = κυρίου 74[1]
25.8   τροπώσεταί σε / κύριος tr. with 44
36.11   ܒܪ =υἱός R

The large measure of agreement with O indicates clearly that this group is Syh's next of kin over the area covered by the extant portions of Syh. These portions are in fact representative enough to warrant the same conclusion for Par generally. As to the cases where Syh sides with G alone, among which should be included the omission of I 1.17-23 and the form in 3.8, where g and h are obviously influenced by G,[2] it is plain that Syh attests in these instances an unrevised text. Ziegler noticed the same phenomenon in Jer, Lam and Baruch, where there exists for comparison a Hexaplaric ms. of the same calibre as Syh.[3]

What of the agreements with L which are not echoed in O or G? Margolis observed a similar feature in the Syh of Jos, in the middle part of the book.[4] Here the answer may be a simple one. According to Rahlfs[5] and Ziegler, Lucianic-type readings are found in the margin of Syh in III-IV Rg and Isa. It must be remembered that the extant portions of Syh of Par have been extracted from a Syh ms. and incorporated into compositions of a different type. In the extraction they were stripped of their Hexaplaric signs, and it may well be that L-type marginal readings were copied into the text. This conclusion is consonant with the different position of the addition at II 30.3.

It is of interest to note that the O mss. statistically closest to these Syh texts are a c i n.[6] Although the extracts lack the value of a complete Syh ms. and time and change of milieu must have taken their toll where accuracy is concerned, this result is a significant pointer to the Hexaplaric quality of mss. within the O group.

---

[1] Baars omits this variant.

[2] And too i's form in 2.14.

[3] "An einer Reihe von Stellen überliefert deutlich 88 allein die hexaplarische Lesart, während Syh den alten, unrezensierten Text bezeugt." (p. 70).

[4] *JQR* i, p. 260.

[5] Rahlfs, *LXX-Studien*, iii, pp. 30-32.

[6] Relatively little of i is extant, but where it is, it compares well with a c n.

(vi) *Hexaplaric signs in Gk mss.*

Hexaplaric signs are scanty in Par according to the apparatus of BM. One obelus is to be found, at I 10.13, in e₂, which is within the L group. It marks the last clause, which is lacking in MT. Hexaplaric signs in "Lucianic" mss. are not unknown elsewhere.[1]

Fifteen asterisks, including three *vid*, appear among three cursive mss. according to BM's apparatus. They are distributed as follows:

I 1.11-23	sub ※ c n	3.4 καὶ ... ἐξάμηνον sub ※ i
vv. 13-16	sub ※ i	v.19 καί¹ pr ※ i
v. 17	υἱοὶ ... Αρφαξαδ sub ※ i	9.5 καὶ υἱοὶ αὐτοῦ ※ i
vv. 18-23	sub ※ i	v. 28 ὅτι pr ※ i
v. 32	υἱοὶ ... Λοωμειν sub ※ i	28.9 ἐάν pr ※ c
v. 38	καὶ (Δησων) sub ※ vid i	II 15.12 ἐξ ¹ ... καί² pr ※ n
v. 43	οἱ ... Ισραηλ sub ※ vid i n	

The mss. which contain asterisks are thus c i n. c has 2, i 10 and b 3. These mss. belong to the group designated O and, together with a, have just been noted as having the closest affinity with Syh. If the use of the asterisks corresponds to Origen's methods, it is reasonable to conclude that they are relics of Origen's work.

I 1.11-23 is grouped together under an asterisk by c n, but i uses three to cover the same section: one to cover vv. 13-16, another for v. 17a and a third for vv. 18-23.

I 1.11-16 is missing in B g h c₂ only. Origen's basic text apparently lacked these verses and he added them to correspond to MT. But according to i the missing verses were only 13-16. The asterisk is surely misplaced, as so often in Hexaplaric mss.[2] The καί which begins v. 13 was mistaken for the one at the beginning of v. 11. The position of ἐγέννησεν as third word in both verses encouraged the error. The asterisks before v. 11 in c n confirm that i's is misplaced.

v. 17 is present in all mss. as far as Αρφαξαδ, but thereafter B g h c₂ have no equivalent for the Heb. However, i places this first part of the verse under an asterisk and c n include it among material added to fill up an omission in the Gk text! The asterisk in i has clearly been carelessly put on the wrong half of the verse. The inclusive ones of c n seem to be copyists' false generalisations.

---

[1] Cf. Rahlfs, *op. cit.*, iii, p. 247f.; Soisalon-Soininen, *Der Charakter der asterisierten Zusätze in der LXX*, p. 16.

[2] Cf. Rahlfs, *Ruth*, p. 66; Ziegler, *Jeremias*, p. 72f.

vv. 18-25 are lacking only in B g h c₂ (and Syh). Apparently they were missing in Origen's basic text: the asterisk of i, as well as the inclusive ones of c n. records their insertion.

v. 32. Apart from B b g h c₂ e₂ (= G L) the mss. continue with a plus enumerating Dadan's progeny. The plus of O R is not found in MT: it emanates from Gen. 25.3 LXX by assimilation. Perhaps the asterisk is an error for an obelus, or more likely it is a later imitation, simply marking an addition. At any rate the asterisk can hardly be Origen's own.

v. 38. $\varDelta\eta\sigma\omega\nu$ is preceded by $\kappa\alpha\iota$ in O⁻ᴬᴺ ᵃ ⁿ ᴬʳᵐ R⁻ᵈ L. MT has ודישן. At first sight i is simply marking this addition. But it is perhaps significant that not only B c₂ but also A N a n Arm lack the conjunction. Is i here following a reading found in R, with which it is associated in the context?[1] If so, the asterisk is post-Origenic, inserted by a copyist to mark a later addition. Or has the asterisk been misplaced from $\kappa\alpha\grave{\iota}\ A\sigma\alpha\rho\ \kappa\alpha\grave{\iota}\ P\iota\sigma\omega\nu$ which in some form replaces B c₂'s $\varOmega\nu\alpha\nu$ in the other mss. except g?

v. 43. Apart from B g h c₂ a long plus is found in the mss. after $\alpha\mathring{\upsilon}\tau\hat{\omega}\nu$, corresponding to MT אשר מלכו···ישראל. The apparent asterisks of i n are thus justified. Presumably $\alpha\mathring{\upsilon}\tau\hat{\omega}\nu$ was obelized by Origen: it replaced the omitted clause in G.

3.4. The words וימלך־שם··· חדשים lack equivalents in B h c₂: O L R restore the clause. The asterisk is valid.

v. 19. There seems to be no valid reason for the asterisk before the first $\kappa\alpha\iota$. It is significant that five adjacent words, not in B c₂ or d p, are supplied by the other mss. to correspond to ושמעי ובן־זרבבל: $\kappa\alpha\grave{\iota}\ \Sigma\epsilon\mu\epsilon\iota\ ...\ Z\sigma\rho\sigma\beta\alpha\beta\epsilon\lambda$. This evidence points to another wrong placing: the asterisk in i should be in front of the second $\kappa\alpha\iota$.

9.5. B a g h c₂ do not represent ובניו; the omission is supplied in the other mss. The asterisk in i corresponds to Origen's principles.

v. 28. The asterisk before $\mathring{o}\tau\iota$ is apparently groundless: $\mathring{o}\tau\iota\ \mathring{\epsilon}\nu$ $\mathring{\alpha}\rho\iota\theta\mu\hat{\omega}\ \epsilon\mathring{\iota}\sigma\sigma\acute{\iota}\sigma\sigma\upsilon\sigma\iota\nu\ (\alpha\mathring{\upsilon}\tau\acute{\alpha})$ is found in all mss. But the following $\kappa\alpha\grave{\iota}\ \mathring{\epsilon}\nu\ \mathring{\alpha}\rho.\ \mathring{\epsilon}\xi\sigma\acute{\iota}\sigma\sigma\upsilon\sigma\iota\nu\ \alpha\mathring{\upsilon}\tau\acute{\alpha}$ (= ובמספר יוציאום) is lacking in B S a g h c₂. Clearly the similarity of the clauses caused its false placing.

28.9. Why this asterisk? It is obviously out of place beside $\mathring{\epsilon}\acute{\alpha}\nu$, which all LXX evidence supports. Earlier in the verse only c e put $\mathring{\epsilon}\nu$ before $\psi\upsilon\chi\hat{\eta}$ (= בנפש). Probably a later asterisk, referring to the

---

[1] i joins R in reading $A\beta\iota\lambda\alpha$ in v. 33 and $\delta\acute{\epsilon}$ in v. 35f.

reading of the sub-group, has been put by mistake not between καὶ ἐν but between the similar -κει ἐάν.

II 15.12. The asterisk seems to be inappropriate here. General LXX tradition has ἐξ ὀλῆς τῆς καρδίας (αὐτῶν) καὶ = בכל לבבם ו. But d m omit, obviously by haplography. Did Origen's basic text, like d m, omit it too? Or is the asterisk in n merely a copyist's imitation of the Origenic method as he restored an accidental omission?

Of the fifteen asterisks five are certainly valid as they stand: I 1.18-23, 43; 3.4; 9.5. Four have probably become wrongly placed: 1.13-16, 17; 3.19; 9.28; the one at 1.38 may have done so. The two at 1.11-23 are falsely generalising. The rest are doubtful.

Some slight evidence of Origen's work has survived in the valid asterisks of c i n. It is not surprising that the loss of most of his signs should have been accompanied by the incorrect placing of some of those that are left. The results, slight though they are, do corroborate the results of the study of Syh. Syh and c i n, as important witnesses to the labours of Origen, together confirm that the third group of mss., with which they are closely associated, reflects the Hexaplaric tradition more faithfully than any other group.

Analysis of a different kind confirms the non-Hexaplaric character of G. The cases where little or no mystery surrounds the asterisks yield the significant fact that B c₂ consistently omit the asterisked additions. In the light of the evidence presented earlier in this section, concerning O's dependence on a G-type text, it may be affirmed that G is not merely of a non-Hexaplaric type but forms the best witness to the pre-Hexaplaric type of LXX text which Origen used as the basis of his revision. Torrey's view of A's superiority to the "Hexaplaric" B is erroneous. Since his view was so wedded to a theory of a second century A.D. translation, serious doubt is cast by implication upon this theory.

(vii) *O and the Three*

One might have expected O to be the home of large numbers of Hexaplaric readings derived from the Three. Certainly there must be many more than can be now recognized: nondescript readings that might be anybody's foil the investigator again and again. However, the textform of O does not exhibit the careful quantitative approximation to the Heb which is a mark of R and even more of L. G and O often have a common lacuna in comparison with MT.

At I 19.13 O L R have ἀνδρίζου καὶ ἐνισχύσωμεν περὶ τοῦ λαοῦ ἡμῶν καὶ περὶ τῶν πολέων τοῦ θεοῦ ἡμῶν. ἀνδρίζου for חזק (= θ′ Isa 41.6) and περί for בעד (= θ′ III Rg 13.6; Prov 20.16; 27.13: = σ′ Isa 37.4) pinpoint the addition as a quotation from θ′. In 28.8 καὶ κατακληρονομήσητε (αὐτήν) O L R for והנחלתם has verb equivalence with θ′ in Jud 11.24. Field, vol. i, p. 741, may well have been correct in attributing to σ′ ὑποδεικνύ(ο)ντος O L R for מורה at II 15.3: b^mg ascribes to σ′ a phrase which in m is read just before ὑποδ. O's reading οφλα (cf. οφλαα L) at II 33.14 has evidently been taken from θ′ according to the ascription of o^mg.

The c e g group occasionally preserve readings which can be traced back to the Three. At II 8.16 c e have ἐτέλεσε in place of O's ἐτελείωσεν for כלתו, a typical Aquilanic substitution.[1] In 35.19 c e g n join R in reading ἤδρασεν, probably taken from σ′.[2]

2. GROUP iv

(i) Mss. in the group

B c₂ are regular members of the group throughout most of Par, but c₂ moves to R from II 31.6b, leaving only B to represent the group in the last six chapters.[3] S, extant only from I 9.27 τὸ πρωί to 19.17, belongs to this group. Of the O mss., A N h sporadically exhibit readings of the group; i shares its readings at times in I 1-3; g sometimes sides with group iv. The mixed mss. f j (in II Par) m at times reflect its readings.

The two uncials B and S are often of help in correcting each other's errors. On the whole B offers a slightly better text:[4] S shows signs of careless writing.

Although c₂ usually closely supports B, it does now and then have readings suspiciously akin to those of other groups. Here are some examples which point to adaptation in c₂ to the text of groups other than its own.

I 3.19   פדיה : Σαλαθιηλ B O : Φαλδαια c₂ cf. Φαδαια L
6.50/65   יקראו : ἐκάλεσεν B A d h i n : -σαν c₂ O^mss. R
12.20/19   עזרם : ἐβοήθησαν B S h m : -σεν c₂ O L R

---

[1] See p. 82.

[2] See p. 82.

[3] It sporadically joins R in a few preceding chapters, e.g. twice in 29.12.

[4] The correctors B^ab often introduce readings from other types of text and so cannot be cited as necessarily giving a G reading.

14.14   בכאים : αἰτίων B* S: απ ἐτίων c₂: ἀπίων O R. απ is a
correction.

18.8   ערי : πολέμων B S h; πολέων c₂ O L R

22.13   תצליח: εὐοδώσει B N h m: + σε c₂ R: the imperative
middle was taken as 3rd singular future active after the
middle fell out of circulation.[1]

II 8.9   המה : ἰδού B: αὐτοί c₂ O L R

10.3   וישלחו ויקראו: καὶ ἀπέστειλεν καὶ ἐκάλεσεν B h: κ. -
λαν κ. - σαν c₂ O L R

15.11   הביאו: ὧν ἤνεγκεν B m: ἀνήνεγκεν c₂: ὧν ἤνεγκαν
O L R. ἀν - in c₂ was intended as a correction of - εν
but instead displaced ὧν.

In view of this evidence of revision it is at times difficult to decide
whether c₂ represents a later correction or the text of G which was
subsequently corrupted in B.

(ii) *The identity of the group*

It has already been shown that at the roots of O L R there lies a
text-form which is very similar to that of group iv. O L R are in turn
revisions of a Gk *Vorlage* most like group iv or G. They show their
dependence upon an earlier form of text very like G by their unique
sharing of G's unusual readings: here only O agrees with G, there
only L, somewhere else only R, in readings clearly overlooked in the
process of revision. Moreover, each of the three other groups in turn
exhibits readings closer to MT than those of G. Also to a varying
extent each contains readings, different from G's, which cancel out
characteristics of the translator deduced in ch. iv from readings
common to all four groups. On these grounds O L R have been classi-
fied as revisions of a type of text similar to G.

There is an interesting confirmation of the priority of G. II 1.1
occurs twice in B* c₂ only. It is generally agreed that the division of
Chron into two books originated in the LXX (cf. e.g. Rudolph, p. III).
The comment of Pfeiffer concerning Sam-Ki applies here: "The division
into two books was introduced in the Greek version (LXX) because
the Greek, in which vowels were written, required one and three-
quarters more space than the Hebrew, in which no vowels were used
until after A.D. 600. Thus one large scroll sufficed for the Hebrew,

---

[1] Cf. Rahlfs, *LXX-Studien*, iii, p. 204.

while two were required for the Greek."[1] Rahlfs, *LXX*, notes at the end of I Rg that the addition of the first verse of the next volume at the end of a scroll was a frequent device to help the reader find the sequel.

In the case of Par it seems likely on the surface that the device goes back to the translator himself. This probability is confirmed by a literary trick used in the two sentences. ויגדלהו is rendered καὶ ηὔξησεν αὐτόν at the end of I Par, but κ. ἐμεγάλυνεν αὐτόν at the beginning of II Par. This is a feature already seen to be characteristic of the translator.[2] O L R, followed by B^c, remove the extra sentence at the end of I Par, obviously because there was no counterpart in Chron. Part of the translator's work, attested only in G, was destroyed by the revising activity of O L R. It is interesting to note that Curtis temporarily forgets Torrey and states that the LXX adds the first verse of II Chron to the end of I.

All these results throw light on the alliance of A N h with G. h frequently has the readings of G: the instances cited in connection with c₂ above incidentally show this trend, and in II Par h exhibits G's form of name in 46 certain cases out of 422. In addition h often has a mixed form of name, combining G and O. Here are some examples. The first Gk form is that of G, the second of O, the third of h.

I 2.26	Οζομ : Ουνομ : Ουζομ
6.69	Εγλαμ Β : Ηλων : Ηγλων
11.30	Νοοζα : Βαανα : Ναανα
14.8	Σαμαίας Β : Σεμαια : Σεμαίας
25.3	Τουνα : Γοδολίας : Τοδίας
II 14.8/9	Μαρισηλ : Μαρησα : Μαρησαλ
17.8	Τωβαδωβεια Β : Τωβαδωνια(ν) : Τωβαδωνβίαν
29.13	Ἀζαρίας : Ζαχαρίας : Ζαρίας

The substantial number of G readings and the "half and half" readings in h combine to suggest that h is derived from a G-type ms. extensively corrected according to O.

The same conclusion is most probably true of N. Torrey was observant enough to notice recurring links with the B text, and decided that it either represented an intermediate stage between the A and B texts or that it was eclectic. Below are set out examples of its following G.

---

[1] *Introduction to the OT*, p. 338.

[2] See p. 55.

I 8.33	Μελχεσουε B : Μεχεσουε N : Μελχισουε c₂ O
11.18	Βαιθσεεμ G N : Βηθλεεμ
15.18	Μακελλεια G : Μακεδια (Λ/Δ) N : Μακενια O
19.16	Σωφαρ B N : Σωφαχ, etc. O
21.5	μαχαίραν G N : μαχ. καὶ … μαχ. O
26.7	Αχιουδ G N h : Αχιου O
II 11.5	εἰς B N : ἐν c₂ O
24.6	ἐξεκλησίασεν G N : -εκκλ- O
29.16	ἕως G N m : ἔσω O
31.10	ἐπί G N : ἔτι O
32.22	Ασσουρ G : 'Ασσουρίων N, 'Ασσυριων O

The third case of a ms. exhibiting widespread Hexaplaric corrections of G's form of text is A, e.g.

I 2.19	Γαζουβα B A : Αζουβα O
4.17	Μαιων B A : Μαρων O
11.47	Εσσειηλ G A : Ιεσιηλ O
27.4	Δωδεια B* : Δωεια A : Δωδαι O
II 17.14	Εδναας B A : Εδνας c₂ O
20.21	ἔλεγεν G A : ἔλεγον O
25.18	ἦλθαν G A : ἦλθεν O
30.15	ἐν οἴκῳ B A : εἰς οἶκον c₂ O

This conclusion concerning A is confirmed by the evidence of Egerton Papyrus 4 (= 971 in Rahlfs' numeration) examined by H. I.

This conclusion concerning A is confirmed by the evidence of Egerton Papyrus 4 (= 971 in Rahlfs' numeration) examined by H. I. Bell and T. C. Skeat.[1] The papyrus comprises two fragments forming the upper and lower portions of a single leaf of a codex, tentatively dated by the editors about the middle, rather than the end, of the third century A.D. II 24.17 Ιουδα -27 τῶν is all that remains, and the authors describe it textually as about midway between A and B. But the question must be asked: where does the codex stand in terms of groups? In v. 18 the order 'Αστάρταις — εἰδώλοις indicates G L R. ἐπί 2 is apparently omitted with B* a c₂. In v. 22 the order μετ' αὐτοῦ Ιωδαε betokens G O. καὶ ὡς is read with G O R. In v. 24 παρεγένετο is read with B O-ᴬR. Unfortunately the names in v. 26 are telescoped together so that no grouping is possible. But the grouping in the preceding verses clearly points to G. There are two

---

[1] *Fragments of an Unknown Gospel*, pp. 52-55.

close links with A: in v. 23 [κατέφθ]ειρεν is read with A g m and in
v. 27 Ιουδα for ἰδού with A only. As Bell and Skeat remark, the history
of a glaring corruption in A is thus carried back two centuries. The
links of the codex with G and A respectively, viewed together, suggest
that its text is related to A in its pre-Hexaplaric form.[1]

R. Roca-Puig has published (in Catalan !) details of Papyrus Barcinonensis 3, which comprises three fragments of a codex containing
recto and *verso* II Par 29.32 κ]αὶ ἐγένετο — 35 ὁλοκαυτωσεω[ς ; 30.2
κ]αὶ ἐβουλεύσατο — 5 ἐ[ποίησεν] with lacunae of varying length.[2]
On good palaeographical grounds Roca-Puig dated the papyrus as
not later than the second half of the third century A.D. and perhaps
even as early as the second half of the second century. In fact, W. Baars,
who has rightly described it as "one of the two oldest available witnesses
for the Greek text of 2 Chronicles", subsequently adduced convincing
reasons for considering it part of the same codex as 971.[3] Baars'
Holmesian deduction is the most exciting thing that can be said about
this papyrus. The portion of Par it preserves contains little in the way
of violent disagreement between the four textforms. There are eleven
significant variants for the purpose of group allocation. In ten cases
Pap. Barc. 3 shares readings with mss. of three groups out of the four:
it sides seven times with G O R against L,[4] and three times with G O L
against R.[5] Thus far the papyrus agrees equally with G and O. In
29.34 it reads [προ] θύμως [ἠνίσθησαν] with R only. There is a quadruple reading at this point. O reads ἠγνίσθησαν προθύμως and L
προθύμως ἡγιάσθησαν.[6] G's προθύμως ἤγνισαν is a not uncommon

---

[1] Rahlfs discovered that in Ruth A's text was originally not Hexaplaric but corrected
according to the Hexaplaric text; its *Grundlage* was pre-Hexaplaric (section 23).

[2] *Boletín de la Real Academia de buenas letras de Barcelona*, xxix, pp. 219-227.

[3] *VT* xv, p. 528f.

[4] 29.34 [αλλ]η : πλήν L ;

30.3 ηδυνασ[θησαν] : ἠδυνήθησαν L ;

ibid. ηγνισθησαν : ἡγιάσθησαν L ;

v. 4 There is no room for πάσης added in L ;

v. 5 [Βηρσαβεε εως] δαν : Δαν ἑως B.

ibid. ελθον [τες G or -τας O R : τοῦ ἐλθεῖν L ;

Cf. too 30.2 φασεκ with G O^mss R against φασεχ O^mss L.

[5] 29.32 ̅ς = διακόσιοι : ὀκτακόσιοι R ;

v. 34 ολιγοι [ησαν] : tr. R.

Cf. too 29.32 ̅κω G O e₂ : ̅κυ R b.

[6] The papyrus could hardly have read like L. Roca-Puig's reconstruction of the verb
is confirmed by its reading in 30.3, cited above. The spacing requires a longer words
than G's verb.

corruption.[1] R has preserved its original reading, now supported by Pap. Barc. 3. Here then it significantly sides with (G) R against O. Its text can therefore be assigned to the G group.[2] The detailed analysis given above serves to confirm J. W. Wevers' statement: "Obwohl das Blatt nur bruckstückhaft ist, bleibt doch genug Material um zu zeigen, das es B als den besten Vertreter des Vorrezensionstextes unterstützt."[3]

Although Josephus has a number of readings apparently in common with L and a couple recurring in R, there are also two places where he sides exclusively with G, the first already cited by Gerleman.[4]

II 11.21 שְׁשִׁים : τριάκοντα G, *Ant.* viii. 250 (ἑξήκοντα O L R).

13.19 יָשׁוּב : Κανα B, Καναν c₂ from Ισ-[5] = 'Ισάναν *Ant.* viii. 284. (Ανα o, (Ι)εσ(σ)ηνα L R).

Compare another case cited by Gerleman:[6] *Ant.* viii. 291 refers to 250,000 Benjaminites in Asa's army with 14.7/8 G O, while L R read 280,000 with MT.

Justin shares G's unique error at I 16.28: his text develops πατρί G into τῷ πατρί. He omits completely v. 24 together with G O.

(iii) *A revised text*

The textform of G has been shown to be very similar to that lying at the base of the revised forms O L R. But G itself is by no means devoid of revision. The text in its present form has been tampered with, and many instances of this secondary activity will be adduced in ch. viii.

3. THE OLD LATIN

A complete Old Latin text of II Par has been preserved in a tenth century Complutensian Bible, whose text in I Par is that of the Vulgate. This Old Latin text has been well edited by R. Weber, who has also included other evidence, notably quotations from the Latin Fathers.[7]

---

[1] Cf. part II, p. 46.

[2] There are three unique readings: 29.32 ηνεγκεν for ανήνεγκεν, v. 34 διειραι, a scribal error for δειραι, read by all mss. except B (ἐκδεῖραι); in 30.5 either παντι or εν παντι ιηλ was probably omitted.

[3] *TR* n.f. xxxiii, p. 56.

[4] See p. 16.

[5] See part II, p. 25.

[6] See p. 16.

[7] *Les anciennes versions latines du deuxième livre de Paralipomènes.*

He has shown that there is evidence of several Old Latin versions. The one preserved for the whole of II Par appears to have been most widespread and to go back at least to the time of Lucifer of Calaris in the fourth century. It was apparently made from a Gk text closer to the Heb than the LXX. Weber suggests that it was the version, or revision, of Theodotion. This basic text had already been revised by the time of Augustine; another attempt was made before the tenth century.

La sides with L again and again. But its frequent divergence from L, whether agreeing with L only partially or reflecting R or O or going its own way, indicates that it cannot be treated merely as dependent upon some form of L. Very often La not only keeps to G O R where L diverges according to the Heb, but also approximates to the Heb where L keeps more or less to G O R. Weber's suggestion that it is a Latin rendering of Theodotion's work does not stand up to investigation. Rudolph noted that transcription is not a feature of the version.[1] In fact La has readings typical of each of the Three.[2] La apparently depends upon yet another revised textform, which like L and R made use of the Three either via the Hexapla or directly, but frequently in a different combination from both L and R. Once again the basic text of this Gk textform appears to have been of the G-type. It preserves the text of G in such small details as a reviser might not have bothered to change. La readings shared only with G are:

25.14   *ipse eis* = αὐτὸς αὐτοῖς.
26.10   *agricola* = γεωργός.
27.1; 28.1 υἱός O L R is not represented: contrast *filius* 34.1 = υἱός L f.
28.5   *nam et* = καὶ γάρ.
v. 12   *Zacarias* = Ζαχαρίας.
36.23   *domum ipsi* = οἶκον αὐτῷ.

In I Par, which falls outside the scope of Weber's work, La has ben preserved in patristic readings collected by Sabatier.[3] Weber's general

---

[1] *Chronikbücher*, p. vi.

[2] E.g. from θ′ probably come II 2.3/4; 13.11 *aromatum* (see p. 75); 20.13 *turbe* (see p. 75). In 15.8 *obtinuit* = κατελάβετο L (cf. 22.9 La) : of the Three only α′ uses this rendering (Reider-Turner, *Index*, p. 129) for לכד. In 3.16 *oraculo* = χρηματιστηρίῳ, ascribed to σ′ in *b*ᵐᵍ. At 21.15, 19 *intestina* = τὰ ἔντερα L for מֵעִין, מֵעִיך, an equivalent used by σ′ in Cant. 5.4.

[3] *Bibliorum sacrorum latinae versiones seu Vetus Italica*, i.

conclusions appear to be equally applicable to these fragments, except that they reveal a good deal of assimilation to parallel texts.

It has not been deemed worthwhile to list in this book every instance of La's agreement or otherwise with extant Gk textforms. Mention has been restricted to readings which have a bearing on the text of G, such as cases where it helps to get behind conflation in the Gk or where it appears to preserve an older reading. Rudolph has noted four places where La is of use to correct a corrupt LXX text: II 6.41; 24.18; 28.10; 35.15. In fact, there are a number of other instances where La throws valuable light upon the early text of Par, viz. II 5.6; 6.30; 7.11; 9.12; 15.4, 9; 20.25; 24.27; 35.11.

CHAPTER SEVEN

FURTHER TECHNIQUES OF THE TRANSLATION

In ch. iv a study was undertaken of the style of Par on the basis of readings shared by all the four groups. Now that the fourth group or G has been seen to be substantially basic to the other three, the translator's methods may be studied further from the readings of G. It will be found that these readings have been very often taken over by one or more of the other groups. M. Rehm worked on the assumption that B c₂ represented the original text of Par. He outlined with examples a number of traits to be discussed below.[1] It is clearly important to discover how the translator handled his Heb material, when the text is clear, in order that correct conclusions may be drawn concerning doubtful places in the text.

1. Longer renderings

The translator did not invariably follow the principle that one Heb word should be rendered by a single Gk one. It was noted, for example, in ch. iv[2] that at times he added possessive pronouns. There are other places where a fuller rendering is given or for the sake of clarity additions are made which may be fairly judged to go back not to the Heb *Vorlage* nor to later Gk accretions but to the translator himself. Rehm, p. 18, gave three instances:

II 12.13 שבטי ישׂראל: φυλῶν υἱῶν Ἰσραηλ B (L) R

16.3 ברית : διάθου διαθήκην G O L R, as in the parallel III Rg 15.19

32.1 אלה : τούτους ... ταύτην G O L R.

The first case more probably depends upon a fuller Heb text.[3] The

---

[1] *Textkritische Untersuchungen*, pp. 15ff.

[2] p. 48f.

[3] See part II, p. 101. It may be mentioned here that such sigla as G O L R refer to group readings, which are not necessarily shared by every ms. in the group. G O (L) R means that L has a different reading which may legitimately be compared for present purposes.

second may well be a case of subsequent assimilation to Rg, but Rehm
is doubtless right in seeing here paraphrase of the Heb elliptical
construction *contra* BH which posits כרת־ברית. The third case is typical
of the demand for fuller rendering which the Gk language sometimes
makes.

Further instances may be given of these fuller renderings:

I 27.10 הפלוני : ὁ ἐκ Φάλλους G O R, "the man from Phallo"

28.1 המשרתים: τῶν περὶ τὸ σῶμα G O R

v. 2 לבנות² : τὰ ἐπὶ τὴν κατασκήνωσιν ἐπιτήδεια G O (L) R, a
flash of excellent Gk which is none too common in Par.

II 5.12 מלבשים בוץ : τῶν ἐνδεδυμένων στολὰς βυσσίνας G O (L R)

11.23 לרב : πλῆθας πολύ G O L R

20.12 לפני : τοῦ ἀντιστῆναι πρὸς G O L R, inspired by v. 6.

v. 24 ויפנו אל : καὶ ἐπέβλεψεν καὶ εἶδεν G O L (R)

22.9 ויבקש : καὶ εἶπεν τοῦ ζητῆσαι G O L R, preparing for the
following plural verbs.

30.14 המקטרות : ἐν οἷς ἐθυμίων τοῖς ψευδέσιν G O L R, an
explanatory paraphrase, as Curtis notes.

Additions are sometimes made for clarity, e.g.

I 9.27 ולבקר לבקר: τὸ πρωὶ πρωὶ ἀνοίγειν τὰς θύρας τοῦ ἱεροῦ
G O L R, a longer rendering to integrate the adverbs of time after
rendering מפתח earlier as κλειδῶν. So too may be explained II 13.11
לבער בערב : τῆς καύσεως ἀνάψαι δείλης G O R : this is not a doublet,
but ἀν. is added to fit the adverb.

21.13 καὶ τὰ τρία G O L R, as a subject for צר. It also appears
in the proto-Lucianic text of the parallel II Rg. 24.14.

v. 30 + οὐ G R, added to harmonise with v. 27[1]

28.15 + ἔδωκεν αὐτῷ G O (L R in doublet)

v. 18 + ὑπέδειξεν αὐτῷ G O L R

II 6.13 העזרה : τῆς αὐλῆς τοῦ ἱεροῦ G O L R

26.18.+ τοῦτο G O L R, to clarify the subject

30.26 כזאת : τοιαύτη ἑορτή G O L R, to avoid "joy" being taken
as the antecedent, as Rudolph notes.

34.16 + ἀργύριον G O L R (Rehm, p.19).

In II 27.5 carelessness earlier in the verse caused the translator to
expand his rendering. κατ᾽ ἐνιαυτὸν ἐν τῷ πρώτῳ G O R is "an

---

[1] Cf. Ziegler, *Beiträge*, p. 50f., for the translator's addition of negatives in Jer LXX.

unnecessary addition due to the mistranslation of בשנה ההיא" (Curtis)
as κατ᾽ ἐνιαυτόν. The translator obviously rendered the earlier phrase
with the end of the verse in mind and then was forced to adapt what
follows.

2. SHORTER RENDERINGS

Rehm, p. 17. gives a list of concise renderings whereby two or more
words are combined in smaller compass in the Gk. Some of his examples
are questionable, but here is a selection from them which do correspond
to his claim, with the present writer's comments.

I 17.9   בני עולה : ἀδικία G O, and so the preceding plural verb
is made singular. This is a further instance of the method of rendering
the Heb figurative use of בן illustrated in ch. iv.[1] BH ineptly posits a
Vorlage יוסיף עולה

II 1.16   יקחו במחיר : ἠγόραζον G O R.

2.3/4   קטרת סמים : θυμίαμα G O R.
Contrast 13.11 θ. συνθέσεως. The translator's inconsistency has been
illustrated abundantly in ch. iv.

4.2   משפתו אל־שפתו : τὴν διαμέτρησιν G O (L in doublet) R.

8.6   ארץ ממשלתו : τῇ βασιλείᾳ αὐτοῦ G O (L in doublet) R.
According to BH the LXX omits ארץ, but this is hardly a fair statement: it is included in the Gk. S. Talmon claims that the *Vorlage* read
א׳ ממלכתו : he contrasts 32.9 where στρατ(ε)ιά G O L R renders
ממש׳.[2] But the sense is different in 32.9 and so a different rendering is
not surprising. Note the similar case of נגיד : generally it is rendered
ἠγούμενος, but in I 29.22 it becomes βασιλέα G O L R and in 28.4
βασίλειον G O R. The translator freely uses related words and cannot
be relied upon to provide a single equivalent.[3]

Some further cases may be cited where shorter renderings are employed:

I 15.16   בכלי־שיר : ἐν ὀργάνοις G.
Cf. II 30.21 בכ׳ עז : ἐν ὀργ. G O R.

26.6   גבורי חיל : δυνατοί G O R.
There is no need to add ἰσχύι L or δυνάμεως to the text with Schleusner.[4]

---

[1] p. 45f.

[2] *Scripta Hierosolymitana* viii, p. 381.

[3] Cf. the illustrations on p. 57.

[4] *Lexicon*, i, p. 649.

28.12 לאצרות בית האלהים : εἰς τὰς ἀποθήκας κυρίου G.
Or has οἴκου O L R fallen out before κῡ ? But there are other examples
of the omission of בית where the place is sufficiently determined:
II 5.1 באצ' בית הא' : εἰς θησαυρὸν κυρίου G (οἴκου O L R omitted
again ?) and 12.10 פתח בית המלך : τὸν πυλῶνα τοῦ βασιλέως G O R,
where Rehm, p. 60, considers that בית has been overlooked after
פתח. Compare I 23.28 עבדת בית האלהים : λειτουργίας τοῦ θεοῦ G.

29.9 שמחה גדולה : μεγάλως G O R, cf. II 29.34 ישרי לבב : προθύμως G O L R and II 6.8 הטיבות כי : καλῶς B * (B^ab c₂ add ἐποίησας ὅτι
with O L R).

II 25.16; 35.21 חדל־לך : πρόσεχε G O R.

28.9 עדד שמו : Ωδηδ ὄνομα B*. B^ab c₂ O L R add αὐτῷ, but the
rendering is good Gk.

v. 10 לכבש ... לכם : κατακτήσε/ασθαι G O L R.

3. Omission of synonyms

There are numerous cases where a single Gk word is used to render
two Heb words which are synonymous or related in meaning.

I 12.2 בחצים בקשת : τόξοις G O R.

v. 18/17 ויען ויאמר : καὶ εἶπεν G O, avoiding a Hebraism.
Rudolph suggests on the basis of Par's omission that ויען was a marginal
comment on v. 19, but the phrase is idiomatic Heb.

v. 24/23 החלוץ לצבא : τῆς στρατιᾶς G O R.
According to BH Par omits הח' but this is not so.

v. 37/36 צבא ... מלחמה : εἰς πόλεμον G O L R.
πόλεμος renders צ' in II 25.5; 28.12 G O L R.

v. 38/37 צבא מלחמה : πολεμικοῖς G O;
Cf. II 26.13. צ' : πολεμική G O L R. It is not fair to say "dl צבא c G"
as BH and Rothstein do.

23.29 משורה ומדה : μέτρον G O R.
It is unfair to claim that Par omits מש' ו, as BH does. Rudolph per-
tinently remarks that there was no other Gk equivalent in common use.

26.8 חיל בכח : δυνατῶς G O R.

v. 16 במסלה העולה : τῆς ἀναβάσεως G O R.
מס' is so rendered in II 9.11 G O L R and מעלה in II 20.16; 32.33
G O L R. Yet Torrey claims that העולה is not translated.[1]

27.26 השדה ... האדמה : τὴν γῆν G O R.

---

[1] *Ezra Studies*, p. 104.

28.8 תירשו ... והנחלתם : κληρονομήσητε G.

Cf. κληρονομία G O L R for נחלה I 16.18 and for ירשה II 20.11.

28.9; 29.18 יצר מחשבות : ἐνθύμημα G O R, διανοίᾳ G O R.
In the first case Par omits יצר according to BH.

v. 20 אלהים אלהי : ὁ θεός μου G O L R, the only natural way
of rendering.

II 4.22 פתח הבית דלתותיו : ἡ θύρα τοῦ οἴκου G O L R (Rehm,
p. 17).

9.12 ותהפך ותלך : καὶ ἀπέστρεψεν G O L (R).
Par omits ותלך according to BH. Cf. 10.5 וילך : καὶ ἀπῆλθεν G O L R.

15.14 בקול גדול ובתרועה : ἐν φωνῇ μεγάλῃ G O R.
ובת' is omitted according to BH. תר' is elsewhere in Par σημασία,
but cf. II Esdr. 3.11, 13 תר' גדולה : φωνὴ μεγαλή, whereas the noun
is rendered σημασία in v. 12. ibid. בחצצרות ובשופרות : ἐν σάλπιγξιν
G. BH claims that ובש' is omitted. O L R's addition is Hexaplaric
according to H. St.J. Thackeray,[1] recensional according to Barthélemy.[2]

20.13 טפם ... ובניהם : τὰ παιδία αὐτῶν G O R.

v. 17 התיצבו עמדו : σύνετε G O R.
התי' is omitted according to BH.[3]

24.11 וישאהו וישיבהו : καὶ κατέστησαν G O R.
ויש' is omitted according to BH. השיב is so rendered in I Rg 5.3;
Jer 23.3.

v. 27 מדרש ספר : γραφήν G O R.
Elsewhere in Par γραφή renders forms from כתב. O. Eissfeldt considers that ספר is a gloss partly on the grounds that it is not rendered
in the LXX,[4] but his assumption is doubtful.

25.4 בתורה ספר משה : τοῦ νόμου (κυρίου) G O R.[5]

v. 10 ויחר אפם : καὶ ἐθυμώθησαν G O R.
Cf. חרון אף : ὀργή in 28.11 G, 13 G R.

26.11 צבא לגדוד : εἰς παράταξιν G O L.
צבא is frequently rendered παρατ., e.g., I 5.18; 7.40 G O R.

28.4 ויזבח ויקטר : καὶ ἐθυμία G O L R.
Cf. ἔθυεν G O L (R(for הקטיר in v.3; the pair are regarded as synonyms.

---

[1] *JTS* viii, p. 267.

[2] *Devanciers*, p. 62.

[3] Cf. further p. 52.

[4] *Einleitung in das AT*[3], p. 753.

[5] For the addition of κυρίου see part II, p. 83.

32.5 שלח ... ומגוים : ὅπλα G O L R.

Benzinger and Curtis make the ill-founded suggestion that ומ׳ is a gloss because Par omits.

34.3 הפסלים והמסכות : τῶν χωνευτῶν G O.

Contrast v. 4 τὰ γλυπτὰ καὶ τὰ χωνευτά. The translator is inconsistent, as so often.

4. Omission of repeated words

Frequently where words are repeated within a sentence or two the second element is not represented in Par where the reference is clear. In the light of the preceding section it is reasonable to assume that the translator himself was generally responsible for this type of omission. A translator who felt it unnecessary to render a pair of synonyms separately would be even more reluctant to repeat himself at the bidding of his *Vorlage*.

Prepositions tend to be repeated before co-ordinate nouns in Heb, but this practice is less common in Gk. Repeated prepositions are sometimes omitted (cf. Rehm, p. 17) :

אל : II 11.3 G (= B: c₂ sides with O L R); 33.7 G.

ב : I 16.5 G O L R

Rothstein, BH and Rudoph counsel that וכנרות be read, comparing 15.16; but there is no need to assume that Par's *Vorlage* lacked the preposition. 28.9 G O L R; II 33.7 G O.

בין : I 21.16 G; II 16.3 G O R; 23.16 G O R twice

ל : II 25.5 G O L; 28.10 G O L

מן : I 9.3 G; II 24.6 G O L

Other elements are omitted apparently because they have already occurred in identical or similar form in the preceding context:

I 11.42 לראובני G O R after הר׳.

There is no need to deduce a gloss in MT with Rothstein.

20.3 ובמגרות G O after במגרה.

Rehm, p. 40, argues from the omission that Par must depend on Rg here, but his conclusion is unwarranted: the omission may be adequately explained within the bounds of the translator's general practice.

21.21 ויבט (ארנן) וירא את־דויד omitted in G O after reading את־המלך in v. 20.[1]

---

[1] See further p. 197.

26.19 לבני ²G : sc. υἱοῖς.

28.1 שרי⁴ G O L R.

v. 13 בית יהוה ² G.

vv. 14-17.   The Heb is heavily repetitive. Apparently the translator skims over it to give the basic sense, rendering only 22 out of 56 Heb words in G. As examples of the abridgment in v. 14 לזהב ... לזהב becomes χρυσῶν in G O and the repeated לכל־כלי עבודה ועבודה is omitted completely after the similar phrase in v. 13. That the translator himself is rendering into Gk idiom is suggested by the renderings ὁμοίως and ὡσαύτως in G O L R to replace repeated nouns in v. 16. Benzinger supposed in view of Par that MT had been worked over and supplemented in vv. 13ff.

29.2 לזהב, etc.

In G O the second mention of materials is omitted in all five cases.

אבני G O R after אבן : sc. λίθον. Curtis' statement that the translator probably did not read אבני is hazardous.

v. 4 זהב מזהב אופיר is rendered χρυσίου τοῦ ἐκ Σουφιρ G O L R.

v. 5 לזהב ... מלאכה G O. Six words of involved and repetitive style are omitted, as in 28.14ff.

v. 27 מלך² G O, מלך³ G O L R (Rehm, p. 17).

II 1.15 ; 9.27 נתן G O R after ריתן.

3.8 הבית G O after בית. Rehm, p. 59, supposed that it was overlooked before אמות, but more probably it was intentionally omitted.

4.4 פנים ², ³, ⁴ G.

7.9 שבעת ימים ² G O R and consequently ו is omitted before החג. BH's note "G^BA sol חן" should read" ... sol ἑορτήν".

16.4 ערי² G O L R (cf. Rehm, p. 17) : πόλεις is to be understood.

v. 11 הנם after הנה G O L R.

18.27 ויאמר ² G O: the same person is speaking.

20.27 וישבו ... ו יר׳ לשוב אל־ירושלם G O after which was read in G O L R as וישי׳ ... יר׳ (εἰς Ιερουσ. : cf. v. 28).

21.1 עם אבתיו ² G. But B's omission in the parallel I Ki 22.51 may suggest that it was absent from the *Vorlagen* of both.

23.10 הבית ² G O (cf. Rehm, p. 17).

24.14 וכלי G O R after כלי.

27.4 בנה ² G O R.

34.9 מכל ² G O R.

v. 17 על־יד ² G (Rehm, p. 17).

II Ki 24. 2/36.5b גדודי⁴ G O L R.

ibid. וישלחם ביהודה G O L R after בו ... וישלח:בו, rendered
ἐπ' αὐτούς O L R¹ was taken to refer to Judah in the light of ביהודה
later.

36.18 בית יהוה G O after בית האלהים.

5. Omission of unknown words

It has already been observed in ch. iv that one way the translator
had of dealing with words outside his vocabulary was simply to omit
them.² More examples, based on the text form of G, may be added to
the previous list.

I 16.3 ואשפר G O R.
According to S. R. Driver,³ Rothstein and Myers ἀρτοκοπικόν is the
equivalent, but in fact ἀρτὸν ... ἀρτοκ. represents ככר־לחם. The
word is ἅπ. λεγ. in the O.T., found only in these parallel places.

II 9.18 לכסא וכבש בזהב לכסא מאחזים : τῷ θρόνῳ ἐνδεδυμένοι
χρυσίῳ G O L (in doublet) (R).
Rudolph explains Par as due to loss of וכבש לכסא by homoeoteleuton
and claims that it is correct in placing בזהב after מאת'. But insight into
the translator's methods permits the assumption that he was rendering
the same text as MT. The ἅπ. λεγ. כבש was omitted as unknown;
לכסא was rendered only once; and probably בז' and מאת' were transposed in translation as a more suitable Gk order. Rehm, p. 60, unnecessarily infers that נשבך was read for וכבש. According to Curtis Par
omits וכבש ... מאח'. BH betrays the same lack of understanding in
claiming Par's omission of the clause and listing ἐνδεδ. χρυσίῳ as an
addition.

9.21 ותוכיים G O R.
The word is ἅπ. λεγ. in the parallel passages.

28.19 הפריע ביהודה G O R.
The verb occurs only here in Chron. The omission could be that of a
Heb line,⁴ but it may be adequately explained as due to a defective
vocabulary.

---

¹ G is corrupt : see part II, p. 8.
² p. 61.
³ *Samuel, ad.* II 6.19.
⁴ See part II, p. 133f.

6. Omission of words not understood

Sometimes words are not represented in Par which came well within the limits of the translator's vocabulary. In many cases their omission appears to be due to poor understanding of the context.[1] They were considered ill-fitting and simply not rendered. This type of rationalising omission may be reasonably laid at the translator's door.

I 5.41/6.15 בְּהַגְלוֹת יהוה את : ἐν τῇ μετοικίᾳ μετά G O.

את was mistaken for the preposition instead of the object sign. The earlier word was consequently taken as בְּהַגְלוֹת[2] on the lines of II 10.7 להגדוד 29.27; להמזבח 25.10; להעם. This view of the text naturally left no room for יהוה. There is no need to posit בַּגֹּלוּת with BH. It is most unlikely that this is a deliberate attempt to avoid a theological difficulty.

20.3 ערי בני־עמון : υἱοῖς Ἀμμων G L (R).

ערי has been omitted in the LXX probably because the clause has been taken to mean not "so David did in the case of all the cities ..." but "so D. did *to* all ...", referring to his treatment of the people of Rabbah earlier. This misunderstanding of ל demanded a personal object for it.

II 4.10 נגבה G O R.
The word is omitted as apparently inconsistent with קדמה.

v. 21 והפרח G O L R.

In v. 5 the noun is rendered βλαστούς. Here floral ornamentation was perhaps thought out of place in a list of cultic utensils.[3]

8.8 לא G O.
The suffix of אחריהם was taken as the antecedent of אשר instead of בניהם. Chron actually speaks of the descendants not being destroyed, but Par refers the clause to their forebears and so is forced to omit the negative.

14.6/7 ויבנו G O R.
After וינח and before ויצלח which the translator read by haplography

---

[1] This type of omission occurs in Isa LXX (Ziegler, *Untersuchungen*, pp. 48ff.).

[2] R. Loewe has privately suggested a pointing בְּהַגְלוֹת underlying the Gk, comparing the Midrashic treatment of והוצאתי אתכם Exod. 6.6 as וְהוֹצֵאתִי אֶתְכֶם

[3] It is interesting to note that in the parallel III Rg. 7.35 (MT 49) the more substantial λαμπάδια occurs after using βλαστός in v. 12 (MT 26). The rendering was probably inspired by the association of βλαστοί and λαμπάδια in Exod. 38.15f., for which see Gooding, *The Account of the Tabernacle*, p. 56f.

before ויה',[1] both the number of the verb and the verb itself were thought out of place and consequently omitted.

16.3   בריתך G O R.

הפר ... את־בעשא is rendered διασκέδασον ... τὸν B., את being wrongly taken as the object sign instead of the preposition. This view of the Heb renders בריתך superfluous. ἀπ' ἐμοῦ is borrowed from the next clause (= מעלי) for sense. Rehm, p. 60, suggests that מתֹכִי was read for בריתך, but this is unlikely.

21.4   ממלכת אביו : τὴν βασιλείαν αὐτοῦ G O R.
Whether this represents ממלכתו (BH) is a matter of opinion. The change is clearly in view of v. 3: the kingdom is no longer his father's but his own. This may be simply rationalisation on the translator's part.

23.13   עם־הארץ : ὁ λαός G O.
Rehm, p. 17, rightly lists this as a shorter rendering, but why is it curtailed ? This is the only place in Par where the phrase is abbreviated in this way. Probably the omission of הארץ is due to rationalising. The term was misunderstood to mean the population of the whole country. Since they could not all be crammed into the Temple area the genitive was omitted as incongruous.

31.18   טפם ונשיהם ובניהם ובנותיהם : ἐπιγονῇ υἱῶν αὐτῶν καὶ θυγα-
τέρων αὐτῶν G O (L) R.
The later words are taken as explanatory of the first, and the wives are omitted as out of keeping after "offspring" thus construed.

v. 19   בשדי מגרש : οἱ ἀπό G O R.
The translator knew what מג' meant, but apparently he could not see the relevance of the phrase here.

33.14   בשער הדגים וסביב : τὴν πύλην τὴν κυκλόθεν G O R (in doublet).

הדגים seems to be omitted deliberately. The translator was apparently unaware of the existence of a gate called the Fish Gate.[2] Similar topo-graphical ignorance appears to underly Zeph 1.10 שער הדגים : πύλης ἀποκεντούντων = שער הרגים.

35.21   כי אל־בית מלחמתי : πόλεμον ποιῆσαι O L (in doublet) R.[3]

---

[1] See further p. 160.

[2] Yet on p. 51f. it was claimed that the translator knew his way round the Temple area. It may be conjectured that he had visited Jerusalem for religious festivals, but had spent no considerable period there.

[3] G is corrupt: see part II, p. 14.

According to Benzinger and BH Par read להלחם, but it is more likely that the rendering merely reflects difficulty in dealing with the present text. כי אל־בית was omitted as incomprehensible and מל׳ was translated loosely. Compare the frequent rendering of מלחמה with an infinitive, listed in section 9.

II Ki 24.2/36.5b את־גדודי כשׂדים : τοὺς Χαλδαίους G O (L) R.
Yet גדודי ², ³ are represented by λῃστήρια. Probably the omission is deliberate, and due to an equation of כשׂדים with the main Babylonian army, as in II Ki 25.10 (cf. II Chron 36.17). It was felt that guerrilla raids hardly suited such a force.

7. Omission of superfluous words

There comes a point in LXX study when it is very difficult to decide whether omissions go right back to the Heb *Vorlage* or merely as far as the pen of the translator. But Gk usage is often a useful criterion. When the subject of a verb is clear from the context, Par often lacks the subject expressed in MT. This feature accords with the succinctness of Gk in such a case, and probably the Gk translator has intentionally suppressed the fuller style of the Heb before him. Here are the instances:

I 10.1   איש־ישׂראל G O.
11.5; 14.16; 21.18   דויד   G O, G O, G O L R respectively.
In the third case Rothstein advises omission with Par as a gloss. Cf.
29.10 ויאמר דויד : λέγων G O L R.
18.6 ארם G O L R.
19.5 האנשׁים G O.
II 11.22 רחבעם G.
14.1/2; 15.16 אסא G O R.
27.5 בני עמון ² G.
II Ki 24.1/36.5a יהויקים G O L R.
36.7 נבוכדנאצר G O L R.

Chron often uses the formal appellation of the type "Solomon king of Israel". Names coupled with epithets in apposition are plentiful; but sometimes either the name or the epithet, usually the latter, is missing from Par. In one of these cases there is evidence which suggests that the translator is consciously abbreviating his *Vorlage*. In II 30.24 חזקיהו מלך־יהודה הרים לקהל is rendered ᾽Εζεκίας ἀπήρξατο τῷ Ιουδα τῇ ἐκκλησίᾳ G O (R). The last two words are clearly secondary.[1] Apparently the translator has seen but passed over מלך יהורה and then rendered קהל by a loose synonym inspired by יהודה. But it would be going completely beyond the evidence to blame all omissions of this type on the translator. Heb mss. obviously varied in the matter of appositional phrase, as parallel passages in Ki and Chron reveal: e.g., in II Par 7.5 the omission of המלך in G O significantly coincides with the shorter text in I Ki 8.63, and likewise in 22.5 מלך ישראל is omitted in G O with II Ki 8.28. Accordingly it will be safer to list the instances of this type of omission in Par under *Vorlage* omissions with the warning that some of the instances may well be due simply to the translator.

8. Traces of theological bias

The degree of theological bias reflected in the LXX has been a subject of controversy. On the one side are ranged writers like C. T. Fritsch,[2] D. H. Gard[3] and V. M. Rogers; on the other side are to be found H. M. Orlinsky[4] and A. Soffer.[5] Orlinsky, while not denying theological bias outright, draws a cautionary distinction between theological and philosophical factors and the factor of literary style; often "what is involved is not theology but stylism and intelligibility".[6]

In Par it is conceivable in a number of instances that the translator is deliberately avoiding a word-for-word rendering on dogmatic grounds. It will be argued that in many cases, but not all, this possibility is to be rejected.

I 5.41/6.15   בהגלות יהוה את־יהודה : ἐν τῇ μετοικίᾳ μετὰ Ιουδα G O. It is unlikely that the omission of יהוה is by theological intent.[7]

12.24/23   כפי יהוה : κατὰ τὸν λόγον κυρίου G O L R. This is doubtless to be understood as a natural paraphrase, just as the Revised Standard Version has "according to the word of the LORD".

---

[1] See p. 153.

[2] *The Anti-Anthropomorphisms of the Gk Pentateuch.*

[3] *The Exegetical Method of the Gk Translator of Job.*

[4] E.g. in the review of Fritsch's work in *The Crozer Quarterly* xxi, pp. 156-160 and in "The Treatment of Anthropomorphisms and Anthropopathisms in the LXX of Isaiah", *HUCA* xxvii, pp. 193-200.

[5] "The Treatment of Anthropomorphisms and Anthropopathisms in the LXX of Psalms", *HUCA* xxviii, pp. 85-107.

[6] *The Crozer Quarterly*, xxi, p. 159.

[7] See p. 117.

A literal rendering is not beyond the scope of the translator: contrast the translation of מפי אלהים in II 35.22 as διὰ στόματος θεοῦ G O (L) R and of מפי יהוה in 36.12 as ἐκ στόματος κυρίου G O L R.[1]

16.10f.   מבקשי יהוה : דרשו יהוה : ζητοῦσα τὴν εὐδοκίαν αὐτοῦ G O L R. ζητήσατε G (+ τὸν κύριον O L R).

The omission of the second יהוה is most probably an inner-Gk error.[2] αὐτοῦ is clearly a good Gk equivalent for יהוה, the reference being clear in the context.[3] Rothstein and BH invoke a *Vorlage* מבקש רצונו. There appears to be no possibility of influence from a similar passage elsewhere. Prov 11.27 יבקש רצון (LXX ζητεῖ χάριν ἀγαθήν) is set in a completely different context. Goettsberger finds here "das Bestreben der späteren Zeit, den Herrn nicht unmittelbar zum Gegenstand menschlicher Tätigkeit zu machen"; similarly Rogers, p. 9f. Two questions arise: does the Gk go back to a Heb variant and, if not, is the translator fighting shy of the immanence of the Heb rather like Targ תבעו מימרא דיהוה? Both questions may be answered in the negative. Here surely is an instance of stylistic variation so characteristic of the translator. To ring the changes he renders the objects of the verbs differently, first loosely then literally, a technique of the type illustrated in ch. iv.[4] Had theological scruple been the motive, the translator would hardly have gone on to write ζητήσατε τὸ πρόσωπον αὐτοῦ G O L R in v. 11b.

29.14   מידך : (ἐκ) τῶν σῶν G O L R.

The translator was forced to paraphrase by the pregnant construction of the Heb; cf. Targ מן ברכת ידך. But is it significant that יד is removed? It is not. In ch. iv it was observed that the translator likes to avoid a literal rendering of יד even in non-theological contexts.[5]

---

[1] Targ in all three cases variously tones down the Heb. At first sight there is here a parallel with Targ, which elsewhere at times renders such a phrase literally and at times scrupulously paraphrases. J. Shunary's article "Avoidance of Anthropomorphism in the Targum of Psalms" in *Textus* v, 1966, pp. 133-144, has some relevance here. He has suggested that since "in general TPs saw no theological difficulty in literal anthropomorphic translation", initially the translation was literal but in the course of time circumlocutions penetrated into it (p. 143f.). In other words the divergence there is to be viewed as a mark of secondary influence. However, these three cases in Par may be simply taken as a further illustration of the translator's tendency to translate now literally, now with a looser literary style.

[2] See part II, p. 58.

[3] cf. p. 46.

[4] p. 56f.

[5] p. 52.

It is important to notice that at v. 12 ἐν χειρί σου G O (L) R twice renders the repeated בידך : if theology had played any part, such a translation would not be found in the same context. Style, not scruple, explains the rendering: it is a stylistic continuation of σά G O L R for ממך earlier in the verse.

v. 23 על כסא יהוה למלך תחת־דויד : ἐπὶ θρόνου Δαυιδ G O (R). Was the translator embarrassed by the notion of Solomon sitting on Yahweh's throne ? Apparently not: he can freely reproduce the thought in II 9.8 that Yahweh ἠθέλησεν (ἐν) σοι τοῦ δοῦναί σε ἐπὶ θρόνον/ου αὐτοῦ. This is rather a case of Heb line omission.[1]

II 2.5/6 לא יכלכלהו : Targ יסוברון יתיה ... : οὐ φέρουσιν αὐτοῦ τὴν δόξαν G (O R).

6.18 לא יכלכלוך : Targ שכנתך יקר יסוברון ... : οὐκ ἀρκέσουσίν σοι G O L R = III Rg 8.27. In the second case the Gk is an echo of the parallel in Rg where according to J. W. Wevers the LXX deliberately avoids the concrete Heb idea that the heavens could impose physical limitations upon God even though it is expressed in the negative.[2] This view surely applies even more definitely to 2.5/6 where the Gk strikingly places an intermediary between God and creation, just as Targ does in 6.18. BH posits a *Vorlage* יכלכלו כבודו, but it is more likely that the translator was responsible for the bridge of δόξα between God and the universe, as Rogers, p. 20f., claims.

6.2 בית־זבל לך : οἶκον τῷ ὀνόματί σου ἅγιόν σοι G O L R. H. S. Gehman finds here a theological interpretation: the idea of God's dwelling in the Temple is removed by inserting τῷ ὀν. σου and rendering זבל simply οἶκον;[3] similarly his student Rogers, p. 22. But in fact τῷ ὀν. σου is not original.[4] For the rendering οἶκον ἅγιον compare Isa 63.15 מזבל קדשך : ἐκ τοῦ οἴκου τοῦ ἁγίου σου. Did the translator feel here that the specific concept of dwelling was already sufficiently expressed in οἶκον ? He had no scruples in using κατα-σκηνῶσαι with Yahweh as implied subject in this very verse.

7.6 להדות ליהוה : τοῦ ἐξομολογεῖσθαι ἔναντι κυρίου G O L R.

12.1 מעלו ביהוה : ἥμαρτον ἐναντίον κυρίου G O (L R). In the first case τῷ κῷ c₂ Boh (vid) is doubtless revised according to

---

[1] See part II, p. 134.

[2] *OTS* viii, p. 318.

[3] *VT* iv, p. 338.

[4] See part II, p. 36.

the Heb. These are less direct renderings, paralleled in Targ משבחין
קדם יהוה in 7.6. Similar use of "before" for ל and אל with reference to
God is found in the Pentateuch and in Job.[1] Elsewhere Par has the
dative or occasionally the accusative after verbs of praising. In 7.4
ἔναντι κυρίου renders לפני יהוה and at v. 6 the translator is lazily
giving the same rendering.[2] מעל ב is variously rendered in Par:
ἀθετεῖν ἐν I 5.25 G O L R, ἀνομεῖν + dative I 10.13 G O (L) R,
ἀδικεῖν ἐν II 26.16 G O L R, ἀποστῆναι ἀπό 26.18; 28.19,22; 30.7
G O L R. These free renderings suggest that the translator is simply
giving a literary paraphrase. On a non-theological level compare
לכל־ישראל : ἐναντίον Ισραηλ G O (L R) in II 1.2.

16.14 וישרפו־לו שרפה : καὶ ἐποίησαν αὐτῷ ἐκφοράν G O R.

21.19 עשו ... שרפה : ἐποίησεν ... ἐκφοράν G O R.

The thought of burning is changed to one of carrying out a corpse to
burial. Wutz, p. 154, suggested that the translation perhaps reflects
modification on theological grounds. Ziegler mentions these passages
in connection with Jer 34/41.5 where וכמשרפות ... ישרפו is rendered
καὶ ὡς ἔκλαυσαν, κλαύσονται, on which he comments "Der Übers.
konnte nicht wörtlich wiedergeven, weil es für ihn und für seine Leser
unvorstellbar gewesen ist, dass die Israeliten ihre früheren Könige
'verbrannt' hatten und auch den König Sedeqia 'verbrennen' werden".[3]

18.31 ויסיתם אלהים : καὶ ἀπέστρεψεν αὐτοὺς ὁ θεός G O L R.

It is often assumed that ויסירם was read (Curtis, BH, Rehm, p. 60,
Rudolph). But it is more likely that the translator toned down the verb
by paraphrase in order to remove the suggestion of deceit implicit in
the Heb verb, as Rogers, p. 29f., observed. For הסית Par uses twice
ἀπατᾶν (18.2 f j;[4] 32.11 G O L R) and once, of Satan, ἐπισείειν
(I 21.1 G O L R). Here it is significant that a verb empty of any
derogatory sense is used. Targ is strikingly similar: ורחקנון. This does
not necessarily imply ויסירם (BH, etc.) but may simply represent a
common exegetical tradition. Comparable is the rendering σὺ δὲ εἶπας
for ותסיתני in Job 2.3 where, however, God is the object: the translator
"eliminated the sinister connotation of the verb".[5]

20.7 לזרע אברהם אהבך : σπέρματι Αβρααμ τῷ ἠγαπημένῳ σου
G O R.

---

[1] Fritsch, *op. cit.*, p. 58; Gehman, *JBL* lxviii, p. 239.

[2] On the lines of ch. iv, section 12 (p. 53).

[3] *Beiträge*, p. 32f.

[4] See part II, p. 20.

[5] Gehman, *JBL* lxviii, p. 232.

Cf. Isa 41.8 זרע אב׳ אֹהֲבִי : σπέρμα Αβ. ὃν ἠγάπησα. The two renderings are significantly akin in their assumption of divine initiative: God is
not merely the object. Since this is a legitimate interpretation of the
unpointed text,[1] little importance can be attached to it, but it may be
noted as a straw in the theological wind.

29.25 ביד נביאיו ... ביד־יהוה : δι᾿ ἐντολῆς κυρίου ... ἐν χειρὶ τῶν
προφητῶν G O (L) R.
Is a literal translation avoided as anthropomorphic, as the second
phrase might pointedly suggest and Rogers, p. 37f., claims? It is
important to note that the two used of ביד are not synonymous: in
the first case it denotes agency and in the second instrumentality.
Surely the translator is merely bringing out the difference, and ἐντολῆς
reflects literary insight rather than theological inhibition.

No consistent policy of dogmatic re-writing can be detected in Par.
Anthropopathisms are not eliminated : e.g. I 21.15 וינחם על־הרעה :
καὶ μετεμελήθη ἐπὶ τῇ κακίᾳ G O L R. In II 18.18 εἶδον τὸν κύριον
moves in a different world from Targ חמית ית איקר שכנתא דיהוה. But
there are a few indications that the translator stood on the fringe of a
new approach to the text dictated by the development of religious
doctrine.

9. STRIKING RENDERINGS

It is a commonplace to stress that the LXX is an interpretation of
the Heb text rather than a mechanical translation. The same emphasis
needs to be made in the case of Par, probably the more so since on the
surface it does give the misleading impression of extreme literalness.
But paraphrase and stylistic variation have already, both in ch. iv
and in the preceding section, been shown to be an integral part of the
translation. Nowhere is the element of interpretation more evident
than in the title of the books. In place of MT דברי הימים stands
Παραλειπομένων G L R. O mss. expand into Π. βασιλέων Ιουδα Α,
Π. τῶν βασιλείων a, Π. τῶν βασιλείων Ιουδα i n.[2] The Gk title
clearly "characterises the book as a supplement to Samuel and Kings".[3]

---

[1] As אֲהֵבְךָ. On the other hand Targ has here רחמך and in Isa רְתֹמִי (Sperber
mentions a variant רחימי in the apparatus).

[2] Similarly at the end of I Par An have Π. τῶν βασιλειῶν Ιουδα, which is repeated at
the beginning of II Par (but n omits Ιουδα). This is also read at the close of II Par by
A*Ncn (in A βασ. is corrected to βασιλέων).

[3] Pfeiffer, Introduction to the OT, p. 782.

Curtis, in view of the high value he places on A, naturally takes the longer title to be original, but he does add that it is attested by the nomenclature of the Ethiopic Church and by Pesh. In the light of A's association with the G textform, illustrated in ch. vi,[1] it may indeed be the survival of the translator's own title, usually abbreviated, but the confinement of "the king(dom)s of Judah" to O mss. does raise a little doubt. Certainly, however, it reflects the intent of the translator. W. Bacher was surely correct in explaining the origin of the title as follows.[2] It is an allusion to יתר which begins the customary formula of a reign in Ki from I 14.19 onwards. The formula refers the reader to ספר דברי הימים. The translator understood the Heb title of Chron in terms of the Ki formula.

Some of the renderings in Par, at first sight anomalous, may be paralleled elsewhere in the LXX Old Testament. חנית is sometimes rendered "sword" in Par. ῥομφαία is the rendering in I 11.11,[3] 20 G O L R and μαχαίρα in II 23.9 G O R. The first rendering occurs also in Psa 35/34.3 and the second in Job 39.23.

The liturgical formula ... כי טוב כי לעולם חסדו occurs three times in Chron: I 16.34; II 5.13; 7.3. In each case the adjective is rendered not ἀγαθός, agreeing with יהוה just before, but ἀγαθόν G O L R,[4] agreeing with ἔλεος following: "for good, for everlasting is ..."[5] The rendering, though grammatically permissible, is unusual. In the LXX there are two parallels: ἀγαθόν in II Esdr 3.11 and καλόν in I Macc 4.24. Doubtless this interpretation was inspired by the phrase כי־טוב חסדך in Psa 69.17; 109.21.

ἐπιφανές G O L R for נראות in I 17.21 is a common LXX rendering for the Niphal of ירא, treating it as if it was from ראה : cf. Jud 13.6; II Rg 7.23; Joel 2.11; 3.4; Hab 1.7; Mal 1.14; 3.22. The treatment is based on an exegetical tradition attested outside the LXX.[6]

ὑψηλόν G O L R for נטויה in II 6.32 is a frequent rendering, found,

---

[1] p. 140.

[2] *ZAW* xv, p. 307.

[3] The *kaige* text of II Rg. 23.8 copies Par here : contrast Rg. v 18.

[4] In the first case d e p have ἀγαθός and c₂ χριστός (= χρηστός); in the second a has ἀγαθός.

[5] It could also conceivably mean "it (i.e., thanksgiving) is good".

[6] See Geiger, *Urschrift*[1], p. 339f. In Deut 4.34; 26.8; 34.12; Jer 32.21 Targ renders (מורא(ים as חזינא/ין as if it were מַרְאָה, while the LXX uses ὁράμασιν (but θαυμάσια in Deut 34.12).

e.g., in Exod 6.6; Deut 4.34; Isa 3.16. It corresponds to the Targumic
מרמם (בדרע).

In II 36.5b (= II Ki 24.2) καὶ ἀπέστησαν G O L R represents
להאבידו. At first sight one is tempted to posit להעבירו : ἀφιστάναι
stands for עבר in Isa 40.27 LXX. But J. Ziegler has drawn attention
to the rendering ἐξαποστελῶ for האבדתי in Jer 49.38/25.18.[1] He does
not cite Par, but he compares Ezek 28.16 ואבדך : καὶ ἤγαγέ σε
and Dan 2.12 LXX להובדה : ἐξαγαγεῖν, and asks whether the LXX
knew of another root אבד. The rendering here in Par surely raises the
same question: it seems to reflect a similar tradition.

Par shows numerous signs of Aramaic influence. A number of
instances fit better in other chapters, but here may be mentioned a
few cases where the translator's knowledge of Aramaic has influenced
him.

I 15.21   לנצח : τοῦ (ἐν)ισχῦσαι G O L (in doublet) R.
29.11   נצח : ἰσχύς G O L (in doublet) R.[2]
Most probably the verb is given the sense of the Aramaic root "be
victorious" : cf. Isa 25.8 לנצח : ἰσχύσας.[3]

At times words beginning with מ are rendered as Gk infinitives.
The Aramaic infinitive of the type מכתב no doubt suggested this
rendering to the translator's mind.

I 15.16   משמיעים : τοῦ φωνῆσαι G O R.
16.42   למשמיעים : τοῦ ἀναφωνεῖν G O L R.[4]
II 5.13   למחצצרים ולמשררים : ἐν τῷ σαλπίζειν G O L R καὶ ἐν τῷ
ψαλτῳδεῖν G O L.
19.7; 35.3   משא : θαυμάσαι, ἆραι G O L R.
20.22   מארבים : πολεμεῖν G O L (in doublet) R.
v. 23   למשחית : τοῦ ἐξολεθρευθῆναι G O R.

The renderings πολεμῆσαι G O L R and πολεμεῖν G O L R for
מלחמה in I 19.7,10[5] may be reminiscences of the Pael and Aphel
infinitives of the type מכתבה and מְכַתְבָה.[6]

---

[1] Beiträge, p. 47.

[2] See further p. 169f.

[3] cf. Driver, Samuel, ad I 15.29.

[4] Rothstein urged that להשמיע be read on the basis of Par.

[5] cf. πόλεμον ποιῆσαι O L R for מלחמתי in II 35.21. G is corrupt: see part II, p. 14.

[6] cf. Leander, Laut- und Formenlehre des Ägyptisch-Aramäischen, p. 51.

The translator appears to have equated the roots עזר and עצר
with עזז. עזר is rendered (κατ)ἰσχύειν in I 5.20 G O R; 15.26 G O L R;
II 14.10/11 G O R; 25.8 G O R; 26.7 G O L R; 28.23 G O L R.
In II 32.3 ויעזרוהו is translated καὶ συνεπίσχυσεν αὐτῷ G (O L R).
In I 5.20 BH, following Rothstein, notes "1 c G^{BA} ויגברו", but Rudolph
rightly points out Par's consistency in so rendering. Schleusner likewise
commented long ago that the parallels rule out the assumption of some
that ויעזזו was read.[1] Par can also use βοηθεῖν, and synonyms, for
עזר. It thus finds two meanings for the word: (i) "help", (ii) "be
strong".

H. M. Orlinsky has given some interesting LXX references outside
Par for the opposite tendency: to regard עזז as a synonym of עזר.[2]
He cites renderings with βοηθ- in Exod 15.2; Isa 30.2; Jer 16.19 and
so on. G. Brin has explored fully the many semantic links to be found
in the Heb Bible.[3] He finds no etymological link between the two
roots, but traces the association to their phonetic similarity.[4] Brin
does not refer to Par's verbal renderings, but it is clear that the translator knew and shared the common tendency to confuse the two words.

עצר also is translated κατισχύειν in II 14.10/11; 22.9 G O L R.
In the last case עצר כח becomes κατισχῦσαι δύναμιν : cf. ἰσχύειν for
the same phrase in I 29.14; II 2.5/6 G O L R. Note κατισχύειν for
עצר כח in Dan. LXX 10.8; 11.6. The presence of כח may have encouraged the rendering, but the case in II Par. 14.10/11 suggests that
עצר has been confused with עזר in the sense of עזז. Comparable
phonetic confusion can be detected in Isa LXX: Wutz, p. 76, noted
that אזר is frequently rendered (κατ/ἐν)ἰσχύειν. Compare καὶ
ἐνισχύσω σε for ואצרך in Isa 42.6 ,although different explanations are
offered by Wutz, p. 510, and Fischer.[5]

Less easy to explain is the translation καὶ κατισχύσαι σε G O L (R)
for ויצוך in I 22.12. It accords with κατισχύσει σε for וצוך in Exod.
18.23, as Wutz notes. Do both cases depend upon a ו/ר confusion? Is
the translator using this Pentateuchal dictionary? Do they merely

---

[1] *Lexicon*, ii, p. 239.

[2] *A Stubborn Faith*, p. 121.

[3] *Leshonenu* xxiv, pp. 8-14.

[4] There may be mentioned here the suggestion of another root עזר "be strong"
claimed by H.L. Ginsberg, *JBL* lvii, p. 210f. But recourse to it leaves עזז: βοηθεῖν
unexplained.

[5] *In welcher Schrift* ..., p. 55.

represent a paraphrase of "appoint, authorise"? Rothstein consider it a free rendering.[1]

פרץ is rendered in a variety of ways in Par apart from verbs of breaking.

I 4.38 פרצו : ἐπληθύνθησαν G O R.
This is a legitimate rendering since the verb develops the meaning "break over (limits), increase".[2] καὶ ηὐξήθη G O L (in doublet) R for ויפרץ in II 11.23 is similar.

I 13.2 נפרצה : εὐω/οδώθη G O L R.
Benzinger, following Stade, considered that this represented נחרצה. BH suggests נרצתה on the basis of Par. Rothstein, on the other hand, claims that the translator read MT and paraphrased. This view is surely right: cf. Hos 4.10 יפרצו : κατευθύνωσιν for a similar paraphrase.[3]

II 31.5 כפרץ : ὡς προσέταξεν G O L R.
Did the translator know of another root "command", cognate with the Accadian paraṣu?[4] It may well be so, but the similar καθὼς προσέτ. G O L R for במפקד in v. 13 could possibly indicate that in v. 5 the translator is guessing from the context.

It was noted in ch. iv that instead of keeping one Gk word for one Heb word the translator was apt to think in terms of a synonym or related word.[5] In II 26.11; 34.13 שטר is rendered κριτής G O L R. The usual rendering is γραμματεύς, but in both cases that word has just been used for סופר. The translator's mind went to κριτής, obviously because in I 23.4; 26.29 שפט and שטר are associated.[6] Cf. Ezra 7.25 שפטין ודינין : γραμματεῖς καὶ κριτάς. In I 5.12 ושפט, rendered ὁ γραμματεύς G O R, is annotated in BH "...שפט vel שטר" after citing Par. The second suggestion is akin to Rothstein's, who con-

---

[1] R. Loewe has suggested privately that the key may be the combination הלא צויתיד חזק ואמץ in Jos. 1.9.

[2] BDB, p. 829b.

[3] Here again there is no need to read יתרצו on the basis of the LXX with BDB, p. 953a.

[4] See Wutz, p. 153; G.R. Driver, *JTS* xxiii, p. 72f. In *JTS* xxv, p. 177f. he agreed with Guillaume that the Arabic faraḍa IV "imposed laws" was the same root. In *JTS* xxxii, p. 365 he agreed further that ڢـرـڊ too was cognate.

[5] p. 55.

[6] And also because in Ptolemaic Egypt the two words were close in meaning: see p. 23.

sidered that הַשֹּׁטֵר underlay Par. But once again the words have been related in the translator's mind.

Now some individual cases of unusual renderings are to be considered and explanations suggested.

I 6.63/78 למזרח : κατὰ δυσμάς G O R.

The Gk is the very opposite of the Heb. Mention of Jericho caused the rationalisation that the reference was to the west side of the Jordan.

9.38 נגד ... עם : ἐν μέσῳ G O L R ... ἐν μέσῳ G.

Rothstein argues that the section 9.35-44 was not originally in Chron and that the corresponding Gk is a later addition in Par, mainly on the ground that the rendering in the parallel 8.32 is κατέναντι ... μετά. The inconsistency of rendering is a proof for him that the passage was subsequently inserted in Par. Rudolph, arguing against him, considers that κατέναντι originally stood here for the first ἐν μέσῳ and has suffered assimilation to the second. The second one he claims is a legitimate rendering of עם : it recurs in I Rg 10.11. Had Rothstein made a close study of Par as a literary document in its own right instead of considering it merely as an aid to Heb textual criticism, he would not have been so surprised by inconsistent renderings. This trait was observed frequently in ch. iv. The first ἐν μέσῳ may be kept as an instance where Par uses identical translations which suit the second case much better than the first, a type of rendering illustrated in ch. iv.[1]

10.3 וַיָּחֶל : καὶ ἐπόνεσεν S O R.[2]

MT takes from חיל but Par from חלה (Curtis, Goettsberger and Rudolph). Compare the same rendering for the Hophal in II 18.33, 35.23. Either the same conjugation was inferred here or, as Rudolph considers, a Niphal וַיֵּחַל.

11.8 ויואב יחיה את־שאר העיר : καὶ ἐπολέμησεν καὶ ἔλαβεν τὴν πόλιν G O (in doublet).

The rendering has caused much perplexity. Rothstein, Rehm, p. 58, and Rudolph assume that Par had a completely different *Vorlage*. Goettsberger considers that מלוא in the preceding clause was confused with לחם and that סביב was related to the Aramaic נסב "take". But Rudolph rightly points out that these words are in fact missing in Par through homoeoteleuton. The Gk takes David as the continued

---

[1] p. 56

[2] B c₂ have a plural by error: see part II, p. 8.

subject, as Rudoph and Curtis note. Underlying it may be a desire to give David the glory of capturing Jerusalem, and so to minimise Joab's work, as Rogers, p. 48, claims. The difficulty of the Heb clause, perhaps coupled with an indistinct ms., may be sufficient explanation. ויואב was doubtless read as ויארב : cf. II 20.22 מארבים : πολεμεῖν G O L (in doublet) R. יחיה, it may be suggested was read as וחיה, related to חוח as a denominative Piel, under the influence of II 33.11 בחחים ... וילכדו : καὶ κατέλαβον ... ἐν δεσμοῖς G O (L) R; "fettered" was interpreted as "captured". שאר was then omitted as superfluous: "the city" was sufficient to distinguish from the fortress captured in v. 5.

12.17/16   עד־למצד : εἰς βοήθειαν G O L R.

G. Bertram expresses uncertainty concerning the rendering and suggests a divergent *Vorlage*[1]. On the other hand, Orlinsky is convinced that paraphrase is the explanation.[2] He cites analogous cases in the LXX Old Testament where words like מעוז and צור are rendered with forms of βοηθεῖν. BH notes "למעוז?". Rothstein suggests לעזר with a query, but inclines to the view that the translation is a loose one. But his former suggestion does raise the question whether there is not some link between the rendering here and the absence from G O R of לעזרנו in v. 18/17 and/or of לעזור in v. 23/22. Did a marginal replacement displace the present Heb ?

13.5   שיחור מצרים : ὁρίων Αἰγύπτου G O L R.

The translator correctly interpreted שיחור as Wadi el-Arish[3] and paraphrased "boundary" in the light of II 9.26 גבול מ' (ὁρίων Αἰγ.). Presumably a transliteration was not used because the name was not in current use: cf. the paraphrase τῆς ἀοικήτου "desert" in Jos 13.3.[4] A translation "river" would have suggested the Nile.

29.11   המתנשא : ταράσσεται G O L (in doublet) R.

The translator takes the verb to mean "rise up" in revolt: in Ezra 4.19 the Aramaic מתנשאה does have this meaning.[5]

---

[1] *ZAW* lvii, p. 94, note 2.

[2] *A Stubborn Faith*, p. 121f.

[3] Cf. Curtis, Rudolph and Simons, *Geographical Texts*, p. 27, for the identification.

[4] In Isa. 23.3 סחר was read. In Jer. 2.18 Γηων may well be an adaptation from Σιωρ to the more familiar river name via a C/Γ error (cf. Γωρ 88) *contra* Ziegler, *Beiträge*, p. 63: cf. the opposite error Σειων G for Γιων in II Par. 32.30. Wutz, p. 29, considered Γιων original here in Par by a Γ/P error and dittography.

[5] Cf. התרוממת in this sense in Dan. 5.23. In Dan. 8.11 Montgomery, *ICC*, p. 356, was surely wrong in explaining Θ ἐταράχθη for הרים as representing a form of מור.

II 4.5 פרח ... כמעשה שפת : ὡς χεῖλος ... διαγεγλυμμένα βλασ-τούς G O (L) R.

According to Rehm, p. 72, the participle represents an extra word פֶּתַח in the *Vorlage*, but it is merely the loose equivalent for מעשה in the sense "artistic work". The plural refers back *ad sensum* to the generic χεῖλος.

v. 18 לא נחקר : οὐκ ἐξέλιπεν G (O) R.

Compare οὐκ ἦν τέρμα in the corresponding III Rg.7.32. The renderings are reminiscent of the translation of the cognate noun in Psa LXX: 95/94.4 πέρατα; 145/144.3 πέρας.

6.28 בארץ שעריו : κατέναντι τῶν πόλεων αὐτῶν G O R.

It is usual to read בּאחד ש' on the basis of the parallel III Rg.8.37 ἐν μίᾳ (BH; cf. Curtis). In turn κατέναντι is frequently taken to be a corruption of κατὰ μίαν (BH; Kittel, *SBOT*, following Kloster-mann; Katz[1]). Rehm, p. 59, attempts to justify κατέναντι on the ground that בארע was read by a ע/צ confusion: ארע means "meet" in post-Biblical Hebrew and Aramaic. Gk corruption from κατὰ μίαν would be by no means easy to explain. It may be suggested that the translator is merely paraphrasing MT, which he took to mean "in the countryside outside the towns" and so thought of a siege. κατέναντι is used of a siege in I 19.7 G O R.

18.34 ותעל המלחמה : καὶ ἐτροπώθη ὁ πόλεμος G O L R.

The parallel II Rg.22.25 reads the same. The verb is a favourite one in Par, occurring for כנע I 18.1, נגף 19.16; II 20.22; 25.22, כשל II 25.8, all in G O L R. In Rg it occurs only in II 8.1, a different section, for כנע. So the rendering may well be original in Par and assimilated in Rg. The paraphrase "the battle was lost" evidently depends upon the sense "withdraw, defeat" for עלה.[2]

21.17 ונשיו : καὶ τὰς θυγατέρας αὐτοῦ G O L R.

This does not necessarily imply ובנותיו, as BH claims. It may be simply a free rendering: "women" just after בניו suggested "daughters".

v. 20 חמדה : ἐπαίνῳ G O L R.

It is customary (cf. BH) to refer to the cognate Arabic *ḥamada* which has the meaning "praise". The translator evidently knew this meaning for the Heb verb.

23.15 וישימו לה ידים : καὶ ἔδωκαν αὐτῇ ἄνεσιν G O L (in doublet) R.

---

[1] *TLZ* lxi, col. 269.

[2] Cf. BDB, p. 748b.

The rendering "made way for her" provides no cause to posit a *Vorlage* רפות with Rehm, p. 60. Par correctly paraphrases ידים in the sense of "place".¹ There is hardly "royal deference" here (Rogers, p. 82).

30.16 זרקים : ἐδέχοντο G O L R.

Wutz, p. 15 finds here an error for ἐκχέοντες, but Par uses προσχεῖν in 29.22; 35.11. It is probably a loose rendering in reminiscence of ויקבלו את־הדם in 29.22.

10. ORDER OF WORDS

In ch. iv it was observed that the translator generally tied himself to the Heb order.² Only a few examples of changed order could be cited on the shared evidence of all four groups. But a different picture comes to light when G is taken as the earliest textform of the four. There emerge several different categories of change of order which is apparently due to the translator. Often an idiomatic Gk order is found.

(i) *Subject before verb*³

I 12.18/17   ויצא דויד : καὶ Δ. ἐξῆλθεν G O

27.23   אמר יהוה : κύριος εἶπεν G O

II 8.11   העלה שלמה : Σαλ. ἀνήγαγεν G O

(ii) *Genitive before nomen regens*

II 17.4   מעשה ישראל : τοῦ Ισραηλ τὰ ἔργα G O

22.8   שרי יהודה : τοὺς Ιουδα ἄρχοντας G

v. 10   בנה : αὐτῆς ὁ υἱός G O

31.2   עבדתו : τὴν ἑαυτοῦ λειτουργίαν G O

(iii) *Pronominal suffix represented before verb*

II 28.6   בעזבם : ἐν τῷ αὐτοὺς καταλιπεῖν G O

30.3   לעשתו : αὐτὸ ποιῆσαι G L

(iv) *Conjunction and verb separated or juxtaposed*

Since it would be necessary to posit drastic changes of verbal forms

---

¹ Cf. Rudolph, *Bertholet Festschrift*, p. 475.

² p. 39.

³ For I 11.5 see part II, p. 51.

in the *Vorlage* if the differences were attributed to the Heb stage, it is more likely that they are post-Heb.

I 8.36	וזמרי הוליד	καὶ ἐγέννησεν Ζαμβρει G
II 26.21	וישב בית החפשות	καὶ ἐν οἴκῳ ... ἐκάθητο G O R
28.19	ומעול מעל	καὶ ἀπέστη ἀποστάσει[1] B O L R.
33.14	ואחרי־כן בנה	καὶ ᾠκοδόμησεν μετὰ ταῦτα G
36.6	(ו)עליו עלה	καὶ ἀνέβη ἐπ᾽ αὐτόν G O L R
v. 13	ויאמץ את־לבבו	καὶ τὴν καρδίαν αὐτοῦ κατίσχυσεν G O

(L)

(v) *Miscellaneous changes*

In these cases a change on the translator's part is more likely, either because a more natural Gk order is followed or because otherwise one would have to assume unlikely upheaval in the *Vorlage*.

I 27.31	למלך דויד	Δ. τοῦ βασιλέως G O
v. 34	ושר־צבא למלך יואב	καὶ Ιωαβ ἀρχιστράτηγος τοῦ βασ. G O R
29.1	See part II, ch. i.[2]	
II 4.11	למלך שלמה	Σ. τῷ βασιλεῖ G L
9.16	זהב שחוט	ἐλατὰς χρυσᾶς G O L R (except f j)
15.9	מישראל לרב	πολλοὶ τοῦ Ισραηλ G O
17.11	צאן אילים (in apposition)	κρίους προβάτων G O
21.18	כל־זאת	ταῦτα πάντα G O^mss. L R
22.4	יועצים אחרי מות אביו	μετὰ τὸ ἀποθανεῖν ... σύμβουλοι G O. Otherwise two Gk infinitives would be too close for easy comprehension.
26.3	עזיהו במלכו	ἐβασίλευσεν Ὀζιάς c₂ O R.[3]
v. 14	לאבני קלעים	σφενδόνας εἰς λίθους G O.[4]
v. 22	דברי עזיהו הראשנים והאחרנים	λόγοι οἱ πρῶτοι καὶ οἱ ἔσχατοι Ὀζείου G.
29.17	ביום ... לחדש הראשון כלו	τῇ ἡμέρᾳ ... συνετέλεσαν τοῦ μηνὸς τοῦ πρώτου G
v. 25	דויד וגד חזה־המלך	Δ. τοῦ βασιλέως καὶ Γαδ τοῦ

---

[1] For this method of rendering an infinitive absolute see Thackeray, *Grammar*, p. 48.

[2] p. 54.

[3] See part II, p. 51.

[4] See part II, p. 88.

προφήτου G. BH gives the wrong impression that המ׳ is missing.

v. 34   היו למעט : ὀλίγοι ἦσαν G O L
30.22   See ch. viii[1]
36.23   לבנות־לו בית : οἰκοδομῆσαι οἶκον αὐτῷ G La

(vi) *A persistent pattern*

Frequently, when Chron has the normal Heb order of verb + subject + direct or indirect object or adverb, Par puts the subject third in the sequence instead of second. Most probably this new pattern has been created by the translator.[2]

I 19.2   דויד/מלאכים G O R
22.11   יהוה/עמך G O
v. 12   יהוה/שׂכל ובינה G O
II 1.6   שׁלמה/שׁם G O L
2.2/3; 21.12   דויד/אבי(ך) G O, G
8.2   שׁלמה/אתם G O L R
14.5/6   יהוה/לו G O L
15.15   יהוה/להם G O L
18.14   המלך/אליו G O L R, as MT in v. 15
21.10   אדים/מתחת יד־יהודה G
23.7   הלוים/את־המלך B
24.17   המלך/אליהם G O L
v. 22   יהוידע אביו/עמו G O
v. 27   המשׂא/עליו G O R
33.20   אמון בנו/תחתיו G O

11. STANDARD FORMS OF NAMES

Names abound in Par, very often in a corrupt form in the text of G.[3] It will be observed in part II, ch. i that the corruption much more often took place in a Gk setting than in a Heb one. But one must not be too hasty in denying the originality of certain forms. Thackeray called attention to the strange mixture of declined and indeclinable

---

[1] p. 154. under 34.12.

[2] By this criterion the transposition בו/בני ישׂראל in II 10.18, attested only in B, is probably a Gk copyist's change.

[3] For references to the principles of transliteration of names see part II, p. 1.

forms of names in lists in Par and II Esdr.[1] He suggested that possibly the lists were originally shorter and were subsequently supplemented from another source. However, the reader of ch. iv will have seen that the translator's very characteristic is a propensity to oscillate between loose and literal forms of rendering. Hellenized and non-Hellenized forms fit aptly into this established pattern. (זכריה(ו can become not only $Za\chi a\rho\iota as$ but also the indeclinable $Za\chi a\rho\iota a$ and $Za\chi a\rho\iota o\nu$. זרח becomes $Za\rho\epsilon$ G O L R I 1.37 and $Za\rho a$ G O L R v. 44. ידיעאל turns into $Ia\delta\iota\eta\lambda$ I 7.6,[2] $Ie\delta\iota\eta\lambda$ 11.45[3] and $I\delta\epsilon\iota\eta\lambda$* 26.2.[4]

There is a danger not only of being too hasty in claiming Gk revision but also of wrongly positing a different *Vorlage*. Par has quite a few stylised equivalents of Heb names, which were taken over from earlier writings and/or were commonly used in an oral setting. It is conceivable, as Rehm, p. 43, concedes, and indeed probable, that certain names had been as it were frozen into a standard Gk form by the translator's time, and that he would feel a natural compunction to use them even though they did not quite correspond letter for letter to the *Vorlage*.

I 2.13; 8.33; 9.39; 10.2; 13.7   אבינדב : $A\mu\epsilon\iota\nu a\delta a\beta$ G O L R. This is a form used in Rg, e.g. I 16.8 (Rehm, p. 43). Gilbert posited a ב/מ error in the first case,[5] but it is not likely that Par's Heb text had this error. אבינדב was confused with עמינ׳ in their Gk dress.

v. 16; 11.20   אבשי : $A\beta\epsilon\iota\sigma a$ G e₂ R, G 18.12; 19.11 $A\beta\epsilon\sigma\sigma a$ G L, B Oᵐˢˢ L. The same twofold tradition is found in Rg: see Rahlfs' note to I Rg. 26.6 in his edition of the LXX.

v. 17; 3.1   אביגיל : $A\beta\epsilon\iota\gamma a\iota a$ G O L R. Originally a Λ/A error, this form goes back to II Rg 3.3 (Rehm, p. 42f), and was doubtless the Gk equivalent current at a very early period.

v. 23; 3.2   גשור : $\Gamma\epsilon\delta\sigma o\upsilon\rho$ B. This form is found in II Rg. 13.37, etc. (but not in II Rg 3.3). $\Gamma\epsilon\sigma\sigma o\upsilon\rho$ c₂, etc., is secondary.

3.5   בת־שוע : $B\eta\rho\sigma a\beta\epsilon\epsilon$ G O (L) R This form occurs in II Rg 11.3. "Nomen feminae et nomen loci antiquis

---

[1] *Grammar*, p. 162.

[2] See part II, p. 43.

[3] See p. 158.

[4] See part II, p. 20.

[5] *AJSL* xiii, p. 292.

temporibus inter se permutata sunt"[1]. Uriah's wife was given the name of the town in Gk: there is no warrant to posit an original $Ba\theta\sigma a\beta\epsilon\epsilon$* in Par with Rothstein.

v. 21 אֲרָנ : $O\rho\nu a$ G O R.

Reference must be made to the same equivalent in G O L R for אֲרָנ in 21.15ff. (In v. 21 the accusative $'O\rho\nu \hat{a}\nu$ G is probably to be replaced by the indeclinable $O\rho\nu a$ O L R: cf. v. 22). $O\rho\nu a$ is found in II Rg 24.16 as the name of the Jebusite farmer. The procedure of the Gk translator of Chron is clear. He took over the Gk name in ch. 21 and used it too for the name with the same consonants in ch. 3, where Rothstein unnecessarily queried whether אֲרנה was read. It would be equally bad policy to suspect the *Vorlage* reading in ch. 21.

4.21 שֵׁלה : $\Sigma\eta\lambda\omega\mu$ G O.[2]

5.29/6.3; 24.1f. אביהוא : $A\beta\iota\sigma\upsilon\delta$ G O L R.

This equivalent is the standard one in the LXX, occurring too in Exod 6.23; Lev 10.1; Num 3.4 (Curtis *ad* 24.1; Fischer[3]). BH wrongly posits אביהוד in 5.29. There was evidently early confusion of $A\beta\iota\sigma\upsilon$ with a similar name,[4] which had probably already occurred in the Gk Pentateuch before Par was translated.

11.22f., etc.[5] יהוידע : $I\omega\delta a\epsilon$ G O R.

Ziegler suggested that in Jer 29/36.26, where the same form occurs in the LXX, probably $I\omega\iota a\delta a\epsilon$, which A often has, was the original form and that ιa fell out.[6] It is more likely that this abbreviated form antedates both Jer LXX and Par. In IV Rg 11.4,9 all mss. read $I\omega\delta a\epsilon$ except A which has $I\omega\iota a\delta a\epsilon$ and $I\omega a\delta a\epsilon$.

15.29 מיכל : $M\epsilon\lambda\chi o\lambda$ G O e₂ R.

This form is found in I Rg 14.49, etc. Probably the original form suffered corruption by assimilation to $M\epsilon\lambda\chi\epsilon\iota\sigma a$ in the same verse in Rg.

20.2 מלכם : $Mo\lambda\chi o\lambda$ B

See ch. viii.[7]

29.4; II 9.10 אופיר : $(\dot{\epsilon}\kappa)$ $\Sigma o\upsilon\phi\epsilon\iota\rho$ G O L R.

II 8.18 אופירה : $\epsilon\iota s$ $\Sigma\omega\phi\epsilon\iota\rho a$ G (O) L R.

---

[1] Rahlfs, *LXX*, *ad* II Rg. 11.3.

[2] See p. 186.

[3] *Das Alphabet*, p. 10.

[4] Cf. Rahlfs, *LXX-Studien*, iii, p. 122.

[5] For BH's error in 9.10 see part II, p, 30; for 11.24 see p. 158; for 12.28/27 see part II, p. 5.

[6] *Beiträge*, p. 75.

[7] p. *162f.*

Rahlfs drew attention to III Rg 10.11 ἐκ Σουφειρ, parallel with II Par 9.10; to III Rg 16.28f (= I Ki 22.49) εἰς Σωφειρ(α), not parallel with Par; and also to Ecclus 7.18 χρυσίῳ Σουφειρ.[1] The initial Gk error of dittography was carried over into the common Gk forms of the name.

II 12.2,5 שִׁישַׁק : Σουσακειμ G O L R.
Rahlfs called attention to this form, found also in the parallel III Rg 14.25 and rightly explained it as due to dittography of (מֶ(לֶךְ), which follows in every case, at some stage.[2] The erroneous Gk form had become established as the standard equivalent before Par was translated, and the translator took it over. In II 12.10 he added Σ. as an amplifying subject.

32.1ff. סַנְחֵרִיב : Σενναχηρειμ (vel sim) G O L R.
Rehm, p. 43, observes that this Gk form, which he regards as initially a β/μ error, occurs constantly in the LXX and is echoed in Josephus' form Σεναχει/ηριμός.

v. 20, 32; 33.20ff. אָמוֹן : Aμως G O L R (in ch. 32), G O R (in ch. 33).
Ziegler observed that this form occurs also in IV Rg 21.18ff. (but L has Aμων and A x Aμμων) and in Jer 1.2; 25.3.[3] He traced the form back to a נ/ז error, following Spohn, but added that "die starke anderweitige Bezeugung von Aμως lässt erkennen, dass keine zufällige Verlesung in Frage kommt, sondern eine exegetische Tradition". Rehm, p. 42, regarded the form as a rendering "unter Erinnerung an der bekannten Namen" and this is more likely. It is much less probable that אָמוֹן was read at some early stage, as Ziegler preferred to think, than that the error occurred in a Gk setting and the common Aμως (= אָמוֹץ and עָמוֹס) became the standard form.

12. RELATION TO THE *kaige* RECENSION

A number of references have been claimed for the proto-Theodotionic recension discovered in Rg and elsewhere.[4] The question springs naturally to mind whether anything comparable can be detected in Par. In part this question has already been raised and answered: D. Barthélemy frequently compared and contrasted the evidence of Par with that of the *kaige* recension (KR) in Rg. [5]

---

[1] *LXX-Studien*, iii, p. 100 note 1.

[2] *Op. cit.*, p. 97 note 2.

[3] *Beiträge*, p. 63.

[4] For references see chapter ix.

[5] *Les devanciers d'Aquila*, pp. 41-43, 48-67.

He himself found nine characteristics. Par's relation to them will be analysed in turn.

1. καίγε (καί) for גם(ו). In G there are two cases, both secondary: at II 6.37 (misplaced from v. 32) G O;[1] 14.14/15 G O L R.[2] Elsewhere there are two cases in O, five in R and fifteen in L. The normal rendering in G is καί, but there is also a sporadic use of καὶ γάρ, seven times 'in II Par,[3] while, to supplement Barthélemy's own observations, I Par employs it for ואף once.[4]

Barthélemy compared the use of καὶ γάρ in Psa and part of Ezek, and spoke of "le groupe καὶ γάρ" (p. 51) with "cette même préoccupation" as the KR group for representation of גם, "mais étrangers et vraisemblablement antérieurs" to the KR group (p. 47). One should not be too dogmatic in assessing Par. The sporadic use of καὶ γάρ must be stressed: גם(ו) introducing a clause is so translated in I Par only seven times out of 27. As Barthélemy himself observes, καὶ γάρ is used in Gen LXX three times,[5] and is good Gk. So the translator of Par may well have been inspired by his Pentateuchal model rather than by scholastic constraint.

2. ἀνήρ for איש in the sense of "each". Barthélemy, p. 51, has presented the evidence. None of the fourteen instances is rendered in G in this stereotyped way. But L uses ἀνήρ thus in four cases.[6]

3. ἐπάνωθεν or ἀπάνωθεν for מֵעַל. There are nine instances of מֵעַל, for none of which does this equivalent appear in any textform.

4. στηλοῦν for נצב־יצב. The four cases in Chron are never so rendered.

5. κερατίνη for שׁופר. As Barthélemy, p. 62, notes, of the two cases in Chron the Heb is transliterated once, in I 15.28 G O L R, and omitted in G at II 15.14, while O L R supply a secondary καὶ ἐν κερατίναις. Evidently the translator did not know the Gk word; although he knew the meaning of שׁופר he was at a loss for a translation. חצוצרות is adjacent in both cases: in the first the translator distinguished by transliteration, in the second he made σάλπιγξ do for both words.

---

[1] See p. 146.

[2] See p. 167; Barthélemy, p. 42.

[3] 12.12 G O R; 19.8 G O; 21.11 G O R; 24.7 G O R; 26.20 G O L R; 28.2 G O L R, 5 G.

[4] 8.32 G R. In I 16.30 L has καὶ γάρ for אך, harmonizing with the Psa parallel.

[5] 16.13; 20.12; 35.17.

[6] II 6.29; 10.16; 20.23; 23.7. Barthélemy omits the second case.

6. Elimination of historic presents. Par does not employ this device.[1]

7. οὐκ ἔστιν for אֵין in past or future time. Barthélemy p. 67, observes that the only instance is II Par 15.5 G O L R, apart from 35.15 L. He might also have compared ἔστιν for יֵשׁ in future time in G at II 16.9. He finds confirmation of "la place marginale" of Par as a predecessor of the KR group. But it would be unwise to lay too much weight upon the phenomenon. Par normally renders both אֵין and יֵשׁ in strict accord with their temporal context.

8. ἐγώ εἰμι for אנכי. Barthélemy mentions no cases in Par, and the present writer has discovered none.

9. εἰς συνάντησιν for לקראת. This equivalent is the standard one is the Gk Pentateuch. In Par there is one case out of five, at II 35.20, while the Gk is also used for לפני at II 14.9/10. However, there is no elimination of εἰς ἀπάντησιν, such as is claimed for KR : it occurs seven times, once for לקראת.[2]

J.D. Shenkel has claimed ten more KR criteria in Rg.[3]

1. ἐν ὀφθαλμοῖς for בעיני, instead of ἐνώπιον. In Par G normally has ἐνώπιον or ἐναντίον (twelve and thirteen times respectively), for which L twice substitutes ἐν ὀφθ.[4] ἐν ὀφθ. in O L R at I 19.13 is secondary.[5] But it is used in I 13.4 G O L R; cf. τοῖς ὀφθ. G O L R in II 29.8. These are occasional literalisms, to be compared with κατ᾽ ὀφθαλμούς for לעיני in II 32.23 alongside ἐνώπιον in I 29.10 and ἐναντίον I 29.25 (all G O L R).

2. θυσιάζειν for זָבַח in place of θύειν. Of the 17 cases of זבח in Chron, Par renders θυσιάζειν four times.[6] This phenomenon is to be explained as stylistic variation for θύειν, employed ten times in G. L uses θυσιάζειν for θύειν in II 15.11, and Rmss Theodoret supply it in 33.17. θυσιάζειν occurs three times in the Gk Pentateuch, standing for the verb זבח once, at Exod. 22.19.

3. διώκειν for רדף, instead of καταδιώκειν. Par uses only the compound verb, at II 13.19; 14.12/13 G O L R.

---

[1] See p. 181a.

[2] I 19.5 G O L R. Also for לפני I 12.17; 14.8; II 15.2; 20.17; 28.9 and for אל־פני II 19.2 - all G O L R.

[3] *Chronology and Recensional Development in the Gk Text of Kings*, pp. 13-17, 113-116.

[4] I 19.3; II 22.4.

[5] See part II, p. 52.

[6] I 21.28; II 7.5 (in b ἔθυσεν is borrowed from the Rg parallel); 33.16 (ἔθυσεν Omss Thdt); 34.4.

4. ἄρχων τῆς δυνάμεως for שַׂר (ה)צבא, instead of ἀρχιστράτηγος. Par does indeed use the literal KR equivalent, in accord with its frequent literal renderings.[1]

5. φρον - for the root חכם, instead of σοφ-. The latter is used for the 17 cases in Chron, as indeed it is in the Gk Pentateuch.

6. KR distinguishes between חרשׁ and חשׁה. Unfortunately Chron uses neither.

7. ἀνομία for עון, in place of ἀδικία. In the single case at I 21.8 G O R read κακίαν, while L has ἀδικίαν in line with "L" in the Rg parallel.

8. ταχύνειν for מהר, instead of σπεύδειν. In the two cases where a verb is used, at II 24.5, G O R and (G O) R[2] have the latter, while L substitutes the former.

9. ἐν γαστρὶ ἔχειν / λαμβάνειν for הרה, in place of συλλαμβάνειν. Interestingly, at I 17.23 L reads συνέλαβε, while G O R render ἔλαβεν ἐν γαστρί.[3] The latter phrase is employed in the Gk Pentateuch.

10. (ἐ)θέλειν for אבה (לא) instead of βούλεσθαι. Both are found in the Gk Pentateuch. The translator of Par did not mind which he used: he employed them both as stylistic variants, the former in I 11.18; 19.19 and the latter in I 10.4; 11.19; II 21.7.

M. Smith has adduced the rendering of הורה as φωτίζειν as another criterion of the *kaige* recension.[4] The verb occurs a few times in Chron, but there is no trace of such a translation in Par.

J. M. Grindel has suggested yet another characteristic of the recension.[5] His concern was to test a wide range of OT Gk material previously claimed as belonging or allied to KR. His new characteristic is the rendering νῖκος for נצח. Examining seven cases in Chron, he found nothing positive, apart from εἰς νῖκος in a doublet of L at I 15.21. From the presence of KR-type readings in L, Barthélemy had deduced simply that readings of this recension had penetrated the textform of L. However, Grindel found a little evidence to suggest a different solution: the text of L is witness not specifically to KR but to a later recension of Par executed on the basis of the Hexapla. His conclusions

---

[1] ἀρχιστράτηγος in I 19.16, 18 is due to harmonization with the parallel passage in the proto-Lucianic text of Rg.

[2] See part II, p. 13.

[3] In I 4.17 G O L R follow a different Heb text.

[4] *Biblica* xlviii, pp. 443-445.

[5] *CBQ* xxxi, pp. 499-513.

would be equally applicable to the whole range of L's apparent approximations to KR characteristics, in the light of L's links with the Three demonstrated in ch. v.

Grindel issued a necessary warning against jumping to unwarranted conclusions in labelling material: "None of these characteristics is *in se* absolute... It is, rather, the systematic use of a certain group of correspondents that distinguishes the *kaige* recension".[1] His words are relevant for evaluating the primary G text of Par. There are occasional links here and there with the recensional characteristics outlined above. Of nineteen suggested characteristics the translator completely violates ten. With four he complies throughout, but in two cases his inspiration can be traced back to the Gk Pentateuch. With five characteristics he betrays a nodding acquaintance, following the LXX of the Pentateuch in each instance save one. It is blatantly obvious that the translator had nothing in common with a systematic reviser producing KR material on consistent and dogmatic lines. It was observed in ch. ii that S. Jellicoe married Torrey's estimate of Par to the discovery of proto-Theodotionic material in Rg and produced the theory that Par itself is proto-Theodotionic. The evidence adduced in this section does not seem to support this theory.

---

[1] *Loc. cit.*, p. 499f.

CHAPTER EIGHT

REVISION IN THE OLDEST TEXTFORM

Although it has been established that G contains the oldest text of Par, there remains the task of isolating every possible element which may be traced as secondary. The extent of Gk assimilation to parallel passages demands consideration : ch. ix will be partically devoted to this task. The text has been tampered with in other ways. The text-form of G contains many attempts to improve the Gk version.[1] Some may well be Hexaplaric in source, and have seeped into the G group. But in many cases the revision has a more ancient air. Evidently Origen was not the first to feel discontent with the Gk text. Traces of pre-Hexaplaric revision are not difficult to discover in Par, as in other books of the LXX.[2] Usually the new words or phrases are to be found added to the text : doublets are tell-tale signs of revision. Occasionally one can detect replacements and the addition of material originally omitted, with the aid of the characteristics of the translation discovered in chs. iv and vii. Some of the revision had a stylistic aim. Most of it was concerned with closer conformity with the Heb. It takes many forms: the supply of omissions and supposed omissions, correction of corruptions and erroneous renderings, literal rendering of para-phrase, translation of transliterations and a number of other adap-tations.

1. OMISSIONS OR SUPPOSED OMISSIONS SUPPLIED

It was noted in ch. iv that the Gk definite article often appears to correspond to את before names in cases where the four textforms agree.[3] But there are suspicious signs that the Gk article is secondary at times. For example, in I 1.46 for את־מדין only L uses τήν. In 2.13 B* L have Ελιαβ for את־אליאב, but c₂ O R prefix τόν. At 7.24

---

[1] Revision attested only in c₂ is ignored: cf. p. 101.

[2] For pre-Hexaplaric revision in the LXX cf. Katz, *Studia Patristica*, i, p. 346f.; in Rg and the Minor Prophets cf. Barthélemy, *Devanciers, passim*; in Isaiah cf. Seeligmann, The *LXX Version of Isaiah*, pp. 31-38; in Daniel cf. Montgomery, *Daniel*, p. 36.

[3] p. 40f.

only L represents the first and third את with τήν. In II 11.22 c₂ O L R have τὸν Αβια for אבי׳־את, but B significantly has simply Αβια. In vv. 6-10 there are fifteen place-names preceded by את : G uses the article eleven times, O thirteen and L R fifteen, an interesting progression illustrating respective care in revision. One wonders how many of G's eleven are in fact original. In quite a few places elsewhere it is obvious that the article is a later insertion in G, added no doubt to correspond to את at a subsequent period which was more sensitive to such niceties. A reviser in unanimity with Aquila, but no doubt a "devancier",[1] has been at work.

I 2.18 ואת־יריעות : καὶ τὴν Ελιωθ G (R).
The article was added after haplography of *iota*: Par originally read καὶ Ιεδιωθ* (ד/ר, Δ/Λ).

4.18 ואת־יקותיאל : καὶ τὸν Χετιηλ G.
The name was originally Ιχετιηλ.[2] τόν is secondary.

6.44/59 (ואת־יטה Jos 21.16) : καὶ τὴν Ατταν G.
The ending has been assimilated to Ασαν.[3] τήν was added after Ιαττα* had become corrupted by haplography.[4]

8.7 ואת־אחיחד : καὶ τὸν Ιαχειχωλ B (-ωα c₂) (O).
The name was originally Αχιχωη* (Ra.;[5] Δ/Λ) which suffered dittography before τόν was added.

v. 8 ואת־בערא : καὶ τὴν Ιβααδα B (... βααδα c₂).
B's reading can only have arisen from an original ΚΑΙΒΑΑΔΑ* (ד/ר), and καὶ Βαλαα L is significantly derived from this very reading. τόν is a later addition, found also in O R, to represent את. נשיו following is rendered γυναῖκα αὐτοῦ G O R, for which BH posits אשתו. It is rather an inner-Gk adaptation of γυναῖκας* αὐτοῦ made after the addition of τὴν which gave the wrong impression that חושים was not a wife. But the translator knew that she was, as v. 11 makes clear. Later Ιβ. was equated with Αδα γυναικὸς αὐτοῦ (v. 9).

v. 9 ואת־צביא : καὶ τὸν Ιεβια G.

---

[1] See Barthélemy, *op. cit.*, p. 17.

[2] See part II, p. 76.

[3] Albright, "List of Levitic Cities", p. 66.

[4] See part II, p. 140.

[5] "Ra." after a Gk form refers to the reading in Rahlfs' edition of the LXX. Although initial *aleph* and *yod* sometimes interchange in Heb in certain words, this is unlikely to be the case here.

Dittography again reveals the secondary nature of the article. The name was $\Sigma\epsilon\beta\iota\alpha$ O R (Ra.) before pseudohaplography of Γ.

v. 10 ואת־מרמה : $\kappa\alpha\grave{\iota}\ \tau\grave{o}\nu\ I\mu\alpha\mu\alpha$ G.
This is a similar case. $M\alpha\rho\mu\alpha$ O R (Ra.) was the original form of the name before ρ dropped out.

The conjunction is a common source of textual variety and doubtless was liable to be added or omitted by copyists more than any other word. There is evidence that $\kappa\alpha\acute{\iota}$ at times has been added to the original translation.

I 1.9 ודדן : $\kappa\alpha\grave{\iota}\ Iov\delta\alpha\delta\alpha\nu$ B ($\kappa\alpha\grave{\iota}\ I\delta ov\delta\alpha\nu$ c₂).
$Ov\delta\alpha\delta\alpha\nu$* (Ra.) was the earlier form : ו was taken as part of the name, and $\kappa\alpha\acute{\iota}$ was added later for Gk style or to correspond to the Heb.

v. 37 ומזה : $\kappa\alpha\grave{\iota}\ O\mu o\zeta\epsilon$ B ($Mo\zeta\epsilon$ c₂ = O).
$\kappa\alpha\acute{\iota}$ has again been supplied.

2.33 וזא : $\kappa\alpha\grave{\iota}\ O\zeta\alpha\mu$ G.
$\kappa\alpha\acute{\iota}$ is secondary, ו being originally regarded as part of the name. It was at first $O\zeta\alpha\zeta\alpha$ A N Arm (Ra.), and became $O\zeta\alpha$ i by parablepsis, then $O\zeta\alpha\mu$ by assimilation to $(P)\alpha\mu(\epsilon\eta\lambda)$.

v. 53 והפותי : ($A\iota\theta\alpha\lambda\epsilon\iota\mu$) $\kappa\alpha\grave{\iota}\ M\epsilon\iota\phi\epsilon\iota\theta\epsilon\iota\mu$ ($Mo\phi\theta\epsilon\iota\nu$ c₂) G R.
M has come about by dittography before $\kappa\alpha\acute{\iota}$ was added. Cf. $H\phi\iota\theta\epsilon\iota\nu$ A N.

4.29f. תולד : ובבתואל : $\Theta ov\lambda\alpha\epsilon\mu$. $\kappa\alpha\grave{\iota}\ B\alpha\theta ov\nu$ (-ov c₂) G.
This originally read $\Theta ov\lambda\alpha\delta$ a c e n (Ra.; assimilated to $\epsilon\rho\mu\alpha$) $\dot{\epsilon}\nu$ $B\alpha\theta ov\eta\lambda$ L R (Ra.; H/N error and λ omitted). $\kappa\alpha\acute{\iota}$ is a later addition, probably to render ו.

8.30 בעל ונדב : $B\alpha\alpha\lambda\alpha\kappa\alpha\iota\mu$ ($B\alpha\lambda\alpha$- c₂) $A\delta\alpha\delta$ G.
Wrong division has again occurred in this example. The text originally read $B\alpha\alpha\lambda\ \kappa\alpha\grave{\iota}\ N\alpha\delta\alpha\beta$ (cf. O L; N/M; internal assimilation). The second $\kappa\alpha\acute{\iota}$ was added subsequently.

There are other, miscellaneous cases where omissions, apparent or real, are supplied to the original text.[1]

I 8.8 שלחו אתם חושם : $\dot{\alpha}\pi o\sigma\tau\epsilon\hat{\iota}\lambda\alpha\iota\ \alpha\dot{v}\tau\grave{o}\nu\ \Sigma\omega\sigma\iota\nu$ B, ... $\alpha\dot{v}\tau\grave{\alpha}s\ \Omega\sigma\iota\nu$ c₂.
c₂ has the earlier text. B exhibits dittography of *sigma* which occurred when $\alpha\dot{v}\tau\grave{\alpha}s$ preceded. $\alpha\dot{v}\tau\acute{o}\nu$, shared by O L (in doublet) is a replace-

---

[1] I 4.43 will be discussed in part II, p. 72.

ment to correspond to ‎־ו. The name was originally $\Omega\sigma\iota\mu$ O L R
(Ra.; M/N error): cf. v. 11.

11.11 ‎על־שלש מאות חלל בפעם אתת : $\ddot{a}\pi a\xi\ \dot{\epsilon}\pi\dot{\iota}\ \tau\rho\iota\alpha\kappa o\sigma\acute{\iota}o\upsilon s\ \tau\rho a\upsilon\mu$-
$a\tau\acute{\iota}as\ \dot{\epsilon}\nu\ \kappa a\iota\rho\hat{\omega}\ \dot{\epsilon}\nu\acute{\iota}$ G O R.
$\ddot{a}\pi a\xi$ represents the original rendering. $\dot{\epsilon}\nu\ \kappa.\ \dot{\epsilon}\nu\acute{\iota}$ is the product of
revision, reproducing the Heb phrase more literally and in MT's
position.

13.10 ‎ויחר־אף יהוה : $\kappa a\dot{\iota}\ \dot{\epsilon}\theta\upsilon\mu\acute{\omega}\theta\eta\ \kappa\acute{\upsilon}\rho\iota os$ B = II Rg. 6.7, $\kappa a\dot{\iota}\ \dot{\epsilon}\theta.$
$\dot{o}\rho\gamma\hat{\eta}\ \kappa.$ S c$_2$ O$^{mss\cdot}$ L R.
The shorter rendering in B has the more authentic ring.[1] S c$_2$ have
suffered revision.

21.24 ‎לך ליהוה : $\sigma o\dot{\iota}\ \kappa\upsilon\rho\acute{\iota}\omega$ ... $\kappa\upsilon\rho\acute{\iota}\omega$ G O (L) R.
The second $\kappa\upsilon\rho\acute{\iota}\omega$ is probably original and the first a case of supplying
an apparent omission. Doubtless it was put later to avoid the awkward
juxtaposition of two datives. Then BH's note "G + ‎ליהוה" is erroneous. Arm omits the first noun, testifying at least to its awkwardness if
not to a tradition of its non-originality.

23.9 ‎האבות ללעדן : $\pi a\tau\rho\iota\hat{\omega}\nu$ B N $\tau\hat{\omega}\nu$ G O$^{mss\cdot}$ e$_2$ $\epsilon\delta a\nu$ G.
$\tau\hat{\omega}\nu$ has displaced $\tau\hat{\omega}$ O^{mss}. R (Ra.) : it was intended to go before
$\pi a\tau.$ where c$_2$ O L R have it.

26.21f. ‎ללעדן ראשי האבות ללעדן הגרשני יחיאלי : בני יחיאלי : $\tau\hat{\omega}$
$\Lambda a a\delta a\nu\ (\Lambda a\delta a\nu$ B) $\kappa a\dot{\iota}\ I a\iota\epsilon\eta\lambda\ (I a\iota a\iota\pi a$ c$_2)\ \tau o\hat{\upsilon}\ \upsilon\acute{\iota}o\hat{\upsilon}\ (\tau o\hat{\upsilon}\ I o\upsilon\ \upsilon\acute{\iota}o\acute{\iota}$ B)
$I\epsilon\iota\eta\lambda\ \ddot{a}\rho\chi o\nu\tau\epsilon s\ \pi a\tau\rho\iota\hat{\omega}\nu\ \tau\hat{\omega}\ \Lambda a\delta a\nu\ \tau\hat{\omega}\ \Gamma\eta\rho\sigma\omega\nu\epsilon\iota\ I\epsilon\iota\eta\lambda.\ \upsilon\acute{\iota}o\dot{\iota}\ I\epsilon\iota\eta\lambda$ G.
In the earlier form of G ‎ר' האׄ' לל' was evidently missing through Heb
homoeoteleuton,[2] the repeated ‎הגרשני was omitted as superfluous[3]
and $\kappa a\acute{\iota}$ was inserted between the two names. c$_2$'s original $\tau o\hat{\upsilon}\ \upsilon\acute{\iota}o\hat{\upsilon}$
was caused by haplography of yod : B's reading represents corruption
by haplography of upsilon plus correction for the singular noun. The
remaining words are an addition (= O L R : Hexaplaric ?) to represent
the words originally missing in G. The name $I a\iota\epsilon\eta\lambda$ is probably a
mixture of $I\epsilon\eta\lambda$, as in 27.32 G, and $I a\iota\eta\lambda$, as in 27.32 R. The first
$I\epsilon\iota\eta\lambda$ was probably in one of those forms originally, but was changed to
the form in the addition.

27.1 ‎את־המלך לכל דבר המחלקות : $\tau\hat{\omega}\ \lambda a\hat{\omega}\ \kappa a\dot{\iota}\ \epsilon\dot{\iota}s\ \pi\hat{a}\nu\ \lambda\acute{o}\gamma o\nu\ \tau o\hat{\upsilon}$
$\beta a\sigma\iota\lambda\acute{\epsilon}\omega s\ \kappa a\tau\dot{a}\ \delta\iota a\iota\rho\acute{\epsilon}\sigma\epsilon\iota s\ \epsilon\dot{\iota}s$ (G omits by haplography) $\pi\hat{a}\nu\ \lambda\acute{o}\gamma o\nu$
G O L (R).

---

[1] Cf. p. 113, especially the examples in II 25.10; 28.11.

[2] See part II, p. 135.

[3] Cf. p. 114.

The centre of this textual maze may be reached by positing two marginal notes referring to the previous verse, 26.32 : (i) εἰς πᾶν λόγον Ιαω[1] and (ii) τοῦ βασιλέως. The first gave a closer rendering of דבר and used an older form of the divine name, in place of Par's εἰς πᾶν πρόσταγμα (λόγον O L) τοῦ κυρίου. The second gloss supplied the article to Par's βασιλέως for המלך (cf. τοῦ βασ. a f L). In 27.1 there is no reason to doubt that Par originally read τῷ βασιλεῖ * κατὰ διαιρέσεις εἰς πᾶν λόγον. The glosses referring to 26.32 in due course came into the text of 27.1, encouraged by its similar vocabulary, with a slightly different word order, displacing τῷ βασιλεῖ. The final stage was reached when τῷ Ιαω was corrupted to τῷ λαῷ by haplography of iota and pseudo-dittography of A as ΛΛ.[2] BH's note "G ... aliter" for לכל וג׳ is thus irrelevant to the student of Chron. Rudolph's comment is incorrect : "Der merkwürdige G-text legt nahe in M eine Verkürzung anzunehmen".

II 6.32　וגם : καί G O R.

v. 37　ושבו : καίγε ἐπιστρέψωσιν G O.

It was observed in ch. iv that וגם is often rendered simply καί in Par.[3] Here an attempt was made to give a separate rendering for גם, but it was misplaced and put 12 lines away in BM's text and 17 in Swete's. This is clearly a case of a marginal note being attached to the wrong column. J. C. Dancy has found three cases where comments evidently standing at the head of one column in the archetype of the mss. of I Maccabees were incorporated into the next column.[4] The verses concerned are 5.28 and 35 ; 9.34 and 43 ; 9.61 and 69. In Swete's text these places are 16, 20, 16 lines away respectively. It is significant that here in Par a similar distance lies between the revising addition and the place to which it refers. Many other cases will be noted, both in this chapter and in ch. x, where material relating to or found in one column appears in what was evidently the corresponding place in the preceding or next column, either via a marginal note or through a horizontal slide of a copyist's eye. The addition of γε is reminiscent of Barthélemy's καίγε group. This too may well be a first century A.D. attempt to make Par conform more exactly to the Heb text.

---

[1] ΙΑΩ appears in 4Q LXX Levᵇ, "a form previously known to us in manuscript only from the margin of the codex Q of the Prophets" (Skehan, Supplements to VT iv, p. 151).

[2] Cf. II 9.8 ליהוה אלהיך : τῷ κυρίῳ θεῷ σου G, τῷ λαῷ σου O, τῷ λαῷ αὐτοῦ L R ; Jer. 31/38.38 ליהוה : λαῷ S* corrected to κυρίῳ..

[3] Cf. Barthélemy, p. 41f.

[4] A Commentary on I Maccabees, pp. 9, 61, 106.

9.2 דבר משלמה אשר : λόγος ἀπὸ Σαλωμων λόγος ὅν B. ἀπὸ
Σαλομων λόγος λόγον ὃν c2.

The first λόγος is in fact the intruder: the antecedent was originally
put next to the relative by stylistic transposition. The addition is a
pedantic restoration of an equivalent for דבר in its correct place. O L R
took λόγος² as superfluous and so omitted the original rendering.

12.16 עם־אבתיו ויקבר : καὶ ἐτάφη μετὰ τῶν πατέρων αὐτοῦ καὶ
ἐτάφη (ἐν ταφῇ c2) G.

The second καὶ ἐτ., omitted by O, has been put in to correspond to the
Heb order.

17.8 הלוים ועמהם : Λευῖται οἱ μετ᾽ αὐτῶν G.

The translator rendered ה : לוים was lost by haplography. οἱ is a
correction according to the MT (cf. οἱ Λ. L), but it was misplaced, and
displaced καί. Par originally read Λ. καὶ μ. αὐτῶν f h j m.

v. 14 גבורי חיל : υἱοὶ δυνατοὶ δυνάμεως G O R.

The last two words render the Heb phrase in v. 16. The first two are
doubtless original, an instance of the translator's stylistic variation.[1]
υἱοὶ δυνατοί usually renders בני חיל, e.g. 26.17. The translation was
evidently inspired by בני חיל which the translator read in v. 7 and
retained in the back of his mind. The addition both renders the Heb
noun more exactly and conforms to v. 16. La has only the last two
words, i.e. a revised, non-conflated text.

20.22 מארבים על־בני עמון מואב : πολεμεῖν τοὺς υἱοὺς Αμμων ἐπὶ
Μωαβ G O R.

ἐπί is clearly a misplaced addition to correspond to the ostensibly
missing על.

v. 25 בהם : κτήνη G O L R; in illis La.

ibid. להם : ἐν αὐτοῖς B R, ἑαυτοῖς c2 O L.

Par attests an obviously correct Heb Vorlage, reading בהמה.² The
text of La has been "corrected" according to the MT. Later in the
verse להם is reflexive. B R's reading, obviously drawn from the same
Gk source as that of La, came in from the margin and was wrongly
taken to be a correction for the later, similar-looking word.

v. 35f. ויחברהו עמו לעשות אניות ללכת : לעשות : ἐν τῷ ποιῆσαι καὶ
πορευθῆναι πρὸς αὐτὸν τοῦ ποιῆσαι πλοῖα τοῦ πορευθῆναι G O (L)
(in doublet) (R).

---

[1] See pp. 53ff.

[2] See part II, p. 89.

The original form of text probably ran ἐν τῷ[1] ποι. πλοῖα καὶ πορ. πρὸς αὐτόν. The main verb was omitted as superfluous after אתחבר earlier, and so was לעשׂות,[2] according to a principle of ch. vii.[2] עמו was then linked with ללכת as πρὸς αὐτόν. Later it was assumed that not only לעשׂות[2] but ללכת was left untranslated: both were supplied and πλοῖα was moved to its "proper" place.

22.7 עם־יהורם ... ובבאו : καὶ ἐν τῷ (ἐξ)ελθεῖν G O ... μετ' αὐτοῦ Ιωραμ G O (L) R.

R adds αὐτόν to correspond to the suffix. In G's text, taken over by the other groups, an earlier attempt to add thus was mistakenly adapted to αὐτοῦ and linked with μετ'.

23.4 זה הדבר : νῦν ὁ λόγος οὗτος G O (L R).

זה was originally taken as an emphasising particle: cf. the renderings ἤδη Gen 43.10; Zech 7.3 and ἰδού Deut 8.4. οὗτος was added to give an equivalent for the supposedly missing זה : cf. O's addition of τοῦτο to ἰδού νῦν for עתה זה in IV Rg 5.22. In the parallel IV Rg 11.5 the earlier textform L has τοῦτο τὸ ῥῆμα and the later KR οὗτος ὁ λόγος.[3]

24.27 המשׂא עליו (Kethib; ירב Qere) ובניו ורב : καὶ οἱ υἱοὶ αὐτοῦ πάντες καὶ προσῆλθον αὐτῷ οἱ πέντε G O R.

πάντες is in an unusual position: it normally precedes its noun. L, with the support of La, has πέντε at this point, surely a survival of the original translation, which must have read simply καὶ οἱ υἱοὶ αὐτοῦ πέντε. The translator failed to understand the phrase after ובניו and discarded it, salvaging only המשׂא read as חמשׁה. Later an attempt was made to translate the whole phrase. ורב, the uncertainty of which is reflected in the existence of a Qere, was assumed to be a corruption: cf. Curtis "G ... read וקרבו, also חמשׁה". The "insight" of the first translator into המשׂא was repeated, although later the first πέντε was corrupted. It is tempting to trace back the presence of ק to a marginal abbreviation for קרי in a Heb ms., indicating a correction. For an abbreviated marginal note creeping into the text compare Perles' view, cited by G. R. Driver, that in Psa 61.8 מן is derived from מ'נ' = מלא נון, referring to יוצרו.[4]

25.18 ותעבר :καὶ ἰδοὺ ἐλεύσεται G O (L) R.

v. 26 הלא הנם : οὐκ ἰδού G O L.

---

[1] For ἐν τῷ see Soisalon-Soininen, *Die Infinitive*, p. 45f.

[2] p. 114.

[3] For textforms in Rg see pp. 175, 189.

[4] *Textus* i, p. 125.

οὐκ ἰδού is the standard rendering for הלא, but there he translator may well have had MT before him. ἰδού was set in the margin to correspond to the apparently missing הנם. But it was incorporated into the wrong column in v. 18, thirteen lines away in BM.

v. 22f. ויביאהו ... לאהליו : εἰς τὸ σκήνωμα ... καὶ εἰσήγαγεν αὐτούς G.

αὐτοῦ O L R was added to correspond to the suffix. It displaced αὐτόν O L R (Ra.) in an adapted form.

29.8 ויהי קצף : καὶ ὠργίσθη ὀργῇ B (O).

c₂ R omit ὀργῇ : it is most probably an addition to correspond to the Heb noun. Compare I 13.10 and comment earlier in this section. There is no need to posit ויחר with Wutz, p. 197.

v. 9f. עתה : על זאת : ὃ καὶ νῦν ἐστίν. ἐπὶ τούτοις νῦν ἐστίν G (O). It is not difficult to trace the growth of the text. V.10 must originally have begun καὶ νῦν ἐστὶν ἐπὶ τούτοις. The translator took על זאת with this verse, as Curtis, BH and Rudolph note. It and עתה were transposed because νῦν generally begins a sentence in Par. The translator or perhaps an early copyist prefaced νῦν with καί : καὶ νῦν is sometimes found for עתה, e.g. in 30.8 G O L. Later καὶ νῦν was linked with v. 9 by adding ὅ, influenced by the appeal to present experience at the end of v. 8. When a reviser studied the adapted translation alongside a Heb text or a close rendering of it, עתה seemed to be missing: the apparent omission was rectified by adding another νῦν ἐστίν.

v. 10 ברית ליהוה : διαθήκην μου διαθήκην κυρίου G.

μου was intended as a correcting addition to ἐπὶ καρδίας for עם־לבבי (L adds μου) : cf. I 22.7 G O ; 28.2 G O L R for the non-representation of the suffix in this phrase. The pronoun was attached by mistake to the next noun, which then had to be repeated to make sense of κυρίου.

30.10 משחיקים : ὡς καταγελῶντες G O L R

v. 18 בלא ככתוב : παρὰ τὴν γραφήν G O L R.

ὡς was probably originally a marginal addition to correspond to כ. It was placed in the wrong column (12 lines away in BM).

II Ki 24.2/36.5b עמון : + τῆς Σαμαρίας G O L R ;

v. 3/5c בחטאת : διά B* = G.

The last rendering was originally διὰ τὰς ἁμαρτίας Bᵃᵇ O L R. Eleven letters were lost, a clear case of line omission.[1] The omitted words were added in the margin and then incorporated into v. 5b in a slightly

---

[1] Cf. part II, p. 150.

different form to fit the preceding names. O L R duly took over the error, and it even travelled as far afield as the L text in Rg, where *contra* Burney it does not go back to a Heb original.

36.17 וְלֹא חָמַל עַל־בָּחוּר וּבְתוּלָה : καὶ οὐκ ἐφείσατο τοῦ Σεδεκίου καὶ τὰς παρθένους αὐτῶν οὐκ ἠλέησαν Gₐ(O) L (R).

Originally the clause ran καὶ τοὺς νεανίσκους* (so בָּחוּרֵיהֶם is rendered earlier in the verse) καὶ τὰς κτλ. οὐκ ἐφείσατο was later added under the impression that לֹא חָמַל was not represented, an impression strengthened no doubt by the fact that φειδόμενος G O L R renders חָמַל in v. 15; the translator is varying his vocabulary.[1] Since this verb takes the genitive case ΤΟΥCΝΕΑΝΙCΚΟΥC was easily corrupted to ΤΟΥCΕΔΕΚΙΟΥ (ᴀ/ᴧ, c/є), especially as the event took place in Zedekiah's reign. Rogers, p. 44f., tortuously endeavours to ascribe the present Gk to the translator.

2. PARAPHRASE LITERALLY RENDERED

I 4.2 בֶּן־שׁוּבָל : υἱὸς αὐτοῦ καὶ Σουβαλ G O (R).

The last two words are secondary. αὐτοῦ was originally put for the name because the person had just been mentioned.[2]

4.22 בְּעָלוּ : κατῴκησαν G O R

v. 23 יָשְׁבוּ : ἐνίσχυσαν καὶ κατῴκησαν G O (L) R.

The first verb in v. 23 is a misplaced correction of the verb in v. 22, an equivalent found also in Isa 62.5 LXX. It was evidently felt to be too weak and a verb expressing control was preferred : cf. ἐξουσίασαν L.

6.39/54 לְמִשְׁפַּחַת הַקְּהָתִי : τῇ πατρίᾳ αὐτῶν τοῦ Κααθει G (R).

Originally τῶν Κ. * must have stood here: cf. 9.5 הַשִּׁילוֹנִי : τῶν Σηλωνει G (R). τοῦ was added for a closer rendering, just as in 9.5 τῶν becomes τοῦ in O L. Then τῶν was adapted to αὐτῶν for sense.

8.24 וַחֲנַנְיָה : + καὶ Αμβρει (Αμρι c₂) G O ;

v. 36 וְזִמְרִי הוֹלִיד : καὶ ἐγέννησεν Ζαμβρει G.

The addition in v. 24 must originally have read καὶ Ζαμβρει*. It was intended as a gloss on v. 36, correcting the order according to the Heb. The correction was placed instead in the preceding column (11 lines away in BM) and the initial letter was dropped by assimilation to the sequence of names beginning with A in the new context.[3] BH wrongly notes "Gᴮᴬ + וְעָמְרִי"; Rudolph suggests omission in MT.

---

[1] Cf. p. 55.

[2] This practice was illustrated on p. 46.

[3] The two names are confused elsewhere in the LXX: cf. Rahlfs, *LXX-Studien*, iii, pp. 128, 285.

12.2 בקשת ... נשקי קשת : τόξῳ G O R ... τόξοις G O R.

τοξόται* most probably once stood at the beginning of the verse: cf. II 17.17 נ' ק' : τοξόται G O L R. τόξῳ was intended as a closer rendering for בקשת (cf. τόξῳ L), but it displaced the similar looking word in v. 2. It is unlikely that Par omitted נשקי *contra* Benzinger and Curtis. In v. 1 עזרי המלחמה becomes βοηθοῦντες ἐν πολέμῳ G O (L) R. Was ἐν originally part of a marginal correction ἐν τόξῳ ?

16.8 קראו בשמו : ἐπικαλεῖλεῖσθε αὐτὸν ἐν ὀνόματι αὐτοῦ G O L. The last three words are secondary. The translator paraphrased, using simply αὐτόν, a good Gk construction. f Boh omit αὐτόν, attesting a revised, non-conflated text.

22.12 לשמור את־תורת : τοῦ φυλάσσεσθαι καὶ τοῦ ποιεῖν τὸν νόμον G O (L) R.

τοῦ ποιεῖν is surely original: Par is being typically free in the interchange of synonymous terms. Compare 28.7 לעשות : τοῦ φυλάξασθαι G O L (in doublet) R, where Rothstein and BH unnecessarily posit לשמור, and 29.19 לשמור : ποιεῖν G O L R. Here the correction of the paraphrase has been incorporated into the text. BH's view "G ins ולעשות" is less likely.

26.1 לקרחים : υἱοὶ Κορεειμ G.

G doubtless originally read υἱοῖς O¹ Κορε O L, a loose rendering which does not require BH's recourse to לבני קרח. The name-ending is an adjustment to the Heb.

v. 20 האלהים ... הקדשים : τοῦ κυρίου G O L R ...τῶν καθηγιασμένων G O R.

v. 28 ההקדיש שמואל : τῶν ἁγίων τοῦ θεοῦ Σαμαυηλ G O L R.

τοῦ θεοῦ, omitted only by A, is out of place in the context of v. 28. According to Schleusner the words were added because a copyist thought ἅγια Σαμ. not fitting.[2] A more likely suggestion may be put forward. In the margin of v. 20 at some stage stood two correcting glosses: τῶν ἁγίων correcting to the standard rendering, as in v. 26, and τοῦ θεοῦ according to MT. These notes were read together and falsely taken as a correction of τῶν ἁγίων in v. 28.

29.11 והמתנשא לכל לראש : ἀπὸ προσώπου σου ταράσσεται πᾶς βασιλεὺς καὶ ἔθνος G O L (in doublet) R.

v. 12 מלפניך ואתה מושל בכל : παρά σου G O L (in doublet) R

---

¹ See part II, p. 7.

² *Lexicon*, ii, p. 48. Similarly Rogers, p. 16, suggests that the translator added to stress that the holy things really belonged to God.

(ditto) ... σὺ πάντων ἄρχεις κύριε ὁ ἄρχων πάσης ἀρχῆς G O L R ... παντοκράτωρ G O (L R).

Several factors have been at work and created a rather tangled textual skein, which may, with patience, be unravelled.[1] ἀπὸ π. σου is a misplaced literal rendering of מלפניך in v. 12: compare L R's addition of ἐκ π. σου. κύριε ... ἀρχῆς represents another attempt to render the clause in v. 11, as Rudolph has seen and briefly noted. κύριε is an error for καί* via κ̄ε̄.[2] The new version was misplaced due to its similarity to the Gk of v. 12. παντοκράτωρ later in the verse has no equivalent in MT.[3] It was probably intended as a standardizing alternative for ὁ ... ἀρχῆς, conceived after the corruption of καί to κύριε. According to Rogers, p. 19, the translator made both additions, to amplify God's prestige.

II 9.17 כסא־שן : θρόνον ἐλεφάντινον ὀδόντων G O (L) R.
Second thoughts reject the idea of a gloss assimilating to the parallel III Rg 10.18 which has θρ. ἐλεφ. ἐλεφάντινος is a common enough LXX rendering of שן in the sense of ivory; cf. v. 21 שנהבים : ὀδόντων ἐλεφαντίνων G O L R. ὀδόντων could conceivably be an addition from v. 21, but it looks very much like a literalist's correction: cr. Psa 45/44.9 שן היכלי : βάρεων ἐλεφαντίνων LXX; ναῶν ὀδόντος Aquila according to Eusebius.[4]

14.7/8 נשא צנה ורמח : ὁπλοφόρων αἰρόντων θυρεοὺς καὶ δόρατα G O L R La.
The last four words represent a gloss providing a more literal and complete rendering. The translator varies in translating such phrases: cf. I 12.9/8 ערכי צנה ורמח : αἴροντες θυρεοὺς καὶ δόρατα G O R; v. 25/24 נשאי צ׳ ור׳ : θυρεωφόροι καὶ δορατοφόροι G O (R). Here a compound noun is in keeping with πελτασταὶ καὶ τοξόται G O L R for נשאי מגן ודרכי קשת later in this verse. Probably one noun is used because the Heb refers to a single type of soldier. ὁπλο — must refer to the large shield or צנה as in several cases in the LXX, e.g. I Rg 17.7, even though ὅπλον is not found with this meaning in Par: the alternative meaning "weapon-bearers" would be out of place alongside other specialized troops in the verse. The translator loosely used one noun to cover the three Heb words: a reviser ignored the style of the

---

[1] For καὶ ἔθνος see part II, p. 102f.

[2] Cf. et Boh for κύριε ὁ ἄρχων, and also καί c2 for κύριε in 17.20.

[3] κύριος παντοκράτωρ is Par's standard phrase for יהוה צבאות (as in LXX of Jer and the Minor Prophets), which is why L R insert κύριε.

[4] Cited in Field, Origenis Hexaplorum, ad Psa.

verse as a whole and provided a more literal rendering. Jos. *Ant.*
viii. 291 evidently paraphrased an already revised text of Par :
ὡπλισμένων θυρεὸν καὶ σιρομάστην.[1]

15.17 והבמות לא־סרו מישראל : πλὴν τὰ ὑψηλὰ οὐκ ἀπέστησαν
ἔτι ὑπῆρχεν ἐν τῷ Ἰσραηλ G (O L R).
The type of paraphrase whereby a positive statement is rendered
negatively has already been noted in Par.[2] The opposite is found in
20.33 אך הבמות לא־סרו : ἀλλὰ τὰ ὑψηλὰ ἔτι ὑπῆρχεν G O (R), and
Rehm, p. 25, compares at this point the significant rendering there.
Here the paraphrase naturally extended to ἐν for מ-. οὐκ ἀπ. is the
product of a literalistic revision which even reproduces a plural verb,
despite the neuter plural subject, in keeping with the Heb.

16.4 וישלח את־שרי ... אל־ערי : καὶ ἀπέστειλεν πρὸς τοὺς ἄρχοντας
G ...ἐπὶ τὰς πόλεις G O L R.
πρός is a correction of ἐπί, rendering אל more exactly. It was misplaced
by analogy with ἀπέστειλεν πρός in v. 2. Rehm, p. 60, wrongly
states that Par read אל for את.

29.12 בן־יואח : οὗτοι υἱοί (c₂ omits) Ἰωαχα G. ὁ τοῦ O L is original:
it has occurred four times before in this verse, and so is stylistically
fitting. υἱοί is a literal correction according to a Heb text which read
בני by dittography. Subsequently ὁ τοῦ was adapted to οὗτοι for
sense. BH's suggestion "G^{BA} אלה בני" is less likely.

30.24 מלך־יהודה הרים לקהל : ἀπήρξατο τῷ Ἰουδα τῇ ἐκκλησίᾳ G
O (R).
See ch. vii.[3] For the loose rendering compare τῷ λαῷ G O L R for
קהל.[2]

31.18 להתיחש : ἐνκαταλοχίσαι G.
ἐν καταλοχίαις O R (Ra.) is doubtless original, although the form of
noun is ἅπ. λεγ. according to Liddell and Scott. G has artificially
adapted to an infinitive form according to the Heb. Cf. v. 17 התיחש :
καταλοχισμός.

32.31 עליו : πρὸς αὐτὸν ... παρ' αὐτοῦ G O L R.
The second phrase was doubtless παρ' αὐτόν* originally, a closer
translation of the Heb. It was incorporated into the text a little further
on and adapted slightly to suit its new position.

34.12 הלוים כל־מבין : πᾶς Λευείτης πᾶς συνίων G (L R).

---

[1] Cf. the substitution of σιρομάσται in *Ant.* viii. 247 for δόρατα II Par. 11.12.

[2] p. 41.

[3] p. 119f.

The translator rendered loosely, as in 30.22 לֵב כָּל־הָלְוִים : πᾶσαν καρδίαν τῶν Λευιτῶν G O R. The second πᾶς is an attempt to render the Heb more exactly.

35.7 בְּנֵי עִזִּים : ἐρίφους ἀπὸ τῶν τέκνων τῶν αἰγῶν O R (L).
G reads as O R apart from the error ἀγίων for αἰγῶν. בְּנֵי is obviously doubly represented. Probably ἐρίφους was glossed with a more literal τὰ τέκνα* which was in due course incorporated into the text in the genitive.[1] In the parallel I Esdr. 1. 7 b Syh, which frequently assimilate to Par, omit ἐρίφους, either citing loosely, as the omission of πάντα after αἰγῶν may suggest, or revealing the hand of a subsequent reviser who struck out ἐρίφους as otiose without adapting the rest of the phrase.

3. Correction of Gk corruption

Many names appear in a notoriously corrupt form in G. This fact was clearly recognised at an early stage, and attempts were made to repair the damage at various points.

I 1.4f. בְּנֵי יֶפֶת : וָיֶפֶת : Αφεθ B*vid υἱοὶ Ιαφεθ G O L (R).
Probably Αφεθ stood in v. 5 at an earlier stage by haplography, and the name in v. 4 was made to conform. Later only the form in v. 5 was corrected.

I 2.10/9f. וָרָם : καὶ Αραμ. καὶ Αρραν G.
The second form is the earlier one.[2] The correction was no doubt originally Ραμ* but the phrase was linked with v. 9 and then differentiated from Ραμ earlier in the verse, as a fourth son.

v. 25 אָרָן : Αραια καὶ Αραν h (...Αραμι, Αβραμ c₂, Αμβαμ B).
Rothstein rightly saw a doublet here. The second name is a revision which itself deteriorates step by step in the G mss. Αραια was doubtless originally Αραν, but its ending became assimilated to the adjacent Βαναια.

v. 32 יָדַע : Ιδουδα B, Ιδουλα c₂.
Ιδα* (cf. Ιεδα e m) became Ιδου, a familiar word, and then the correction was added on.

v. 51 אֲבִי בֵית לֶחֶם : πατὴρ Βαιθα Λαμμων πατὴρ Βαιθαλαεμ B, π. Βαιθλαμμων π. Βαιθλεεμ A N g, π. Βαιθαλαεμ c₂.

---

[1] For the insertion of the preposition cf. Gen 38.20 גְּדִי הָעִזִּים : ἔριφον ἐξ αἰγῶν and also p. 45.

[2] See p. 186.

The first rendering in B A N g became corrupted under the influence of Σαλωμων just before, and was corrected by the second form, which in turn became partially corrupted: it was Βαιθλαεμ at first, as in G at v. 54. c₂ has excised the worse of the forms.

3.18 נדביה : Δενεθει G;

4.7 אתנן : Σεννων G.

The first part of the name in 3.18 has suffered metathesis.[1] But what of the second part ? εθει was surely intended as a partial correction of Σεννων in the next column (13 lines away in BM) : cf. Εθηναν i. It displaced -αβια L or the like in 3.18.

ibid. חלאה : Λοαδας B*, Θοαδας Bᵇ, ʼAωδας c₂.

Bᵇ is original: cf. Θοαδα v. 5. In B* Λ, a correction of Δ, displaced Θ. c₂ has a corruption of B*, assimilated to ʼAωδας (= נערה) in v. 6.

v. 16 יהללאל זיף : Γεσεηλ Αμηαχει G.

Rothstein calls the basis of Γ. an "unlösbares Rätsel". It is clearly a corrupted secondary representation of the first name. It probably became assimilated to Ισερεηλ c₂ (-ρα- B O is surely influenced by -ρα just before) at the end of the verse, then dropped ερ by parablepsis and suffered a I/Γ error. The second name in G is a combination of two: ΑΛΛΗΛ. ΖΕΙ* (ΛΛ/Μ, Λ/Α, Ζ/Χ). Φ has been dropped.

v. 17 שמי : Σεμεν B, Σεμερ c₂.

Σεμεν comes from Σεμεαι* : ΑΙ was intended as a correcticn of the itacism E, but became incorporated as N. Cf. Σεμ(μ)αι O R. ερ in c₂ is a cursive error for εν.[2]

v. 42 ישעי : Ιεσθεν B (Εσθ-c₂).

The name was originally Ιεσσαι*, cf. Ιεσαι g. It became Ιεσσε*, then ΑΙ was added to the name as a correction, but it became N. A c/Θ error completed the corruption.

5.5f. בעל ... בארה : Ιωηλ G L (in doublet) ... Βεηλ (Βαιηλ c₂) G. The first name has become assimilated to the name in v. 4. The second is a revising gloss which displaced the equivalent for בארה.

v. 19 נפיש ... נודב : Ναφεισαδαιων B i (-εσ- c₂) ... Ναδαβαιων B Oᵐˢˢ, Ναβαδαιων c₂ Oᵐˢˢ.

Ναβ. must earlier have stood in B to influence the preceding word. It has evidently been corrected according to the Heb or a better preserved Gk mss.

6.27/42 איתן : Αιθαν B, Αιθαμ c₂.

---

[1] Gilbert, *AJSL* xiii, p. 291.

[2] Cf. Rahlfs, *LXX-Studien*, iii, p. 62, for this type of error.

In v. 44 G L have $Aιθαμ$. The next name in v. 42 is $Zαμμαμ$ in B for זמה, a form clearly influenced by a preceding $Aιθαμ$, which has since been corrected in B.

v. 53f./68f. אילון ... יקמעם : $Iνικααμ$ c₂, $Iκααμ$ B ... $Eκλαμ$ c₂, $Eγλαμ$ B.

A correction has displaced the equivalent for אילון. The first and earlier form was originally $Iκμααμ$* (cf. c₂ : M/NI and metathesis); the second form was $Iεκμααμ$ = N n in v. 68 (haplography of $ι$ after $καί$). G often represents initial *yod* with *iota*, while the other textforms prefer IE or IA.

7.3 עזי יזרחיה ... מיכאל ועבדיה : $Zειρρει$ $Zαρεια$ G ... $Mειχαηλ$ G ...$Mειβδεια$ B, $Aβδια$ c₂.

$Zαρεια$, originally $Iζ$.*, is a correction. $Zειρρει$ was formed by a fusion of $Oζι$ O L R and $Iζαρεια$*. A similar phenomenon is found in B in the second case.

v. 15 שפים : $Mαμφειν$ ($Aμφειν$ c₂) G.

The form comes from $Σαπφειν$* ($Π/M$), as in v. 12. M, a correction for the final consonant, displaced $Σ$.

v. 19f. תחת ... אניעם : $Aλιαλειμ$ B, $Eλιαμειν$ c₂ ... $Nοομε$ B, $Nοεμε$ c₂, $Nομεε$ O.

The second name has displaced the equivalent for תחת. It is another attempt to render the first name.

v. 25 בנו ו. : $υἱοῦ$ B*.

B^b rightly corrects the parablepsis of B* to $υἱοὶ$ $αὐτοῦ$: later in this verse בנו ו. was read as $υἱοὶ$ $αὐτοῦ$ G O R, and the same occurred here. But another corrector had been at work in earlier times: $υἱοί$ before $Oζαν$ in v. 24 has no equivalent in MT and is surely a misplaced marginal correction in part of $υἱοῦ$ in B*. It does not stand for בני in place of את *contra* Rothxtein. The misplaced correction was taken over in G O R.

v. 31 מלכיאל : $Mελλειη$ B ($Mελιη$ c₂).

$Mελχιηλ$ O L R (Ra) is original. $Λ$, intended to complete the end of the name, displaced X.

v. 32 יפלט : $Iφαμηλ$ G.

$Λ$ was probably originally a correction of M but it displaced the wrong consonant.

v. 36 ברי : $Σαβρει$ G.

v. 37 בצר : $Σοβαλ$ G.

It is most likely the form in v. 36 has suffered Gk corruption, which may have come about in the following way. The name in v. 37 is probably corrupted from $B\alpha\sigma\alpha\delta*$.[1] ʙᴀᴄ was put in the margin to correct the first syllable. It displaced the first syllable of $B\alpha\rho\iota$ O R immediately above $\Sigma o\beta\alpha\lambda$ in the preceding line, creating the form $B\alpha\sigma\rho\epsilon\iota*$ which was subsequently transposed into $\Sigma\alpha\beta\rho\epsilon\iota$.

8.1 אשבל ... בעל : $B\epsilon\lambda\epsilon\lambda\epsilon\eta\lambda$ ($B\epsilon\sigma$- c₂) ... $\Sigma\alpha\beta\alpha$ G.
-$\eta\lambda$ on the first name is a misplaced correction for the end of the second: cf. $A\sigma\beta\eta\lambda$ O L R. The first name was originally probably $B\alpha\lambda\epsilon$ O L R (so G in v. 3): $B\epsilon$ is due to $B\epsilon\nu\iota\alpha\mu\epsilon\iota\nu$, then errors of A/Λ and dittography occurred. The second name comes no doubt from $E\sigma\alpha\beta\alpha\lambda*$ (AI dropped after KAI; pseudo-haplography of A): cf. 4.21 אשבע : $E\sigma o\beta\alpha$ G O R.

v. 5 שפופן וחורם : $\Sigma\omega\phi\alpha\rho\phi\alpha\kappa$ G $\kappa\alpha\grave{\iota}$ $\Omega\iota\mu$ G O.
P was inserted by way of correction into the wrong word. The phrase was originally $\Sigma\omega\phi\alpha\phi\alpha\nu*$ (κ by dittography, ending assimilated to $\Gamma\epsilon\rho\alpha$) κ. $\Omega\rho\iota\mu*$. BH wrongly cites L as "G^B" with respect to שׁ.

v. 9 מלכם ... חדש : $A\delta\alpha$ G O R ...$M\epsilon\lambda\chi\alpha\varsigma$ (-$\epsilon\alpha\chi$- c₂) G.
The first name was originally $A\delta\alpha\varsigma*$; the ending was assimilated to $B\alpha\alpha\delta\alpha$ v. 8. Rothstein and BH wrongly take it back to a *Vorlage* בעדא, as Rudolph observes. ς was added as a correction to the wrong name. The second name was earlier $M\epsilon\lambda\chi\alpha*$, assimilated to the -$\alpha$ endings, and originally $M\epsilon\lambda\chi\alpha\mu$ O.

v. 15 זבדיה :$A\zeta\alpha\beta\alpha\beta\iota\alpha$ G.
The form was originally $Z\alpha\beta\alpha\delta\iota\alpha$ b i, as in v. 17. A was originally Δ, intended as a correction of the second B caused by internal assimilation, but misplaced.

v. 24 ענתתיה : $A\nu\omega\theta\alpha\iota\theta$ $\kappa\alpha\grave{\iota}$ $A\theta\epsilon\iota\nu$ G (O).
The form was earlier $A\nu\omega\theta\alpha\theta\iota*$,[2] perhaps assimilated in ending to $A\mu\beta\rho\epsilon\iota$. After the ending was transposed, an attempt was made to correct it. -$\alpha\theta\epsilon\iota$ in $M\alpha\chi\alpha\nu\alpha\theta\epsilon\iota$[3] G (O) R for מחנת 8.6 appears to be a correction displacing -$\alpha\theta$, placed in the wrong column (12 lines away in BM). The name here was later glossed $\alpha\theta\epsilon\iota\alpha*$ to indicate its ending in accordance with the Heb. This gloss was taken as a separate name and incorporated with $\kappa\alpha\iota$. The final A became N by partial dittography of K.

v. 26 עתליה : $O\gamma o\theta o\lambda\iota\alpha$ G.
The name was originally $\Gamma o\theta*$. It became $O\gamma\theta*$ by metathesis. The second o was intended as a correction. Cf. 24.13 below.

---

[1] Cf. part II, p. 113.

[2] From $A\nu\alpha\theta\omega\theta\iota*$? cf. $A\nu\alpha\theta\omega\theta\iota\alpha$ O L.

[3] BH mis-spells the Gk form.

v. 27 וִיעֲרְשִׁיה : καὶ Ιασαρια καὶ Σαραια G.

The pre-revision is the second, corrupted under the influence of Σαραια in v. 26. A correction has been added, no doubt Ιαρασαια*, but P and Σ became transposed owing to three cαp syllables in the context. It is unnecessary to ask with BH whether וִיעְשְׂרָא should be read with G^B.

v. 36 וְאֶת־יְהוֹעֵדָה וִי׳ : τὸν Ιαδ καὶ Ιαδα καὶ Ιαδα B.

c$_2$ omits one κ. Ιαδα. It probably represents not simply dittography in B but a correction of the corrupt name earlier.

v. 39 יְעוּשׁ ... אֱלִיפֶלֶט : Γαγ ... Ελιφαλεις B.

ς on the second name is a misplaced correction of Ιαι*, the original of Γαγ, into Ιαις c$_2$. The name was originally Ελιφαλετ O R (T/I).

9.12 מַעֲשַׂי : Μαασαια (Μασ- h c$_2$) G.

v. 21 מְשֻׁלֵּמִיה : Μασαλαμι G (O).

The two words were adjacent (12 lines away in BM). After an accidental omission of A in v. 21 A was put by way of correction on the similar-looking word in the previous column. There is no cause to posit מַעֲשִׂיה with BH.

11.40 גֶּרֶב : Γαρηοβαι (-βε S c$_2$) G.

The form was originally Γαρηβ O L (Ra.). Iota has come by dittography; the name was earlier Γαρηβα*, with the ending assimilated to Ιρα. o was meant as ό, a misplaced correction to correspond to (יתדי)ה following. Ιοθηρει G is an error for ό Ιθηρει*, as in S earlier.

v. 45 יְדִיעֲאֵל : Ελθειηλ G.

The form was earlier Εθιηλ*, having suffered assimilation to the original Εθθι* (cf. Εθθει O) in 12.11 in the next column (13 lines away in BM). It was originally Ιεδιηλ O L R (Ra) : iota was lost by haplography. Λ was originally Δ, an attempt to correct Θ.

ibid. יַחָא ... הַתִּיצִי : Ιωαζαε G O ... ό Ιεασει G.

In the first name AE was intended as a correction of Ιωαδ, read by parallel assimilation to Rg, for Ιωδαε O R, the usual form for יְהוֹיָדַע in v. 24 in the preceding column (13 lines away in BM). The name was probably originally Ιχα* (cf. Ηλα L, probably from Ηχα*) or Ιαχα*, which developed into Ιωχα* by assimilation to Ιωσαφατ v. 43 and then into Ιωαζ* by X/Z error and metathesis. R reads Ιεεας, which suggests that Ιεασ- in the second form is a correction according to R's form which displaced part of the equivalent for הַתִּיצִי.

24.13 חֻפָּה : Οχχοφφα B, Οχοφφα c$_2$.

The name was originally Χοφφα*; it became corrupted by metathesis. Χο or o is a correction. Cf. 11.26, discussed above.

26.14 יוֹעֵץ : Σωαζ G.

The name was earlier *Ιωαζ** and originally *Ιωας* O L R (Ra.). *Σ* is a correction of *ζ*, which was no doubt written under the influence of *Ιωζαβαθ* in v. 4 in the previous column (11 lines away in BM).

II 20.14 יעיאל : *Ελεαηλ* B a c e.
Originally עיאל was read by wrong word-division.[1] *ΑΙΑΗΛ** became first *ΕΑΗΛ** and then *ΕΛΗΛ**. *EA* was added above the line by way of correction, but became wrongly incorporated. *Ελεηλ* c₂ O R is an adaptation of B's form. BH wrongly suggests that אליאל may underlie the Gk.

22.11 אחזיהו : + *καὶ Ιωραμ ἀδελφοί* c₂, *καὶ Ιωδαε* ("δαε sup ras" BM) *ἀδ.* B*.
Ιωραμ was doubtless the earlier form in B. The correction *Ιωδαε* appears to be an attempt to remove the awkward mention of Jehoram at this point. *Ιωραμ* was intended as a correction of *Ιωας* for יהורם earlier, an error due to assimilation to *Ιωας* at the beginning of the verse. It has been falsely incorporated into the text. *ἀδελφοί* is apparently a subsequent harmonising gloss noting that this particular Jehoram must have been a brother of Ahaziah.

26.11 מעשיהו : *'Αμασαίου* B.
A is a correction which was misplaced due to *'Αμασείας* in v. 4 adjacent in the preceding column (12 lines away in BM). The name was originally *Μααυαίου** (Ra.) : cf. *Μασαίου* c₂.

Apart from names attempts were made to correct other types of inner-Gk corruption.

I 9.1 הגלו : *μετὰ τῶν κατοικισθέντων* B, *μ. τῶν μετοικισθ.* c₂, *μ. τῶν ἀποικισθ.* O R.
At an earlier stage G must have had simply *τῶν κατ.*, a corruption of an original *τῶν μετ.* (cf. c₂) agreeing with *τῶν βασιλέων.*[2] The corruption was due to the influence of *κατοικοῦντες* in v. 2 and *κατῴκησαν* in v. 3. *μετοικίζειν* is Par's standard rendering for גלה (e.g. 8.6) except at II 36.20 where *ἀποικίζειν* is used. *μετά* has developed from *μετ*, a correction of the prepositional prefix but it became incorporated into the text. Rothstein and BH wrongly assume that בַּמְגִלִים underlies Par.

15.28 בנבלים וכנרות : *νάβλαις* G O^mss *καὶ ἐν κινύραις* G O L R.

---

[1] See part II, p. 106.
[2] For the style of rendering cf. p. 42.

ἐν Omss. L was omitted before ναβ. after -ες and later replaced in the wrong position.

26.32   בני חיל : υἱοὶ οἱ δυνατοί G.

υἱοὶ δυνατοί O L R (Ra.) is original. It became οἱ δυν. by the same error as in v. 30.[1] The correction has come into the text.

II 1.16f.   ויעלו ... מקרא : πορεύεσθαι B Omss (c₂ omits) ... ἐνέβαινον G.

The infinitive was originally ἔμπορ. a c e m n = מִקְרָא.[2] ἐμ was omitted by error. ἐμ or ἐν was added to correct the error, but it was associated with the wrong verb and displaced ἀν(έβαινον) O L R.

11.12   ובכל עיר ועיר : κατὰ πόλιν καὶ κατὰ πόλιν G.
The last three words, absent from O L R, are secondary.[3] καί fell out before κατά. The corrected phrase was added to the text.

14.6/7   ויצליחו ... וינח לנו : καὶ κατέπαυσεν ἡμᾶς G O L ... καὶ εὐόδωσεν ἡμῖν G O.

ἡμᾶς is an error for ἡμῖν R: it was assimilated to ἡμᾶς three words before. For the dative cf. v. 5/6 לו ... הניח : κατέπαυσεν αὐτῷ G O L (R). The correction was incorporated into the text after the next verb, which presupposes ויצלח, read by haplography of ו. There is no cause to assume that לנו was read in the *Vorlage* with Curtis, BH and Rudolph, still less to read ויצלח לנו for MT with Winckler[4] and Benzinger. Rogers, p. 27f., ascribes the Gk to the translator, in order to emphasise God's activity.

28.2f.   הקטיר בגיא ... עשה לבעלים : ἐποίησεν ἐν τοῖς ... ἔθυεν Γαι. G.

ἐν O L R (Ra.) was dropped by haplography after ἔθυεν. Later it was wrongly restored after ἐποίησεν.

v. 21f.   ובעת הצר : לו : αὐτῶν G. ἀλλ' ἢ τῷ θλιβῆναι G O R.
That the translator freely rendered the suffix with a plural is unlikely in view of לו : αὐτόν G O L R a few words later. It is merely an error for αὐτῷ ἦν L R. The missing letter was added, above the line doubtless, but it was taken with ἀλλ' following in view of the frequent phrase ἀλλ' ἢ, and displaced ἐν*. ἀλλ' is a good rendering for ו.[5] ἐν τῷ renders בעת in 20.22 G O L R; 29.27 G O L R. Kittel, unaware

---

[1] See part II, p. 44.

[2] See part II, p. 122.

[3] For the rendering cf. p. 46.

[4] *Alttestamentliche Untersuchungen*, p. 187.

[5] Cf. p. 41.

of this complex Gk development, reconstructed and read a *Vorlage*
כי אם לצרה לו[1] which BH follows, urging "frt 1". Rudolph rightly calls
the change graphically impossible. In fact it has no basis.

31.2 בשערי מחנות יהוה : ἐν ταῖς πύλαις ἐν ταῖς αὐλαῖς οἴκου κυρίου
G (O L).
Rudolph, with uncharacteristic lack of caution, reads חצרות for מח'
on the basis of Par, taking οἴκου as a Gk amplification. But the change
is both graphically and logically inconceivable. Curtis rightly takes
οἴκου as a free rendering of מח'.[2] The archaic Heb expression occurs in
I 9.18f., though in the singular in v. 19. The repetition of ἐν ταῖς points
suspiciously to a doublet. Goettsberger suggests that αὐλαῖς depends
upon a reading חצרי by transposition of שערי. But the doublet is more
likely to be Gk. The terms πύλη and αὐλή are frequent variants in Gk
mss.: cf. I 23.28 αὐλάς : πύλας h i y. Par generally uses πύλη for שער.
The corrupt variant was encouraged by the frequency of the phrase
αὐλὴ οἴκου, e.g. 24.21; 29.16; 33.5. The correction has here been
incorporated into the text.

32.21 ויכחד ... גבור חיל : ἐξέτριψεν ... δυνατὸν καὶ πολεμιστήν G.
KAI B[ab] O L R (Ra.), omitted after N, was subsequently inserted in
the wrong place.

4. CORRECTION OF RENDERINGS AT VARIANCE WITH THE POINTED MT

I 1.41 בני ענה : υἱοὶ Σωναν (Σωνα c2) G.
The beginning of the name suggests that υἱός earlier stood in the text,
causing dittography of ς. Then the name in v. 40 was changed accordingly in B (Ωναν c2). There is a significant Heb link with the Sebir בן. (The
name has been assimilated to Ωναν in v. 40).) A ע/צ error, claimed by
Gilbert,[3] is a less likely explanation.

4.8 בן־הרום : υἱοῦ Ιαρειμ (Αρειμ c2 vid) G O.
Again the beginning of the name suggests that υἱοῦ is a correction. υἱοί
R was probably its predecessor, leading to dittography of *iota*. This
may well go back to a *Vorlage* בני.

5.2 נְבַר באחיו : δυνατὸς ἰσχύι καὶ ἐν τοῖς ἀδελφοῖς αὐτοῦ G O L
R.

---

[1] Cf. Winckler, *op.cit.*, p. 167 : כי אם להצר לו.
[2] See p. 51 for this type of paraphrase in Par.
[3] *AJSL* xiii, p. 285.

ἰσχύι presupposes בחיל for באחיו via omission of א and dittography (ול follows).[1] What follows in the Gk is a correction according to MT.

v. 4   בנו[1] : καὶ Βαναια υἱὸς αὐτοῦ καὶ υἱοί G O (R).

Originally בנו was read as בני.[2] It was linked with the preceding name by the conjunction. Remarkably the error has been corrected twice: once by υἱοί = בני and again by the correct υἱὸς αὐτοῦ. Frankel[3] and Curtis noted a doublet here but did not mention the third representation. BH's note surely lacks a plus sign.

6.12/27   ירחם : Ἰδαερ G.

In v. 19/34 the name is rendered Ἀαλ B, Ἠδαδ c₂, from Ἰδααμ* (ד/ר). This name once stood here no doubt. EP is a correction which displaced the end of the name: cf. Ἰεροαμ O and Ἰερδααμ h, mixing O with the original G form.

7.25   תלח בנו ו : Θαλεες υἱοὶ αὐτοῦ B (c₂ omits).

Par read בניו. The *sigma* is probably a misplaced correction according to MT.

v. 26   בנו[1] : υἱῷ αὐτοῦ υἱοί G O.

Par read בני as later in the verse. The first two words are a correction according to MT.

8.21   בראיה : Βεριγα καὶ Βαραια G.

Par read בריעה, a corruption caused by the proximity of בריעה in the preceding column at 7.30.[4]

11.43   המתני : ὁ Βεθανει S, ὁ Βαιθ. B c₂.

v. 44   שמע : Σαμαθα G.

הבתני was read by the translator (מ/ב). ΜαΘΑ was placed in the margin as a correction: cf. Μαθανι O R. It affected the second form, which was originally Σαμα h m.

12.2   מאתי : ἐν τοῖς ἀδελφοῖς B.

The Gk stands for באחי. S c₂ O L R correct to ἐκ τῶν ἀδελφῶν.

20.2   מַלְכָּם : Μολχολ βασιλέως αὐτῶν B (O R).

The parallel II Rg 12.30 has the same doublet. B's form Μολχολ is the standard one for מַלְכָּם, as Ziegler observes;[5] it is generally accepted

---

[1] The error depends on MT pointing: cf. I Sam 2.9 לֹא בכח יגבר־אישׁ. But the translator took the verb as גֻּבַּר.

[2] Cf. part II, p. 84.

[3] *Vorstudien*, p. 75.

[4] Cf. part II, p. 91.

[5] *Beiträge*, p. 68.

as original. The last two words correct according to MT.[1] c₂ has simply
Μολμοχ, probably a corruption of revision according to Μολχομ O.

v. 4 ספי : Σαφουτ G.

The Gk was probably originally Σαφου R (Ra.) = ספו. τ was originally
ι, correcting according to MT: cf. Σαπφι L.

24.31 אבות הראש : πατριάρχαι Ααραβ G.

The translator had הראב before him.[2] Doubtless he originally wrote
πατριαὶ Ααραβ : אבות in this sense is generally πατριαί in Par. -άρχαι
is a rendering according to MT.

25.4 ירימות : Αμσου καὶ Ιερεμωθ G.

The first form, going back to ידמות, is original.[3]

v. 9 השני הוא י : ὁ δεύτερος Ηνια G O R.

P. Katz rightly detected a doublet here and postulated an original
Σηνι*, corrupted by haplography of *sigma* and dittography of *alpha*. [4]
But the original form and its relation to the *Vorlage* and MT require
further investigation. הוא י is apparently not represented in Par. It
may be suggested that in fact Σηνια* was the original form, standing
for שניהו : names ending in הו- are rendered in the same way as those
ending in ה-. ה was lost after הו, and או in front of אח by parablepsis.
Katz regarded ὁ δεύτ. as Hexaplaric.

26.7 סמכיהו : Σαβχεια καὶ Ισβακωμ G (O L R).

Rothstein correctly saw a Gk doublet here, in which ב was read for מ.
The ending of the second and earlier form he explained as going back
to ום for יהו via י/ו, ה/מ and haplography of ו (but how can this last
be ?) But inner-Gk correction may have to be reckoned with even in
this form : perhaps ωΜ is a corruption of CEΜ intended as the
beginning of the word.

v. 27 מן־המלחמות : ἃ ἔλαβεν ἐκ (+ τῶν c₂ O R) πόλεων G O (L) R
... ἀπ᾽ αὐτῶν G O L R.

The translator read אשר נשא מן־המ׳.[5] ἀπ᾽ αὐτῶν was originally
ἀπὸ τῶν*, rendering according to MT, article and all. It was incorporated into the Gk in an adapted form.

27.34 אחרי : μετὰ τοῦτον ... ἐχόμενος G O L R.

---

[1] For the revision represented in the Massoretic vocalisation see Geiger, *Urschrift*,[2]
p. 306.

[2] See part II, p. 92.

[3] See part II, p. 77.

[4] *TZ* v, p. 13. Katz was in fact anticipated by Wutz, *op. cit.*, p. 56.

[5] See part II, p. 102.

Originally אַחֲרָו was read. ἐχόμενος is a misplaced correction of the error.

II 15.9 הַגֵּרִנם : τοὺς προσηλύτους τοὺς παροικοῦντας G O L R. The second element is a correction according to MT. La omits it, attesting a pre-revised Gk text. The first implies הַגֵּרִים, which is frequently so translated in Par, e.g., 2.16/17.

25.18 וְתַעֲבֹר חית : καὶ ... ἐλεύσεται τὰ θηρία ... καὶ ἦλθαν τὰ θηρία G (O L R). Rehm, p. 25, saw here a Gk doublet. The first clause is earlier, taking the *waw* as weak and making the clause part of the thistle's message. The plural verb in the second clause is a sign of a different translator.

31.13 בניהו : Βαναίας καὶ οἱ υἱοὶ αὐτοῦ G O L R. Curtis remarks that the second element is based on an ancient dittography or conflated. BH mistakenly notes "G + בניו". The translator pointed בְּנֵיהוּ

32.5/4f. וַיְּחֲזַק : καὶ κατισχύσῃ. καὶ κατίσχυσεν Ἐζεκίας G O L R. The translator took the verb with v. 4, as וַיְתְּ, making it part of Hezekiah's fear that Sennacherib would use the water supply for his own ends. The next clause is the work of a reviser, who added the name to make it quite clear that Sennacherib was not the subject.

35.9 כונניהו Kethib : Χωνενίας καὶ Βαναίας G O R. Two possibilities present themselves. Either an original misreading on the translator's part has been subsequently corrected or the doublet represents a correcting gloss already in the *Vorlage*. The scales are tipped in favour of the former possibility by the reading of b Syh in the parallel I Esdr 1.9: Βαναίας in place of Ἰεχονίας for כ. b Syh often assimilate to Par and here they clearly used a Gk ms. preserving an original reading בניהו without the correcting gloss incorporated into the text.

5. TRANSLATION OF TRANSLITERATIONS

Transliteration was seen in ch. iv to be an integral part of the translator's method under the three categories of rendering names, real or imagined, technical terms and unknown words.[1] But there are indications that the number of transliterations was originally greater than at

---

[1] pp. 62ff.

present appears. Indeed, L has some unattested in the other textforms. Torrey has studied all the transliterations to be found in mss. of Par.[1] He considers that in places L has preserved the original Gk with its unique transliterated forms. Torrey has of course a vested interest in amassing transliterations: he considers that Par has emanated from the pen of the noted transliterator Theodotion. A less biased investigation induces more caution.

I 16.3 כֹּכַּר לֶחֶם : ἄρτον ... ἀρτοκοπικόν B O R, χελχαρ ἄρτου L.

But the use of an adjective instead of a noun in the genitive is quite in keeping with the translator's usage.[2]

II 9.21 תוכיים : G O R omit, τε(κ)χειμ L.

This example has already been claimed as a case of omission of an unknown word, a proven feature of the translator's technique.[3] It is probable that L drew upon a separate source for transliterations. Was the second column of the Hexapla this source?

But there are in Par some more sure examples of subsequent changes from transliterations, strange to the reader's eye, to familiar Gk words. Kahle on the subject of transliterations being thus replaced remarked that it was not done with the same thoroughness in different books.[4] He considered that the changes were due to the use of the LXX by non-Jewish Christians, who, unlike Gk-speaking Jews, would be unfamiliar with common Heb transcriptions.

I 2.53 קִרְיַת יְעָרִים : πόλ(ε)ις Ιαειρ G.[5]

13.5 πόλεως Ιαρειμ G O L R

13.6 πόλιν Δαυιδ G O R.[6]

II 1.4 πόλεως Καριαθιαρειμ G O L R.[7]

In I 2.50,52 Καριαθιαρειμ is used. An attempt has been made to replace Καριαθ with πόλις.

I 14.11 בַּעַל פְּרָצִים : Διακοπὴ(ν) Φαρισιν G O R.

---

[1] *Ezra Studies*, pp. 70-81.

[2] See p. 46.

[3] p. 116.

[4] *Cairo Geniza*,[2] p. 254f.

[5] See further part II, p. 87.

[6] See part II, p. 5.

[7] Swete, *Introduction*, p. 325, gave examples of doublets created in the LXX by adding a translation to a transliteration. Further instances in Par are noted by Wutz, pp. 58,135: I 2.55 מֵחַמַּת ; ἐκ Μεσημα G; 18.8 מִטְבֳּחָת : ἐκ τῆς Μεταβηχας G: 26.31 בִּיעֶזֶיר : ἐν Ριαζηε (for Βιαζηρ*) G. Cf. also II 3.1 הַמּוֹרִיָּה : τοῦ Αμορια G O (L R).

Earlier in this verse בעל is transliterated, and the same treatment is expected here. Διακ. is a translating gloss on Φαρ., which displaced the equivalent for בעל. Rogers, p. 8, claims that the translator was avoiding mention of a pagan god, but why then did he leave the first case intact ?

21.23   מנחה : θυσίαν G O L R.

23.29   θυσίας G O L R.

II 7.7   μαναα G O R, θυσίας L.

In these three cases מנחה is the technical "cereal offering". In eight other cases where "gift" is the meaning δῶρα is used, e.g. I 16.29.[1] Evidently the translator used the transliteration for the cultic term as well-known among Gk-speaking Jews. Revision was later carried out in the two adjacent instances, but the case in II Par was overlooked, except in L, where S. Daniel ascribes the rendering to Theodotion.[2]

II 1.3   לבמה : εἰς τὴν ὑψηλήν G O L R.

The singular במה occurs elsewhere in I 16.39; 21.29; II 1.13, always in connection with Gibeon as here. In each case the rendering is Βαμα.[3] The plural במות is always τὰ ὑψηλά in Par, where the gender can be discerned. Therefore τὴν ὑψ. is a double surprise, Βαμα or at the very least τὸ ὑψηλόν being expected. The literalistic feminine for במה has the air of a revision of Βαμα*. La reads here in baama; this may well preserve the original text. A survey of the passages listed in Hatch and Redpath's *Concordance*, reveals that the Three never use ἡ ὑψηλή for במה, but mainly τὸ ὑψηλόν. But at Ezek. 17.22 τῆς ὑψηλῆς renders הרמה in the Three according to Q j and at Jer 31/38.15 S* has τῇ ὑψηλῇ for רמה. One wonders, therefore, whether Βαμα* was corrupted into Ραμα before the translation occurred: compare Ραμα L R for Βαμα in v. 13.[4]

---

[1] S. Daniel, *Recherches*, p. 212, wonders whether the translator felt repugnance at the idea of foreigners usurping Israel's prerogative. But there is no inconsistency in the rendering.

[2] *Op. cit.*, p. 223. She claims that θυσία is used in Par for the rite of the מנחה, and μαναα for the actual offering. But it is not easy to apportion both the instances of θυσία to the former category.

[3] B has Βαμωθ in I 21.29 and Μαβα in II 1.13. S. Daniel, pp. 43f., 48, observes that in I Rg and Par the transliteration was used in order to differentiate the special, official במה at Gibeon from the other במות.

[4] The change to Ραμα could be due not simply to confusion of letters but to an exegetical tradition: cf. Targ Onqelos רמתא and רמת for במות in Num. 21.19f.; 22.41.

3.5 שַׁרְשְׁרֹת : χαλαστά G O R.

v. 16 שַׁר׳ ... שַׁר׳ : σερσερωθ ... χαλαστά G O R.

The transliteration has an original ring: the translator did not know the meaning of the word. If this is so, a translation has been supplied in two cases at a later period.[1] The rendering χαλαστά is ascribed to Theodotion in Exod. 28.14 (Syh), 22 (M Syh).

4.12 ג׳ ... גֻּלּוֹת : γωλαθ ... τὰς κεφαλάς G O R.

v. 13 γωλαθ G O R.

The translation sticks out like a sore thumb. Again it looks as if the translator resorted to transliteration out of ignorance ; that he should hazard a guess only in the second of the three instances is unlikely. The rendering is found elsewhere : in Arm in the first instance in v. 12 and in Eth at the parallel III Rg. 7. 27f. (= I Ki 7.41f.). Unless it is merely an inference from the context, it has been linked with גֻלְגֹּלֶת. Rehm, p. 59, supposed that the *Vorlage* actually so read by dittography, but the explanation given above follows the pattern of partial revision of σερσερωθ in ch. 3.

14.14/15 וְגַם אָהֳלֵי מִקְנֶה : καί γε σκηνὰς κτήσεων τοὺς Ἀμαζονεῖς G O (L R).

This is a Gk doublet in which the first element is a correction according to MT.[2] The transliterated form, lacking in La, has been changed to a familiar Gk name via a X/Z error. It was probably something like Αλαιμαχανα* originally.[3] F. Hommel, followed by Barnes, found here an ancient Heb variant מֹזְנִים.[4] H. St. J. Thackeray supposed a mythological allusion similar to the rendering "Titans" for רְפָאִים at II Rg 5.18,22.[5] Gerleman sees evidence of Egyptian colouring, noting that the Amazons were fabled to live in or near Ethiopia.[6] His reference to "the tents of cattle ... called 'the Amazonian' " is inaccurate: the masculine article shows that the phrase is not adjectival. Rudolph criticises Gerleman for seeing here a reference to the Amazons at all: τούς would not fit this female tribe. Instead he views Ἀμαζ. as a corruption of Ἀλιμαζονεῖς added here from 22.1. Such is the

---

[1] Although the word does occur in Exod. 28.14, 22 ; 39.15/36.22, it may have slipped the translator's memory or he may deliberately have rejected LXX κροσσωτά, κρόσσους "tassels" as unsuitable here.

[2] Winckler, *Alttestamentliche Untersuchungen*, p. 165; Barthélemy, p. 42.

[3] For ק becoming χ see Rahlfs, *LXX-Studien*, iii, p. 226, and Ziegler, *Beiträge*, p. 60.

[4] *ET* viii, p. 378.

[5] *JTS* viii, p. 267.

[6] *Studies in the LXX*, p. 21.

variegated history of the study of this doublet. καίγε is most probably secondary, having replaced an original καί, as Barthélemy suggests.[1] It recalls his first century Palestinian καίγε group.[2]

26.7 בגור : ἐπὶ τῆς πέτρας G O L R.
Wutz, p. 95, surely grasped the vital clue when he traced τῆς πετ. back to coyp* and saw it as an error for ΓΟΥΡ* (Γ/C). Unfortunately he visualised the translator misreading his supposed Graecised *Vorlage*. More probably גור was transliterated as a place-name and, after the transliteration was corrupted (cf. 1.3), was translated. Perhaps the translation had Petra in view, as Bertheau and Curtis suggest. Codex Amiatinus of V reads *Turbaal* for גור־בעל: this may go back to another Gk corruption, ΤΟΥΡ* for ΓΟΥΡ* (Γ/Τ). As Rudolph notes, a confusion of ג and ט is hardly likely *contra* BH's suggested בטור ; בצור, proposed by Kittel,[3] has the same disability.

6. Miscellaneous alternative renderings

I 4.11 כלוב אחי־שוחה : Χαλεβ G O L R πατὴρ G O R Ασχα G (O) R. Curtis, etc., have rightly seen here a correction according to 2.49 בת־כלב עכסה : θυγατὴρ Χαλεβ Ασχα G R. Similarity of names must have caused confusion, as Goettsberger remarks. In spite of the reading אֲבִי in "Ec 1.11 MSS" (BH) one cannot help thinking that the error is an inner-Gk one in Par. Ασχα here is transposed from Σαχα* = שחה; in 2.49 the original must have been Αχσα O, as Gilbert saw.[4] After these errors had taken place the way was clear for ἀδελφός L to become πατήρ.

5.12 יעני : Ιανειν G.
The form was originally Ιανει*, which was corrected according to Ιαναι O. Then *AI* was corrupted to *N*.

6.7f./22f. אסיר : Ασερει G.
In v. 22 Αρεσει B has suffered metathesis, as Gilbert observed.[5] G's form was originally Ασερ L (in v. 23). It was corrected to Ασειρ O L R (in v. 22), O R (in v. 23; so G O in v. 37).

v. 56/71 מגרשיה[1] : τὰ περιπόλια αὐτῆς G L.

---

[1] *Op. cit.*, p. 42.
[2] Cf. the comment on II 6.32, 37 on p. 146.
[3] *Handkommentar*, ad loc.
[4] *AJSL* xiii, p. 291.
[5] *Ibid.*

Elsewhere in vv. 40-66 περισπόρια is used in G O R, as Ra. notes. Probably G has been revised according to L.

7.3 וִיוֹאֵל יִשִׁיָה : καὶ Ραηλ Εισια B (c₂)

v. 10 וְתַרְשִׁישׁ : καὶ Ραμεσσαι B (c₂).

Rothstein rightly remarked that B's form in v. 10 does not go back to תר' but he could not detect its source. It is in fact a variant to the names in v. 3.[1] It was placed in the margin and displaced a name in the next column (10 lines away in BM). Compare the corruption of Ραμα* into Ραηλ in 27.27.[2]

v. 26 עַמִּיהוּד : Αμιουειδ B.

c₂ O L R read Αμιουδ. ει is a misplaced alternative for ι.

12.22/21 בַּצָּבָא : ἐν τῇ στρατ(ε)ιᾳ ἐν τῇ δυνάμει G (L) R. Either translation is possible. δύναμις stands for צבא twelve times elsewhere in Par and στρατ(ε)ιά seven times. Since צבא became στρατ. in vv. 15/14, 24/23 and δυν. is used for מחנה in v. 23/22, the former is the more obvious rendering. For that reason it is to be regarded as secondary. δυνάμει is original, an example of the translator's liking for variety. It was later corrected to distinguish from δυν. in v. 22 and to harmonise with the rendering of צבא elsewhere in ch. 12.

24.12 אֶלְיָשִׁיב : Ελιαβιει B, Ελιαβει c₂. The form in B is earlier, but a complicated history may be glimpsed behind it. It was earlier Ελιαβις*, transposed from Ελιασ(ε)ιβ O (Ra.). ει was intended as a replacement for ι, but it displaced ς.

v. 22 יַחַת : Ιναθ G O. This was earlier Ιαιθ*: cf. Ιεθ G O R in 4.2; 23.10f. α is a correction to the form Ιαθ R. ΑΙ became Ν.

29.6 לְשָׂרֵי מְלֶאכֶת הַמֶּלֶךְ : οἱ προστάται τῶν ἔργων καὶ οἱ οἰκόδομοι (οἰκόνομοι O) τοῦ βασιλέως G O (L) R. The first phrase is original: προστάται was used for שׂרי in 27.31 G O R and ἔργα frequently stands for מלאכת in Par, e.g., in 22.15 G O L R. οἰκόνομοι O is obviously correct in the alternative version: it was changed to the common οἰκόδομοι. In this case the revision, probably. Hexaplaric, is marked by more free and better Gk.

v. 11 הַנֵּצַח וְהַהוֹד : ἡ νίκη καὶ ἡ ἰσχύς G O R. The second equivalent is most perplexing at first sight. But a glance at 15.21 reveals the history of the text:

לְנַצֵּחַ : ἰσχῦσαι G, ἐνισχῦσαι O R,

ἐνισχῦσαι εἰς νῖκος L.

---

[1] For Ραηλ see part II, p. 121.

[2] See part II, p. 17.

L's addition εἰς νῖκος to the original in 15.21 corresponds to the way
the Three rendered למנצח in the Psalms.[1] Aquila translated it
τῷ νικοποιῷ, Theodotion εἰς τὸ νῖκος and Symmachus ἐπινίκιος.
Here ἰσχύς was evidently the original rendering for נצח.[2] It was
revised with νίκη, and the equivalent for הוד was displaced as a
result.[3]

II 4.16 ואת־הסירות ואת־היעים ואת־המזלגות : καὶ τοὺς ποδιστῆρας
καὶ τοὺς ἀναλημπτῆρας καὶ τοὺς λέβητας καὶ τὰς κρεάγρας G OL R.
The second pair is original. λεβ. stands for סירות, a standard rendering
in the LXX generally. (It is translated πυρεῖα in v. 11, where the
translator is borrowing from Exodus, as so often in this chapter.)
κρεάγρας is used for יעים in v. 11: there יעים ... סירות are transposed
in translation.[4] In I 28.17 מזלגות is translated κρεαγρῶν. יעים and מז׳
are accordingly regarded as synonymous by the translator, and he
renders them with a single term.[5] ἀναλ. was probably intended to
represent the missing term. ποδ. is based on a misreading, יסודות.[6]
The first pair of terms is ascribed to Theodotion and to Aquila by Q at
Jer. 52.18, and the second term is said to be Theodotion's equivalent
for יעים at Exod 38.3/23 according to Syh. Accordingly Field ascribes
these two terms to Theodotion here.[7] In fact Josephus' Gk text already
had the addition. He mentions ποδιστῆρας καὶ ἀναλημπτῆρας ...
λέβητας καὶ ἁρπάγας in *Ant.* viii. 88. The last word is surely an
error for, or an adaptation of, κρεάγρας.

5.12 ולבניהם ולאחיהם : καὶ τοῖς υἱοῖς αὐτοῦ G O καὶ τοῖς ἀδελφοῖς
αὐτοῦ G.
L inserts τοῦ before Ασαφ a few words before: probably this displaced
(αὐ)τῶν L R (Ra.) in the first case, and then a second αὐτῶν O L R
(Ra.) was adapted accordingly.

---

[1] Cf. p. 140.

[2] Cf. p. 126.

[3] Targ apparently renders הוד in terms of strength in Prov. 5.9; Zech 10.3. In the
first case חילך was most probably read (cf. LXX ζωήν σου = חייך) by assimilation to
31.3. In the second case a war-horse's הוד may not unnaturally be defined in terms of
strength, hailed as the equine virtue in Job 39.19; Psa 147.10.

[4] *Contra* Gerleman, *Studies*, p. 25: "הסירות is rendered by τοὺς κρεάγρας".

[5] In accordance with ch. vii, section 3 (p. 112).

[6] The error is a fairly common one: cf. Exod. 38.3/23 סירות : βάσιν A, misread as
יסודות according to Gooding, *Account of the Tabernacle*, p. 53; Nahum 1.10 סירות :
θεμελίου.

[7] *Origenis Hexaplorum, ad loc.*

10.17 עליהם : ἐπ' αὐτῶν G R, ἐπ' αὐτούς L.

v. 18 וישלח : + ἐπ' αὐτούς G L R.

The addition in v. 18 was a marginal alternative to the phrase in v. 17.

11.15 לשעירים : τοῖς εἰδώλοις καὶ τοῖς ματαίοις G O L R.

The translator produced the second term, using his Pentateuchal dictionary. שעירים in the sense of "devils" occurs only at Lev 17.7 in the Pentateuch, and is so rendered.[1] The translation has been glossed with a clearer rendering to avoid misunderstanding.

20.23 ויעמדו ... עזרו : καὶ ἀπέστησαν G ... ἀνέστησαν G O L R.

ἀνέστησαν O L R (Ra.) is expected in the first case and is doubtless original. Then the second verb may be satisfactorily explained on the lines of ch. iv, section 12.[2] απ, it may be suggested, was a marginal variant for ἐπ' (ἄκρου) in v. 16, where b c₂ read ἀπ' ἄκρου. It was connected with the wrong column and displaced αν in v. 23 (about 12 lines away in BM).

23.12 המהללים : ἐξομολογουμένων καὶ αἰνούντων G O L R.

Rehm, p. 25, was most probably right in seeing a Gk doublet here. BH's comment "G BAL + המודים" is less likely. Elsewhere in Par הלל is rendered ἐξομολογεῖσθαι four times and αἰνεῖν eleven times. The second term apparently supplies the more common rendering. La has only the second : doubtless its source was the same as that of the amplification in the Gk mss.

24.19 ויעידו בם ולא האזינו : καὶ οὐκ ἤκουσαν · καὶ διεμαρτύραντο αὐτοῖς καὶ οὐχ ὑπήκουσαν G (O).

The first clause is an alternative to the last one. O so reads in the last case; so do L R, but they lack the first clause.

25.11 ויך : + ἐκεῖ G O L R;

v. 16 שמעת : ἐπήκουσας G O R, εἰσήκουσας n y.

31.12 ויביאו : καὶ ἤνεγκαν ἐκεῖ G, καὶ εἰσήνεγκαν ἐκεῖ O L R, et intulerunt La.

33.19 והעתר : καὶ ἐπήκουσεν G O L R;

ibid. והעמיד : + ἐκεῖ G O L R.

In each case ἐκεῖ is the corruption of a reviser's prepositional prefix. EIC became EK and was incorporated into the text as the adverb. In the first case the variant must have been put in the margin. It was attached to the next column (11 lines away in BM).

28.13 הנה ... עלינו : ὧδε πρὸς ἡμᾶς ... ἐφ' ἡμᾶς G O L R.

---

[1] The Gk expression is borrowed from a Heb concept: cf. Jer. 8.19 הבלי : ματαίοις.

[2] p. 53.

πρὸς ἡμ. was originally a marginal gloss on the phrase two lines further on. It linked the phrase with λέγετε and "improved" the style of the Gk.

29.17 **באחד לחדש** : τῇ ἡμέρᾳ τῇ πρώτῃ [1] νουμηνίᾳ τοῦ μηνός G O (R).

The translator elsewhere uses νουμηνία only in the plural in the sense of "new moon festivals", e.g., in 31.3. νουμ. is a gloss : the longer phrase stylistically matches the two indications of date later in the verse. For the gloss cf. Exod 40.2 **ביום־החדש הראשון באחד לחדש** : ἐν ἡμέρᾳ μίᾳ τοῦ μηνὸς τοῦ πρώτου νουμηνίᾳ. It is unlikely that νουμ. is original. Walde so assumed;[2] Rudolph considers the first element of the doublet, as found in B*, to be a correction of νουμ., which was rendered superfluous by the further correction of τρίτῃ to πρώτῃ.

v. 35 **השלמים** : τῆς τελειώσεως τοῦ σωτηρίου G O L R.

The latter is original : it is the standard equivalent in Par. τελ. occurs only here in Par, and nowhere else in the LXX renders **שלמים**. This etymological gloss is also found in the same rôle, but as a marginal note, in M, at Lev 4.35; 6.12; 7.19. It hardly comes from any of the Three.[3] Aquila and Theodotion are credited with τελείωσις for **תמים** at Lev 8.8 by j; it does not sound like Symmachus.

32.33 **וכבוד עשו** : καὶ δόξαν καὶ τιμὴν ἔδωκαν G O L R.

Curtis posited **והוד וכבוד** and wondered whether a misread dittography of **דויד** was the cause. But Rehm, p. 25, rightly saw here a Gk doublet. Presumably the first phrase is the older : δόξα renders **כבוד** sixteen times elsewhere in Par; τιμή occurs only once, for **מקוא** in II 1.16. Was the gloss prompted by religious sensitivity? διδόναι δόξαν is used with a human object in I 29.25, but it is generally a term of divine worship, e.g., in II 30.8.

33.7 **פסל־הסמל אשר** : τὸ γλυπτὸν τὸ χωνευτόν, εἰκόνα ἦν G (O L R).

פסל becomes γλυπτόν also at 33.19; 34.4. **סמל** is rendered γλυπτόν in v. 15. Here having already used it, he resorts with characteristic looseness[4] to χωνευτόν, a word which he elsewhere (34.3,4) reserves for **מסכות**. Rehm, p. 108 note 1, not appreciating the translator's freedom, regards χωνευτόν as the intruder because it does not render

---

[1] For the error τρίτῃ in B* see part II, p. 33.

[2] *Esdrasbücher*, p. 36.

[3] Cf. S. Daniel, p. 296. She too sees a gloss here (p. 287).

[4] Cf. p. 55.

פסל or סמל elsewhere. In fact the range of the translator's vocabulary is the determining factor. εἰκών does not occur anywhere else in Par. Evidently a reviser desired a clearer rendering for סמל and added εἰκόνα, which translates סמל in Deut. 4.16 and is probably derived from Theodotion in Ezek 8.5.[1] ἦν must originally have been ὅ, and was changed after the gloss entered the text. Theoretically τὸ γλυπτόν could be a gloss from the parallel IV Rg 21.7, but its use in v. 15, referring to the same image, rules out assimilation.

34.8 יואחז ... יואח : Ιουαχ ... Ιωαχ G.

Ιω renders the first syllable of יואח elsewhere : I 6.6/21 Ιωαβ G, 26.4 Ιωαθ G, II 29.12 Ιωαχα G O L R. Ιωαχ was doubtless intended as a more usual rendering and displaced Ιωαχαζ O L R (Ra.)

35.16 ותכון כל־עבודת : καὶ κατο/ωρθώθη καὶ ἡτοιμάσθη πᾶσα ἡ λειτουργία G O.

In this chapter ἑτοιμάζειν renders כון, except at v. 10 ותכון העבורה : καὶ κατο/ωρθώθη ἡ λειτουργία G O L R. At first glance καὶ κατ. looks suspiciously like an addition from the similar phrase at v. 10. Or did the translator render as in v. 10, and καὶ ἡτοιμ. come in later as a standardising correction ? Probably the latter explanation is the true one. ἡτοίμασαν αὐτοῖς has just gone before. It would be true to character for the translator to vary his rendering, and moreover his translation in v. 10 would readily have come to mind. L and Lao mit καὶ ἡτοιμ. and may well be preserving the original text. The secondary character of ἡτοιμ. is confirmed by its appearance in L at 29.35 as a variant for κατ. G O R in a similar context.

The evidence of revision in Par points to a long history in the course of which several hands worked over the text in the interests of accuracy and intelligibility. In many cases O, L and/or R apparently found the text already conflated and generally merely eased glosses more smoothly into place. The revision is manifold. There are the pedantic and literalistic revision and standardising glosses that are so reminiscent of Barthélemy's "devanciers d'Aquila".[2] The addition of the article to correspond to את with a name, and of γε for גם is particularly suggestive. On the other hand, the changes from transliteration to

---

[1] At v. 5 the Hexaplaric reading is given no source, but in v. 3 Q attributes εἰκόνος to Theodotion.

[2] R. Loewe has suggested privately that the vestiges of an Aquila-type revision reflect an attempt to produce a text suitable for use in connection with Midrashic exegesis of the Heb, noting the Talmudic dictum לא נתנו דברי הימים אלא לידרש.

translation have a Hellenising ring about them: they suggest another hand at work, more concerned with the meaning of the text for the plain man than with scrupulous trifles. The ancient revision in Par is definitely heterogeneous. It presents a kaleidoscopic picture of keen desire for clarity and closeness to the Heb text.

CHAPTER NINE

ASSIMILATION TO PARALLEL TEXTS

Previous research into the problem of assimilation in Par was discussed in chapter ii;[1] it must now be evaluated and coordinated. Before individual passages may be examined in detail principles of approach have to be laid down. It should first be made clear that Barthélemy's investigation of Rg has vitiated some of the detailed examination of parallel texts undertaken by Rehm and Gerleman, both of whom relied upon Codex B in Rg. "La pretendue 'recension lucianique' ... des sections $\beta\gamma$ [= II Rg 10.1[2] -III 2.11] et $\gamma\delta$ [= III Rg 22, IV Rg] des Règnes est en réalité le témoin le plus fidèle de la Septante ancienne, tandis que les témoins que nous avons rattaches au groupe $\kappa\alpha i \ \gamma\epsilon$ (et entre autres le codex Vaticanus) n'attestent ni las Septante ancienne ni une traduction nouvelle, mais une *recension* de la Septante ancienne."[3] Barthélemy deliberately excluded from consideration passages which had parallels in Par since there the factor of assimilation complicates the textual tradition and beclouds the evidence he attempted to reveal.[4]

F. M. Cross has used the evidence of 4Q Sam[ab] to confirm Barthélemy's conclusion about a first century A.D. *kaige* recension.[5] But he points out that because the text of the so-called Lucianic mss. antedates the recension it is not therefore necessarily identical with the primitive Gk text, which he assumes to be lost in the $\beta\gamma$ and $\gamma\delta$ sections. He suggests rather that it represents a proto-Lucianic recension of the first or second century B.C. His reasoning is based on the 4Q Sam mss. In I Sam 1-II 11.1 their text follows closely the common readings of B and the Lucianic mss., and sporadically the Lucianic text against B; in II Sam 11.2-24.25 4Q Sam[a] normally stands with L against B. He sees in 4Q Sam[a] an Old Palestinian text, later superseded by a proto-Massoretic text on which the proto-Theodotionic *kaige* recension was

---

[1] pp. 26ff.

[2] J.D. Shenkel, *Chronology*, pp. 117-120, has demonstrated that the section begins here rather than at 11.1.

[3] *Devanciers*, p. 91.

[4] *Op. cit.*, p. 91f.

[5] *HTR* lvii, pp. 292ff.

based. Although Cross' claims may be overstated and further research is necessary to substantiate his claims, it must be said that he has made out an impressive case for a proto-Lucianic recension.[1]

How does this discovery affect the question of assimilation where the two sections of Rg are concerned ? It might appear to be impossible to track down either Heb or Gk assimilation if the important controlling factor of witnesses to the earliest text of Rg is irretrievably lost. But the picture is not so black : two considerations are reassuring. First, the proto-Lucianic has completely replaced the primitive text : it may well have done so at a very early stage, so that for very much of Par's history the only Gk text in circulation to be compared with Par was that of the early recension, joined from the first century A.D. by the *kaige* text. Secondly, according to Cross the proto-Lucianic recension was based on an Old Palestinian text of the second or first century B.C., while the basic Rg was itself translated from a very similar Egyptian Heb text which separated from the Old Palestinian textual tradition no later than the fourth century B.C. The closeness of 4Q Sam[a] to the B group in I Sam 1-II 11.1 underlines the closeness of their *Vorlage* to a first century B.C. text. It is therefore unlikely that the revision was very extensive.[2]

Cross has stressed the similarity of the 4Q Sam mss. not only to Rg but also to Chron.[3] This similarity materially affects the question of assimilation on the side of Rg, a subject with which this study is little concerned. It implies that common ground between Rg and Chron is due to their common underlying text, which was later revised

---

[1] As S.P. Brock, *Studia Evangelica* v, pp. 176ff., has observed, b o c₂ e₂ contain secondary elements in Rg βγ. He points to Atticisms, such as also appear in these mss. in I Rg where they contain a late textform, and demonstrates the existence of stylistic improvements. He finds some evidence that this textform received its final formulation at a time close to Lucian. He issues a warning that readings in both the "Lucianic" and the *kaige* textforms must be checked against recensional changes in other places and against the traits of the original translation insofar as it can be discerned. J.W. Wevers, *TR* xxxiii, p. 74f., has similarly stressed that b+ contain late elements in Rg βγ. G. Howard, *VT* xxi, pp. 440-450, has attacked Cross' theories of Heb and Gk recensions and some of Barthélemy's conclusions fundamental to Cross' work. E. Tob, *RB* lxxix, pp. 101-113, considers that the substratum of b+ contains either the Old Greek or any single Old Greek translation.

[2] Cf. Shenkel, *op. cit.*, p. 10: "Despite the demonstrable differences between the Old Greek and proto-Lucian in a number of readings, these two text types have much in common in comparison with Greek texts of a later provenance."

[3] *Loc. cit.*; *The Ancient Library of Qumran*, pp. 141ff.

according to a proto-Massoretic text. Therefore not subsequent assimilation but original identity of text must frequently be assumed as
the reason for their present closeness. But by the same token assimilation in the *Vorlage* of Par shines out all the more clearly. The
temptation would doubtless have been strong to conform Heb mss.
of Chron to a proto-Massoretic text of Sam as it became current. The
many differences between the Chron-Rg text on the one hand and the
MT of Sam on the other serve to confirm that when Par sides with
Sam against Chron its text has indeed suffered contamination.

Rehm and Gerleman disagree in principle about Par's *Vorlage*.
Rehm is unwilling to admit parallel contamination at the Heb stage
apart from the last chapters of II Chron, where it can hardly be
denied. One is surprised at this inconsistent attitude : if it is present in
certain chapters, then *prima facie* its presence is not unlikely elsewhere.
Has Rehm fallen victim to the view which he feels obliged to bolster,
that the translator of Par used Rg ? So resolutely does he set his face
towards the establishment of this view that he tends to ignore or to
play down factors which might point in another direction.

Against the possibility that Par's *Vorlage* had suffered assimilation
to Sam-Ki Rehm claimed that when Par wrongly corresponds to the
Vorlage of Rg, it is generally impossible to trace palaeographical links
between the two Heb texts. But this is begging the very question of
parallel assimilation within the Heb ms. tradition, upon which palaeographical considerations have no direct bearing. For example, a case
may be considered which is among those cited by Rehm as instances
of the translator's incorporation of Rg into the text of Par. In I Par
14.13 ἐν τῇ κοιλάδι τῶν γιγάντων stands for בעמק, while II Rg 5.22
has ἐ. τ. κ. τ. τιτάνων for בעמק רפאים. Gerleman needs no recourse
to any device of lower criticism in order to assume here the presence of
רפאים in the Heb text of Par: it is for him a straightforward case of
Heb parallel contamination.[1]

Rehm finds another obstacle to the assumption that Par's Heb text
wrongly agreed with Sam-Ki. He considers it unlikely that a Heb ms.
of Chron would contain readings of the parallel text which are inferior
to those of Chron: rather, it is easier in his eyes to assume the adoption
of Gk renderings of these worse readings. In making this assumption
Rehm is surely ignoring the psychological probability that Sam-Ki

---

[1] *Studies in the LXX*, p. 31.

would be regarded as authoritative by virtue of their wider use. Even
a corrupted reading might well carry greater weight for a copyist of
Chron. Often heard, it would creep into his mind and whisper its
plausible message that here Chron needed "correction" as from a
master text.

Sometimes Par corresponds to Sam-Ki when there is no equivalent
at all in Rg or when Rg itself seems to translate the text of Chron.
The latter cases Rehm analyses : he is reluctant to find *Textkreuzung*
in the Heb texts of the translators in the sense that both were deliberately similar.[1] At times he gives the impression of wriggling away from
the simplest and most obvious solution. Rehm seems to be partially
aware of the problem posed by cases where Rg omits equivalents for
Sam-Ki readings echoed in Par. At II 5.1, 5 the MT is judged degenerate
and the parallel readings are judged original in Chron : כל is a dittograph
of הכלים ; for העלו read ויעלו by error of וי/ה; insert ו before הליים -
"hapl. ו vor ה?" (p. 70). In 6.36 εἰς γῆν ἐχθρῶν εἰς γῆν μακράν
appears for אל ארץ רחוקה. One might consider himself justified in
seeing here conflation with Ki אל ארץ האויב,[2] but Rehm, p. 100, can
discover in the first phrase merely an explanatory addition prompted
by the context. In 8.12 the omission of יהוה with Ki is plausibly
explained as an omission perpetrated by the translator because
τῷ κυρίῳ precedes. But Rehm has left breaches in his defences. In
two other cases Rg omits, I 16.3 and II 10.3 : the former is ignored and
the latter is mishandled.[3] One might of course suggest that Rg originally
had equivalents for the Heb, but this would be special pleading. In
fact the cumulative impression given by all these cases is that Par's
Heb text had been assimilated to Sam-Ki.

The text of the famous Qumran ms. Is[a] lends support to this conclusion. P. W. Skehan has drawn attention to the exegetical process of
harmonization evident in its text, whereby similar passages in Isa and
elsewhere are echoed.[4] He suggests that in this respect 1QIs[a] resembled

---

[1] Textkritische Untersuchungen, pp. 99-101.

[2] Details of chapter and verse are given later in the chapter.

[3] On p. 45 Rehm cites the reading of A in III Rg 12.3, corresponding to II Par 10.3,
although he usually follows B's text (cf. p. 13). He presumably considers A to be original
here, but he says nothing as to how the reading fell out of B. Syh includes the words
under an asterisk.

[4] *VT* iv, p. 151f.

the Heb ms. used by the Gk translator of Isa, replete with harmonizing glosses and readings in the text. Skehan does not mention parallel assimilation, but in those chapters of Is[a] that overlap with II Ki there are in fact twelve readings which are most probably to be explained as case of parallel assimilation.[1] If this second century B.C. Heb ms. had yielded to the bombardment of parallel texts, it is not unlikely that the Chron ms. which lay before the Gk translator had been overwhelmed in similar fashion.

Another defect in the conclusions which Rehm draws from the evidence concerns his readiness to jettison the text of Chron MT in favour of Sam-Ki. In this respect he takes over the attitude of older commentators such as Benzinger and at times Curtis. For all such, if Par supports Sam-Ki, then Chron is immediately suspect and liable to be judged corrupt, as if in the evidence of a majority of witnesses. There are occasions when this is undoubtedly true and Chron does exhibit a corrupt text : such cases will be considered separately in later chapters. But in very many cases the more obvious explanation is that the textual variation goes back to the Chronicler's time or earlier. It is clear that Chron is a revised text compared with its sources.[2] Rehm often seems to overlook the possibility that Chron's textual variation ante-dates Par. Once the principle of assimilation is admitted, the possibility must ever be faced that Par in supporting the parallel text is by no means an independent witness but merely an echo of its neighbour. For instance, II Chron 34.21 reads שָׁמְרוּ but Par and Rg ἤκουσαν = Ki שָׁמְעוּ. Rehm, p. 72, adopts the Ki reading, following a number of other scholars. A predilection of the Chronicler is thereby ignored, as will be noted later. Here is one case out of eight assimilations to Ki in this single chapter. Rehm, by rewriting Chron according to Par, is undoing the Chronicler's work.

Did the translator of Par use Rg ? There are clearly many close links between the two books. To explain them Gerleman, p. 37, thinks of

---

[1] 36.11, 21; 37.6, 7, 9 (conflated), 11, 14, 20, 27; 38.3, 6; 39.2. Cf. J.R. Rosenbloom, *The Dead Sea Isaiah Scroll*, 1970, pp. 44-46.

[2] Cross has stressed the similarity of 4Q Sam[ab] to Chron and concluded that "the usual picture painted of the Chronicler violently or wilfully distorting Samuel and Kings to suit his fancy must be radically revised" (*HTR* lvii, p. 294). Cf. Gerleman, *Synoptic Studies*, especially p. 12. But the use of Aramaisms in the parallel texts of Chron points to some measure of post-exilic revision: cf. Kropat, *Syntax*, especially pp. 73ff. W.E. Lemke (cf. *HTR* lviii, pp. 349ff.) has concluded from close study of the synoptic passages that theological changes, though present, are less frequent than is commonly supposed.

both Heb and Gk assimilation and compares the textual contamination
of the NT Gospels. Rehm is disinclined to admit Heb assimilation, but
thinks rather in terms of the translator's taking over Rg, intact or
with stylistic changes, and also of subsequent Gk assimilation to Rg.
The present writer considers Rehm's recourse to stylistic changes
unsatisfactory and unnecessary, once the principle of Heb assimilation
is admitted as a regular feature in Par's Heb text. With Gerleman it is
assumed in the following textual study that a different rendering
from Rg's, which nevertheless suggests the same *Vorlage*, implies a
Heb text similar to Rg's.

More recently J. D. Shenkel has endeavoured to bring Par into line
with the evidence of redaction in Rg, arguing that the translator of Par
worked over the synoptic passages in I-II Rg and produced a recension
marked by regular substitutions.[1] He finds six recensional characteristics:

1. Elimination of the historic present.
2. Omission of the definite article.
3-6. Substitution of $\check{\epsilon}\rho\chi\epsilon\sigma\theta\alpha\iota$ for $\pi\alpha\rho\alpha\gamma\acute{\iota}\nu\epsilon\sigma\theta\alpha\iota$, $\pi\alpha\hat{\iota}s$ for $\delta o\hat{\upsilon}\lambda os$,
$\dot{\epsilon}\nu\alpha\nu\tau\acute{\iota}o\nu$ for $\dot{\epsilon}\nu\acute{\omega}\pi\iota o\nu$, $\sigma\omega\tau\eta\rho\acute{\iota}o\upsilon$ for $\epsilon\dot{\iota}\rho\eta\nu\iota\kappa\acute{\eta}$.

It is claimed that apart from these deliberate changes the translator
took over Rg, virtually lock, stock and barrel. In order to interpret
the evidence Shenkel has to indulge in a "heads I win, tails you lose"
kind of reasoning. Different renderings in Par betoken redactional
changes made in conformity with the translation techniques of the rest
of I and II Par. However, a case of identical readings in Par and the
older text of Rg which violates Par's norms elsewhere "clearly shows
the dependence of P [= Par] upon the Old Greek text form of Reigns".[2]
Shenkel's essential task in order to prove his thesis was (a) to establish
norms by comparison with the rest of Par and (b) to show that they
had been rigorously employed in the synoptic passages, since he equated
the redactor with the translator. The use of the word "recension"
presupposes that the characteristics of a redactor are consistently and
comprehensively reproduced.

How does the text of I Par (Shenkel follows the text of B) in the
synoptic passages stand up to an investigation of this kind ? Some of
his characteristics will now be examined.

---

[1] *HTR* lxii, pp. 63ff.

[2] p. 71 note 10.

1. He admits that two cases of the historic present survive in Par contrary to normal practice. One case is in I Par 19.17 (= II Rg 10.17). In the other case, Par v. 9, he notes that Rg v. 8 has no corresponding historic present.[1]

2. A number of cases of omission of the definite article are mentioned, but not analysed. Gerleman had earlier defined it as in most cases applying "to genitival constructions where the lack of an article must be regarded as a Hebraism, corresponding to the use, in the original text, of the noun without the article in *status constructus* or with a suffix."[2] Shenkel apparently includes cases of proper nouns after a preposition. An examination of his comparative layout of portions of the texts of Rg and Par clearly shows that this elimination was not consistently carried out, although Shenkel does not remark on the lack of consistency. In fact there are over a hundred instances in the synoptic material of I Par where the article appears in violation of this redactional characteristic.

3. Indeed ἔρχεσθαι appears for παραγίνεσθαι as the rendering of בוא. But is it not curious that παρέσῃ in II Rg 5.23 is allowed to stand in I Par 14.14 ?

4. Four cases of δοῦλος are left in the synoptic passages: I Par 17.4, 7, 18, 26. In fact Par does occasionally use δοῦλος as a stylistic variant for παῖς and this may well be so in v. 26, but the other instances look like Rg unrevised.

Shenkel claims six redactional characteristics, on the basis of the differences actually exhibited in the overlapping material of I Par in its present form. If, however, one starts from a wider perspective and compares the treatment in Par as a whole with the synoptic text of I Par, it is possible to establish a number of theoretical norms to which the synoptic chapters ought to adhere, but unfortunately do not.

1. He admits that in I Par 19.12, parallel with II Rg 10.11, occur, as in Rg, "the only two instances in both books of Paraleipomena where κρατεῖν is used to translate the verb חזק, which occurs with comparatively high frequency".[3]

2. καθίζειν for ישב in the developed sense of "dwell, remain" occurs in Par three times (I 11.7; 13.14; 19.5), each time agreeing

---

[1] Has not Par preserved the correct text of Rg here ?

[2] *Op. cit.*, p. 40

[3] *Loc. cit.*, p. 71 note 10.

with its parallel (II Rg 5.9 ; 6.11 ; 10.5). This equivalent occurs nowhere else in Par.[1]

3. שׁוּב is a very frequent verb in Chron : ἀνακάμπτειν, its occasional equivalent in Rg, is never employed to render it in Par except at I 19.5, where it agrees with the older text of II Rg 10.5.

4. In I 19.16, 18 Par's ἀρχιστράτηγος δυνάμεως completely violates the translator's renderings of שׂר (ה)צבא elsewhere : ἄρχων / ἀρχηγός (τῆς) δυνάμεως.[2] ἀρχιστράτηγος appears in the older text of II Rg 10.16, 18 : the present text of Par has obviously suffered conflation.

5. In I Par 11.17 ἐξ ἐναντίας for לקראת, agreeing with II Rg. 10.10, 17, is never found elsewhere in Par.

6. (ὁ) Σύρος for ארם ten times in I Par 18, 19 smacks of Rg not of Par which uses Συρία or οἱ Σύροι.[3]

Finally, it should be remarked that Shenkel finds two "substitutions" which he admits are not characteristics of Par : τῷ αἴροντι and ἐφοβεῖτο in I 10.4 for πρὸς τὸν αἴροντα and ἐφοβήθη in I Rg 31.4.

All this mass of contradictory evidence prompts the question: where is the ruthless redactor who works out a rigorous pattern of stock changes ? Is not Gerleman's haphazard assimilator a better candidate for the composition of the present mixed text of Par than the translator-redactor in whom Shenkel would have us believe ? It was noted in the survey in ch. iv that he claims his hypothesis to be both "simpler and more in accord with what is known of the recensional history of Reigns" than Gerleman's explanation. The second claim begs the question; the first is open to the charge of confusing simplicity with superficiality unless the hypothesis yields a convincing solution of all the problems.

It was also noted earlier that Shenkel points to the paucity of mss. now extant in which the earlier text of II Rg. 10-24 is found, and suggests that parallel assimilation would have reproduced the later text exhibited in Codex Vaticanus and the majority of our mss. In terms of parallel assimilation this merely means that for the most part[4]

---

[1] κατοικεῖν is nearly always used (66 times) ; καθῆσθαι occurs three times in the sense "sit (= stay) at home".

[2] I 25.1 ; 26.26 ; 27.3. 5/4 ; II 33.11.

[3] In I 19.18f. does Par's singular attest the original of II Rg. 10.18f., where the earlier text of Rg unexpectedly has the plural ?

[4] But Shenkel himself states that in I Par. 11.11-25 (= II Rg. 23.8-23) "Even though R [= Codex Vaticanus] exhibits the καίγε recension here, 68% of the words in P[ar] correspond to R".

the text of Par succumbed to the pressure of its rival before the first century A.D. recension became widely used. It is not unlikely that the latter met with long resistance before it managed to swamp the earlier textform.

The theory that the translator of Par used Rg overlooks a significant factor : his treatment of unknown words. It has already been observed that he turns to the Gk Pentateuch virtually as to a dictionary. If he had a copy of Rg before him, would he not have sought from it the meaning of words unknown to him ? In ch. iv were noted his methods of dealing with such words.[1] Here are two cases, together with the equivalent in the parallel text :

II 4.12f. גלות : γωλαθ : III Rg 7.27f. στρεπτά.

15.16 גבירה : omitted ; III Rg 15.13 ἡγουμένην.

On this score it appears unlikely that the translator made direct use of Rg.

It may well be that Par in its original form contained reminiscences, especially of well known stories in Rg. Gerleman observed that certain chapters are now very close to their counterparts: he could have added I Par 18, II 10 and 22-23 to his list. All these chapters are likely to have been well known. The fame of their contents may have influenced even the translator to a certain extent in his choice of vocabulary and thus provided a substratum of unconscious assimilation which would have invited further development.

In the subsequent study attention is generally paid only to cases which go back directly or indirectly to Heb variants.[2] An attempt will be made to distinguish between assimilation which had already occurred in the *Vorlage* and that which entered after Par had been translated. It must often be frankly admitted that the period of assimilation cannot be specified from the reading itself. But the context is helpful at times, as Gerleman rightly saw. Frequent Heb harmonization in the context is taken to suggest that a sporadic, nondescript rendering shared by Rg is in fact coincidental.

Assimilation which is indubitably Gk leads to the corollary that it is impossible to conclude that Par's *Vorlage* necessarily contained a different text. Therefore, when, as often, commentators and BH

---

[1] pp. 59ff.

[2] Cases where the Heb texts of both Rg and Par evidently shared a reading different from Sam-Ki and Chron are not listed in this chapter because of uncertainty as to the source of the different reading. Such cases are listed in part II with an indication that Rg's Heb text shared the reading.

translate or transcribe the Gk back into Heb in such cases, there is actually no evidence for so doing. All that Par is attesting is in fact the text of Rg.

The early chapters of Chron draw heavily upon portions of the Pentateuch. Podechard has shown that in the first chapter Par very often leans on the Gk Genesis.[1] Translator or copyist could be responsible: he thought that the former alternative was often the case. Gerleman's discovery that the translator made use of Pentateuchal vocabulary supports this view. Nevertheless one would probably be unjustified in laying all links which names have with the Gk Pentateuch at the translator's door. Copyists have no doubt lent a hand in smoothing out differences: this is suggested by the fact that some differences still remain. One feels that, had the translator gone so far himself, he would have gone the whole hog.

What is left in I Par of 1.5-23 has four Gk links with its source, Gen 10.

1.5   יון : + $E\lambda\epsilon\iota\sigma a$ G O L R.

Kittel and BH derive from v. 7, but Podechard, p. 376, rightly points out that it has come from Gen 10.2 LXX, where the name was taken from v.4.

v. 6   תוגרמה : $\Theta o\rho\gamma a\mu a$ G L = Gen 10.3 LXX (D E)

v. 9   סבתכא : $\Sigma\epsilon\beta\epsilon\kappa a\theta a$ G L, cf. Gen 10.6 $\Sigma a\beta a\kappa a\theta a$.

v. 10   נמרוד : $N\epsilon\beta\rho\omega\delta$ G O L R = Gen 10.8,9 LXX.

ibid.   גבור : + $\kappa\upsilon\nu\eta\gamma\acute{o}s$ G O R, derived from Gen 10.9.

As Podechard, *ibid.* argues, there is no reason to attribute the addition to Par's *Vorlage* since Par so often approximates to Gen LXX. Actually the name-form confirms the Gk origin.

1.28-34 comes from Gen 25. The following Gk parallels are found.

1.29 אלה : $a\mathring{\upsilon}\tau a\iota\ \delta\acute{\epsilon}$ G O R = Gen 25.12 LXX (MT ואלה) : cf. Podechard, p. 379.

ibid. אדבאל : $Na\beta\delta a\iota\eta\lambda$ G (O) = Gen 25.13 LXX (Podechard, *ibid.*).

ibid. מבשם : $Ma\sigma\sigma a$ G cf. Gen $Ma\sigma\sigma a\mu$ (Pod., *ibid*). μ has been lost by haplography before $Ma\mu a$.

v. 30 ודומה : $I\delta o\upsilon\mu a$ G (O L R) = Gen v. 14 LXX.

ibid. משא : $Ma\nu a\sigma\sigma\eta$ B (from $Ma\sigma\sigma\eta$ c₂) = Gen LXX D (Pod., *ibid.*)

---

[1] *RB* xiii, pp. 363ff.

ibid. תימא : Θαιμαν G O L = Gen LXX v. 15 (Pod., *ibid.*)

v. 32 דדן : Δαιδαν G O = Gen 25.3 LXX (Pod., *ibid.*)

v. 32f. מדין : Μαδιαμ (transposed) G (O L) = Gen 25.2,4.

v. 33 עפר, עיפה : Γαφερ G, Οφερ G O R; cf. Gen 25.4 A Γεφαρ, Αφερ (Pod., p. 380)

vv. 35-54 are derived from Gen. 36 and there is considerable Gk assimilation. This fact suggests that in the few cases where Gen MT or mss. of Chron agree with Par the contamination is nevertheless independent and inner-Gk.

v. 36 צפי : Σωφαρ G O = Gen 36.11 LXX = צפר, a corruption of צפו (MT) (Pod., *ibid.*).

ibid. קנז : καὶ Κενεζ G O b R = Gen LXX = וקנז MT. ותמנע ועמלק : καὶ τῆς Θαμνα Αμαληκ G. MT seems to represent these last two as further sons of Eliphaz. Par harks back to Gen v. 12 which makes Timna his concubine and mother of Amalek. Pod., p. 381, sees here an attempt to harmonise Chron with Gen, and an indirect witness to the difficult MT.

v. 39 הומם : Αιμαν G O = Gen v. 22 LXX (Pod., *ibid*).

v. 40 שפי : Σωβ G. cf, Σωφ Gen v. 23. Σωβ is assimilated to Σωβ(αλ) nearby.

v. 40f. ענה : Σωναν B, Ωναν c_2 in v. 40, Σωνα(ν) in v. 41: cf. Gen Ωναν (Pod., p. 382).[1]

v. 42 זעון : Ζουκαμ B h = Gen 36.27 LXX (Pod., *ibid.*).

v. 43f. בלע : Βαλακ G O L R = Gen 36.32f. LXX. According to Curtis and Pod., p. 383, Par has been influenced by Num 22 LXX.

v. 44 יובב : Ιωβαβ c_2 O L R, as also B in v. 45. But here B has Ιωαβαβ. Gen 36.33 LXX has Ιωβαδ here and Ιωβαβ v. 34. In B probably Δ was written over the name as an assimilating gloss and was incorporated as Α.

v. 45 חושם : Ασομ G O L R = Gen 36.34f. LXX (Pod., *ibid.*).

v. 46 בדד : Βαραδ G O = Gen 36.35 LXX.

ibid. עיות : Γεθθαιμ G O R = Gen LXX (Pod, p. 394). As Rudolph says, dittography of וימ(ת) has caused the error. But it probably did not occur in Par's Heb text.

v. 47/51 משרקה : Μασεκκας BOR = Gen 36.36 LXX.

v. 50 בעל חנן + υἱὸς Αχοβωρ G O = Gen 36.39 LXX = בן ב׳ח׳ עכבור MT. The addition in Heb mss. is probably dependent on Gen MT, and that in Par on Gen LXX, as Pod., *ibid.*, remarks.

---

[1] For the *sigma* see p. 161.

ibid.   הדד : +υἱὸς Βαραδ G L = Gen LXX D E L (Βαραθ A) (Pod., *ibid.*).

ibid.   פעי : Φογωρ G O = Gen LXX for פעו MT (Pod., *ibid.*).

v. 51   עליה : Γωλα G O = Gen 36.40 LXX (עלוה MT) (Pod., p. 386).

v. 52   אהליבמה : Ἐλειβαμᾶς G O R = Gen 36.41 LXX (Pod., *ibid.*).

v. 53   מבצר : Μαζαρ G = Gen 36.42 LXX (Pod., *ibid.*).

v. 54   עירם : Ζαφωειν G = Gen 36.43 D E (Pod., *ibid.*). LXX and MT record different alternative readings (אלוף צפו, cf. vv. 36, 40), as Podechard, *ibid.*, and Goettsberger say; but there is no evidence that the other reading occurred in Par's *Vorlage.*[1]

2.1 has a link with Exod 1.1:

אלה : ταῦτα τὰ ὀνόματα G (O R) = Exod. 1.1 LXX = אלה שמות MT.

This could be Heb assimilation but it may well be Gk.

The next two cases are Gk assimilation from Gen 46:

v. 3   שלה : Σηλωμ A N h c₂ L R (-ων B) = Gen 46.12. Since this rendering occurs in 4.21 without a parallel, it seems to be a standard one.[2]

v. 5   חמול : Ιεμουηλ G O R = Gen 46.12 LXX.

Members of Hezron's progeny are listed in various places besides 2.9-17. There are two links by assimilation with Ruth 4, one Gk and the other Heb:

v. 10   רם : Αρραν G = Ruth 4.19 LXX.

v. 11   שלמא[1,2] : Σαλμων G L R = Ruth 4.21 שלמון (LXX Σαλμαν). The same change was made in vv. 51, 54, where Σαλωμων, probably corrupted from Σαλμων, appears for שלמא.

Ch. 3 has one case of contamination, and that Gk:[3]

v. 3 שפטיה : Σαβατεια = II Rg 3.4.

4.28-33 has at two points suffered assimilation at the Heb stage to its parallel Jos 19.

---

[1] Torrey, *Ezra Studies*, p. 94, derived Ζαφ. from an earlier Αιραμ* as follows: "The Z came from the final N of the preceding word; ρ = φ as very often; the confusion of α with ω can be found on almost every page of B; μ becomes ιυ, νι, etc., very frequently". Torrey's high view of A, which reads Ηραμ here, doubtless prompted this text-critical *tour de force.*

[2] Cf. Fischer, *Das Alphabet der LXX-Vorlage im Pentateuch*, p. 9.

[3] For Ἀβειγαίᾳ in 3.1 see p. 135.

4.28 בבאר שבע‎ : + καὶ Σαμα G O (L). Cf. Jos 19.2 ושבע‎ : καὶ
Σαμαα B, and also Jos 15.26 ושמע‎ : καὶ Σαλμαα B, κ. Σαμαα A.
Gk harmonization with either verse in Jos is unlikely since the rest of
the names are quite dissimilar, even taking Gk corruption into account.
Moreover two distinct transcriptions of שמע‎ seem to be represented in
Par and Jos respectively. So the assimilation must be Heb. The
influence of Jos 15.26 is hardly likely since the context is so different.
Probably at some point a copyist of Chron knew of a reading ושמע‎ in
a Jos ms. at 19.2, as did the LXX translator cf Jos: ושבע‎ had been
changed to ושמע‎ by assimilation to 15.26. The pre-assimilated form
ושבע‎ was in fact merely a dittograph, as Rudolph clearly shows.

v. 33 בעל‎ : Βαλατ B = Jos 19.8 בעלת‎ (B Βαρεκ = בעל‎[1]). BH
rightly sees here Heb contamination.

The next cases of assimilation are in ch. 6.1-13/16-28. Here are the
Gk ones.

6.1ff./16ff. גרשום‎ : Γεδσων G L = Exod 6.16 LXX. This is a
frequent equivalent.

v. 4/19 מושי‎ : Ομουσει G O L R = Exod 6.19 LXX. This form
occurs too in I Par 23.21; 24.26.

v. 8/23, 22/37 אביסף‎ : v. 23 Αβιαθαρ G, v. 37 Αβιασαρ G. cf.
Αβιασαρ Exod. 6.24 (MT אביאסף‎). The first Gk form is simply a
c/ө error; BH wrongly claims a *Vorlage* אביתר‎.

Heb assimilation occurred in v. 4/19 and comes from Num 3.20.
In v. 33/48 appears an addition κατ᾽ οἴκους πατριῶν αὐτῶν G O L R.
This represents a gloss on לאבותיהם‎ in 6.4, assimilating to Num לבית
אבותם‎. Evidently it was put in the margin and has strayed into the
next column in the *Vorlage*.[2]

The list of Levitical cities in 6.39-66/54-81 echoes Jos 21. There
seem to have been three extra links in the *Vorlage*.

v. 50/65 וממטה בני בנימן‎ : G O and Jos 21.9 MT omit. Jos LXX
has it, but it looks suspiciously like a later insertion.

ibid. קראו‎ : ἐκάλεσεν B A d h i n = קרא‎ : cf. Jos יקרא‎ (LXX
ἐπεκλήθησαν).[3]

---

[1] κ stands for χ = ע‎ (cf. I Par. 5.8 בלע‎ : Βαλεχ h c₂, Βαλεκ B) and ρ is used instead
of λ as a Coptic pronunciation (cf. Montgomery, *Daniel*, p. 52): so Jos LXX points back
to בלע‎, a transposed form of בעל‎.

[2] Cf. part II, p. 90.

[3] αὐτῷ, standing for להם‎ in v. 52/67, seems to be a consequence of this change.

It is characteristic of Chron to change an indefinite 3rd singular into a plural.[1]

v. 61/76 חַמּוֹן : χαμωθ : cf. Jos v. 32 חַמֹּת דֹּאר. Jos LXX has two forms, Νεμμαθ and Θεμμων. Albright considers that the LXX is there original and that one name fell out of Jos MT and the other out of Chron,[2] but Rudolph rightly points out that the total "thirteen cities" in Jos 21.6 and here in v. 47/62 does not favour this view. The second form may well be a correction according to Chron (cf. v. 50/65 above). Is Chron's form a ונ/ת error? Par probably attests a Heb assimilation back to Jos.[3]

7.29 has an affinity with Jos 17.11. There was an addition from Jos at the Heb level:

+καὶ Βαλαδ καὶ αἱ κῶμαι αὐτῆς G (O L R) = ויבלעם ובנותיה (Jos LXX omits). The Gk form was no doubt Ιβαλααμ* originally: cf. Βαλααδ O L R.

I Par 10 is the first major link with Sam-Ki/Rg. There are three approximations to I Sam 31.

v. 1 וינס : καὶ ἔφυγον G O = I Rg 31.1 = וינסו MT
v. 5 החרב : τὴν ῥομφαίαν αὐτοῦ G O L R = Rg v. 5 = חרבו MT
v. 6 בניו : +ἐν τῇ ἡμέρᾳ ἐκείνῃ G O L R = Rg v. 6 = ביום ההוא MT.

On the surface the approximations could have occurred at a Heb or Gk stage. The first case is conceivably not assimilation at all, but merely a rendering *ad sensum*. But if it is, then it is probably not Gk since the rest of the verse is quite different. The same applies to v. 5 : here Benzinger characteristically adopts the Sam reading. If the first two cases are Heb in origin, then the third probably is too. Rehm, p. 44, claims that here the translator is taking over Rg.

Ch. 11.1-9 comes from II Sam 5. Extensive Heb assimilation had taken place in Par's Heb text.

11.1 : ויקבצו : καὶ ἦλθεν G O R : cf. Sam v. 1 ויבאו (Rg καὶ παραγίνονται). ויבאו was in the *Vorlage* and rendered according to a principle laid down in ch. iv.[4] BH wrongly posits ויבא. Rehm, p. 36, and Shenkel, p. 67f., imply that the translator took over Rg with a stylistic change.

---

[1] See Kropat, *op. cit.*, p. 7.

[2] "List of Levitic Cities", pp. 53, 71f.

[3] *Contra* Ziegler, *Beiträge*, p. 73.

[4] p. 43.

v. 2   גם (בהיות) : G O L omit with Sam and Rg v. 2. Probably this is Heb assimilation as often in the context. Rehm, p. 69, considers גם a post-LXX corrupted dittograph of ־ום with ג for ו.

ibid.   יהוה אלהיך לך : κύριός σοι G = Sam יהוה לך (Rg κύριος πρός σε). Kittel, *SBOT*, and Benzinger adopt Sam. Rehm, p. 44, thinks that the translator is taking over Rg.

ibid.   נגיד : εἰς ἡγούμενον G O L R = Rg (so most mss. B* is apparently corrupt)[1] = Sam לנגיד. Again probably Heb assimilation.

ibid.   על עמי ישראל : ἐπὶ Ισραηλ G O R = Sam על־ישראל (Rg ἐπὶ τὸν I.).

Kittel, *SBOT*, and Benzinger follow Sam. Rehm, *ibid.*, and Shenkel, p. 68, consider that Par is following Rg.

v. 3   דויד : ὁ βασιλεὺς Δαυιδ G O L R = Rg v. 3 = Sam ד' המלך. This is once more probably Heb assimilation. One Ken. ms. so reads. Rehm, *ibid.*, and Shenkel, p. 69, find here the translator's use of Rg.

v. 4   דויד וכל־ישראל : ὁ βασιλεὺς καὶ ἄνδρες αὐτοῦ G = Sam v. 6 המלך ואנשיו (Rg Δαυιδ κ. οἱ ἄ. α.). Kittel, *SBOT*, adopts Sam and Benzinger favours it, but v. 1 authenticates MT here. The translator is adapting Rg according to Rehm, *ibid.*; he considers the link between Rg and Chron coincidental (p. 99)!

v. 7   קראו : ἐκάλεσεν G O b R = קרא, read under the influence of Sam v. 9 ויקרא (Rg καὶ ἐκλήθη). Rehm, p. 69, reads קרא, but see the comment on 6.50/65.

11.10-47, paralleled in II Sam 23, was also marked by extensive contamination in Par's Heb text. In Rg the chapter falls within the βγ section, where what was formerly regarded as the late Lucianic recension has been shown by Barthélemy and Cross to be substantially a much older text.[2]

v. 12   דודו : Δωδαι G O L (R) = Sam v. 9 דדי Kethib (Rg : Δουδαι L, πατραδέλφου αὐτοῦ KR). Curtis adopts Sam's text, but דודו : Δωδω(ε) G (O) R in v. 26 seems to support MT here.

v. 13   נסו : ἔφυγεν G O L R = Rg v. 11 = Sam נס. If this really is assimilation, it is probably Heb.

v. 14   ויושע : καὶ ἐποίησεν G O L R = Rg v. 12 = Sam ויעש. BH,

---

[1] Or is it ? Its reading εἰσηγούμενος may be the result of partial assimilation to Par, which other mss. either made sense of or completely assimilated. In that case Rg attests an earlier Sam reading נגיד = Chron.

[2] The "Lucianic" mss. are here cited as L and the B group as KR (= *kaige* recension) in the βγ and γδ sections of Rg; when they agree they are called Rg.

Rothstein and Goettsberger follow Sam, but Rudolph rightly regards this as unnecessary.

v. 20 וְלֹא Kethib : καὶ οὗτος G O L R = וְלוֹ Qere and Sam v. 18, cf. Rg οὗτος L (καὶ αὐτῷ KR). The Qere is generally followed, e.g. by BH and Rehm, p. 69 (see Rudolph for another view), with the presumed support of Par. Is the Qere assimilation or has Chron MT been corrupted according to v. 21c ? Reading וְלוֹ necessitates reading בִּשְׁלִשִׁים or כִּשְׁלוֹשָׁה later : but Par did not do so. לֹא may well be the Chronicler's correction of a Sam text which read בִּשְׁלֹשָׁה just as Sam MT does. It is most probable that Chron took over the corrupted Sam text and made of it the best it could. But Par is probably merely echoing L in Rg and has no independent value.

v. 22 בְּנָיָה : καὶ Βαναια B (S) a : cf. Sam v. 20 וּבְנָיָהוּ (Rg καὶ Βαναίας). Rehm, ibid., reads with Sam, but Chron may well have omitted ו in the course of changing the form of the name from -יָהוּ to -ָה (cf. Rehm, p. 104).

v. 23 אִישׁ מִדָּה : ἄνδρα ὁρατόν G O R = Rg v. 21 KR (ὁρ. ἄν. L) = Sam Qere אִישׁ מַרְאֶה (Kethib מִ'אֲשֶׁר), Par is probably following Rg (Rehm, p. 45).

v. 24 יְהוֹיָדָע : Ιωαδ B L. Contrast Ιωδαε G O R in v. 22. This is] a further case of Gk assimilation. B has been affected by Rg v. 20 L (Shenkel, p. 27).

v. 27 שְׁמוֹת : Σαμαωθ G = שְׁמָהוֹת (BH). Sam v. 25 reads שַׁמָּה : ה, a correction according to Sam, has been incorporated. For the process cf. שְׁמָהוֹת 27.8, which Noth explains as a combination of variants שַׁמָּה and שְׁמוֹת.[1] Rehm, p. 120 note 3, wrongly derived G's form from Σαμμωθ L R.

ibid. הֲרוֹרִי : Αδι G O. Rehm, p. 58 seeks to explain in terms of errors of ד/ר and parablepsis. But it is significant that חוֹרִי in v. 32 stands for הֲדִי in Sam v. 30 (Rg : Αδδαι L, KR omits). The wrong word was changed in the Heb Vorlage according to the parallel.

v. 34 שָׁגֵה : Σωλα G. BH helpfully refers to the parallel שַׁמָּה in Sam v. 33: cf. Σαμαια(ς) L here. שַׁמָּה was read by assimilation in Par's Heb text (Rg: Σαμαα L, Σαμνας or the like KR). M/Λ confusion has occurred in the Gk : cf. the equivalent Σομε 1.37. Rehm, pp. 58, 115, wrongly reads Σωα*, assuming a ג/ו error in MT.

v. 35 אֱלִיפַל : Ελφατ B S from Ελφαλατ*: cf. Sam v. 34 אֱלִיפֶלֶט. BH so reads with many scholars (see Curtis; add Rothstein). But

---

[1] Personennamen, p. 259.

Noth defends Chron.[1] Probably assimilation had occurred in the *Vorlage* (Rg : ὁ Φελλει L, Αλειφαλεθ KR).

v. 37 חצרו : Ησεραι S (-ερε B, -αιραι c₂) = חצרי Sam v. 35 Qere (Kethib = Chron) (Rg : Εσσερει L, Ασαραι KR).

v. 38 אחי : υἱός G = Sam v. 36 בן (Rg : ἀδελφός L, KR = Par). Kittel, Benzinger and Curtis follow Sam. Rehm, p. 45, wrongly thinks that Par is taking over Rg.

12.20/19 alludes to the incident recorded in II Sam 29.1-9. In Par the verse has been rewritten at three points.

בבאו עס-פלשתים : ἐν τῷ ἐλθεῖν τοὺς ἀλλοφύλους G O R, conformed to the account in Sam, in which the satraps object and David is sent away. Rothstein posits בבוא הפ'.

שלחהו : ἐγένετο παρά G O R, another change echoing the narrative of the satraps' decision. Rothstein considered that it was not clear what Par read.

בראשנו : ἐν ταῖς κεφαλαῖς τῶν ἀνδρῶν ἐκείνων G O R = Rg v. 4 = Sam בראשי האנשים ההם. Rothstein comments that the text has been influenced by Sam.

At what stage was the text altered ? In the second case probably the translator is rewriting in terms of the Sam narrative which was doubtless well known. The same is probably true of the first instance too. In the third case there is no telling whether the *Vorlage* was already assimilated or whether the assimilation occurred in the course of Gk transmission. Rogers, p. 51f., overlooks the factor of harmonization.

In 12.24/23 τὰ ὀνόματα G O L R = שמות (BH) stands for (אלה) מספרי. The variant did not arise in view of v. 28f. *contra* Rudolph nor from the careless notion that the verse was a subscription of the preceding verses *contra* Curtis. It is rather a case of misplaced harmonization. In 11.11 the similar מספר (אלה) corresponds to שמות in II Sam 23.8. The change had probably already taken place in the *Vorlage*.

13.6-14 is based on II Sam 6.1-11. The assimilation is mainly Heb. In v. 13f. occurs the phenomenon of Gk assimilation superimposed upon Heb.

13.10 ויכהו : καὶ ἐπάταξεν αὐτὸν ἐκεῖ G O L (R) = Sam v. 7 ויכהו שם (Rg κ. ἔπαισεν a. ἐ.). Rehm, p. 44, considers that Par is using Rg.

v. 13 עבד-אדם : Αβεδδαρα G O R = Rg v. 10. Par's own form is

---

[1] *Op. cit.*, pp. 187 note 5, 237.

$A\beta\delta o\delta o\mu$ (15.25; 16.38) or $A\beta\delta\epsilon\delta o\mu$ (15.21), and so this is clearly Gk influence. Rehm, p. 40f., ascribes the name here and in v. 14 to the translator or to a Gk copyist.

v. 14 עַם־בֵּית עֶבֶד אֲדֹם בְּבֵיתוֹ : ἐν οἴκῳ $A\beta\epsilon\delta\delta\alpha\rho\alpha$ G O (R) = Sam v. 11 בֵּית ע׳ א׳ (Rg εἰς οἶκον $A\beta\epsilon\delta\delta\alpha\rho\alpha$). The name goes back to Rg, but the rest appears to go back to Sam *contra* Rehm, p. 44.

ibid. אֶת־בֵּית ע׳ א׳ : $A\beta\epsilon\delta\delta\alpha\rho\alpha$ c₂ O (-ραμ B, -ραν S) = Sam אֶת־ע׳ א׳ (Rg ὅλον τὸν οἶκον $A\beta\epsilon\delta\delta\alpha\rho\alpha$). Here again the name probably depends upon Rg. No doubt originally $A\beta\delta o/\epsilon\delta o\mu$* stood here, rendering a *Vorlage* assimilated to Sam. According to Rehm, p. 58, בֵּית was lost after אֶת in Sam but this is dubious.

Ch. 14 has II Sam 5.11ff. as its source. There is a certain amount of Heb assimilation; but Rehm may well be right in seeing here assimilation to Rg, not involving variants in Chron, in vv. 9 and 13 (p. 35) and 14 (p. 34), and this likelihood warns against supposing that the assimilation involving Heb variants is solely Heb.

14.3 וַיּוֹלֶד דָּוִיד : καὶ ἐτέχθησαν $\varDelta$. G : cf. Sam v. 13 וַיִּוָּלְדוּ עוֹד לְדָוִד (Rg καὶ ἐγένετο τῷ $\varDelta$. ἔτι). Rehm, p. 44, supposes that Rg is used.

v. 11 קָרְאוּ : ἐκάλεσεν G O L R = קָרָא Sam v. 20 (Rg ἐκλήθη). Rehm, p. 69, unnecessarily adopts Sam: see the comment on 6.50/65.

v. 13 בָּעֵמֶק : ἐν τῇ κοιλάδι τῶν γιγάντων G O L R = Sam v. 22 בְּעֵמֶק רְפָאִים (Rg ἐν τ. κ. τ. τιτάνων) : a clear case of Heb contamination (so Gerleman, p. 35) *contra* Rehm, p. 44. One de Rossi ms. adds thus. Rudolph observes that the omission of an original רְפָאִים in Chron would be inexplicable.

v. 15 כְּשָׁמְעֲךָ : ἐν τῷ ἀκοῦσαί σε G O L R = Rg v. 24 = Sam בְּשָׁמְעֲךָ. The stage of assimilation cannot be specified. Rehm, p. 69, adopts Sam.

15.25-16.3 is based on II Sam 6.12-19.

15.29 מִיכַל : $M\epsilon\lambda\chi o\lambda$ G O L R = Rg v. 16. This is the standard form throughout Rg and was doubtless taken as the standard equivalent in Gk. It is based not upon a ל/י error (Rehm, p. 40), but upon confusion with the equivalent for מַלְכָּם [1].

16.3 כִּכַּר־לֶחֶם : ἄρτον ἕνα ἀρτοκοπικόν G O R. Cf. Sam v. 19 חַלַּת לֶחֶם אַחַת (Rg omits אַחַת). The contamination here is clearly pre-LXX. According to BH אֶחָד was added to the *Vorlage*, but Exod 29.23 כִּכַּר לֶחֶם אַחַת justifies the feminine.

---

[1] See Ziegler, *Beiträge*, p. 68.

The psalm of thanksgiving in 16.8ff. is paralleled in parts of the fourth book of Psalms. Vv. 8-22 correspond to Psa 105/104.1-15: 23-33 to Psa 96/95; and 34-36 to the beginning and end of Psa 106/105. The assimilation appears to be mostly Heb.

16.25 וֹנּוֹרא : φοβερός G O L R = Psa. 96.4 LXX = MT נוֹרא. The whole verse is the same in LXX Psa : so Gk assimilation is not improbable.

v. 26 וַיְהוה = Psa 96.5 = LXX ὁ δὲ κύριος. But G O L read καὶ ὁ θεὸς ἡμῶν, which is out of place here. It is significant that, for אלהי ישׁענו in v. 35, Psa 106.47 reads יהוה אלהינו. This looks like a careless correction according to Psa 106 : אלהינו was added to the wrong verse and displaced יהוה.

v. 27 וחדוה : καὶ καύχημα G O R = Psa 96.6 וֹתפארת (LXX κ. μεγαλοπρέπεια). 'תפ is rendered καυχ. also in 29.13.

v. 29 בהדרת־קדשׁ : ἐν αὐλαῖς ἁγίαις αὐτοῦ : cf. Psa 96.9 LXX ἐν αὐλῇ ἁγίᾳ αὐτοῦ (also in Psa 29/28.3). BH in a confused and misplaced note intends to posit בחצרת here, and Rothstein posits בחצרותיו, but the link was more probably forged at the Gk level. This appears to be a reminiscence (on the part of the translator?) of the rendering in the Gk Psalter.

v. 36 ויאמרו : καὶ ἐρεῖ G O L R = Psa 105.48 LXX = Psa 106.48 MT ואמר. In view of the next case the link is probably Heb.

ibid. והלל ליהוה : καὶ ἤνεσαν τῷ κυρίῳ G O L R : cf. Psa הללו־יה (LXX puts before Psa 106 as Ἀλληλουια). In the *Vorlage* (ו)הללו (לי') had been read by assimilation. BH unnecessarily posits ויהללו.

In ch. 17 Chron takes up the thread of Sam again : it runs parallel to II Sam 7. This is one of the chapters which Gerleman noted as closely linked in wording with Rg; Rehm before him enumerated many of the links. But the superficially indeterminate assimilations cannot thereby be neatly labelled Gk, for there are some clear cases of Heb contamination, as might be expected on reflection. These are two in number:

17.3 דבר־אלהים : λόγος κυρίου G O L R = Sam v. 4 דבר־יהוה (Rg ῥῆμα κυρίου). Par is taking over Rg according to Rehm, p. 44, but Par would probably have had ῥῆμα in that case.

v. 21 לך : αὐτῷ G (O L R) = Sam v. 23 לו (Rg σε). Rehm, p. 69, considers Chron MT a textual error: "כ־ו ?".

Four instances are pretty clearly Gk:

v. 5 מאהל אל־אהל וממשכן : ἐν σκηνῇ καὶ ἐν καταλύματι G O: cf.

Rg v. 6 ἐν κ. καὶ ἐν σκ. = Sam באהל ובמשכן. Rehm, p. 83, rightly says that Par is very probably dependent on Rg; nevertheless he reads according to Sam, but see Rudolph.

v. 6 את־אחד שפטי : πρὸς μίαν φυλήν G = Rg v. 7 = Sam שבטי ... Rg is taken over in Par, as Rehm, p. 45, states.[1]

v. 21 הלך : ὡδήγησεν αὐτόν = Rg v. 23, cf. Sam הלכו. The Hiphil with a personal object does not occur in II Sam; for II Chron 33.11; 35.24; 36.6 (ἀπ)άγειν is used. These latter data confirm that Par is taking over Rg, as Rehm, ibid., claims.

Then there are a number of parallels of indeterminate source because the Gk vocabulary is not distinctive enough; agreement with Rg does not infallibly indicate dependence thereon. But Rehm, p. 45, claims this in the case of vv. 4 and 11.

v. 4 הבית לשבת : οἶκον τοῦ κατοικῆσαί με G O L R = Rg v. 5 = Sam בית לשבתי.

v. 9 לבלתו : τοῦ ταπεινῶσαι αὐτόν G O L R = Rg v. 10 = Sam לענותו. Rehm, p. 35, claims Rg as the source, but it might well have been Sam: The Gk verb is common in Par.

v. 11 ללכת : καὶ κοιμηθήσῃ G L R = Rg = Sam ושכבת.

ibid. מבניך : ἐκ τῆς κοιλίας σου G O L R = Rg = Sam ממעיך.

v. 14 והעמדתיהו : καὶ πιστώσω αὐτόν G O R, cf. Sam v.16 ונאמן and Rg κ. πιστωθήσεται. This is an indirect influence. Rehm, p. 69, posits a Vorlage והאמנתיהו, superior to Chron MT.

v. 25 אלהי : κύριε O L (in doublet) R² = Rg v. 27 = Sam יהוה. In v. 24 G O R read κύριε κύριε for יהוה : the second word is probably a misplaced restoration of the omission in G.

Ch. 18 is taken from II Sam 8. Rehm points out a number of links with Rg. But he overlooks the fact that Gk assimilation can be a two-way process. So far as instances involving Heb variants are concerned, there appear to be three cases of Gk contamination and two of Heb. First the Heb ones:

v. 6 עבדים : εἰς παῖδας G O R = Sam v. 6 לעבדים (Rg εἰς δούλους).

v. 10 הדורם : Ἰδουραμ S (-ααμ B, Ἰλουρααμ c₂) = ידורם. Cf. Sam v. 10 יורם. Apparently the Vorlage had a mixed reading. י was intended

---

[1] In this verse ὅτι, representing למה both here and in Rg, is doubtless interrogative, as probably in certain cases in the NT, for which see C.F.D. Moule, An Idiom Book of NT Greek, p. 159; D. Tabachovitz, Die LXX und die NT, p. 107.

[2] For the omission in G see part II, p. 58.

as an assimilating correction of הד, but it displaced ה. Rg Ἰεδδουραν attests the same mixed reading in its Heb text.

v. 16 אבימלך : Ἀχιμελεχ B c₂ O L = Rg v. 17 for אחימלך. Curtis, Rehm, p. 69, Goettsberger and Rudolph read according to Sam. But it is significant that S R read Ἀβειμελεχ. It is probable that B c₂ have suffered assimilation to Rg, while S represents a *Vorlage* identical with MT.

ibid. שׁוֹשָׁא : Σους S, Ἰησοῦς B (Σουσα c₂ O L R). The list of David's officers is not only paralleled in Sam v. 16ff., but also has affinity with the list in 20.24f. Cf. Rg. 20.25 Ἰησοῦς KR (Σουσα L) for Sam Kethib שׁיא, Qere שׁוא. Par has been assimilated to the text of KR in Rg. B's form has developed from dittography of *iota*. Σους probably preserves KR's original form, rendering שׁואס, read by dittography of (פר)ס. L's text in Rg is based on a text of Sam with the reading of Chron.

v. 17 הכרתי : τῶν ἱερέων B S b h (c₂) as if הכהנים. הראשׁנים ליד replaces כהנים (Rg αὐλάρχαι) in Sam v. 18: כהנים is a harmonizing gloss which was taken to refer to כרתי nearby and displaced it.[1] It is significant that Rehm does not mention this case.

The Gk cases are as follows:

v. 6 דויד : + φρουράν G O L R = Rg v. 6 for Sam נציבים. It is generally assumed, e.g. by BH, that נציבים stood in the *Vorlage* of Par and has fallen out of Chron. But compare v. 13 φρουράς with Rg v. 14 φρουράν for the same Heb. Par is witnessing only to Rg here: the whole of the first clause has been borrowed from Rg.

v. 8 מכון : ἐκ τῶν ἐκλεκτῶν G O L R = Rg v. 8 for Sam מברתי, read as מבחרי.[2] This reading involves a ת/ח error and metathesis; it seems better than Benzinger's מבררות or ממבחר. The distinctiveness of the rendering points to Rg as the source (cf. Rehm, p. 45).

v. 15 אחילוד : Ἀχεια G = Rg v. 16. Par is leaning on Rg, as Rehm, p. 42, observes: he plausibly assumes an original Ἀχειλαδ in Rg.

Ch. 19 is parallel with II Sam. 10. At this point in Rg the βγ section begins, as Shenkel has convincingly demonstrated. There are a large number of small differences between Sam and Chron. Par mainly follows the text of Chron, but not infrequently it has taken over the text of Rg in cases not involving Heb variants.

---

[1] Wutz, p. 24, explained the Gk as a corruption of χερεθθι via a χ/ι error. Torrey, Ezra Studies, p. 78, thought in terms of an original χερηθι corrupted via χ/ι and Θ/Ω. But palaeography does not seem to be the right key here.

[2] Cf. the suggestion מבחורי made by Smith, *Samuel, ad loc.*

There appear to be three instances of assimilation at the Heb level, in vv. 1-2.

v. 1   נחשׁ : G omits with Sam/Rg v. 1.

ibid.   וימלך: +*Avav* G O (L) R = חנן (BH) = *Avvav* Rg L (*Avvων* KR). In both cases Rehm, p. 45, claims that Par has taken over Rg. Slight differences between the texts of Par and Rg L suggest pre-Gk contamination. Five Chron mss. read חנון, as in Sam.

v. 2   כי : ὡς G O L R = כאשׁר Sam v. 3 (Rg : καθώς L, ὃν τρόπον KR)

On the other hand, in vv. 3, 17 Rg has invaded Par.

v. 3   בעבור לחקר ולחפך : ὅπως ἐξεραυνήσωσιν τὴν πολιν G (O L) R = Rg v. 3 L (ἐξέρευν-) = Sam בעבור חקור את־העיר. There is no need to insert את־העיר into Chron with BH: Chron replaces it with הארץ, as Rudolph observes.

v. 17   ויערך דויד לקראת ארם מלחמה : καὶ παρατάσσεται Σύρος ἐξ ἐναντίας Δαυιδ G = Rg v. 17 L (but ὁ Σύρος) = Sam ויערכו ארם לקראת דוד. Practically every word is an echo of typical Rg L usage and a contrast to the norms of Par. The reading of d ἀπέναντι τῶν Σύρων εἰς πόλεμον may well represent part of the original Par text.[1] Rehm, p. 69, considers מלחמה a dittograph of וילחמו ("ו/מ").

20.1-3 has a parallel in II Sam 11.1; 12.26-31. There is one case of assimilation, of uncertain origin, in v. 1. ויך יואב את־רבה ויהרסה : καὶ ἐπάταξεν τὴν Ραββα ... G. Par reads as if David were the subject. The omission clearly depends upon the parallel narrative, in which Joab merely besieges Rabbah and David actually captures it.

20.4-8 echoes II Sam 21.18-22. Par's *Vorlage* was altered to Sam in two places.

v. 4   ותעמד : καὶ ἐγένετο ἔτι G O L R = Sam v. 18 ותהי־עוד (Rg telescopes the first two clauses and has a different order). Most commentators, BH and Rehm, p. 69 ("מ/ה" and transposition"), read as Sam and Par (and also Pesh). But this late use of עמד is paralleled elsewhere in Chron.[2] The removal of עוד suits the new context, which has no previous reference to the Philistines. Thus MT may well go back to the Chronicler.

v. 8   בגת : +πάντες ἦσαν τέσσαρες γίγαντες G O L R: cf. Sam v. 22

---

[1] ἀπέναντι belongs to Par's vocabulary. It is used four times for לפני; the translator was not addicted to strict equivalence in translation.

[2] See BDB, p. 764, *s.v.* עמד Qal 6.a,c.

ארבעת. γίγαντες is Par's consistent rendering of (רפא(ים).[1] The addition alludes to the parallel verse, although the Chron/Par narrative deals with only three of Sam/Rg's giants. Although the addition could be a later Gk one (Gerleman, p. 38; cf. Rehm, p. 47) it more probably goes back to a Heb gloss כלם ארבעת רפאים.

Ch. 21 is paralleled in II Sam. 24. Two assimilations are apparently Heb and four are ambiguous.

v. 2 דויד : ὁ βασιλεὺς Δ. G L R : cf. Sam 24.2 המלך = Rg ὁ βασιλεύς. Synoptic conflation has occurred in Par or its *Vorlage*.

ibid. העם : τῆς δυνάμεως G O L R = Sam החיל (Rg τῶν δυνά-μεων L; τῆς ἰσχύος KR). According to Rehm, p. 45, the translator has used Rg.

v. 3 הלא אדני המלך : καὶ οἱ ὀφθαλμοὶ κυρίου μου τοῦ βασιλέως βλέποντες G O (L R) = Rg v. 3 (KR has ὁρῶντες) = Sam ועיני א׳ה׳ ראות. Rehm, *ibid.*, and Shenkel, p. 80, claim that Par has used Rg.

v. 10 נטה : αἴρω B h e₂ : cf. Rg v. 12 ἐρῶ L, an error for αἴρω KR. Sam has נוטל.

v. 19 בדבר : κατὰ τὸν λόγον = Sam v. 19 כדבר (Rg κατὰ τὸ ῥῆμα L; KR = Par). Many change MT (see Curtis; BH "1 c G V S T 2 Sam"; Rehm, p. 69), but Rudolph rightly regards the change as unnecessary.

v. 20 המלאך : τὸν βασιλέα G O L R = Rg v. 20 = Sam המלך. Ms. Ken. 587 so reads. On the surface the contamination could be either Heb or Gk, but two factors in the context suggest that the translator read as Sam : (i) בניו is taken in Par as the second object of וירא and the suffix is taken to refer to the king; (ii) in v. 21 וירא ... ויבט is omitted, obviously as otiose with the reading המלך in v. 20 (cf. Rehm, p. 24). That the translator omitted the words is shown by the fact that ארנן was retained and put *before* the verb according to a Gk order of words. Kittel, BH and Rehm, pp. 70, 83, consider Par original; Rudolph points out that its reading does not suit v. 21 and affords no reason for the sons to hide. Rogers, p. 15, suggests that the translator "played with" המלאך, objecting to "the idea that Ornan should have the same insight into the supernatural as David".

II Chron 1.6-13 comes from I Ki 3.4-15. There are two cases of Heb influence in v. 12.

---

[1] Cf. vv. 4, 6; Ραφα in v. 8 is assimilated to Rg v. 22. The text of Rg seems to have been worked over: it is probable that the occurrences of γίγαντες in Rg were inspired by Par (contrast τιτάνων Rg L v. 18; 23.13).

נתון : δίδωμι G O L R = Ki v. 12 נתתי (Rg δέδωκα). Rehm, p. 21, finds here not assimilation but a form without vowel-letter : נִתֶן. This is less likely.

ibid. כן : ὅμοιός σοι G O L R = Ki כמוך (Rg ὥς συ). Rehm, p. 36, infers stylistic adaptation of Rg.

1.14-17 is parallel to I Ki 10.26-29/III Rg 10.29, 31-33. V. 14 contains an instance of Gk conflation: וְעַם המלך : καὶ ὁ λαὸς μετὰ τοῦ βασ. G O L R : cf. Rg v. 29 καὶ μετά = Ki v. 26 וְעָם. μετά has been inserted in Par. Gerleman, p. 38, rightly sees here a secondary attempt at harmonization in Par. Rehm, p. 27, strangely thinks in terms of a Heb doublet וְעָם עָם.

In 1.18-2.17/2.1-18, paralleled in I Ki 5.15-30/III Rg 5.1-16, there is one case of conflation in Par, at 2.9/10:

מכות : εἰς βρώματα ... εἰς δόματα B (O L) R. The former rendering is the intruder as comparison with the Heb word-order shows. δόματα is a conjectured rendering inspired by δέδωκα earlier.[1] εἰς may have been imported by the translator, as at 36.1. Or does it represent למכ(ו)ת in the *Vorlage*? If so, then מכלת in Ki v. 25 (Rg v. 11 μαχειρ) may have become למכת by metathesis and then, dropping the predicative ל, מכ(ו)ת in Chron : if this is what happened, Par's text represents an intermediate stage between Ki and the corruption in Chron. To return to the assimilation in Par, the repeated εἰς in the secondary phrase suggests that revision took place in a Gk ms., undertaken by comparison with the Heb of Ki or with a non-LXX Gk version close to MT, other than α' or σ', who render differently. Rehm, p. 27, discovers here a Heb doublet מתן ... מכלת ; on p. 70 he holds that εἰς βρώμ. supports Ki against the erroneous form in Chron ("ו/ל").

3.1-5.1 is based on I Ki 6 ; 7.13-51. Extensive assimilation to Ki had occurred in Par's Heb text.

3.4 והאולם : καὶ αιλαμ G O R : cf. Rg v. 7 καὶ τὸ αιλαμ. Rehm, p. 40, suspects Par's use of Rg, but in fact this is a standard form of transliteration in the LXX.[2]

ibid. על־פני : κατὰ πρόσωπον τοῦ οἴκου G O L R = הבית על־פ' Ki v. 3 reads here היכל הבית ע' פ' and Rg v. 7 κ. π. τοῦ ναοῦ. Some commentators (see Curtis) insert הבית with Par, but Rudolph rightly

---

[1] Cf. pp. 59ff. Schleusner, *Lexicon*, i, p. 631, unnecessarily suggested a corruption of κόμματα, comparing σῖτος κεκομμένος "pounded grain".

[2] Cf. Montgomery, *Kings*, ad I Ki. 6.3.

warns that its omission cannot be explained graphically. Where then
has the addition come from? It is probable that it was added to the
corrupt text under the influence of עַל־פְּנֵי הַבַּיִת : κατὰ πρόσ. τοῦ
οἴκου at the *end* of the parallel verse. It doubtless occurred before the
composition of Par because Par would hardly make sense without it
and also in view of the tendency towards Heb contamination in the
context.

v. 10 וַיְצַפּוּ : καὶ ἐχρύσωσεν G O L R = Ki v. 28 וַיְצַף (Rg
κ. περίεσχεν). Benzinger, Curtis and Rehm, p. 70, adopt the Ki
reading, but Rudolph ("man") reasonably keeps Chron MT.[1]

4.3 סָבִיב סָבִיב : κύκλῳ G O (L) R = סָבִיב Ki 7.24 (Rg v. 11
κυκλόθεν). Rehm, *ibid.*, would delete the second, but the repetition
has parallels in Chron.[2]

v. 11 הַמִּזְרָקוֹת : +καὶ πάντα τὰ σκεύη αὐτοῦ G O L R: cf.
Ki 7.45, which is parallel to v. 16, וְאֶת־כָּל־הַכֵּלִים (Rg v. 31 κ. π. τὰ
σκεύη). This is a case of assimilation to the wrong verse in Ki. The
phrase is already represented in v. 16; the fact that מִזְרָקוֹת ends both
lists of equipment in Ki vv. 40, 45 caused the erroneous assumption
that it belonged here too.

ibid. אֶת־הַמְּלָאכָה : πᾶσαν τὴν ἐργασίαν G O L R = Ki v. 40
אֶת־כָּל־הַמְּ׳ (Rg v. 26 πάντα τὰ ἔργα). Rehm, *ibid.*, unnecessarily
sides with Ki and Par.

v. 14 עָשָׂה : ἐποίησεν δέκα G O L R : cf. Ki v. 43 and Rg v. 29
δέκα. Rehm, p. 44, thinks in terms of Gk conflation, but it is more
likely to be Heb in view of the Heb influence upon this section.

v. 16 עָשָׂה : ἃ ἐποίησεν G O L R = Rg v. 31 = Ki v. 45 אֲשֶׁר עָשָׂה.
Rehm, p. 70, prefers Ki and Par to Chron. But it is more likely to be
another case of Heb contamination. Evidently this was not the only
attempt to assimilate this place to the parallel. At v. 4 ᾗ ἐποίησαν
αὐτούς G O R appears for עַל עוֹמֵד. Rehm, p. 59, posits there a
different unknown *Vorlage*. Benzinger, positing עָשִׂים, suggests that a
Heb copyist was trying to make sense of הַבָּקָר in v. 3. Curtis, likewise,
finds a re-writing "to fit the *oxen* misread for *knops*". It may be
suggested that the rewriting was facilitated by a marginal reading
אֲשֶׁר עָשָׂה, really referring to v. 16 in the next column. The plural verb
has come about by local assimilation to the three preceding plural

---

[1] Cf. Kropat, p. 7.
[2] Cf. Kropat, p. 13.

verbs at some stage.[1] After the first attempt at harmonization had
gone astray, another, more successful attempt was made.

v. 19 בית האלהים : οἴκου κυρίου G (O L) R = Ki v. 48 בית יהוה
(Rg v. 34 ἐν οἴκῳ κ.).

v. 22 ודלתי : εἰς τὰς θύρας G O = Ki v. 50 לדלתי (Rg v. 36
καὶ τὰς θύρας). Rehm, p. 79: considers Ki erroneous; Par is merely
adapting to εἰς τὰ ἅγια before (p. 100)! He seems to be evading the
clear impression that criss-cross assimilation had taken place in the
Heb texts of both Rg and Par.

5.1 ואת־כל־הכלים : καὶ τὰ σκεύη G O R = Ki v. 51 ואת־הכלים
(Rg v. 37 omits), read by many Chron mss. Rehm, p. 10, considers כל
a dittograph.

ibid. באצרות בית האלהים : εἰς θησαυρὸν [2] κυρίου G (O L R) =
Ki בא׳ ב׳ יהוה (Rg εἰς τοὺς θησαυροὺς οἴκου κυρίου). Par tends to
omit בית as superfluous with אצרות : cf. I 28.12; II 36.18.

5.2-14 has I Ki. 8.1-13 as its source. There are three cases of Heb
contamination.

v. 5 העלו : καὶ ἀνήνεγκαν G O L R = Ki v. 4 ויעלו (Rg omits).
Rehm, *ibid.*, thinks Chron MT has suffered an error of וי/ה.

ibid. הלוים : καὶ οἱ Λευῖται G O L R = Ki והלוים (Rg omits).
Many read with Ki;[3] but Curtis points to 23.18; 30.27 as confirmation
that the Chronicler's text omitted the *waw*. MT certainly has the merit
of being the harder reading. Rudolph regards הלוים as a gloss, which
implies the corollary that Par is either simplifying or assimilating.

v. 10 ממצרים : ἐκ γῆς Αἰγύπτου G O L R = Rg v. 9 = Ki
מארץ מצ׳. According to Rehm, p. 45, Par is taking over Rg, but the
trend towards Heb assimilation in the context suggests otherwise.

Ch. 6.1-40 is parallel with I Ki 8.14-52. Gerleman mentions this
chapter as an instance of close fusion with Rg; Rehm specifies much
of the common ground. It must not be overlooked that at times Rg is
probably the borrower, as clearly in v. 20. The assimilation involving
Heb variants is not all Gk: here are the Heb ones: v. 28 אויביו : ὁ ἐχθρός
G O R = Ki v. 37 איבו (Rg ἐχθρὸς αὐτοῦ). BH, Rehm, p. 118, and
Rudolph adopt in Chron, but the plural accords well with v. 34.

---

[1] Probably the corruption was Gk: note ἐχώνευσαν just before for יצקים. Is αὐτούς a
corruption of τούς? Boh reads *fecit* and omits αὐτούς : it may well have preserved an
original ἐποίησεν τούς*.

[2] For the singular see part II, p. 89.

[3] See Curtis, *ad loc.*; add BH and Rehm, p. 70 ("Hapl. ו vor ה ?").

v. 32 אל־הנכרי : πᾶς ἀλλότριος G O L R. It is significant that for
בני in v. 30 Ki v. 39 has כל־בני. πᾶς doubtless goes back to a misplaced
marginal gloss, which displaced אל. It is hardly a direct textual change,
as Rehm, p. 59, seeks to explain it (כ derived from the preceding מ
and א ignored).

v. 36 שוביהם : + εἰς γῆν ἐχθρῶν G O L R : cf. Ki v. 46 אל־ארץ
האויב (Rg omits האויב). Rehm, p. 100, sees here merely an explanatory
addition !

Gk assimilation involving Heb variants is as follows:

v. 17 יאמן : πιστωθήτω δή G O b R = Rg v. 26 = Ki יאמן נא.
Some Heb mss. so read, but τὸ ῥῆμά σου for דברך just afterwards
suggests that Rg is the source: Par prefers λόγος. Rehm, p.70, rather
pedantically sides with Ki, explaining the absence of נא in Chron as
due to haplography of נ.

v. 27 תורם אל־הדרך : δηλώσεις ... τὴν ὁδον G O L R = Rg
v. 36 = Ki ת' את־הד'.

v. 37 ורשענו : ἠνομήσαμεν G O R = Rg v. 47 = Ki רשענו.
Rehm, p. 38, observes that this and the two preceding verbs are
identical in Rg and Par, but on p. 70 prefers Ki. Probably Par witnesses
only to Rg.

Finally there are three uncertain cases:

v. 19 לפניך : + σήμερον G O L R = Rg v. 28 = Ki היום. The
loan could be either Heb or Gk. Rehm, p. 45, claims the latter.

v. 21 תחנוני : τῆς δεήσεως G O L R = Rg v. 30 = Ki תחנת.
According to Rehm, ibid., Par has taken over Rg, but the source
cannot be specified so easily, and in fact, it may be that Par is deliberately using the same word it employs for תחנה. The same phenonemon
occurs in v. 39 where the parallel Rg v. 49 omits. This suggests that
the assimilation is either Heb or non-existent. In favour of the former
possibility is the fact that six Chron mss. read תחנתם in v. 39.

Ch. 7 is parallel with I Ki 8.54-9.9. There are two cases of assimilation, one Heb and the other Gk.

v. 5 המלך : G O omit with Ki 8.63. Rg follows Chron, though
Rehm, p. 99, claims that this is accidental !

v. 20 מעל אדמתי : ἀπὸ τῆς γῆς G O L R = Rg 9.7 (Ki מעל פני
האדמה). Rg has been taken over as Rehm, p. 45, rightly states.

Ch. 8, matched in I Ki 9.10-28, has two cases of contamination, in
v. 18.

וישלח־לו : καὶ ἀπέστειλεν G O L R = Rg v. 27 = Ki וישלח. This
case could be either Heb or Gk. The fact that the second case is Gk in
origin suggests the latter.

אופירה : εἰς Σωφειρα G (O) J R = Rg v. 28. Rehm, p. 42, rightly
sees here Gk influence.

9.1-28 corresponds to I Ki 10.1-29. This is another section which
Gerleman noted as having undergone a thorough process of Gk assimilation. Rehm too notes many parallels. Again, in some instances Rg has
taken over Par.[1] But so colourful a narrative as that of the Queen of
Sheba's visit to Solomon and the description of his wealth not unnaturally attracted Heb assimilation too, as follows.

9.6 לדבריהם : τοῖς λόγοις G O L R = Ki 10.7 לדברים (Rg τοῖς
λαλοῦσίν μοι). Rehm, p. 71, alters Chron's text to that of Ki.

v. 21 אניות ... הלכות : ναῦς ... ἐπορεύετο G O L R. Cf. Ki v. 22
אני, Rg ναῦς. The change assumes an ambivalent הלכת. BH's suggestion that Par read הלך is unnecessary since אני can be feminine (cf.
Ki). Chron never uses the singular. Rehm, p. 45, claims Gk influence.

v. 28 ומוציאים סוסים : καὶ ἡ ἔξοδος τῶν ἵππων G O L (R) = Rg
v. 28 = Ki ומוצא הסוסים. Rehm, p. 71, favours Ki, comparing II Chron
1.16, and finds a ה/מ error here. But Kropat, p. 7, includes the
change in a tendency of Chron to introduce third plurals; certainly the
change suits the brevity of the extract. Since vv. 25-26 were apparently
borrowed *en bloc* in Rg from Par, it is not unlikely that v. 28a was also
taken over. Par's *Vorlage* was influenced by Ki, unless II Chron 1.16
was the source of the change.

Here are the cases of Gk influence.
v. 15 שש מאות זהב שחוט יעלה על־הצנה האחת :
ἑξακόσιοι χρυσοῖ καθαροὶ τῷ ἑνὶ θυρεῷ
      ”   ”   ἐπῆσαν ἐπὶ τὸν ἑνὰ θυρεόν G O.
Cf. Rg v. 16 τριακόσιοι χρυσοῖ ἐπῆσαν ἐπὶ τὸ δόρυ τὸ ἕν. The first
part of the doublet is original: καθαρός is frequent in Par. It renders
a text lacking יעלה. The second half is probably leaning on Rg: Par
habitually renders עלה idiomatically in such a sense as this.[2]

v. 18 מקום השבת : τοῦ θρόνου τῆς καθέδρας G O L R : cf. Rg
v. 19 τ. τόπου τῆς καθ. τ. θρ. was originally intended for the
whole phrase; τῆς καθ. was added from Rg.

---

[1] Viz., vv. 14 (see p. 62 note 2), 17, 25 (Curtis, Rehm, p. 97f., Gooding, *VT* xix,
p. 462f.), 26 (Gooding, *ibid.*), 27.
[2] See p.41f.

In some cases the source cannot be tracked down.

v. 7 וְאַשְׁרֵי : μακάριοι G O L (in doublet) R = Rg v. 8 = Ki אַשְׁרֵי. Rehm, p. 71, favours Ki.

v. 8 אֱלֹהֶיךָ[3] : κύριον τὸν θεόν σου G O L R : cf. Ki v. 9 יהוה, Rg κύριον. Rehm, p. 96, finds here not parallel conflation but local assimilation: יהוה אלהיך has occurred twice in this verse.

v. 25 וּמֶרְכָּבוֹת : εἰς ἅρματα G O L R = Rg 2.46i; cf. Ki 5.6 לְמֶרְכָּבוֹ. Rehm, p. 70, reads לְמֶרְכָּבוֹת, comparing Ki. Assumed abbreviation appears to underlie the Gk.

Ch. 10 repeats I Ki 12.1-19. Here too Rehm can draw many parallels between Rg and Par. It is not surprising that so important an episode in Jewish history as the division of the kingdom also encouraged Heb contamination. However, R. W. Klein has emphatically denied Heb parallel harmonization in this chapter.[1] His alternative explanations of certain phenomena will be examined in detail below.

10.2 וַיֵּשֶׁב יָרָבְעָם מִמִּצְרַיִם : καὶ κατῴκησαν Ιερ. ἐν Αἰγ. καὶ ἀπέστρεψεν Ιερ. ἐξ Αἰγ. G O L R : cf. Ki v. 2 בְּמִ יֵשֶׁב (Rg has κ. ἐκάθητο ἐν Αἰγ. at the end of 11.43). Rehm, p. 27f., admits assimilation to Ki in the *Vorlage*. On the other hand, Klein suggests that Chron MT is secondary here, i.e. presumably that the first rendering in Par is true Chron (= Ki) and the second is subsequent revision according to the present corrupted text. In fact, Ki is generally jettisoned by commentators in favour of Chron MT ![2]

v. 3 וְכָל-יִשְׂרָאֵל : καὶ πᾶσα ἡ ἐκκλησία G O L R Ισραηλ O L R καὶ c₂ ἦλθον G (cf. ἦλθε i y). In G Ισραηλ was omitted before καί, exactly as in B at II 5.2; 29.27.[3] The first five words correspond to Ki v. 3 וְכָל-קְהַל יִשְׂרָאֵל (Rg omits). This was read in the *Vorlage* in place of Chron's shorter text. Klein in *HTR* claims omission by homoeoteleuton in Chron MT. In a subsequent article he changes his mind: Ki v. 3a is secondary and depends upon Chron.[4] Ki's different text he explains as a conflation of כָל-יִשְׂרָאֵל (Chron MT) and כָל-הַקָּהָל underlying B in Par. O L R's text he likewise claims to be conflated by the addition of a translation of Chron MT יִשְׂרָאֵל to B's text. But in

---

[1] *HTR* lxi, p. 493f.

[2] Cf. Montgomery, Gray, *ad loc.*

[3] See part II, p. 50.

[4] *JBL* lxxxix, p. 217f. In this respect he follows Montgomery, cf. Gray. But Gooding, *VT* xvii, pp. 173ff, to whom Klein refers, has argued for the retention of Ki MT. Cf. his criticisms of Klein's approach in *JBL* xci, pp. 529-533.

evaluating Par one must never rush into retroversion before considering the possibility of Gk corruption, especially when, as in this case, similar errors occur elsewhere.

The last two words stand for ויבאו. It is significant that in place of ויבא four words earlier in the verse, in Ki the Kethib reading is ויבאו. Evidently the variant was first recorded in a marginal note in a Chron ms. and subsequently intruded into the text, displacing the next verb וידברו.[1]

v. 5 אלהם : +πορεύεσθε G O L R = Ki v. 5 לכו (Rg ἀπέλθετε). Curtis, BH and Klein adopt Ki, the last suggesting "haplography" in Chron MT. But Rudolph rightly regards the addition as unnecessary. Rehm, p. 45, considers that Par has taken over Rg with stylistic changes here and in v. 7.

v. 7 אם : + ἐν τῇ σήμερον G O L R (except f j) = Ki v. 7 היום (Rg ἐν τῇ ἡμέρᾳ ταύτῃ). Curtis, BH and Klein again add with Ki, Klein claiming homoeoteleuton in Chron MT. But Rudolph is on safer ground in seeing here a deliberate omission made by the Chronicler.

v. 10 כה תאמר[1,2] : οὕτως λαλήσεις ... οὕτως ἐρεῖς G O L R. The first phrase implies כה תדבר which actually occurs in Ki v. 10 for the second כה תא' (Rg τάδε λαλ.).. The wrong phrase was adapted in the *Vorlage*. Klein states that "Kings and Par agree" and that "this agreement is a fortuitous result of text development rather than a 'drifting back' towards Kings". But in fact λαλεῖν is the standard LXX equivalent for דבר : Ki and Par do not agree here. In any case, "fortuitous development" is an inadequate plea in view of the many cases of Heb assimilation to Ki underlying Par in the context and elsewhere.

vv. 11, 14 ואני : καὶ ἐγὼ παιδεύσω ὑμᾶς G O L (R), G L = Ki vv. 11, 14 ואני איסר אתכם. Rg has ἐγὼ δέ ... in v. 11, which probably suggests pre-Gk assimilation in Par. In v. 14 Rg reads κἀγώ... : if the assimilation is Heb in v. 11, then it must be here also. Rehm, p. 45, claims Gk influence in both cases.

v. 13 ויענם : καὶ ἀπεκρίθη G O R. Cf. Rg v. 13 καὶ ἀπ. ... πρός

---

[1] BH erroneously notes "1 frt c G^BA ... דברו". Klein, *ibid.*, takes B as authoritative and postulates a *Vorlage* באו, comparing Pesh ملك at this point. But (i) he gives no explanation of this variant, while that of an underlying ויבאו is not difficult to explain: (ii) c₂ very often preserves B's text when B is corrupt; and (iii) the reading of Pesh appears to depend on a factor absent in Par: Pesh omits v. 2 בן־נבט -v. 3 ירבעם by homoeoteleuton, probably a Syriac error; subsequently ملك was added to make sense of ملكا اشر املك left hanging in the air.

τὸν λαόν = Ki את־העם ... ויען. If assimilation has taken place, it probably did so at the Heb level. Rehm, *ibid.*, claims Gk contamination.

15.16-18 is paralleled in I Ki. 15.13-15.

15.16 אם אסא המלך : τὴν μητέρα αὐτοῦ G O R = Rg v. 13 = Ki אמו. The suffix is more suitable in Ki/Rg because Asa is the subject of the preceding verse.

v. 18 וקדשיו : καὶ τὰ ἅγια G O L R = Ki v. 15 Qere וקדשי (Kethib וקדשו; Rg καὶ τοὺς κίονας αὐτοῦ).

ibid. האלהים : κυρίου τοῦ θεοῦ G O: cf. Rg κυρίου, Ki יהוה.

At what stage did the assimilation take place ? The first case in v. 18 is clearly pre-Gk *pace* Rehm, p. 100, who considers Par and Rg independent of Ki and Chron respectively. The second instance in the verse is probably due to Heb conflation: the Heb context of Ki is closer to Chron than Rg is to Par, and so assimilation would be more likely. Rehm, p. 44, thinks that Par is drawing on Rg. If these two cases are Heb in origin, probably the one in v. 16 is too, *contra* Rehm, p. 45.

16.1-6 is based upon I Ki 15.17-22.

16.2 ויצא : καὶ ἔλαβεν G O L R = Rg v. 18 = Ki ויקח.

v. 4 ויכו : καὶ ἐπάταξεν G O L R = Ki v. 20 ויך (Rg κ. ἐπάταξαν). Since the case in v. 4 is pre-Gk, the one in v. 2 may well be too. Rehm, p. 46, judges that Par has used Rg in v. 2 ; in v. 4 he believes it unnecessary to posit different *Vorlagen* (p. 99).

v. 8 לרכב : εἰς θάρσος G O (L). Wutz, p. 785 note 1, postulated a *Vorlage* לרחב, comparing θρασυκάρδιος for רחב־לב in Prov 21.4. But surely Gk parallel contamination is to blame. Rg v. 21, parallel to v. 5, ends with εἰς Θερσα (Ki בתרצה) in a clause which is chaⲗged in Chron. This is the source of the strange equivalent. A marginal assimilating gloss was slightly adapted and displaced the original, similar εἰς ἅρμα*. Compare 36.5b-c for another misplaced adaptation of a name into a common noun.[1]

Gerleman observed how close ch. 18 is to its parallel I Ki 22 in the Gk. Rehm too lists many parallels, but he overlooks the possibility of Par's having influenced Rg, which has occurred in vv. 5, 34 at least. There are some clear cases of Heb contamination:

18.1 ויתחתן לאחאב : καὶ ἐπεγαμβρεύσατο ἐν οἴκῳ Αχααβ G O (L) R. This is not in fact assimilation to an exactly parallel place. The clause refers to the marriage of Jehoshaphat's son Jehoram, mentioned

---

[1] See p. 149.

in 21.6 = Ki 8.18. Jehoram's son Azariah is called חנן בית אחאב in Ki 8.17. An assimilating gloss בית was attached here and displaced ל. It became or was taken as בבית.

v. 3 וכעמך עמי : ὡς ὁ λαός μου καὶ ὁ λαός σου G = Ki v. 4 כעמי כעמך (Rg: κ. καθὼς ὁ λ. σου οὕτως · κ. ὁ λ. μου L; καθ. ὁ λ. μου ὁ λ. σου KR). This is less likely to be a Gk interchange, as Rehm, p. 46, claims (he is using the text of KR in Rg).

v. 5 הנלך : εἰ πορευθῶ B O L R = Rg v. 6 = Ki האלך. Kittel, Curtis and BH adopt the Ki reading here, but Rudolph argues well for MT. According to Rehm, ibid., Par has taken over Rg, but in fact the opposite is true: contrast ἀναβαίνειν for הלך in Rg vv. 4, 15.

v. 12 דברך : οἱ λόγοι σου G O L R = Ki v. 13 Kethib דבריך (Rg: ἐν λόγοις σου L; εἰς λόγους σου KR).

v. 18 על־ימינו ושמאלו : ἐκ δεξιῶν αὐτοῦ καὶ ἐξ ἀριστερῶν αὐτοῦ G O L R = Ki v. 19 מימינו ומשמאלו (Rg ... εὐωνύμων ...). Benzinger so read.

v. 26 ואמרתם : καὶ ἐρεῖς G R = Ki v. 27 ואמרת (Rg: εἶπε L; εἶπον KR).

There is one case of Gk assimilation, conforming to the text of Ki:

v. 14 עלו והצליחו : ἀνάβαινε καὶ εὐοδώσει G O = Rg v. 15 = Ki עלה והצלח. MT is correct as בידכם : εἰς χεῖρας ὑμῶν shows. Rg has probably contaminated Par (cf. Rehm, p. 46): εὐοδώσεις in B A g^b m is a corruption of the middle voice. Contrast Par's own εὐοδωθήσῃ in v. 11.

Three cases are of uncertain origin, either Heb or Gk:

v. 21 לרוח : πνεῦμα G O L R = Rg v. 22 = Ki רוח.

v. 29 ויבאו : κ. εἰσῆλθεν G O L R = Rg v. 30 = Ki ויבא. Rehm, p. 70, reads as Ki. So read "ca 30 mss G V S T I R 22, 30" (BH).

v. 33 ידיך Kethib : τὴν χεῖρά σου G O L R = Rg v. 34 (L; τὰς χεῖράς σου KR) = Qere and Ki ידך.

21.5-10, 20 is dependent upon II Ki 8.17-24. Par has three closer links than Chron.

v. 7 אמר : εἶπεν αὐτῷ G O L R = Rg. 8.19 (L; εἶπεν KR) = Ki אמר־לו.

v. 9 הרכב : +καὶ ἔφυγεν ὁ λαός εἰς τὰ σκηνώματα αὐτῶν G O L R = Ki v. 21 וינס העם לאהליו (Rg : ... αὐτοῦ L; KR = Par).

v. 20 ויקברהו : καὶ ἐτάφη G O L R = Ki v. 24 ויקבר (Rg: κ. θάπτεται L; KR = Par). The active third plural is characteristic of Chron (cf. Kropat, p. 7).

These links were probably all forged before Par came into being. This is certainly the case with v. 20, and probably also with v. 9 *pace* Rehm, p. 46, which suggests that v. 7 in turn should be so grouped (here Rehm, p. 100, considers αὐτῷ a coincidental addition).

22.2-6 is taken from II Ki 8.25-29. It is closer to Ki at four points.

22.3 בדרכי : ἐν ὁδῷ G O R = Rg v. 27 = Ki ברֹרךְ.

v. 5 מלך ישׂראל : G O omit with Ki v. 28 and Rg.

v. 6 וישׁב : + Ιωραμ G O L R : cf. Ki v. 29 יורם המלך, Rg ὁ βασιλεὺς Ιωραμ. One de Rossi ms. so reads.

ibid. הכהו : +οἱ Σύροι G O L R = Rg L (R omits) = Ki ארמים.

The source of these approximations cannot be determined. Rehm, p. 46, attributes the first three to Par's use of Rg and considers the last merely a coincidental amplification of the subject.

22.10-23.21 is another passage in which Par and Rg (ch. 11) bear a very similar look. Rehm lists quite a number of links. It may confidently be assumed that the thrilling story of the prince in hiding and of wicked Athaliah's overthrow captured many an imagination. It is therefore not surprising that Gk assmilation was superimposed upon a section which had already suffered Heb contamination, as follows:

22.12 אתם : μετ' αὐτοῦ G = Ki 11.3 אתה (Rg μετ' αὐτῆς). The word is pointed אֹתָהּ in Ki; the translator of Par took it as אֹתֹה (Rehm, p. 71) referring to the priest: Rehm, p. 84, suggests that this was because of a restriction on women in the Temple when Par was translated, comparing Jos. *Bell. Jud.* v. 199, 206. BH and Rehm read as Ki. Chron's plural suffix refers to the priest and his wife or (Rudolph, following Gk ms. 44) to his wife and the nurse of v. 11.

23.14 ויוצא יהוידע הכהן את : καὶ ἐξῆλθεν I. ὁ ἱερεύς · καὶ ἐνετέιλατο I. ὁ ἱερεὺς τοῖς G O : cf. Rg v. 15 κ. ἐνετ. I. ὁ ἱ. τοῖς = Ki ויצו ו׳. At first sight κ. ἐνετ. I. ὁ ἱ. could be a gloss from Rg. But it is too deeply embedded in Par for that : τοῖς would qualify ἐξῆλθεν, which is hardly likely. The doublet must have been in the *Vorlage*. The verb for "command" is common in both Par and IV Rg. Rehm, p. 44, considers that Rg has been used; even Gerleman, p. 38, finds here secondary Gk assimilation. BH has a misleading note : "1 c G^{BAL} S 2 R 11, 15 ויצו".

v. 18 יהוידע : +ὁ ἱερεύς G O R : cf. Ki v. 18 הכהן = Rg ὁ ἱερεύς. The conflation is probably Heb in origin since the clause is translated quite differently in Rg, which thus presented less occasion for harmonization. But Rehm, *ibid.*, ascribes it to Par's use of Rg.

v. 20 ויורד : καὶ ἐπεβίβασαν G (O L) = Ki v. 19 ויורידו (Rg καὶ κατήγαγον).

Here are the instances of Gk assimilation:

22.10 ותדבר : καὶ ἀπώλεσεν G O L R = Rg v. 1 = Ki ותאבד. The verb bears the hallmark of Rg, not of Par. It occurs only here in Par, a striking fact since Par has a prolific vocabulary for "destroy".[1] On the other hand ἀπολλύναι occurs three times elsewhere in IV Rg for אבד : 10.19; 13.7; 19.18. Therefore Gk assimilation has taken place here. This means that BH's note, voicing the opinion of many commentators (see Curtis) "l c nonn MSS (L*) GVST 2 R 11, 1 ותאבד" has in fact no support from Par, which attests only Rg. G.R. Driver interprets Chron in terms of a second root, apparently correctly,[2] but he is wrong in claiming Par among the versions supporting this lexical rediscovery.

v. 11 יהושבעת בת־המלך יהורם אשת יהוידע הכהן כי היא היתה אחות אחזיהו : Ιωσαβεε θυγάτηρ τοῦ βασιλέως Ιωραμ ἀδελφὴ Ὀχοζειόυ G = Rg v. 2 KR (Ιωσαβεαι ... ἀδελφὴ δὲ Ὀχ. L) = Ki יהושבע בת־המלך יורם אחות אח׳. According to Rehm, p. 46 note 1, the translator is using Rg. Certainly Gk influence seems to have been at work: Par uses the genitive form Οχοζεια in vv. 8, 9, 10, 11 (earlier). Probably the first name has come from Rg as well.[3]

ibid. מפני עתליהו : καὶ ἔκρυψεν αὐτὸν ἀπὸ προσώπου Γοθολίας (G) O L R = Rg KR (...ἐκ πρ. Γ. L); cf. Ki ויסתרו אתו מפני עתליהו Rehm, ibid., finds the translator's hand at work. Par uses the indeclinable form Γοθολια : cf. 23.21. This case and the previous one are interesting because they apparently demonstrate assimilation not to Rg L, as so often, but to the later KR. But L may be secondary in either or both cases.

23.2 ויקבצו : καὶ συνήγαγεν G, probably by partial Gk assimilation to the parallel IV Rg 11.4 καὶ εἰσ (ἀπ-R) ἤγαγεν for ויבא.

v. 3 עם־המלך : +καὶ ἔδειξεν αὐτοῖς τὸν υἱὸν τοῦ βασιλέως G O R = Rg L v. 4 (+Ιωδαε KR) = Ki ירא אתם את־בן־המלך. Rehm, p. 44, considers Rg to be the source, and a study of vocabulary confirms his opinion. ἔδειξεν also occurs in IV Rg at 6.6; 20.13 for the same Heb equivalent. δεικνύναι occurs only here in Par.[4]

---

[1] ἐξολεθρεύειν 18 times, ἐξαίρειν 6, καταφθείρειν 6, φθείρειν 1, ἐκτρίβειν 2.

[2] JTS xxvii, p. 158f. It is significant that at I 21.14 דבר is translated θάνατος, a standard LXX rendering which seems to assume knowledge of this other root.

[3] It is less likely to be simply a Θ/E error, as Wutz, p. 114. claimed.

[4] ὑπέδειξεν is used in I 28.18; II 20.2.

v. 13 בכלי השיר : ἐν τοῖς ὀργάνοις ᾠδοί G O R. The nominative is quite unintelligible in the context. No doubt Par originally read ἐ. τ. ὀ. ᾠδῶν (so f j -by revision or preservation?) : compare the rendering of the same Heb in 5.13 as ἐ. ὀ. τῶν ᾠδῶν. ᾠδοί is a gloss assimilating ἄρχοντες (= Chron שרים) to ᾠδοί (= שׂרים, read by seven Chron mss.) earlier in Rg v. 14. The gloss was taken to refer to ᾠδῶν and displaced it. Rehm, p. 60, wrongly posits a reading בכלים שרים. *Principes cantorum* La for השׂרים represents a conflated text in which the assimilating addition has been incorporated into the text by changing to a genitive.

v. 17 העם : ὁ λαὸς τῆς γῆς G O L R = Rg v. 18 = Ki עם הארץ The last two words are not original in Par. In v. 13 ὁ λαός occurs for עם הארץ : it is the only place in Par where the second element is omitted. The omission appears to be the result of rationalization.[1] The term was misunderstood by the translator: the population of the whole country could hardly be packed into such a confined space as the Temple area. If this explanation is correct, then the addition here cannot be pre-Gk.

There are the inevitable cases of ambiguous assimilation:

23.1 בברית : εἰς οἶκον G (O L R) : cf. Rg v. 4 εἰς (τὸν) οἶκον ... διαθήκην; Ki בבית ... ברית ... בית. Rehm, p. 66, and Rudolph see here merely textual corruption, but parallel assimilation more probably underlies the change.

v. 11 ויתנו ... ויוציאו : καὶ ἐξήγαγεν ... καὶ ἔδωκεν G O L R = Rg v. 12 (L; R ... ἐξαπέστειλεν...) = Ki ויוצא ... ויתן

v. 13 ותאמר : καὶ ἐβόησεν G (OL R) = Rg v. 14 = Ki ותקרא.

24.1-14 is paralleled in II Ki 12.1-17. There is one case of Gk or Heb conflation:

24.6 המלך : +Ιωας G O = Rg v. 7; Ki v. 8 המלך יהואש.

In 24.23-27, based upon II Ki.12.18-22, there is one instance of uncertain origin:

v. 27 ויסוד בית האלהים : καὶ τὰ λοιπά G O L (R) = Rg v. 19 = Ki v. 20 ויתר.

25.1-13, corresponding to II Ki 14.1-7, contains one similar case:

v. 3 עליו : ἐν χειρὶ αὐτοῦ G O L R = Rg v. 5 (KR; L has τῇ) = בידו. Ten Chron mss. so read. Rehm, p. 70, sides with Ki.

---

[1] Cf.p. 118.

25.17-28, parallel with II Ki. 14.8-20, has three closer links, the first two probably Heb and the third probably Gk:

v. 19 להכביד : ἡ βαρεῖα G O L R = הַכָּבֵד : cf. Ki v. 10 הִכְבַּד; Rg : ἡ βαρεῖα (from Par) ἐνδοξάσθητι L; KR just ἐνδ.Rehm, pp. 71, 84, considers Chron corrupt and Par an independent witness to Ki.

ibid. למה : καὶ ἵνα τί = Rg = Ki ולמה. Since the previous instance is Heb in origin, probably this one is too. Rehm, p. 71, again sides with Ki.

v. 24 האלהים : κυρίου G O L R = Rg v. 14 = Ki יהוה. This is probably Gk assimilation, along with τοὺς υἱοὺς τῶν συμμίξεων later.[1]

26.21-23 is parallel to II Ki 15.2-7. One case of Gk influence may be suggested.

26.21 Kethib החפשות, Qere שׂית- : αφφουσιων G. ιωαν is probably a misplaced correction of Ιωαθαμ according to the sporadic reading Ιωναθαν at Rg v. 5 in B b′ e* (cf. v. 7). It is significant that in v. 23 A reads Ιωναθαν for Ιωαθαμ : this too may attest the influence of the Rg variant.

27.1-9, based upon II Ki 15.33-38, has been assimilated once either to Ki or to Rg. Rehm, p. 46, considers the latter, as usual.

v. 9 ויקברו אתו : καὶ ἐτάφη G O L R = Rg v. 38 = Ki ויקבר. Cf. the comment on 21.20.

Fresh contacts continue to occur sporadically. In 28.1-4, parallel with II Ki 16.2-4, the new link is at v. 3, again of uncertain origin:

ויבער : καὶ διῆγεν G O (L R) : cf. Rg v. 3 διῆγεν = Ki העביר. Rehm, p. 71, reads as Ki. But Chron is original and Ki has undergone revision.[2] One de Rossi ms. has ויעבר.

28.26-27 is based upon II Ki 16.19-20. V. 27 has two indefinite links:

ויקברוהו : καὶ ἐτάφη G O L R = Rg v. 20 = Ki ויקבר, read by two Ken. mss. Rehm, p. 46, thinks that Par has used Rg. Cf. 21.20; 27.9.

בעיר בירושלם : ἐν πόλει Δαυιδ G O L R = Rg = Ki בעיר דוד.

32.1-21 corresponds to II Ki 18.13-19.37. There are two cases of Heb contamination in v. 12:

חזקיהו : +ὅς G O L R = אשר II Ki. 18.22 (Rg omits). Rehm, pp. 71, 101, considers that in Chron אשר has fallen out before הסיר;

---

[1] See p. 45 note 1.

[2] Cf. Geiger, *Urschrift²*, p. 305.

but it is to be noted that the Chronicler has changed the order of words and may well have dispensed with אֲשֶׁר in the process.

לִפְנֵי מִזְבֵּחַ אֶחָד : κατέναντι τοῦ θυσιαστηρίου τούτου G O R = לִפְנֵי הַמִּזְבֵּחַ הַזֶּה Ki and also Isa 36.7 (LXX Isa omits; Rg ἐνώπιον τοῦ θυσ. τούτου). Rehm, p. 44, claims Par's use of Rg.

In v. 4 τῆς πόλεως G O L R = הָעִיר (BH) stands for הָאָרֶץ. Cf. Ki 20.20 וַיָּבֵא אֶת־הַמַּיִם הָעִירָה. Probably the *Vorlage* had suffered assimilation to the similar clause in Ki.

33.1-10 is parallel with II Ki 21.1-9. V.8 has three new points of contact. The first two Rehm, p. 46, considers Gk in origin. All three could be either Heb or Gk, but as this is very near the belt of close Heb approximation to Ki the balance of probability inclines towards the former.

לְהָסִיר : σαλεῦσαι G O (L R) = Rg v. 8 = Ki לְהָנִיד. Oettli, Kittel and Curtis adopt Ki, but Benzinger is more likely to be correct in suggesting that a more familiar word has been substituted in Chron.

הֶעֱמַדְתִּי : ἔδωκα G O L R = Rg = Ki נָתַתִּי. Many (see Curtis and BH) follow Ki, but Rudolph rightly regards this as assimilation to Ki. Chron is fond of עמד.

לַאֲבֹתֵיכֶם : τοῖς πατράσιν αὐτῶν G O L R = Rg = Ki לַאֲבוֹתָם. Ki is generally followed (see Curtis, BH, Rehm, p. 71, Rudolph), but to take David and Solomon as the antecedent (cf. v. 7) may well be as old as Chron in view of the importance of both in Chron.

With 34.8-32, parallel with II Ki 22.3-23.3, begins a stage of extensive Heb harmonization which continues till the end of II Par. R. W. Klein has strenuousy denied Heb contamination beneath Par.[1] He avers that Par's *Vorlage* attests the real Chron text and that in each case Chron MT is secondary. Each of his claims will be mentioned in the detailed study below. He shrinks from the proposal that "the Chronicler made changes which were then erased by the *Vorlage* of Par — Occam's razor would seem to apply !" Perhaps the reader of this chapter can be left to decide the justice or otherwise of this judgment. It must be said that Klein's freedom in emending Chron MT — to which his view forces him — harks back to the bad old days of Curtis and Rehm, and runs counter to more recent trends in the study of Chron.

v. 10 וַיִּתְּנוּ[1] : καὶ ἔδωκαν αὐτό G O L = Ki v. 5 וַיִּתְּנֻהוּ (Rg: κ. δοθήτω L; κ. δότωσαν αὐτό KR). Curtis unnecessarily suggested וַיִּתְּנוּ אֹתוֹ in Chron. Klein holds that Par's rendering "can be explained as a legiti-

---

[1] *HTR* lxi, p. 494.

mate interpretation of the consonantal text (*êw* from *ēhû*. Compare
ויקדשיו in the Nash Papyrus, and contrast it with Exodus 20.11 MT
[וַיְקַדְּשֵׁהוּ])", but he seems to argue as if Par's verb were singular, not
plural.

ibid. עושׂי : ποιοῦσι G O (L) R = Ki לעשׂי (Rg τοῖς ποιοῦσιν).
Many (see Curtis, Rehm, p. 71) favour Ki, and Klein claims that "the
argument that Chron MT is original here is not very strong (cf. Syriac)".[1]
But Rudolph justifies Chron MT.

v. 11 לקנות : καὶ ἀγοράσαι G O = Ki v. 6 ולק׳ (Rg: τοῦ κτήσασθαι L;
καὶ τ. κτ. KR). Rehm, p. 72, reads as Ki.

v. 20 מיכה : Μειχαια G O R = Rg v. 12 (L; Μειχαίου KR) = Ki
מיכיה. The link is probably pre-Gk. Chron uses a later abbreviation.[2]
Klein claims a post-Par defective writing in Chron.

v. 21 ונתה : ἐκκέκαυται G O L R = Ki v. 13 ונצתה (Rg ἐκκεκαυμένη).
Rehm, pp. 46, 101, considers that Par has adapted Rg. Some (see
Curtis, BH "frt") adopt Ki, but it should be noted that Chron uses
נתך in connection with anger in 12.7 (Par στάξῃ). Post-Par adaptation
of the verb, suggested by Klein, is therefore less likely than a recensional change associated with the Chronicler's text.

ibid. שׁמרו : ἤκουσαν G (O L R) = Rg = Ki שׁמעו. The assimilation
is probably Heb as in the context. Some (see Curtis, BH, Rehm,
p. 72, Goettsberger) follow Ki. But Chron frequently links שׁמר with
עשׂה and God's commands : cf. I 22.13; 29.19; II 7.17; 19.7; 33.8;
34.31. So the change was probably deliberate.

v. 22 תוקהת : Καθουαλ G from Θακουα* (Wutz, p. 30, Rehm,
p. 72) = תקוה Ki v. 14 (Rg Θεκουε). Rehm considered Chron corrupt.
Klein asks: "With no convincing derivation available for תוקהת, why
not see it as the result of metathesis and the addition of a ת?" But
Noth, p. 260 (cf. Rudolph), judges that in fact Ki Hebraized a non-
Semitic name.

ibid. חסרה : Χελλης G. The middle of the word has been assimilated
to the preceding Σελλημ, but the *sigma* testifies to Ki חרחס (Rg:
Αδρα L, Αρα(α)ς KR). Rehm, p. 72, also traced Par's form back to
Ki, but via a ל/ר error; he considered Chron corrupt (cf. Curtis).

v. 24 כל־האלות : τοὺς πάντας λόγους G O L R: cf. Ki v. 16
כל־דברי (Rg π. τ. λ.). Par presupposes כל־הדברים (BH) under the

---

[1] Pesh is hardly a reliable witness to the text of Chron: "One of its most striking
characteristics is found in the fact that the text has very frequently been conformed to
the text of Samuel and Kings" (Curtis, p. 42).

[2] See Noth, *Personennamen*, p. 107.

influence of Ki; then of course הכתובים must have been written for ‑ות.
Rehm, p. 46, finds here Par's use of Rg. Klein stands alone in hailing
Par as witness to a pre-corrupted text of Chron.

v. 25 ותתך : καὶ ἐξεκαύθη G O L R = Ki v. 17 ונצתה (Rg κ. ἐκ-
καυθήσεται). Cf. v. 21. BH is here more positive: "l c G ..."

v. 31 על־עמדו : ἐπὶ τὸν στύλον G O L R = Rg. 23.3 (L; πρὸς ...
KR) = Ki על־העמוד. At 23.13 על־עמודו in a similar context justifies
Chron here. Rehm, p. 46, thinks that Rg has been used, and he may
well be right. This and the next case comprise a pocket of Gk assimilation.

ibid. אחרי יהוה ... לפני יהוה : ἐναντίον κυρίου ... ἐνώπιον κ. G O
L R : cf. Rg ἐνώπιον κ ... ὀπίσω κ. This is probably not the translator's avoidance of anthropomorphism (Rogers, p. 41) nor a mere
textual error in Par but a misplaced correction according to the first
phrase in Rg.

v. 32 כברית : +ἐν οἴκῳ G O R = בבית. In v. 30 בית stands for
בבית in Ki v. 2 : the Ki reading has been misplaced because ברית
occurs in both contexts. Alternatively, since in the preceding clause
Chron lacks בברית of Ki v. 3, this may be a misplaced and corrupted
gloss: cf. 23.1.

35.18-24, 26-27 corresponds to II Ki. 23.21-23, 28-30a. From now
on the *Vorlage* of Par becomes a kind of omnibus edition. After v. 19
Ki vv. 24-27 was inserted in the underlying Heb, "as is shown by the
transliteration καρασειμ = ... קדשים, not found in 2 K. 23.24".[1] The
Chron ms. used for Par was supplemented with material from Ki
concerning Josiah's reform, his greatness and Yahweh's threat of
exile for Judah. Torrey has argued that the Heb text had a lacuna at
this point which was filled by the insertion of Ki vv. 24-28, but which
originally contained a passage underlying I Esdr. 1.21f.[2] But Rudolph
rightly queries whether the I Esdr passage had a Heb foundation and
criticises Torrey's attempt to create one; he points out that there is no
feasible reason, such as homoeoteleuton, why it should have fallen out.

The addition to v. 19 actually begins at the *athnach*. The second
half of the verse and as far as את־הבית is missing in G O mss. It is
significant that I Esdr. 1.20, 23 contains the words except for את־הבית.
Clearly Par's *Vorlage* too had at some stage lost this last element,

---

[1] Curtis, ad loc. Cf. BH and p. 62 note 2. Rehm, p. 48, wrongly presupposes קרצים
("ר/שׂ").

[2] *Louis Ginzberg Jubilee Volume*, pp. 405ff.

probably because אשר was wrongly taken to refer to the object of הכין. Then the preceding words fell out simply by homoeoteleuton of יאשיהו. (The omission is obviously not Gk: Par always had the additions from Ki and v. 20a would hardly fit before this extra material.) But there is an indication pointing back to an earlier stage when the forerunner of Par's Heb text contained v. 19b, and so presumably v. 20a as far as יאשיהו. At the end of v. 18 Par (except g) has an addition τῷ κυρίῳ. Walde calls it a misplaced gloss on τὸ φασεχ ὃ ἐποίησεν in v. 18.[1] But is it ? Ki v. 23 contains the words נעשה הפסח הזה ליהוה בירושלם, for which the counterpart in Chron v. 19 has only נ' הפ' הזה : this is clearly the counterpart and not כפסח אשר עשה in v. 18. More probably the addition represents ליהוה, which was a Heb assimilating gloss added when the predecessor of Par's Heb text (or that itself if the translator's own eye slipped) contained the words subsequently lost. It was carelessly misplaced: since בירושלם follows in Ki it was put next to ירושלם in v. 18.

Chron v. 20 from עלה onwards appears differently in Par. In view of the changes at the Heb level in the preceding context it is probable that the *Vorlage* was replaced by Ki v. 29 as far as בהלחם לקראתו.[2] המלך ינהר 'פרעה על־מלך אשור בכרכמיש became were added. לקראתו יאשיהו was transposed. The Esdr text confirms Chron MT, as Rehm, p. 50f., notes.[3] Superimposed upon this Heb assimilation was a Gk change: Ἀσσυρίων G O L R is Rg's standard rendering for אשור, while Par generally uses Ασσουρ. The Hellenized form is found besides only at 32.9, 10 where also assimilation has taken place, to Rg 18. 17, 19.

R. W. Klein has drawn attention to the close similarity of the text of the parallel proto-Lucianic mss. of Rg to that of Par in 35.19a-d, 20; 36.2a-c, 3 (second half), 4 (first half), 4a, 5 (second half), 5a-d, 8 and perhaps also 36.1, 4 (second half).[4] The conclusion he has drawn is that either the translator of Par or a Gk editor used old Lucianic material in Rg and put it into Par. The author has opposed this view on three counts.[5] (a) The style of translation in the Gk material fits

---

[1] *Die Esdrasbücher*, p. 66 note 3. Cf. Rehm, p. 46.

[2] εἰς συνάντησιν is not attested in any Rg ms. and is certainly part of Par's vocabulary: it is used for לפניו in 14.9/10. Rehm, p. 48, claimed Gk contamination. According to Seeligmann. *Isaiah*, p. 78, the translator borrowed phrases from Rg in order to interpret בכרכמיש על־פרת : "for him Karkemish was the name of an Assyrian king" !

[3] But Φαραω for נכו in I Esdr 1.25 conforms with Ki. One de Rossi ms. adds פרעה with Par.

[4] *HTR* lx, pp. 93ff.

[5] *HTR* lxi, 483ff.

Par like a glove. It exhibits features which may be closely paralleled elsewhere in Par. This suggests that the translator rendered a Heb text. (b) There are in fact many passages in Par, e.g. II 10, 34, which on close examination betray a Heb *Vorlage* assimilated to the text of Sam-Ki. So a text contaminated at the Heb level would be nothing new. If other crucial and thrilling episodes of Old Testament history inspired a more comprehensive Heb text than the original Chron, how much more the tragic closing years of the southern kingdom? (c) The close similarity between Par and the L text of Rg is to be explained as due to parallel assimilation to Par, a notorious feature of the Lucianic recension.

Klein issued a short rejoinder.[1] (a) He played down the similarity of translation technique between the Ki-type Gk material and the rest of Par. In some cases where Rg L differs from Par he urged subsequent correction in the former. It would have bolstered his own case if he had been able to make the counter-claim that the techniques and renderings characteristic of Par were not uniquely so, but could be matched in old Rg material. He was apparently unable to do this. He did suggest that at times the Par reading has been assimilated to the rest of the book, which inclined him to urge more firmly than before that "the additions from Reigns were made by the Par translator himself". This raises questions which have already been discussed in connection with the views of Rehm and Shenkel. (b) Klein considered "not cogent" the present writer's examples of pre-Gk assimilation in II Par. 10, 34. His criticisms have already been discussed at the appropriate places above.

(c) Finally, he stressed that in Rg we do not have a late Lucianic recension but essentially a proto-Lucianic one. Therefore, it is inferred, we must not appeal to a late Lucianic feature like parallel assimilation. It is noteworthy that although he had been eager to point earlier to late and secondary elements in this group of Rg mss., here he argues from an opposite point of view. Before one can seek refuge at a proto-Lucianic shrine, a good deal of comprehensive work still needs to be done on "proto-Lucian" in IV Rg to analyse just how much is old and how much has been overlaid by later strata. The question of synoptic harmonization is wider than the relation between the Par supplements and IV Rg L. Rahlfs was able to cite many impressive examples in IV Rg 18-20 where the LXX text of the parallel Isa 36-39 has been

---

[1] *HTR* lxi, pp. 492ff.

substituted in L.[1] He himself claimed that the Lucianic text of IV Rg
had been corrected according to Par, including the supplements,[2]
and in this respect he found it to be no different from the L text of
III Rg, in which he found similar assimilation to Par.[3] Certainly
Rahlfs lived in a pre-Barthélemy, pre-Cross era, but the data with
which he wrestled seem to point closest to his own conclusion.

36.1-12 is based on II Ki. 23.30ff.; 24.1-19. It is strongly characterised by changes, omissions and additions according to Ki. I Esdr again
confirms the text of Chron. It has not been realised hitherto that in a
large part of this section it is not a case of the *Vorlage*'s having been
adapted to Ki piecemeal. Rather, 36.1-8 has been abandoned, and
II Ki. 23.30b-24.6 taken over *en bloc*; then some Chron variants have
been inserted into the new text. One insertion from Chron is ויסירהו מלך
מצרים in v. 3: καὶ μετήγαγεν αὐτὸν ὁ βασιλεὺς εἰς Αἴγ. G O (L) R.[4]
Chron v. 6f. has also been inserted into the Ki-type text. Assimilation
back to Chron also takes the form of a replacement: in v. 4 ואת־יהואחז
ואת־יו' אחיו ל' לקח ויבא מצרים has been replaced by נכה ויביאהו
מצרימה. It is not insignificant that the material taken over from Ki
would amount to one whole column:[5] this factor serves to confirm the
Heb origin of the assimilation.

There are a few instances of Gk assimilation, e.g. Ἰωσείου for יאשיהו
in vv. 1,4: Ἰωσεια is Par's genitive, e.g. in 35. 16, 26. It may be noticed
in passing that Rg L frequently depends upon Par. A clear instance
of this dependence is the rendering δύναμιν for ערך in IV Rg 23.25 L =
II Par 36.4a. In IV Rg 12.5/4 both L and KR use συντίμησις, a

---

[1] *LXX-Studien*, iii, pp. 254-257.

[2] *Op. cit.*, iii, pp. 257-259.

[3] *Op. cit.*, iii, pp. 250-252.

[4] Rehm, pp. 61, 72 note 2, unnecessarily assumes a variant המלך.

[5] Observation, especially of local assimilation, has taught the lesson that in the
Vorlage or its forbears one column must have been equivalent to an average-sized page
of BH. See part II, p. 90.

In II Par 36.8 a lost clause of Ki is preserved. After עם־אבתיו of II Ki 24.6 G O L R
add καὶ ἐτάφη ἐν γανοζα (-αν, -αη) μετὰ τῶν πατέρων αὐτοῦ = ויקבר בגן־עזה עם־
אבותיו. According to Rehm, p. 23, the *Vorlage* of Par was filled out from II Ki 21.26.
But the different Gk in Rg L and Par indicates that it was in the Heb texts of both. On
the score that κῆπος is used by the later Gk translators, Klein (*HTR* lx, p. 105 note 42;
lxi, p. 493) finds here a late element in Rg L. But this is an unnecessary supposition.
κῆπος is a good LXX word: in Rg it is used for גן in III Rg. 20.2 (= I Ki. 21.2) as well
as in both L and KR texts of IV Rg. 21.18, 26; 25.4. It is probable that the clause fell
out of Ki by homoeoteleuton and omission of a nineteen letter line, for which cf. part II,
p. 136.

venerable equivalent used in the Pentateuchal LXX. KR so reads here: it is difficult to avoid the conclusion that KR preserves the vintage Rg reading and L has been contaminated by Par.

In v. 5b = Ki 24.2 כדבר יהוה אשר דבר is rendered μετὰ τὸν λόγον τοῦτον κατὰ τὸν λόγον κυρίου G O L R. The last four words are an intrusion from Rg. τοῦτον was doubtless originally αὐτοῦ * τόν *: the former word is a common indirect translation in Par in cases where the antecedent is obvious, and the latter is a not untypical short rendering.[1] After the intrusion of the gloss the original text was adapted for sense. There is no need to assume a *Vorlage* כדבר הזה with Rehm, p. 48.

Par v. 10 affords the last case of assimilation, of uncertain origin: אחיו : ἀδελφὸν τοῦ πατρὸς αὐτοῦ G O L (R) = Rg 24.17 L (υἱὸν αὐτοῦ KR) = Ki דודו. Rehm, p. 72, and Rudolph ("c GSV") read אחי אביו on the strength of Par, but Curtis is on safer ground in regarding it as a correction according to the parallel.

An attempt has been made in this chapter to disentangle the mass of parallel assimilation and to specify wherever possible the stage at which each instance occurred. It is hoped that it has been convincingly shown both by individual analysis and by cumulative effect that not only Par but also the translator's Heb text have absorbed varying amounts of contamination from parallel texts. The contaminated state of the *Vorlage* has a bearing upon Torrey's view of Par. Such a text would hardly be a likely basis for an A.D. revision.

No text is necessarily immune from parallel assimilation. Chron MT is relatively free, but there are a few very probable instances, as follows:

I 6.46/61 חצי is omitted by G O L R. BH annotates "dl c V" and Rudolph states "dl c Vrs". The latter rightly explains the extra word as originally a marginal gloss on מחצית two words before. The position of the word reveals its secondary nature. It has in fact come in from the parallel Jos. 21.5 which reads חצי for מח'.

16.35 וקבצנו והצילנו. Rothstein notes that והצ' is absent from Psa 106.47 and suggests that it is a variant to or a gloss on וקבצנו. But Par points in another direction: it lacks וקבצנו. Chron MT may well have a conflated text. The second word looks like a recensional change native to Chron and the first an import from the parallel text.

II 6.27 השמים : ἐκ τοῦ οὐρανοῦ G O L R = מן־הש'. In this chapter

---

[1] Cf. pp. 46, 50f.

מִן־הֹשׁ׳ stands seven times in place of הֹשׁ׳ in I Ki 8. מִן is generally restored here with the versions. Probably the Ki text has infiltrated into MT here by assimilation.

27.8 is omitted by G O and Pesh. So far as Par is concerned it could be a case of Gk homoeoteleuton : ΙΗΛ and ΙΛΗΜ. But the underlying uncertainty about the verse in Chron itself renders this possibility doubtful. Curtis suggests that it is a repetition of v. 1 or else a marginal gloss on 28.1. Rudolph supports the latter view, seeing here a falsely positioned gloss correcting 20 years to 25. But Rehm, p. 87, notes that the verse is an exact copy of II Ki 15.33a, describing Jotham's reign. It therefore seems more likely that this verse is to be related to 27.1 as an assimilating gloss.

BIBLIOGRAPHY

ACKROYD, P.R., "The Hebrew Root באש", *JTS* ii, 1951, pp. 31-36.
——, "Some Notes on the Psalms", *JTS* xvii, 1966, pp. 392-399.
ALBRIGHT, W.F., "The List of Levitic Cities", *Louis Ginzberg Jubilee Volume*, English Section, 1945, pp. 49-73.
ALLEN, L.C., "Further Thoughts on an Old Recension of Reigns in Paralipomena", *HTR* lxi, 1968, pp. 483-491.
ALLGEIER, A., "Beobachtungen am LXX-text der Bücher Esdras und Nehemias", *Biblica* xxii, 1941, pp. 227-251.
ALLRIK, H.L., "I Esdras According to Codex B and Codex A as Appearing in Zerubbabel's List in I Esdras 5.8-23", *ZAW* lxvi, 1954, pp. 272-292.
AP-THOMAS, D.R., *A Primer of OT Text Criticism²*, 1964.
BAARS, W., "Papyrus Barcinonensis, Inv. No. 3 and Egerton Papyrus 4", *VT* xv, 1965, pp. 528-529.
——, *New Syro-Hexaplaric Texts Edited, Commented Upon and Compared with the LXX*, 1968.
BACHER, W., "Der Name der Bücher der Chronik in der LXX", *ZAW* xv, 1895, pp. 305-308.
BARNES, W.E., *An Apparatus Criticus to Chronicles in the Peshitta Version*, 1897.
——, *The Book of Chronicles*, Cambridge Bible, 1900.
BARTHÉLEMY, D., *Les devanciers d'Aquila*, VT Supplements x, 1963.
BAUDISSIN, W.W. GRAF VON, *Kyrios als Gottesname im Judentum und seine Stelle in der Religionsgeschichte*, 1926-9.
BEGRICH, J., ed. Chronicles, *Biblica Hebraica,³* ed. R. Kittel and P Kahle, 1937 (BH).
BELL, H.I., & T.C. SKEAT, *Fragments of an Unknown Gospel and Other Early Christian Papyri*, 1935.
BENZINGER, I., *Die Bücher der Chronik, Kurzer Hand-Kommentar zum AT*, 1901.
BERTHEAU, E., *Bücher der Chronik, Kurzgefasstes Exegetisches Handbuch zum AT*, 1873.
BERTRAM, G., "Der Sprachsatz der LXX und der des hebräischen AT", *ZAW* xvi, 1939, pp. 85-101.
BEWER, J.A., "Textkritische Bemerkungen zum AT", *Festschrift für A. Bertholet*, ed. W. Baumgartner, etc., 1950, pp. 65-76.
BICKERMAN, E.J., "Some Notes on the Transmission of the LXX", *Alexander Marx Jubilee Volume*, ed. S. Lieberman, 1950, pp. 149-178.
BRIN, G., "השרשים עזר – עזז, במקרא", *Leshonenu*, xxiv, 1960, pp. 8-14.
BROCK, S.P., "Lucian *Redivivus*. Some Reflections on Barthélemy's *Les devanciers d'Aquila*", *Studia Evangelica* v, ed. F.L. Crass, 1968, pp. 176-181.
BROOKE, A.E. & McLEAN N., *The OT in Greek*, vol. ii, 1935 (BM).
BROWN, F., DRIVER S.R. & BRIGGS C.A., *A Hebrew and English Lexicon of the OT*, 1907 (BDB).
BURCHARD, C., *Bibliographie zu den Handschriften vom Toten Meer, ZAW Beihefte* lxxxix, 1965.
BURNEY, C.F., *Notes on the Hebrew Text of the Book of Kings*, 1903.
CHURGIN, P., "The Targum and the LXX", *AJSL* 1 (= *JNES* i), 1933-4, pp. 41-65.

CROSS, JR., F.M., "The Oldest Manuscripts from Qumrân", *JBL* lxxiv, 1955, pp. 147-72.

——, *The Ancient Library of Qumrân and Modern Biblical Studies*, 1958.

——, "The Development of the Jewish Scripts", *The Bible and the Ancient Near East*, ed. G.E. Wright, 1961, pp. 133-202.

——, "The History of the Biblical Text in the Light of Discoveries in the Judaean Desert", *HTR* lvii, 1964, pp. 281-299.

——, "The Contribution of the Qumrân Discoveries to the Study of the Biblical Text", *IEJ* xvi, 1966, pp. 81-95.

CURTIS, E.L. & MADSEN A.A., *The Books of Chronicles, ICC*, 1910.

DANCY, J.C., *A Commentary on I Maccabees*, 1954.

DANIEL, S., *Recherches sur le vocabulaire du culte dans la Septante*, 1966.

DELITZSCH, F., *Die Lese- und Schreibfehler im AT*, 1920.

DRIVER, G.R., "Some Hebrew Roots and their Meanings", *JTS* xxiii, 1922, pp. 69-73.

——, "The Root פרץ in Hebrew", *JTS* xxv, 1924, p. 177f.

——, "On Some Passages in the Books of Kings and Chronicles", *JTS* xxvii, 1926, pp. 158-160.

——, "Studies in the Vocabulary of the OT. IV", *JTS* xxxii, 1931, pp. 250-257.

——, "Abbreviations in the Massoretic Text", *Textus* i, 1960, pp. 112-131.

——, "Once Again Abbreviations", *Textus* iv, 1964, pp. 76-94.

DRIVER, S.R., *Notes on the Hebrew Text and the Topography of the Books of Samuel*[2], 1913.

EHRLICH, A.B., *Randglossen zur hebräischen Bibel*, vol. vii, 1914.

EISSFELDT, O., "Zeilenfüllung", *VT* ii, 1952, pp. 87-92.

——, *Einleitung in das AT*[3], 1964.

ELMSLIE, W.A.L., *Chronicles, Cambridge Bible*[2], 1916.

——, "The First and Second Books of Chronicles", *The Interpreter's Bible*, ed. G.A. Buttrick, etc., vol. iii, 1954.

FAULHABER, M., "Die Katenenhandschriften der spanischen Bibliotheken", *Biblische Zeitschrift*, i, 1903, pp. 151-159, 246-255, 351-371.

FIELD, F., *Origenis Hexaplorum quae supersunt …*, 1875.

FISCHER, J., *Das Alphabet der LXX-Vorlage im Pentateuch, Alttestamentliche Abhandlungen* x, 2, 1924.

——, "In welcher Schrift lag das Buch Amos der LXX vor ?", *TQ* cvi, 1925, pp. 308-335.

——, *Zur LXX-Vorlage im Pentateuch, ZAW Beihefte* xliii, 1926.

——, *In welcher Schrift lag das Buch Isaias der LXX vor ?, ZAW Beihefte* lvi, 1930.

FRANKEL, Z., *Vorstudien zu der LXX*, 1941.

——, *Uber den Einfluss der palästinischen Exegese auf die alexandrinische Hermeneutik*, 1851.

FREUDENTHAL, J., *Hellenistische Studien*, vol. i, 1875.

FRITSCH, C.T., *The Anti-anthropomorphisms of the Greek Pentateuch*, 1943.

GARD, D.H., *The Exegetical Method of the Greek Translator of Job, JBL Monograph* viii, 1952.

GEHMAN, H.S., "The Theological Approach of the Greek Translator of Job 1-15", *JBL* lxviii, 1949, pp. 231-240.

——, "Some Types of Errors of Transmission in the LXX", *VT* iii, 1953, pp. 397-400.

——, "Ἅγιος in the LXX", *VT* iv, 1954, pp. 337-348.

——, "Adventures in LXX Lexicography", *Textus* v, 1966, pp. 125-132.

GEIGER, A., *Urschrift und Ubersetzungen der Bibel in ihrer Abhängigkeit von der innern Entwicklung des Judentums*[1], 1857,[2], 1928.

GERLEMAN, G., *Studies in the LXX II. Chronicles*, 1946.

——, *Synoptic Studies in the OT*, 1948.

——, *Gesenius' Hebrew Grammar*, ed. E. Kautzsch, A.E. Cowley, 1910 (GK).

GILBERT, H.L., "Forms of Names in I Chron. 1-7", *AJSL* xiii, 1897, pp. 279-298.

GINSBERG, H.L., "A Ugaritic Parallel to 2 Sam. 1.21", *JBL* lvii, 1938, pp. 209-213.

GOETTSBERGER, J., *Die Bücher der Chronik oder Paralipomenon, Die Heilige Schrift des AT*, 1939.

GOODING, D.W., *The Account of the Tabernacle, Texts and Studies* vi, 1959.

——, "The LXX's Rival Versions of Jeroboam's Rise to Power", *VT* xvii, 1967, pp. 173-189.

——, "Text-Sequence and Translation-Revision in 3 Reigns ix. 10-x. 33", *VT* xix, 1969, pp. 448-463.

——, "Jeroboam's Rise to Power: A Rejoinder", *JBL* xci, 1972, pp. 529-533.

GORDIS, R., *The Biblical Text in the Making: a Study of the Kethib-Qere*, 1937.

GOSHEN-GOTTSTEIN, M.H., "Neue Syrohexaplafragmente", *Biblica* xxxvii, 1956, pp. 162-183.

——, "The Edition of Syrohexapla Materials", *Textus* iv, 1964, p. 230f.

GRAY, J., *I and II Kings*², 1970.

GREENLEE, J.H., *Introduction to NT Textual Criticism*, 1964.

GRINDEL, J.M., "Another Characteristic of the *Kaige* Recension", *CBQ* xxxi, 1969, pp. 499-513.

GROTIUS, H., *Annotata ad Vetus Testamentum*, 1644.

GWYNN, J., *Remnants of the Later Syriac Versions of the Bible*, 1909.

HATCH, E., and REDPATH H.A., *A Concordance to the LXX and the Other Greek Versions of the OT*, 1897-1906.

HELBING, R., *Die Kasussyntax der Verba bei den LXX*, 1928.

HOLMES, R. and PARSONS J., *Vetus Testamentum Graecum cum variis lectionibus*, 1798-1827.

HOMMEL, F., "Zerah the Cushite", *ET* viii, 1896-7, p. 378f.

HOWARD, G., "Frank Cross and Recensional Critisism", *VT* xxi, 1971, pp. 440-450.

HOWORTH, H., "The Real Character and the Importance of the First Book of Esdras", *The Academy*, xliii, 1893, pp. 13f., 60.

——, "The True LXX Version of Chronicles-Ezra-Nehemiah", *The Academy*, xliv, 1893, p. 73f.

——, "Some Unconventional Views on the Text of the Bible. I. The Apocryphal Book Esdras A and the LXX", *PSBA* xxiii, 1901, pp. 147-159.

——, "... III. The Hexapla and Tetrapla of Origen and the Light They Throw on the Books of Esdras A and B", *PSBA* xxiv, 1902, pp. 147-172.

——, "...VII. Daniel and Chronicles", *PSBA* xxix, 1907, pp. 31-38, 61-69.

HUNT., A.S., *The Oxyrhynchus Papyri*, vol. vii, 1910.

JACOBY, F., "Eupolemos", *Paulys Real-Encyclopëdie der classischen Altertumswissenschaft*, ed. G. Wissowa, vol. vi, 1907, coll. 1227-1229.

JELLICOE, S., "The Occasion and Purpose of the Letter of Aristeas: a Re-examination", *NTS* xii, 1966, pp. 144-150.

——, *The LXX and Modern Study*, 1968.

JOHNSON, Bo, *Die hexaplarische Rezension des I Samuelbuches* der LXX, 1963.

KAHLE, P.E., *The Cairo Geniza*¹, 1947,², 1959.

——, *Die hebräischen Handschriften aus der Höhle*, 1951.

——, "The Age of the Scrolls", *VT* i, 1951, pp. 38-48.

KATZ, P., review of Rahlfs' *Septuaginta*, *TLZ* lxi ,1936, coll. 265-287.

——, "*KATAΠAYΣAI* as a Corruption of *KATAΛYΣAI* in the LXX", *JBL* lxv, 1946, pp. 319-324.

——, "Das Problem des Urtexts der LXX", *TZ* v, 1949, pp. 2-14.

——, *Philo's Bible*, 1950.

——, "Two Kindred Corruptions in the LXX", *VT* i, 1951, pp. 261-266.

——, "Septuagintal Studies in the Mid-century", *The Background of the NT and its Eschatology*, ed. W.D. Davies & D. Daube, 1956, pp. 176-208.

——, "Justin's OT Quotations and the Greek Dodekapropheton Scroll", *Studia Patristica* i, ed. K. Aland & F.L. Cross, 1955, pp. 343-353.

KAUTZSCH, E., *Die Heilige Schrift des AT*. 1894.

KITTEL, R., *The Books of Chronicles*, notes translated by B.W. Bacon, *SBOT*, 1895.

——, *Die Bücher der Chronik*, Handkommentar zum AT, 1902.

KLEIN, R.W., "New Evidence for an Old Recension of Reigns", *HTR* lx, 1967, pp. 93-105.

——, "Supplements in the Paralipomena: A Rejoinder", *HTR* lxi, 1968, pp. 492-495.

——, "Jeroboam's Rise to Power", *JBL* lxxxix, 1970, p. 217f.

KLOSTERMANN, A., *Die Bücher Samuelis und der Könige, Kurzgefasster Kommentar zu den Heiligen Schriften Alten und Neuen Testamentes*, 1887.

KROPAT, A., *Die Syntax des Autors der Chronik verglichen mit seiner Quellen*, *ZAW* Beihefte xvi, 1909.

LAGARDE, P. DE, *Anmerkungen zu griechischen Übersetzung der Proverbien*, 1863.

——, *Librorum Veteris Testamenti Canonicorum pars prior Graece*, 1883.

LEANDER, P., *Laut- und Formenlehre des Ägyptisch-Aramäischen*, 1928.

LEE, S., *The Syriac Old and New Testament*, 1823-6.

LAKE, H. & K. *Codex Sinaiticus, OT*, 1922.

LIDDELL, H.G., & SCOTT R , *A Greek-English Lexicon*, revised by H.S. Jones, 1940.

MARENOF, S., "A Note on I Chron. 17.17", *AJSL* liii, 1936-7, p. 47.

MARGOLIOUTH, D.S., "Sukkiim", *Hasting's Dictionary of the Bible* (HDB), vol. iv, 1902, p. 627.

MARGOLIS, M.L., "*Λαμβάνειν* (Including Compounds and Derivatvies) and its Hebrew-Aramaic Equivalents in OT Greek", *AJSL* xxii, 1905, pp. 110-119.

——, "The Greek Preverb and its Hebrew-Aramaic Equivalents", *AJSL* xxvi, 1909, pp. 33-61.

——, "The Grouping of Codices in the Greek Joshua", *JQR* i, 1910, pp. 259-263.

——, "The Washington MS. of Joshua", *JAOS* xxxi, 1911, pp. 365-367.

——, "Transliterations in the Greek OT", *JQR* xvi, 1925-6, pp. 117-125.

MILLARD, A.R., "*Scriptio Continua* in Early Hebrew: Ancient Practice or Modern Surmise ?", *JSS* xv, 1970. pp. 2-15.

MILNE, H.J., & SKEAT T.C., *Scribes and Correctors of Codex Sinaiticus*, 1938.

MONTGOMERY, J.A., *The Book of Daniel, ICC*, 1927.

——, *The Books of Kings, ICC*, 1951.

MOORE, G.F., "The Antiochian Recension of the LXX", *AJSL* xxix, 1913, pp. 37-62.

MOULE, C.F.D., *An Idiom Book of New Testament Greek*, 1953.

MOZLEY, F.W., *The Psalter of the Church*, 1905.

MYERS, J.M., *I Chronicles, II Chronicles, The Anchor Bible*, 1965.

NAU, F., "Permutations des lettres M, N, B dans le codex Vaticanus", *Revue d'Orient Chrétien*, xvi, 1911, p. 428f.

NOTH, M., *Die Israelitischen Personennamen im Rahmen der Gemeinsemitischen Namengebung*, 1928.

——, *Überlieferungsgeschichliche Studien I*, 1943.

OESTERLEY, W.O.E. & ROBINSON T.H., *An Introduction to the Books of the OT*, 1934.

OETTLI, S., *Bücher der Chronik, Kurzgefasstes Exegetisches Kommentar zum AT*, 1889.

OLMSTEAD, A.T., "Source Study and the Biblical Text", *AJSL* xxx, 1913, pp. 1-35.

ORLINSKY, H.M., review of M. Rehm, *Textkitische Untersuchungen* ..., *JBL* lviii, 1939, pp. 397-399.

——, "The Kings-Isaiah Recensions of the Hezekiah Story", *JQR* xxx, 1939-40, pp. 33-49.

——, "Critical Notes on Gen. 39.14,17, Jud. 11.37", *JBL* lxi, 1942, pp. 87-97.

——, review of C.R. Fritsch, *The Anti-anthropomorphisms* ..., *The Crozer Quarterly*, xxi, 1944, pp. 156-160.

——, "Current Progress and Problems in LXX Research", *The Study of the Bible Today and Tomorrow*, ed. H.R. Willoughby, 1947, pp. 144-161.

——. review of G. Gerleman, *Chronicles*, *JBL* lxvii, 1948, pp. 387-390.

——, "The Treatment of Anthropomorphisms and -pathisms in the LXX of Isaiah", *HUCA* xxvii, 1956, pp. 193-200.

——, "Notes on the Present State of the Textual Criticism of the Judaean Biblical Cave Scrolls", *A Stubborn Faith*, ed. E.C. Hobbs, 1956, pp. 117-131.

——, "The Textual Criticism of the OT", *The Bible and the Ancient Near East*, ed. G.E. Wright, 1961, pp. 113-132.

PAYNE SMITH, P., *Thesaurus Syriacus*, vol. ii, 1879.

PERLES, F., *Analekten zur Textkritik des AT*, 1895.

PFEIFFER, R.H., *Introduction to the OT*, 1948.

——, *History of NT Times, with an Introduction to the Apocrypha*, 1949.

——, "Chronicles I & II", *The Interpreter's Dictionary of the Bible*, 1962, vol. i, pp. 572-580.

PODECHARD, E., "Le premier chapitre des Paralipomènes", *RB* xiii, 1916, pp. 363-386.

POHLMANN, A.A., "Über das Ansehen des apokryphischen dritten Buchs Esras", *TQ* xli, 1859, pp. 257-275.

RAHLFS, A., *Septuaginta-Studien*, vol. i, 1904, vol. iii, 1911.

——, *Verzeichnis der grieschischen Handschriften des AT*, 1914.

——, *Studie über den grieschischen Text des Buches Ruth*, 1922.

——, *Septuaginta, id est Vetus Testamentum Graece iuxta LXX interpretes*[5], 2 vols., 1952 (Ra.)

REDPATH, H.A., "A Contribution Towards Settling the Dates of the Translation of the Various Books of the LXX", *JTS* vii, 1906, pp. 606-615.

REHM, M., *Textkritische Untersuchungen zu den Parallelstellen der Samuel-Königsbücher und der Chronik*, Alttestamentliche Abhandlungen, xiii, 3, 1937.

REIDER, J. and TURNER N., *An Index to Aquila*, VT Supplements xii, 1966.

ROBERTS, B.J., *The OT Text and Versions*, 1951.

ROCA-PUIG, R., "Un papir grec del llibre dels Paralipòmens", *Boletín de la Real Academia de buenas letras de Barcelona*, xxix, 1961-2, pp. 219-227.

ROGERS, V.M., *The Old Greek Version of Chronicles: a Comparative Study of the LXX with the Hebrew Text from a Theological Approach*, unpublished Ph. D. dissertation, Princeton, 1954.

ROPES, J.H., *The Beginnings of Christianity*, edd. J.F.F. Jackson and L. Kake, vol. iii, 1926, pp. lxxxviii-civ.

ROSSI J.B. DE, *Variae lectiones Veteris Testamenti*, vol. iv, 1788.

ROTHSTEIN, J.W. and HÄNEL J., *Das Erste Buch der Chronik*, Kommentar zum AT, 1913.

RUDOLPH, W., *Esra und Nehemia, Handbuch zum AT*, 1949.

——, "Die Einheitlichkeit der Erzählung vom Sturz der Atalja (2 Kön 11)", *Festschrift für A. Bertholet*, edd. W. Baumgartner, etc., 1950.

——, *Chronikbücher, Handbuch zum AT*, 1955.

SABATIER, P., *Bibliorum sacrorum latinae versiones seu vetus italica*, vol. i, 1751.

SCHLEUSNER, J.F., *Novus Thesaurus philologico-criticus sive Lexicon in LXX et reliquos Interpretes Graecos ac scriptores Apocryphos Veteris Testamenti*, 1821.

SCOTT, R.B.Y., "The Pillars Jachin and Boaz", *JBL* lviii, 1939, pp. 145-149.

SCHRENK, G., "'Ἱερός, τὸ ἱερόν", *Theological Dictionary of the NT*, ed. G. Kittel, tr. G.W. Bromiley, vol. iii, 1965, pp. 221-230, 230-247.

SEELIGMANN, I.L., *The LXX Version of Isaiah*, 1948.

——, "Indications of Editorial Alteration and Adaptation in the MT and the LXX", *VT* xi, 1961, pp. 201-221.

SHENKEL, J.D., *Chronology and Recensional Development in the Greek Text of Kings*, 1968.

——, "A Comparative Study of the Synoptic Parallels in I Paraleipomena and I-II Reigns", *HTR* lxii, 1969, pp. 63-85.

SHUNARY, J., "Avoidance of Anthropomorphism in the Targum of Psalms", *Textus* v, 1966, pp. 133-144.

SIBINGA, J.S., *The O.T. Text of Justin Martyr*, vol. i, 1963.

SIMONS, J., *Geographical and Topographical Texts of the OT*, 1959.

SKEHAN, P.W., "The Qumran Manuscripts and Textual Criticism", *Volume du Congrès*, VT Supplements iv, 1957, pp. 148-160.

SMITH, H.P., "OT Notes I", *JBL* xxiv, 1905, p. 27.

——, *The Books of Samuel, ICC*, 1899.

SMITH, M., "Another Criterion for the καίγε Recension", *Biblica* xlviii, 1967, pp. 443-445.

SOFFER, A., "The Treatment of Anthropomorphisms and -pathisms in the LXX of Psalms", *HUCA* xxviii, 1957, pp. 85-107.

SOISALON-SOININEN, I., *Die Charakter der asterisierten Zusätze in der LXX*, 1959.

——, *Die Infinitive in der LXX*, 1965.

SPERBER, A., "NT and LXX", *JBL* lix, 1940, pp. 250-257.

——, *The Bible in Aramaic*, vols. i-iva, 1959-68.

SWETE, H.B., *An Introduction to the OT in Greek*, revised by R.R. Ottley, 1914.

TABACHOVITZ, D., *Die LXX und das Neue Testament*, 1956.

TALMON, S., "A Case of Abbreviation Resulting in Double Readings", *VT* iv, 1954, pp. 206-208.

——, "Synonymous Readings in the Textual Traditions of the OT", *Scripta Hierosolymitana*, viii, 1961, pp. 335-383.

THACKERAY, H. ST. J., "The Greek Translators of the Four Books of Kings", *JTS* viii, 1907, pp. 262-278.

——, *A Grammar of the OT in Greek according to the LXX*, vol. i, 1909.

——, *The LXX and Jewish Worship*, Schweich Lectures for 1920, 1921.

THEIS, J., *Geschichtliche und literarkritische Fragen in Esra 1-6*, 1910.

THOMSEN, P., "Ein Fragment einer Minuskelhandschrift mit hexaplarischen Notizen", *ZAW* xxxi, 1911, p. 308f.

TOB, E., "Lucian and Proto-Lucian. Towards a New Solution of the Problem", *RB* lxxix, 1972, pp. 101-113.

TORREY, C.C., "The Greek Versions of Chronicles, Ezra, and Nehemiah", *PSBA* xxv, 1903, p. 139f.

——, "The Nature and Origin of 'First Esdras'", *AJSL* xxiii, 1907, pp. 116-141.

——, "The Apparatus for the Textual Criticism of Chronicles-Ezra-Nehemiah", *OT and Semitic Studies in Memory of W.R. Harper*, vol. ii, 1908, pp. 55-111 (ATC).

——, *Ezra Studies*, 1910.

——, "A Revised View of First Esdras", *Louis Ginzberg Jubilee Volume*, ed. S. Lieberman, etc., English Section, 1945, pp. 395-410.

VANNUTELLI, P., *Libri Synoptici Veteris Testamenti seu librorum Regum et Chronicorum loci paralleli*, 1931 and 1934.

VAUX, R. DE, "Binjamin-Minjamin", *RB* xlv, 1936, pp. 400-402.

WADDELL, W.G., "The Tetragrammaton in the LXX", *JTS* xlv, 1944, pp. 158-161.

WALDE, B., *Die Esdrasbücher der LXX*, 1913.

WEBER, R., *Les anciennes versions latines du deuxième livre des Paralipomènes*, Collectanea biblica latina viii, 1945.

WELLHAUSEN, J., *De gentibus et familiis Judaeis quae I Chr. 2.4 enumerantur*, 1870.

WESTCOTT, B.F. and HORT F.J.A., *The NT in the Original Greek*, vol. ii, *Introduction*, 1881.

WEVERS, J.W., "Exegetical Principles Underlying the LXX Text of I Ki. 2.12-21.43", *OTS* viii, 1950, pp. 300-322.

——, "Principles of Interpretation Guiding the Fourth Translator of the Book of the Kingdoms", *CBQ* xiv, 1952, pp. 40-56.

——, "A Study in the Exegetical Principles Underlying the Greek Text of II Sam. 11.2-I Ki. 2.11", *CBQ* xv, 1953, pp. 30-45.

——, "Proto-Septuagint Studies", *The Seed of Wisdom*, T.J. Meek Festschrift, 1964, pp. 58-77.

——, "Septuaginta Forschungen seit 1954", *TR* n.f. xxxiii, 1968, pp. 18-76.

WHISTON, W., *An Essay Towards Restoring the True Text of the OT*, 1722.

WINCKLER, H., *Alttestamentliche Untersuchungen*, 1892.

WRIGHT, W., *Catalogue of Syriac Manuscripts in the British Museum, Acquired Since the Year 1838*, 1870-1872.

WÜRTHWEIN, E., *The Text of the OT*, tr. P.R. Ackroyd, 1957.

WUTZ, F.X., *Die Transkriptionen von der LXX bis zu Hieronymus*, 1925, 1933.

ZIEGLER, J., *Untersuchungen des Buches Isaias*, Alttestamentliche Abhandlungen, xii, 3, 1934.

——, *LXX: Vetus Testamentum Graecum*, vol. xiii, *Duodecim Prophetae*, 1943; vol. xiv, *Isaias*, 1939; vol. xv, Jeremias, Baruch, Threni, Epistula Jeremiae, 1957.

——, *Beiträge zur Jeremias-LXX*, 1958.

The following mss. on microfilm in whole or in part were used. The numeration of Rahlfs' *Verzeichnis* is added in brackets.

Bibloteca Naz Marciana, Venice:
    Appendix I.13 (728)
    Graeci 5 (68)
    Graeci 6 (122)
    Graeci 16 (731)
Biblioteca Vaticana, Rome:
    Vaticani Graeci 331 (236)
    Vaticani Graeci 1238 (246)

Biblioteca Mediceo-Laurenziana, Florence:
    S. Marco 700 (74)
Bibliothèque Nationale, Paris:
    Coislin 4 (46)
    Supplément grec 609 (610)
Deutsche Staatsbibliothek, Berlin:
    Phillipps 1405 (350)
Österreichische Nationalbibliothek, Vienna:
    Theologici Graeci 23 (130, cited as 144 in BM)
National Library of Greece, Athens:
    44 (314)
Mt. Athos:
    Βατοπαιδίου 603, formerly 516 (321)
    Πρωτάτου 53 (346)
Real Biblioteca, El Escorial, Madrid:
    Σ-II-19 (98)
    Ψ-I-8 (379)
    Ω-I-13 (381)

The British Museum ms. Add. 17195 has been consulted.

INDEX OF BIBLICAL PASSAGES

A. CHRONICLES/PARALIPOMENA

Asterisks refer to criticism of the apparatus of BH³

I 1.1-4	91	1.44	135, 185	2.53	144, 165
1.4	154	1.45	4, 65, 185	2.54	155, 186
1.5	154, 184	1.46	142, 185	2.55	165
1.6	184	1.47/51	185	3.1-20	91
1.7	184	1.50	185, 186	3.1	77, 135
1.8	78	1.51	186	3.2	94, 135
1.9	71, 144, 184	1.52	186	3.3	96, 186
1.10	184	1.53	186	3.4	94, 98, 99, 100
1.11-23	89, 98, 100	1.54	186	3.5	92, 93, 94, 135
1.11-16	98	2.1	186	3.6	96
1.11	98	2.3	55, 67, 94, 186	3.7	96
1.13-16	98, 100	2.5	186	3.8	94, 97
1.13	98	2.6	90, 94	3.12	78, 92, 94
1.17-24	94	2.8	96	3.16	93
1.17-23	97	2.9	41, 55, 67, 94, 154	3.17	63
1.17	91, 98, 100	2.10-44	68	3.18	93, 96, 155
1.18-25	99	2.10	154, 186	3.19	89, 94, 98, 99, 100,
1.18-23	98, 100	2.11	186		101
1.19	78	2.13	135, 142	3.20	94
1.24-28	91	2.14	33, 94, 97	3.21	79, 136
1.25	92	2.16	86, 92, 94, 135	4.2	33, 83, 150, 169
1.28	97	2.17	135	4.5	155
1.29	184	2.18	143	4.6	155
1.30	184, 185	2.19	104	4.7	155
1.32	72, 77, 98, 99, 185	2.21	40	4.8	75, 161
1.33	32, 99, 185	2.23	79, 86, 135	4.11	168
1.34	91, 96	2.25	154	4.14	71
1.35f.	99	2.26	103	4.16	155
1.35	89	2.29	4, 65	4.17	84, 104, 140, 155
1.36	185, 186	2.32	154	4.18	143
1.37	83, 135, 144, 190	2.33	144	4.21	62, 136, 157
1.38	98, 99, 100	2.42	89	4.22	150
1.39	185	2.46	68	4.23	150
1.40	72, 161, 185, 186	2.48	41, 68	4.24	71
1.41	161, 185	2.49	168	4.27	89
1.42	185	2.50	165	4.28	80, 187
1.43f.	185	2.51	154, 186	4.29f.	144
1.43	98, 99, 100	2.52	165	4.33	187

B. OTHER BIBLICAL BOOKS

C. APOCRYPHA